Classroom Test Construction

CLASSROOM TEST CONSTRUCTION

JON CLARK MARSHALL
University of Missouri, St. Louis

LOYDE WESLEY HALES
Ohio University

ADDISON-WESLEY PUBLISHING COMPANY
Reading, Massachusetts · Menlo Park, California · London · Don Mills, Ontario

This book is in the
ADDISON-WESLEY SERIES IN EDUCATION

Cover photo: DeWys, Inc.

To our wives,
Sharon and Anne

Preface

This material has been designed to provide prospective and in-service teachers with a thorough presentation of classroom measurement procedures. In writing it, the authors have been guided by the needs of classroom teachers, for developing cogent techniques of measuring and evaluating student achievement.

Classroom Test Construction differs from most measurement books in that it is devoted to the construction and analysis of classroom tests and the description and utilization of data obtained from these measures. Standardized tests of achievement, aptitude, interests, and personality are not included in the text, since excellent discussions of standardized instruments, norming procedures, and the like are presented in several books already available. However, there are few books available which offer thorough presentations on classroom testing procedures.

The need for teachers to have good measurement skills prompted the authors to write this book. Teachers continually evaluate student behavior. These evaluations are all-important to the educative process because functions such as teaching procedures, curriculum materials, students' promotions, students' chances to participate in extra-curricular activities, and scholastic honors are dependent upon intelligent evaluations. The introduction of Individual Prescribed Instruction has placed even greater importance on measurement, since diagnosis precedes prescription. It is necessary for teachers to be able to develop and use *good* measurement instruments in their classrooms.

The ordering of material in this text is similar to that which would be followed in the actual classroom: design and administration of the test, treatment of the test scores, evaluation, and improvement of the test (possibly for future use). Classroom testing involves much more than the construction of a few multiple-choice or essay test items. Before constructing the first item, the teacher must decide on the behavioral objectives and content to be measured by the test, the item types to be used, the administrative procedure, the scoring procedure, and other similar issues. The test should be cautiously constructed, with care taken to avoid common pitfalls. After the test is administered, the scores must be analyzed to provide meaningful interpretations. At periodic stages, the teacher will have to translate the obtained measurements into evaluations of student achievement. It should be determined whether or not the test was a good one and which items were good and which were poor. The item results can be used by the teacher as a signal of the areas of relative strengths and weaknesses of the students. All of these issues are treated here.

No previous training in measurements or statistics is required to understand the material presented. The necessary concepts drawn from these areas are presented as needed for the reader to understand test construction. The latter sections of the book contain a treatise of descriptive statistics and item analysis procedures as they pertain to classroom testing. These analytical sections constitute an important segment of this area. Test scores by themselves are worthless pieces of information. They become meaningful when sufficiently analyzed to provide information descriptive of student behavior. The statistical procedures described should fulfill this need.

Good test items are hard to come by. If a teacher is going to teach the same course more than once, it is imperative that he analyze his test items in order to improve his testing instruments. Even though this procedure takes extra time during the first year or two in the classroom, it will save the teacher time later and yet enable him to use better tests. The techiques recommended by the authors are straightforward and will take a minimal amount of the teacher's time. In many schools in which data processing facilities are available, item analysis and other statistical data can be provided for teachers if they know what to do with the information.

This book can be used by either undergraduate or graduate students as a text for test construction courses or as a supplementary text for courses in educational psychology, general techniques, methods, and measurements. It can also be used profitably by in-service teachers as a handbook for test construction.

We are indebted to the many pre-service and in-service teachers and colleagues who read and critiqued portions of the manuscript. We acknowledge a special debt to Arthur Caladarci, Professor of Education and Psychology, Stanford University, for his critical review of earlier drafts of the material, and for his suggestions which helped the authors in their preparation of the final manuscript.

St. Louis, Missouri   J.C.M.
Athens, Ohio   L.W.H.
April 1971

Contents

PART I

CLASSROOM TESTING

Chapter 1

An Introduction

RATIONALE

Presenting high-quality education is a professional endeavor requiring years of preparation. The details of such an undertaking should not be left to chance. However, most teachers have received little if any training in the techniques of classroom evaluation. Prospective elementary and secondary school teachers occasionally obtain a fleeting glance at tests and measurements in educational psychology courses. Even then, however, the course is usually concerned with standardized testing instruments and selected descriptive statistical techniques. Little or no time is spent teaching prospective teachers how to develop and use evaluation instruments for their own specific needs. As contradictory as it may seem, the plight is even worse at the university level. Most university personnel have not had even the little amount of training in classroom test construction that is given to elementary and secondary school teachers. If the proper construction and use of tests is important in the professional performance of teachers, it would seem that there is a woeful need for programs to train teachers in these skills.

The Need for Classroom Testing

It is generally recognized by educators that provisions in instruction should be made for individual differences, and that these provisions should be made on the basis of the abilities and achievements of students. Since the instructional content and the achievements of students are continually changing, up-to-date measures of achievement should be obtained frequently. Good measurement procedures are crucial when working with individual differences because it is impossible to provide for these differences unless the teacher can identify them. How can Billy's teacher help him to conquer his difficulties with syllabification if she does not know where the difficulties lie? The identification of students' strengths and weaknesses is a major purpose of classroom testing.

Tests are also used to determine whether or not a student has mastered a particular skill. This mastery type of test is appropriate in a number of testing situations but is primarily used where the skill being taught is basic to further learning in the area. For example, a child has to learn the meanings of certain numerals before he can continue the study of mathematics; a student must learn the meanings of certain selected words before he can effectively proceed in learning a foreign language. As can be inferred from these examples, mastery tests should be used more often in the elementary grades and courses where the foundation is being laid for further learning.

The teacher is concerned with the academic growth of his pupils. He wants to know whether or not his students are learning what he considers important for them to learn, and learning at a rate commensurate with their ability. Tests are often administered in order to obtain data bearing on this question. Teachers may use standardized tests of achievement and academic potential (available from test publishing companies) to compare the achievement test scores obtained for each pupil in the fall with those obtained in the spring, and to contrast the difference for each pupil with his academic potential. Some teachers may construct achievement tests which they use at the beginning and end of a unit of study in order to determine the amount of student change.

Tests are commonly used for discriminating among students who demonstrate various levels of achievement, particularly at the high school and higher education levels. When teachers are expected to make evaluations of students achievement, to assign marks on the basis of these evaluations, and to report these marks to administrative officials, there is an implicit expectation that they will do so on the basis of identified differences in achievement among the various students. Tests help teachers perform this task of ordering students on the basis of their exhibited differences in achievement.

ORGANIZATION OF THE BOOK

We did not write this book with the expectation that the diligent study of its contents would make of every teacher a measurement specialist. Rather, it is our hope that it will help teachers to become better teachers through the improvement of their measurement and evaluation skills. Furthermore, it is intended that this book will answer many of the teachers' questions concerning the development and use of appropriate test types, use of optional questions, weighting of questions, difficulty of questions, and assigning of marks. Finally, it is designed to help teachers select and develop appropriate classroom tests.

The appropriateness of a classroom test is a function of three factors: (1) the purpose of the test, (2) the confidence which can be placed in the test results, and (3) the relevance of the test questions to the intended purpose of the test. These factors are discussed in detail in subsequent chapters.

We have attempted to present test construction techniques and statistical procedures in a straightforward and easily understood manner. For the purpose of brevity, little evidence is cited to substantiate claims presented for different types of examinations. It should be noted, however, that these claims are based on an extensive review of the literature on testing. For the interested reader a review of this literature is presented in Appendix A.

In the organization of this book an attempt was made to present the basic knowledge and understandings of test construction which are needed by a classroom teacher in the order in which they would naturally occur in the development and execution of a teacher-designed classroom testing program. To this end, the book is divided into four parts: (I) Classroom Testing; (II) Types of Tests: Characteristics, Construction, and Use; (III) Test Scores: Description and Evaluation; and (IV) Test Quality: Assessment and Improvement. Part I consists of discussions of the need for classroom tests, the basic characteristics of educational measures, the general qualities of a good measurement instrument, the need for and methods of determining what one should measure, techniques for developing a test which is relevant to its intended purposes, and general considerations in the development and reproduction of a test.

In the chapters of Part II, we discuss various types of examinations, classified according to the characteristics of the items which comprise them. Advantages, disadvantages, procedures for item construction, and techniques of scoring are considered for several types of items: essay, completion, oral, multiple-choice, true-false, matching, and performance.

The chapter comprising Part III is presented to help teachers describe the results of their tests in terms of the examinees who took the examination: What is average for the group? How variable is the group? And what are the relations between the scores on different tests for the group? Some of the problems of pupil evaluation and marking are also examined here.

The chapters of Part IV are presented to help teachers evaluate their tests and improve their tests through the refinement or replacement of items comprising the test. The chapter on item quality contains a discussion of and comparison among several item analysis techniques. The purpose of this discussion is to explain the anthors' contention that the percentage technique for item analysis is not only easier but also better than many of the more sophisticated procedures.

SOME BASIC PRINCIPLES OF MEASUREMENT AND EVALUATION

Before a teacher can come to grips with the problems associated with the construction, administration, scoring, and interpretation of tests, he should have at least a minimum exposure to the basic principles of measurement and evaluation. The following introductory discussion is presented in this light, and many of the concepts mentioned here will be discussed in detail in subsequent chapters.

Measurement and Evaluation

The concepts of measurement and evaluation are used in everyday school situations. Decisions are continually being made by both school personnel and students. The basketball coach has to select his team. The principal or counselor has to help Billy decide what courses he should take. Gary has to decide whether or not he should attempt to go to college and, if he does, which one. In order to make intelligent decisions, data of many types are needed.

The data which are collected are called measurements, and measurements vary in type. A teacher might measure Billy's height or his ability to read; a counselor might measure his interests or his aptitude; a coach might measure his ability to run. These data are all measurements until we assign degrees of quality to them; when we have done this, we have made evaluations. A teacher measures Billy's height to be 54 inches; she evaluates his height when she says that he is short. Similarly, a coach may measure Billy's speed at 13 seconds for the 100-yard dash, but he evaluates Billy's speed when he categorizes him as being slow.

Characteristics of Educational Measures

Among the measures of interest to the teacher are those of human behavior thought to be expressions of some underlying mental process or characteristic—attitudes, interests, intelligence, aptitudes, achievement. Measures in these areas have certain characteristics in common.

Educational measures are indirect. When attempting to measure intelligence, for example, one cannot weigh it, assess its length, or even see or feel it. How, then, can we measure intelligence? In everyday usage one might say of a person "it was intelligent of him to do that" or "he must lack 'smarts' to do that." In a scientific assessment, experimentally tested behavioral tasks are presented to the individual, and his reactions to these tasks are interpreted as a reflection of his intelligence. Behavior thought to reflect intelligence, rather than intelligence itself, is used as the measure. Thus the measurement of intelligence is indirect. Likewise, behavioral reactions to tasks which are thought to require some specific learning (for example, specific facts or generalizations) in order for a correct response to be given, rather than achievement itself, are used to reflect achievement. All educational and psychological measures of mental processes are indirect. Consequently, whether standardized or teacher constructed, a test is not relevant unless there is a clear relationship between the behavioral tasks of the test and the underlying trait or mental process that the test presumes to measure.

Measurement is incomplete. From all the possible questions which one might write for a test which is being constructed to measure achievement in some area, only a very small number are actually written and selected. If we view the possible items as a hypothetical pool of items for measuring some mental process, we can say that only a sample of items from this pool is actually employed in constructing a test. A test of word knowledge, for example, might have 50 to 100 words in it, but the English language contains thousands of words. Even the most basic vocabulary is thought to contain approximately 4000 words. Not only would the test be incomplete because it employed only a few of the large number of available words, but for each word it would be incomplete in terms of the number of ways the question could have been written. The testmaker must conscientiously endeavor to select behavioral tasks which will be representative of the pool of appropriate tasks for the mental process being measured.

Educational measures are relative. Jimmy answered 50 percent of the items on a history test correctly and missed all the items on a mathematics test. Can we say that he performed poorly in history? Perhaps the history test was very difficult and he did better than all his classmates. What can be said about his knowledge of mathematical concepts? Could you say that he had no mathematical knowledge? What if he were asked "What is 1 plus 1?" These questions cannot be answered from the data furnished, because such measurement is relative. Such measures must be interpreted in terms of some reference group, in this case the members of Jimmy's class who took the examination.

This relative nature of measurement means that we cannot say just how difficult an item is until we try it out on a group of examinees. It also suggests the absence of a true zero score—the score which indicates a complete absence of the trait being measured. Although Jimmy missed all the items on the mathematics test, we cannot say that he has no mathematical knowledge because it is impossible to locate the score point which reflects a complete lack of knowledge. This same limitation prohibits us from saying that a student who got 100 percent right on a test knows twice as much as the student who only got 50 percent right—an erroneous assumption often made when test results are expressed as percentages.

Measures are used for classification. Measures are obtained in order to classify people or objects on the basis of some characteristic or characteristics. When attempting to classify people on the basis of a psychological trait, process, or characteristic, one is normally concerned with continuous data. However, occasionally one uses discrete data when classifying a physical trait. Classification by sex is discrete. Classification by intelligence or weight is continuous. Although we may express weight in pounds, we remain aware that two objects weighing one pound may not remain the same in weight if we refine our measures and include ounces. Likewise, two objects weighing one pound and two ounces may not weigh the same if we refine our scale to measure in tenths of ounces. In fact the characteristic, "weight," is continuous, but superimposed on this continuous characteristic is a scale, in pounds, ounces, etc., which appears to be discrete. Likewise, achievement is continuous but our measures of achievement, expressed in scores, appear to be discrete. Although all individuals receiving the same score on a test are treated as being the same, we are aware that differences might arise if the instrument were more refined. To summarize, most educational and psychological data are continuous in that the measurement categories can be made smaller and smaller through the refinement of the measuring instrument; however, some data are inherently discrete—refining the scale will not change the size of the categories. For example, the number of apples in a bowl is discrete (unless, of course, one is talking about applesauce!).

The simplest form of classification is the "yes/no" dichotomy. A person is either male or female, has blue eyes or doesn't have blue eyes, is a registered Democrat or is not a registered Democrat. Data of this type are considered to be *nominal* measurements. All members of a nominal class are treated the same in regard to the trait used for classification and *only* in regard to that particular trait. Catalog numbers in the Sears, Roebuck and Company catalog comprise a nominal scale because all items of a given number are considered to be similar.

If, within a nominal classification, one can talk about some members as having more of the characteristic than other members, it may be possible to develop an *ordinal scale* for that class. If one can say that Bill has more of the trait than Sue, that Sue has more than Carl, and that Carl and John have the same but more than Jimmy, the data are in an ordinal scale. The scores in Table 1.1 form an ordinal scale.

Table 1.1 Illustration of an ordinal scale

Children	Scores	Problems
Bill	5	A. $2+2=$
Sue	4	B. $3-1=$
Carl	3	C. $4+10=$
John	3	D. $12-6=$
Jimmy	2	E. $276\times312=$

Because Problem E in Table 1.1 is much more difficult than the other problems, one would suspect that the difference between Bill and Sue (scores of 5 and 4) in arithmetic skills is far greater than the difference between Sue and Carl or John (scores of 4 and 3). Nevertheless, on the basis of the scores received on this test, all one can do is rank these children:

$$Bill > Sue > Carl = John > Jimmy.[1]$$

The most refined scale encountered in educational and psychological measurement is the *interval scale*. When data occur on this scale, the scores can be ranked (as can ordinal data), and inferences about the differences between scores can be made since equal differences between scores indicate equal amounts of the trait. Thus if Bill received a score of 40, Dick a score of 30, and Mary a score of 20 on a test, one could say that the difference in achievement between Mary and Dick is the same as the difference between Dick and Bill. However, lacking a "zero point," one could not say that Bill exhibited twice as much achievement as Mary. Well-constructed standardized tests of intelligence and achievement are treated as if they produced interval scales.

Most classroom tests are likely to produce data which convey more than simple rank-order (ordinal) information, but do not convey *equal* interval information. However, it is usually safe to treat most well-constructed classroom tests as though they do provide data which are interval in nature.

---

[1] The symbol $>$ is read as "greater than." The converse, "less than," is symbolized by $<$.

Errors of measurement. All measurements contain error. If we wanted to determine Clyde's weight, we could place him on a bathroom scale and record the weight indicated on the measuring instrument. Would you accept this as his true weight? The measuring instrument may not be accurate for various reasons, including improper tension on the spring, improper calibration between spring and measuring scale, and lack of sensitivity to small weight differences. The observer may not read and record the weight accurately because of a simple error in recording or because of faulty judgment in determining to which of two adjacent weights the indicator is closer. Clyde may just have eaten a large meal, making the measured weight atypical for him. The floor may not be level, causing the indicator to point to the wrong weight. Clyde's observed weight may contain error from several sources: the measuring instrument, the observer, variations in Clyde, and the physical environment in which the measure was taken. These same possible sources of error are present in measures of psychological characteristics and traits. Consequently, we can assume that any observed measure contains two parts: *error score* and *true score*. For an individual these two parts of the observed score cannot be entirely separated.

DESIRABLE TEST ATTRIBUTES

Any test that is to be used effectively as a measuring instrument should be (1) reliable, (2) valid, and (3) practical. A gross deficiency in any of these test attributes can render a test useless.

Reliable

Earlier in this chapter it was stated that measurement is incomplete. In the discussion of this characteristic, reference was made to a hypothetical pool of items containing all the items which might be written to measure the variable in question. In this item pool would be items measuring the same concepts in varying degrees of complexity and from varying vantage points. This very large pool of items would contain items covering all aspects of the variable to be measured. If we were to randomly select several sets of items (tests) from this item pool, the score of a student on one set (test) should be similar to his score on any other set of items. (Perfect agreement cannot be expected because of errors of measurement.) A test is considered to be consistent if students who obtain high scores on one set of items (test) obtain high scores on other sets of items. *The degree of consistency among test scores is called reliability.* (The concept of reliability is discussed in greater depth in Chapter 12.)

Valid

A test may be highly reliable but not relevant to the behavior to be measured. An American history test, for example, may be reliable but would not be relevant for measuring knowledge and understanding of the periodic table of elements. An

English teacher could not use the results of an English grammar-usage test to determine the creative writing ability of his students, no matter how reliable it might be.

A classroom test should be both consistent and relevant; this combination of characteristics is called validity. (A more complete discussion of validity is found in Chapter 12.) Three of the factors which affect the consistency and relevance of test scores are the objectivity, balance, and fairness of the test.

Objectivity. Test scores should be as free as possible of variations due to factors other than the exact behavior being measured, factors such as reader idiosyncrasies in scoring, ambiguities in the test questions or responses made, and simple clerical errors. Preconceived ideas of a student's performance level, writing and composition skills, and time of scoring can influence the score assigned to an examination response. The reader's mood can also be a critical factor in scoring: if the reader is just beginning to score a set of papers, he may be overly critical, expecting too high a level of achievement; if he has just finished dinner, he may be sluggish and "easygoing" when scoring papers; and, as he nears the end of the scoring activity, in exhaustion he may skim over papers and assign to them scores which are too high.

It is quite common to find clerical errors in the scoring of selection-type tests. Even machine scoring is liable to error. Of course, these errors can be minimized through careful scoring procedures.

Regardless of the test method used, careful planning and scoring should be exercised to maximize test objectivity. However, one should avoid sacrificing the often difficult task of measuring higher-order mental processes in this endeavor to achieve objectivity.

Balance. In order for a test to be valid, it must measure the behaviors relevant to the content area being studied. The test should include items measuring the content and objectives of the instructional period being tested. Care should be taken to ensure that one content area or objective is not overtested at the expense of other areas or objectives. Except when careful planning has been exercised, teachers generally write items which overtest the material freshest in their minds. All too often this means that the test is not balanced, since it overemphasizes current material at the expense of material presented earlier in the instructional period. Yet students' results on such a test are generalized as indices of their degrees of goal attainment for the total instructional period. A test will exhibit balance if it is constructed on the basis of an adequately developed table of specifications and if what is taught actually reflects the course objectives. (Objectives are discussed in Chapter 2 and the Table of Specifications is discussed in Chapter 3.)

Fairness. One of the cardinal principles of the testing situation should be fairness. To *trick* an examinee is to *cheat* him. A test built on deceptions, such as verbal tricks, ambiguous items, and unspecified expectations, is not fair to anyone. The student who obtains a low score may actually understand the area being tested, but he is discriminated against because of naiveté, lack of "testwiseness," or misperceived expectations. Lack of fairness can result from a number of sources. However, probably the two greatest sources are trick items and teacher biases. The following true-false example illustrates a trick item.

The tallest mountain in the world is Mt. Eveready.

This is a trick item, since the word "Eveready" is so close to "Everest" that a good student might actually read the key word as "Everest." Such items measure reading detail rather than content achievement.

Teacher biases affect testing during both the construction and the scoring stages. A teacher may consistently use language forms or general concepts in questions which favor one group of examinees over another. This is often true in situations where both affluent and poor children are in the same classes. A teacher may fail to so structure the question that it yields only one interpretation. Differences in the responses to such questions may reflect differences in item interpretation and not differences in achievement. However, it is difficult for a teacher to consider each mode of response equally.

These factors, and many others which impinge upon the testing situation, affect the fairness of the test. *The teacher should make every effort to ensure that the test is fair for all students.*

Practical

When planning a test, the teacher should be cognizant of the practical requirements of the testing situation. Since both the student's and the teacher's time is valuable, the economical use of time in test construction, test administration, and test scoring is important. (Obviously, one should avoid sacrificing validity and reliability in this endeavor to achieve practicality.) These three functions—construction, administration, scoring—are somewhat competitive in that types of items which are easier and faster to construct tend to be less efficient with respect to use of student time during testing and to require a greater expenditure of time and effort to score than do types of items which are more difficult and time-consuming to construct. The number of students to be tested and the probable reuse of items from the test at some future time are relevant to the endeavor to achieve an economical use of time.

Two additional practical considerations should be mentioned. The availability of supplies and equipment needed for the construction and administration of tests may be a valid consideration in tight-money situations. However, a lack of supplies or equipment is often used as an excuse for perpetuating poor measurement practices. Also, the amount of time available for the administration of a classroom test is nearly always limited by the organizational structure of the school, with the possible exception of self-contained classes in the elementary school.

SUMMARY

In this chapter several somewhat diverse topics were considered: the need for classroom tests and for teachers skilled in developing such tests, the organization of the book, some basic measurement principles, and some attributes of tests. It was shown that educational measures are indirect, incomplete, and relative; that they contain error; that they are used for the purpose of classification; and that they occur on one of three scales—nominal, ordinal, or interval. Finally, the test characteristics of reliability, validity, practicality, objectivity, balance, and fairness were discussed.

Chapter 2

What to Measure

Many of the most important decisions in the area of testing are made before the first item is selected for the test—even before a decision is made concerning item format. Unfortunately, the problems which should be considered prior to test construction are too often "solved" the day before the examination, during the process of writing and selecting items for the test—solved far too often by default. This tends to be the case particularly with teacher-made tests. If the primary purpose of testing is to determine the extent to which the objectives of the unit of study have been realized, it would appear that a mandate exists concerning test construction. The test must be so constructed that the distribution of scores on the test will reflect the differences in achievement of the skills, knowledge, and understanding needed to realize the objectives of the unit of study. Consequently, before an adequate test can be constructed, the objectives must be clearly in mind and stated in terms of expected student behaviors.

EDUCATIONAL OBJECTIVES

A distinguished lecturer stands before the podium and states to an audience composed of teachers: "Today I wish to consider with you the relationship between educational objectives and evaluation." With the uttering of the phrase "educational objectives," many teachers moan: "Oh, no! Not another talk about teaching pupils to live in a changing world, teaching for adult life." Other teachers, however, expect a discussion of immediate, specific objectives, such as "to help students learn that you can divide by a fraction by inverting and multiplying." Which group of teachers is correct? What does the term educational objectives mean? Actually, either interpretation could be correct and both are matters of concern for educators.

Ultimate Objectives

In order to justify the demands made by the school on students and the expenditure of large sums of money for education, the educative process must clearly contribute to the ability of the child to cope with the demands of society now and in the world of his future—unless, of course, one considers that the major purpose of the school is simply to serve the custodial function of keeping children off the streets and out of the available labor force. Ultimate objectives are inevitably a concern of education. What are the ultimate objectives of education? Unfortunately, a simple, clear, and generally acceptable answer is not possible. In our society there is no clear and universally accepted set of ultimate objectives. Why this is true may be discovered through an examination of some of the factors which must be considered in the determination of these objectives.

Since objectives are merely the means to further ends, they must be consistent with and must contribute to the achievement of these ends. Consequently, in order to develop the ultimate objectives, the *desired ends* must be determined, and this involves philosophical questions concerning the components of a good life for the individual, the role of the individual in society, and the responsibility of society for the individual.

Although a good life for the individual may be described in many ways, most people in our society would probably accept the inclusion of the following elements, the relative importance of these elements varying with different philosophical orientations: maintenance of life; good health; self-actualization (achieving one's potential), which requires self-understanding, self-direction, and acceptance of self as a person of worth; relating well with others; understanding of and ability to cope with the environment, both social and physical; the achievement of an adequate economic standard of living; and effective participation in the decision-making process of society. Although all these elements are generally acceptable, the interpretation of what is needed to satisfy the requirements of the element (for example, what constitutes "self-actualization" or what is "an acceptable economic standard of living") varies with one's philosophical view of man and society.

A person's philosophical views concerning the nature of society and the individual's role in it influences his selection of desired ends. If he believes that the structure of society must be both maintained and modifiable in order for a civilization to survive, and that this society should survive, this belief will be reflected in the ends he selects. The needs of society and the role of the individual in meeting these needs must be brought into relief.

When trying to determine the role which the school should play in helping the individual and society achieve these goals, one's views about the nature of society's responsibility for the individual, and its authority in meeting this responsibility, will be quite influential.

In order to adequately determine the ultimate objectives for an educational system one must select the desired ends in keeping with the requirements of the philosophical framework in which the school operates. After the desired ends have been determined, the objectives which will serve to achieve these outcomes must be developed. During this development stage, these ends serve as a validity criterion (since the means must be consistent with the ends) and as guideposts to indicate direction. However, they cannot be expected to determine the adequacy of the objectives for realizing these outcomes.

The desired ends considered in the discussion of the "good life for the individual" can be translated into the following list of ultimate objectives for each schoolchild:

1. To develop the skills, understandings, and attitudes which will contribute to the maintenance of life and the achievement and maintenance of good health.
2. To develop the understandings and attitudes needed in order to acquire an acceptance of self as a person of worth and a desire for self-actualization.
3. To develop self-understanding and self-direction.
4. To develop the skills, understandings, and attitudes needed in order to relate well with others.
5. To develop an understanding of and the ability to cope with his physical and social environment.
6. To develop the skills, understandings, and attitudes which will enable him to achieve an acceptable economic standard of living.
7. To develop the skills, understandings, and attitudes needed in order to effectively and productively participate in the decision-making processes of society.

In order to make these broadly stated objectives educationally meaningful, each one must be more carefully defined and specific objectives must be identified to support them. If these specific objectives are to be usable, they must be defined in levels appropriate for the developmental stage of the learner. Consequently, a body of knowledge, drawn from field and laboratory research, judgments and theoretical speculations of experts, and the experiences of educational practitioners, concerning child growth and development, the nature of learning, personality development, and the interactional processes occurring in groups, must be acquired and carefully considered during the process of selecting the more specific objectives. Only then can one hope to select the appropriate "means" for achieving the desired "ends."

Instructional Objectives

With few exceptions, the curriculum, whether it be in a public or a private school, whether it be at the elementary, secondary, or higher education level, is divided into academic and performance areas which function more or less independently of each other. Ideally, the organization of the school and the composition of its curriculum should be consistent with and should contribute to the achievement of the specific objectives which were derived to obtain the desired ends. Unfortunately, one would not expect to encounter this ideal in a normal school setting, since much of the organization and content of the curriculum exists partially as a result of tradition and is sometimes related only coincidentally to the objectives of education. Thus in developing his course objectives, the teacher must operate within a limiting structure which may be far from the ideal. Nevertheless, considerable latitude usually exists within the institutional structure, permitting the ingenious teacher to develop instructional objectives for his particular course which are consistent with the ultimate objectives of education.

In writing the instructional objectives for a course of study, the teacher should keep foremost in his mind that the purpose of education is to promote changes in behavior which will contribute to the eventual realization of the ultimate objectives. Objectives must be stated in terms of observable student behavior, if the teacher intends to measure the degree to which his instructional objectives have been realized. Although every course of study includes factual content, some of which may be unique to it, the objectives should focus on attributes (such as skills, understandings, and attitudes) which will ultimately contribute to the attainment of the goals of education rather than on course content *per se*. This does not mean that facts will not be learned; however, it does mean that the objectives should be something other than "to learn the content of the textbook." The instructional objectives should be attainable, appropriate for the child at his current level of development, and a major determinant of the course content. Obviously, the objectives selected should properly reflect the behaviors considered to be critical.

The following rules should prove useful in writing instructional objectives:

1. Be concise—at most, objectives should be one or two sentences in length.

2. Be singular—an objective should focus on one and only one aspect of behavior.

3. Describe expected behavior—an objective should indicate the desired end product, not merely a direction of change or a teacher activity.

4. Be realistic—an object should focus on observable behavior, not on teacher illusions or undefinable traits.

5. Use definite terms—terms such as "write," "define," "list," and "compare" have definite meanings, whereas terms such as "know," "understand," and "apply" have a multitude of meanings.

The following objectives fail to meet the above guidelines for the reasons indicated:

1. To develop *accuracy* (undefined trait).

2. To *know* the rules for constructing essay tests (indefinite term).

3. To be able to give a verbal definition of the mean, to be able to calculate the mean from a given set of scores, and to be able to explain the uses of the mean (multiple objective).

4. To *read* Chapters 4, 5, and 6 (activity).

5. To be able to act with a sense of responsibility as an adult (teacher illusion).

In terms of the guidelines discussed, the following objectives are much better constructed:

1. To be able to select the correct answer to given division problems, with accuracy to three decimal places.
2. To be able to list five rules for constructing essay tests.
3. To be able to write a definition of the mean.
4. To be able to list the appropriate uses of the mean.
5. To be able to calculate the correct mean for a given set of scores.
6. To be able to differentiate correctly between group-oriented and self-oriented behavior in simulated situations.

However, technically correct instructional objectives are not necessarily good ones. The objectives must also be consistent with the particular concerns of the course of instruction and the ultimate objectives of the school. When evaluating an instructional objective, one must consider all three of these criteria.

A possible list of ultimate objectives was considered in the previous section. These objectives can serve as the school-level criterion for writing instructional objectives. (The list of ultimate objectives for a particular school may differ from the one presented here. However, in most cases there will be a high degree of similarity in the desired ends expressed.)

During the past decade, classroom teachers have become increasingly involved in the initiation and development of improved school programs. One of these programs is the grade eleven American Studies Program at University City High School, University City, Missouri.

The program, involving approximately six history teachers, six English teachers, and 500 students, has been in effect since 1965. It was planned and organized to achieve student-centered learning goals based on a process-oriented philosophy. This philosophy was represented in published statements evolved from the deliberation and the experience of the school's professional staff. These statements were directed toward the school's primary purpose of serving the youth of the community and the society in which they lived by aiding them to become responsible, perceiving, self-directing individuals capable of making decisions and value judgments. This philosophy is explicated in at least four of the ultimate objectives listed in this chapter (objectives 3, 4, 5, and 7).

As part of the developmental process, a set of instructional objectives was developed for the program.[1] These objectives are presented in Table 2.1. They are organized under the following headings: skills in logical thinking; skills in developing and analyzing hypotheses and generalizations; skills in applying logical thinking, hypotheses, and generalizations; and skills in the comprehension

---

[1] The objectives were originally reported in Alvin P. Sokol and Jon C. Marshall, *Inquiry into Innovations*, Research Report I, Demonstration Schools Project, University Senior High School, University City, Missouri, Title III of ESEA, Public Law 89–10, 1968, Part III.

and recall of information. These objectives could be reorganized and listed under the ultimate objectives which they support.

Table 2.1 Tentative behavioral objectives for the American Studies program

I. Skills in Logical Thinking
   a) Can identify the purpose of a statement, argument, document, or literary work.
   b) Can identify the point of view of a statement, argument, document, or literary work.
   c) Can identify the main idea of a statement, argument, document, or literary work.
   d) Can reconstruct goals, attitudes, or policies which were associated with a given action.
   e) Can list the assumptions made in selected materials.
   f) Can identify logical inconsistencies, ambiguities, or fallacies in statements under consideration.
   g) Can generalize to a principle from a set of factual information.
   h) Can translate a principle into a concrete example.
   i) Can explain the similarities and differences among issues, policies, and events within the context of selected recurring themes in American Studies.

II. Skills in Developing and Analyzing Hypotheses and Generalizations
   a) Can identify the problems and their subproblems when confronted with statements of issues, policies, or historical events.
   b) Can list (or select) tentative statements offering explanations for or solutions to selected problems, issues, policies, or events.
   c) Can support or reject arguments, explanations, and proposed solutions with statements of facts, records, historical personalities, and the like.
   d) Can differentiate between relevant and irrelevant information used in the support of arguments, explanations, and proposed solutions.
   e) Can write (or select) logical implications of given problems, issues, policies, or events.
   f) Can logically accept, modify, or reject a hypothesis on the basis of given information.

III. Skills in Applying Logical Thinking, Hypotheses, and Generalizations
   a) Can recognize and state one's own beliefs, opinions, and values.
   b) Can differentiate between objective evidence and personal bias when preparing explanations for or solutions to problems, issues, policies, or events.
   c) Can recognize bias in a given selection of information.
   d) Can prepare explanations for or solutions to problems, issues, policies, or events in a reasonable period of time.
   e) Can demonstrate the willingness and ability to use a variety of types of evidence to support or reject explanations for or solutions to problems, issues, policies, or events.
   f) Can analyze and evaluate the foundations of American political, social, and economic institutions.

V. Skills in the Comprehension and Recall of Information
   a) Can recall selected names, facts, and ideas in American Studies.
   b) Can define selected terms and literary devices in American Studies.
   c) Can present the point of view of selected persons in American history.

The ultimate objective "to develop self-understanding and self-direction" is behaviorally defined as:

Can recognize and state one's own beliefs, opinions, and values (IIIa).

Can differentiate between objective evidence and personal bias when preparing explanations for or solutions to problems, issues, policies, or events (IIIb).

The ultimate objective "to develop the skills, understandings, and attitudes needed in order to relate well with others" is behaviorally defined as:

Can explain the similarities and differences among issues, policies, and events within the context of selected recurring themes in American Studies (Ii).

Can prepare explanations for or solutions to problems, issues, policies, or events in a reasonable period of time (IIId).

Can present the point of view of selected persons in American history (IVc).

Because of the interrelationships among broadly stated ultimate objectives, it is difficult to classify all instructional objectives into unique categories. As is the case with the American Studies objectives, many instructional objectives can logically fit more than one ultimate objective category. For example, the objectives listed above as explicating the ultimate objective "to develop the skills, understandings, and attitudes needed in order to relate well with others" could also logically support the objective "to develop the skills, understandings, and attitudes needed in order to effectively and productively participate in the decision-making processes of society." Conversely, several instructional objectives in Table 2.1 which might logically support the former objective were not included in the above list.

The foregoing discussion is presented to illustrate the consistency between a set of instructional objectives and the ultimate objectives presented in this chapter. The uniqueness of objectives (either instructional or ultimate) is not of prime importance when writing them, because specific behaviors developed are generally interrelated. Of prime concern in writing instructional objectives are (1) the behavioral aspect of the objective, (2) the consistency of the objective with the general goals of the course, and (3) the consistency of the objective with the ultimate objectives of education. This consistency of an instructional objective is best judged in relation to the set of desired ends rather than to a specific goal or ultimate objective.

Study questions. Presented below is a list of instructional objectives written for specific classroom units. Rewrite these objectives in a more acceptable form.

1. The student should, after studying his life, works, and environment, know who Walt Whitman is.

2. To know the issues and events leading to the U.S. involvement in World War II.

3. To understand the cause-and-effect relationships of the events during the years 1932 and 1941.

4. To be able to analyze a poem.

5. Analyze foods that can be canned with best results.

6. Will can three different types of jelly during the week.

7. To develop the vocabulary of the students.

8. Students should be able to associate points on a rational number line with points on a natural number line by using mates and distinguish the difference between rational and natural numbers by use of the density and successor properties.

9. Increase fluency in Spanish by participating in question-and-answer games.

10. To study basic dialogue sentences (in foreign language).

CLASSIFYING INSTRUCTIONAL OBJECTIVES

During the initial planning of a unit of study many objectives will be recorded, but in a somewhat random order. It is necessary to bring organization to this chaos: the objectives must be classified. Two systems of classification will be considered here: (1) content and (2) cognitive-affective.

Content Classification Systems

When the teacher selects his objectives for his unit of study, he is also determining the subject matter he will use in his endeavor to achieve these objectives. Consequently, it is possible to organize them within a content classification system. The exact nature of this system will depend on the objectives to be realized and the content to be organized. For example, although it has been common practice to present history in a time-ordered sequence, it is not uncommon to find the study of government organized on the basis of the major functions of the governmental units being studied or to find social studies classified on the basis of current problems in society and government. In mathematics the building-block model is often encountered, where content is ordered from simple to complex; each new concept builds on the preceding one. If the authors were to develop a content classification system for some of the objectives of this chapter, it might evolve somewhat as shown in Table 2.2. (The table contains a topic outline of the chapter's content in the left-hand column and objectives associated with each topic in the right-hand column.)

Table 2.2 Content classification of some of the instructional objectives of this chapter

Content Outline	Instructional Objectives
I. Ultimate Objectives	
a) Definition and rationale	1. To be able to state (or select) the definition of "ultimate objectives." 2. To be able to list the reasons why ultimate objectives are important to teachers.
b) Relations to "ends"	3. To be able to explain the relationships among the "components of the good life." 4. To be able to evaluate the appropriateness of stated objectives when the "ends" are used as the criteria.
c) Philosophical considerations	5. To be able to identify the philosophical assumptions made in specific ultimate objectives.
d) Construction	6. To be able to identify the ultimate objectives suggested in this book. 7. To be able to develop ultimate objectives for realizing desired "ends."
II. Instructional Objectives	
a) Definition	8. To be able to state (or select) the definition of "instructional objectives." 9. To be able to differentiate between instructional objectives and ultimate objectives.
b) Desirable characteristics	10. To be able to explain the importance of child growth patterns to the selection of instructional objectives. 11. To be able to list the desirable attributes of instructional characteristics. 12. To be able to explain why instructional objectives must be stated behaviorally.
c) Construction	13. To be able to develop a set of instructional objectives for a unit of study. 14. To be able to list the rules for the construction of instructional objectives.
III. Classifying Instructional Objectives	
a) Need	15. To be able to state the major reason for classifying objectives.
b) Classification systems 1. Content	16. To be able to classify a set of instructional objectives in a content classification system.
2. Cognitive-affective	17. To be able to classify a set of instructional objectives in a cognitive classification system.

Cognitive-Affective Classification Systems

Although a content classification of instructional objectives is needed for a meaningful organization of the unit of study, it is also important to consider and classify objectives on the basis of the intellectual activity involved (cognitive domain) and the attitudes, beliefs, interests, and values fostered (affective domain).

When an examination is to be constructed with the intent of assessing student progress, most teachers are inclined to consider only those objectives which fall in the cognitive domain. To mark attitudes, values, and beliefs is sometimes thought to be irrelevant and perhaps even a violation of individual rights. However, an even stronger criticism of classroom tests in the affective domain is the ease with which the examinee can fake the desired responses. Nevertheless, since many objectives do belong in the affective domain, it is important to recognize them explicitly and to measure the extent to which they are achieved, even though one may not wish to base marks on the resulting measures.

Within the cognitive domain, it is possible to order instructional objectives on the basis of the complexity of the intellectual activity required. One of the most comprehensive classification systems is the taxonomy devised by Bloom, Englehart, Furst, Hill, and Krathwohl.[2] The major categories developed for this system, ordered from simple to complex, are knowledge, comprehension, application, analysis, synthesis, and evaluation. Each successive category includes the behaviors appropriate to the preceding category.

The simplest cognitive behavior, *knowledge*, involves the recall of information. Objectives concerned with the individual's knowledge of terms and facts, knowledge of methods and criteria for handling terms and facts, and knowledge of the abstractions of a field are properly classified in this category. Most achievement test items measure objectives at this level.

To be able to state (or select) the definition of "ultimate objectives" (Table 2.2).

To be able to state (or select) the definition of "instructional objectives" (Table 2.2).

Can recall selected names, facts, and ideas in American Studies (Table 2.1).

The vast number of items of this type on a test often overshadows any items measuring higher-order mental processes. This is unfortunate, since many educational objectives call for skills of a much higher order than just knowledge. Nevertheless, the importance of knowledge should not be discounted. Scholarly pursuit is by definition a quest for knowledge. Even though process learning is important, it should not be done at the expense of knowledge.

There are three essential qualities which vegetables must possess in order to obtain the best results when canning. List these three qualities.

Who was Roosevelt's vice-presidential running mate in 1940?

*A. Charles E. Hughes[3]
B. Cordell Hull
C. Elihu Root
D. Henry A. Wallace

---

[2] Bloom, B. S., and others, *Taxonomy of Educational Objectives, Handbook I; Cognitive Domain*, David McKay Co., New York, 1956.
[3] A star is used to indicate the correct answer in multiple-choice items.

Objectives classified as *comprehension* objectives require the ability to reorganize, restate, and intepret the facts, the methods and criteria for handling facts, and the generalizations and abstractions of a field.

To be able to explain why instructional objectives must be stated behaviorally (Table 2.2).

Can present the point of view of selected persons in American history (Table 2.1).

In classroom tests, this level represents the second most common category of items. Items of this type require examinees to make low-level decisions in identical or parallel situations to those presented in the course content.

In two or three sentences, state the theme of the following poem.[4]

> I never saw a moor,
> I never saw the sea;
> Yet know I how the heather looks,
> And what a wave must be.
>
> I never spoke with God,
> Nor visited in heaven;
> Yet certain am I of the spot
> As if the chart were given.

Which of the following was the most important reason Filipinos feared the Hawes–Cutting Act for Philippine independence?

*A. They thought the United States would raise tariff barriers against Philippine products.
 B. They thought the United States would remove the U.S. Naval bases from the islands.
 C. They wanted the United States to maintain control over the islands.
 D. They feared internal struggle once the United States forces left the islands.

When instructional objectives are directed toward the utilization of knowledge in new and different situations, they may be classified as *application* objectives.

To be able to classify a set of instructional objectives in a content classification system (Table 2.2).

Can support or reject arguments, explanations, and proposed solutions with statements of facts, records, historical personalities, and the like (Table 2.1).

Test items in this category require examinees to make decisions in new situations which must be translated first into situations which are identical or parallel to those presented in the course content.

---

[4] Emily Dickinson, "I Never Saw a Moor," in Martha Dickinson Bianchi and Alfred Leete Hampson (Eds.), *The Poems of Emily Dickinson.* Roberts Brothers, Boston, 1890, p. 163.

Explain how

$a(kb) = (ka)b$

is obtained from

$$\frac{a}{b} \sim \frac{ka}{kb}$$

(universe for $a = N$; universe for b and $k = C$).

The following three items consist of word groups. Determine the number of sentences in each group.

Mark A if the group is not a sentence.
Mark B if 1 sentence.
Mark C if 2 sentences.
Mark D if 3 sentences.

1. "Thank you," said Richard as the car started she reached out her hand to him.
2. Before the work of the new day had begun.
3. Come or you may not see the hot rods how disappointed you will be.

The *analysis* category contains objectives which require the individual to determine the elements of some problem or theory under consideration, the relationship among the elements, and the relationship of the elements to the whole. This level can be characterized as taking the "whole" of a problem and breaking it down into its various parts to extract meaning from the situation.

To be able to explain the relationships among the "components of the good life" (Table 2.2).

Can identify the problems and their subproblems when confronted with statements of issues, policies, or historical events (Table 2.1).

Can explain the similarities and differences among issues, policies, and events within the context of selected recurring themes in American Studies (Table 2.1).

Test items of this type require examinees to isolate specifics in an overall problem situation, and use the interrelationships among the specifics to solve the given problem. Items of this type are difficult to construct, particularly in the selection-type format.

"When Lilacs Last in the Dooryard Bloomed" was written by Whitman on the occasion of Abraham Lincoln's death. Describe and explain the format used in this poem, and illustrate how it parallels the general form of an elegy.

The expression $(m - x^3)(ny)$ is negative in sign. If m is positive, what would be the direction of the signs for x, n, and y?

A. x, n, y all positive
B. x, n positive; y negative
C. x positive; n, y negative
*D. n positive; x, y negative
E. n, y positive; x negative

Objectives classified as *synthesis* include behaviors like the development of a plan or a set of abstract relations. This level can be characterized as taking the various parts of a problem and putting them together to derive meaning from the situation.

To be able to explain the relationships among the "components of the good life" (Table 2.2).

Can generalize to a principle from a set of factual information (Table 2.1).

Test items of this type require examinees to organize specifics into an overall problem statement, and from this statement draw conclusions or generalizations. Most items of this type are in the essay format.

A, a minor, was a student at Duncan High School. He purchased an automobile for $500 from B, an adult, with a down payment of $50. The car was subsequently stolen and A refused to pay B the remaining $450. B sued A for the money. What was the decision? Why? (Be specific.)

A study was run comparing three competitive makes of automobiles. The following data were gathered for automobiles A, B, and C.

	Make A	Make B	Make C
Expected retail price	$2650	$2600	$2300
Wheelbase (inches)	111	111	106
Overall length (inches)	193	188	181
Overall width (inches)	71	73	72
Curb weight (pounds)	2900	2800	2700
Displacement (cubic inches)	220	230	195
Horsepower at 4000 rpm	145	135	115
Acceleration time, 0 to 60 mph (seconds)	15.0	19.5	16.5
Minimum distance for controlled stop at 60 mph (feet)	170	150	150
Constant-speed gas mileage at 60 mph (mpg)	22.0	19.5	18.0
General comfort in a) front b) rear	Good Fair	Poor Poor	Fair Poor
Repair record	Good	Average	Average

DIRECTIONS: Consider the hypotheses presented as items 1, 2, and 3 below in light of the data presented above. If a hypothesis is supported by the data, *mark answer space A*; if the hypothesis is not supported by the data, *mark answer space B*.

1. Cars with higher-powered engines get poorer gas mileage (at 60 mph) than cars with lower-powered engines.

2. The greater the disparity between the retail prices of cars, the greater the disparity in other measured characteristics.

3. For comparative purposes, displacement and horsepower yield the same relative information.

4. Relative to the data presented above, which one of the three makes of automobiles would be the best buy as a family car?
   A. Make A
   B. Make B
   C. Make C

The last item (item 4) requires the synthesis of information. However, it also requires the examinee to make a judgmental decision and therefore involves evaluation, the highest level of cognitive behavior.

Objectives requiring the evaluation (or judging) of theory or products according to internal evidence or external criteria are properly classified as *evaluation* objectives.

To be able to evaluate the appropriateness of stated objectives when the "ends" are used as the criteria (*Table 2.2*).

Can differentiate between relevant and irrelevant information used in the support of arguments, explanations, and proposed solutions (*Table 2.1*).

Can logically accept, modify, or reject a hypothesis on the basis of given information (*Table 2.1*).

Measurement at this level requires utilization of the lower-level mental skills. The student is required to decide between right and wrong, good and bad, relevant and irrelevant. These decisions require knowledge and comprehension of relevant concepts, skill in applying these concepts, and ability to analyze and synthesize data in the forming of sound, logical judgments. Items of this type are often difficult to construct because of the necessity of being able to defend one alternative as a better response to an item than all other possible alternatives.

A logical argument is stated below. Analyze it and determine whether it is a valid or invalid argument. State and explain your conclusion.

If a triangle has all three sides equal, it is equilateral. $\triangle ABC$ is equilateral Therefore, $\triangle ABC$ has all three sides equal.

Which of the following is the *best* original source of ideas for classroom test items?
   A. Course objectives
   B. Course outlines
   C. Textbooks
   D. Standardized tests

Because of the difficulty often encountered in determining the proper classification of objectives and to aid in the writing and classification of test items, it is advantageous to use a three-category classification system: knowledge, understanding, and application. Within this system, *knowledge* is defined as the ability to recall previously learned information, whether it be facts, trends, or generalizations; *understanding* is defined as the ability to restate and interpret information; and *application* includes any intellectual activity more complex than simple understanding, such as application of principles to a new problem, analysis, synthesis, and evaluation. The scheme for this system as compared to the six-category one is as follows:

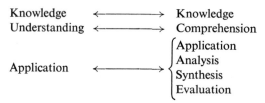

Applying this classification system to some objectives which might be applicable to the topics which we have considered in this chapter could yield the results given in Table 2.3.

Table 2.3 Example of a classification of objectives

Objective	Classification
1. To be able to list the reasons why ultimate objectives are important.	Knowledge
2. To be able to identify the ultimate objectives of education suggested in this book.	Knowledge
3. To be able to reconstruct the content classification system.	Knowledge
4. To be able to differentiate between ultimate and instructional objectives.	Understanding
5. To be able to contrast educational philosophy and educational objectives.	Understanding
6. To be able to explain the importance of child growth patterns to the selection of objectives.	Understanding
7. To be able to develop a set of objectives for a unit of study.	Application
8. To be able to evaluate the appropriateness of stated objectives when the "ends" of education are used as the criteria.	Application
9. To be able to classify objectives.	Application

SUMMARY

Before a test which will measure the differences among students in their acquisition of skills, knowledge, and understandings needed in order to achieve the objectives of a unit of study can be constructed, the instructional objectives must be formulated as concise, precise, singular, realistic statements of expected student behaviors. If the instructional objectives are to be relevant, they should be pertinent to the realization of the ultimate objectives of education; thus the ultimate objectives of education must be determined, and the form which they take is influenced by one's philosophy concerning the components of a good life for the individual, the role of the individual in society, and the responsibility of society for the individual.

The instructional objectives of a unit of study should be organized according to some system of classification. The content associated with the objectives may serve as the system for classification, with the content organized in keeping with some identifiable scheme. A cognitive-affective system of classification may be used in the process of ordering the instructional objectives.

SUGGESTED READING

Ahmann, J. Stanley, and Marvin Glock, *Evaluating Pupil Growth: Principles of Tests and Measurement.* Allyn and Bacon, Boston, 1967, pp. 36–60.

Bloom, B. S., and others, *Taxonomy of Educational Objectives, Handbook I: Cognitive Domain.* David McKay Co., New York, 1956.

"Cardinal Principles of Secondary Education." *U.S. Office of Education Bulletin,* No. 35, 1918.

Dickinson, Emily. "I Never Saw a Moor," in Martha Dickinson Bianchi and Alfred Leete Hampson (Eds.) *The Poems of Emily Dickinson.* Roberts Brothers, Boston, 1890, p. 163.

Dressel, Paul L., "Measurement and Evaluation of Instructional Objectives," in *Seventeenth Yearbook.* National Council of Measurement in Education, Ames, Ia., 1960, pp. 1–6.

Ebel, Robert L., *Measuring Educational Achievement.* Prentice-Hall, Englewood Cliffs, N.J., 1965, Chapter 2.

Educational Policies Commission, *The Purposes of Education in American Democracy.* National Education Association and the American Association of School Administrators, Washington, D.C., 1938.

French, Will, and associates, *Behavioral Goals of General Education in High School.* Russell Sage Foundation, New York, 1957.

Havighurst, Robert J., *Human Development and Education.* Mckay, New York, 1953, Parts I, II, and III.

Henry, Nelson B. (Ed.), "Adapting the Secondary-School Program to the Needs of Youth," in *Fifty-Second Yearbook, National Social Studies Education,* Part I. University of Chicago Press, Chicago, 1953, Chapters 2 and 12.

Kearney, Nolan C., *Elementary School Objectives.* Russell Sage Foundation, New York, 1953, Parts II and III.

Krathwohl, D. R., B. S. Bloom, and B. B. Masia, *Taxonomy of Educational Objectives: Affective Domain.* David McKay Co., New York, 1964.

Lindquist, E. F., "Preliminary Considerations in Objective Test Construction," in E. F. Lindquist (Ed.), *Educational Measurement.* American Council of Education, Washington, D.C., 1951, pp. 119–140.

Mager, R. F., *Preparing Instructional Objectives*. Fearson Publishers, Palo Alto, Calif., 1962.

Sokol, Alvin P., and Jon L. Marshall, *Inquiry into Innovation*. Research Report I, Demonstration School Project, University Senior High School, Title III of ESEA Public Law 89–10, 1968, Part III.

Stoker, H. W., and R. P. Kropp, "Measurement of Cognitive Processes," *Journal of Educational Measurement*, **1**, 1964, 39–42.

Chapter 3

Planning the Test

INTRODUCTION

The teacher makes many decisions during the construction of a classroom test. However, he may not be fully aware that he is doing so or that these decisions influence the test characteristics of reliability, validity, and administration and scoring efficiency. In this chapter, some of the factors which should be systematically considered when planning a test will be discussed.

TABLE OF SPECIFICATIONS

In Chapter 2, it was stated that before an adequate test can be constructed, the objectives must be clearly in mind and should be stated in writing in behavioral terms. This statement was followed by a discussion of ultimate and instructional objectives, and suggested systems for their classification. Since the primary purpose of classroom testing is to obtain individual measures for evaluating students with regard to their acquisition of the instructional objectives, a blueprint for selecting appropriate test items must be developed. This blueprint is called a *Table of Specifications.*

A Two-Way Table

Before constructing a test to determine whether or not an objective has been realized, it is necessary to select the content which is applicable to the objective and to identify the complexity of the intellectual or affective activity involved. That is, the teacher must be able to classify the objectives in two dimensions: content and cognitive-affective. The test blueprint is a two-way table, with content shown on one axis and the cognitive (and/or affective) domain on the other.

Content	Cognitive Domain		
	Knowledge	Understanding	Application
I.			
II.			
III.			

One use of this table is to indicate, for each content area, the relative importance of the different levels of intellectual activity in achieving the instructional objectives relevant to that area. Likewise, it is used to indicate the relative emphasis of each content area to the instructional objectives. The intersection of a content-area row with a cognitive domain column should indicate the relation between intellectual activity and content. Consequently, each item which is written for a cell (a row/column intersection) should reflect the relation between intellectual activity and content for the instructional objective it is intended to measure.

Construction of the Table

If a test is to be valid as a measure of the extent to which the instructional objectives are achieved, the relative emphasis of the various content areas should reflect their relative importance to the instructional objectives. Consequently, the Table of Specifications should indicate the relative value of each content area, perhaps by showing the desired weight as a percentage. These weights are *subjective teacher decisions* reflecting the relative importance of each area.

Many criteria can aid the teacher in formulating the "best" weights. For example, one might expect these weights to be related to class time devoted to each area; thus class time may be used as an indicator of importance. If one-half period is spent on the topic "Scoring the Test" in a five-period unit on "Test Planning," then the expected weight of the content area might be

$$\frac{.5 \text{ period}}{5 \text{ periods}} = .10 \quad \text{or} \quad 10\% \quad \text{(See Table 3.1)}.$$

Similarly, if just less than two days (about $1\frac{3}{4}$ periods) are spent on the topic "Table of Specifications," this category would be expected to account for about

$$\frac{1.75 \text{ periods}}{5 \text{ periods}} = .35 \quad \text{or} \quad 35\% \text{ of the test}.$$

Other common criteria which might be used are (1) total student time and (2) degree to which content areas relate to future learnings.

Regardless of the exact criteria used, the weights assigned indicate the relative importance of content areas as perceived by the teachers. Table 3.1 is a Table of

Table 3.1 Table of specifications for a 26-item test

Content	Objectives:	Knowledge 30%	Understanding 40%	Application 30%	Number of items by content area
35%	I. Table of specifications				
	a) Content classification	1	4	4	9
	b) Level of abstraction				
	c) Weight of elements				
30%	II. Test and item characteristics				
	a) Mastery or discriminatory				
	b) Item difficulty and discrimination	2	3	3	8
	c) Verbal behavior or performance				
5%	VI. Test length	1	0	1	2
5%	IV. Test instructions	0	1	0	1
10%	III. Test layout	1	1	0	2
5%	V. Reproducing the test	1	0	0	1
10%	VII. Scoring the test	2	1	0	3
	Number of items by cognitive classfication	8	10	8	26

Number of items in cell = row weight ∗ column weight ∗ number of test items (for Area I, Understanding) = .35 ∗ .40 ∗ 26 = 3.6 items.

Specifications which might be constructed to examine the acquisition of the objectives of Chapter 3; the desired weights for the content areas are shown in the left-hand column.

Emphasis on the various areas of the cognitive domain should reflect the relative importance of these to the instructional objectives. Thus the three classifications of the cognitive domain (knowledge, understanding, and application) should be indicated. The area weights should equal the accumulations of the weights of the instructional objectives within them: first, the weight should be determined for the individual objectives in a specified category; second, these weights should be added to determine the category weight. For example, if there are six knowledge objectives, each with a weight of 5 percent, then the weight of the knowledge category is 30 percent. The instructional-objective weights are determined in the same manner as for the content areas. For the Table of Specifications shown in Table 3.1 these weights are as follows: knowledge, 30 percent; understanding, 40 percent; and application, 30 percent.

Since it is difficult to write items measuring the more complex intellectual activities and because specific knowledge often aids the teacher in achieving the instructional objectives (and is sometimes itself an instructional objective), it is unlikely that a teacher could, or would even want to, use only application-level items. For many teachers, the weighting given in Table 3.1—knowledge 30 percent, understanding 40 percent, application 30 percent—may be desirable. However, these weights should be viewed as examples only. The relative importance of the different levels of the cognitive domain varies across subject areas and schools.

After the desired weights for each content area and for each of the cognitive-domain areas have been determined, the weight to be attached to any cell may be found. It is the product of the percentages for the row and the column corresponding to the cell. For example, the weight for the cell corresponding to "Test Layout" and "Knowledge" in Table 3.1 is

$$.10 \times .30 = .03 \quad \text{or} \quad 3\%.$$

The number of test items to include in a cell is found by multiplying the cell weight by the desired number of items on the total test. Thus the test of Table 3.1 should contain $.03 \times 26 = .78$ or, in practical terms, 1 item testing knowledge in content area III. However, it might not be desirable to hold rigidly to this number, since the importance of the different levels of intellectual activity could vary across content areas. In Table 3.1, for example, the cell corresponding to "knowledge" in content area I was assigned one item, whereas the weighting percentage indicates that there should be $.35 \times .30 \times 26 = 2.7$ items. In developing this Table of Specifications, it was decided that knowledge was less important to this content area than to other content areas of the test.

Special Considerations in Weighting

Having determined the weight for each component of the Table of Specifications, it would appear to be a rather simple task to achieve the desired weighting on the examination. If it can be assumed that each item in the test carries the same weight, a balanced test should result when each cell weight (expressed as a proportion) is multiplied by the number of items desired in the test. Thus if the test is to contain 100 items and a given cell proportion is .02, two items ($100 \times .02$) should be selected for that cell. Unfortunately, this would not necessarily ensure a proper weighting for the examination.

Correct weights would be obtained in this manner only if each item on the test carried the same weight.[1] If the classroom test is designed to cover several

---

[1] If each item is to carry the same weight on the test, the interrelations between the items must be equal and the variabilities of the scores on the items must be equal. If the test covers several content areas at various levels of abstraction, the interrelations should normally be rather small. If the cells have items of comparable difficulty and of comparable discrimination, the variability of the scores in these cells should be about equal. A more detailed discussion of this aspect of test construction is found in K. W. Vaughn, "Planning the Objective Test," in E. F. Lindquist (Ed.), *Educational Measurements*, American Council on Education, Washington, D.C., 1951, pp. 167–170.

content areas at various levels of abstraction (with items of varying levels in the cognitive domain), and if the cells have items of somewhat equal difficulty and of somewhat equal power to separate those who perform well on the total test from those who perform poorly, an approximation of the desired weighting can be obtained by treating all items as if they have equal weights. Consequently, unless there is reason to suspect that a significant relation exists between the areas to be covered by the examination, the various components of the test (as shown in the Table of Specifications) can be expected to exhibit the desired weighting when the number of items to be used in each cell is determined as discussed in the preceding paragraph and care is taken to use good items of comparable difficulty. In those portions of the test thought to be related, one may use slightly fewer items.

Example of a Table of Specifications

The following Table of Specifications shown in Table 3.2 illustrates the application of this approach to the construction of a 75-item multiple-choice final examination for a research and statistics course. The teacher selected the weights which *he thought* were most appropriate for the content areas and recorded these weights as percentages in the content column of the table. The weights to be used for each mental process of the cognitive domain were recorded under the appropriate column headings. The number of items desired for each content area at each level of abstraction was then determined and placed in the appropriate cell. It should be noted that the cell values in this table are only approximately equal to those which would be obtained by multiplying a computed cell weight by the total number of items on the test. These variations are the result of the impossibility of using fractional items and the judgment of the teacher as to the appropriateness of different levels of the cognitive domain for specific content areas. The computed number of items and the theoretical weights for the cells are shown in parentheses.

Adaptation to Other Test Forms

This format can also be used for constructing the Table of Specifications for an essay or oral examination. The only special adaptation of the table would be in the number of test items in each cell. In these formats, it is usually necessary for individual items to overlap several cells because of the small number of items that can be included in the test.

TEST AND ITEM CHARACTERISTICS

Early in the process of developing a test, decisions must be made about the kind of test it should be and the types of items it should include. The consideration of these factors cannot be fully separated from the consideration of the instructional objectives to be measured, and the decisions made affect the form of the Table of Specifications.

Table 3.2 Table of Specifications for a final examination in a course entitled "Introduction to Research and Descriptive Statistics"

Content	Objectives:	Knowledge 30%	Understanding 40%	Application 30%
5%	I. History of measurement a) Early attempts b) Methodological foundations c) Rapid expansion of testing d) Period of doubt e) Clarification and new programs	2 (1.125) (1.5%)	1 (1.50) (2.0%)	0 (1.125) (1.5%)
5%	II. Nature of educational measurement a) Characteristics b) Types of scales c) Continuous vs. discrete data d) Errors of measurement	2 (1.125) (1.5%)	1 (1.50) (2.0%)	0 (1.125) (1.5%)
5%	III. Frequency distributions a) Purposes b) Characteristics c) Construction d) Adaptations for unusual data	1 (1.125) (1.5%)	2 (1.50) (2.0%)	1 (1.125) (1.5%)
5%	IV. Graphic presentations a) Types of graphs b) Graphing frequency distribution c) Types of distributions	2 (1.125) (1.5%)	1 (1.50) (2.0%)	1 (1.125) (1.5%)
5%	V. Measures of central tendency a) Mean b) Median c) Mode	0 (1.125) (1.5%)	2 (1.50) (2.0%)	2 (1.125) (1.5%)
10%	VI. Measures of variability a) Range b) Semi-interquartile range c) Standard deviation	2 (2.25) (3.0%)	2 (3.00) (4.0%)	3 (2.25) (3.0%)
5%	VII. Normal curve a) Definition b) Characteristics c) Uses	1 (1.125) (1.5%)	2 (1.50) (2.0%)	1 (1.125) (1.5%)

Table 3.2—*continued*

Content	Objectives:	Knowledge 30%	Understanding 40%	Application 30%
10%	VIII. Standard scores			
	a) z-score	1	3	4
	b) Z-score	(2.25)	(3.00)	(2.25)
	c) Normalized scores	(3.0%)	(4.0%)	(3.0%)
	d) Stanines			
5%	IX. Percentiles and percentile ranks			
	a) Uses	1	1	2
	b) Computations	(1.125)	(1.50)	(1.125)
	c) Characteristics	(1.5%)	(2.0%)	(1.5%)
15%	X. Regression and correlation			
	a) Linear regression and correlation	3	3	5
	b) Standard error of estimate	(3.375)	(4.50)	(3.375)
	c) Curvilinear correlation	(4.5%)	(6.0%)	(4.5%)
	d) Multiple correlation			
5%	XI. Characteristics of tests			
	a) Reliability	1	2	1
	b) Validity	(1.125)	(1.50)	(1.125)
	c) Practicality	(1.5%)	(2.0%)	(1.5%)
5%	XII. Item analysis	1	2	1
	a) Indices of difficulty	(1.125)	(1.50)	(1.125)
	b) Indices of discrimination	(1.5%)	(2.0%)	(1.5%)
20%	XIII. Topics in educational research			
	a) Sampling theory			
	b) Strategy of indirect proof	5	8	2
	c) Type I and Type II errors	(4.50)	(6.00)	(4.50)
	d) Hypothesis testing	(6.0%)	(8.0%)	(6.0%)
	e) Basic research designs			
TOTAL	a) Actual number of items	22	30	23
	b) Theoretical number of items	(22.50)	(30.00)	(22.50)
	c) Theoretical percentage of test	(30.0%)	(40.0%)	(30.0%)
	d) Actual percentage of test (=number of items/test length)	29.3%	40.0%	30.7%

Discriminatory or Mastery Test

If the purpose of a test is to determine the extent to which the instructional objectives have been realized, the teacher must still determine the *function* of the test. If it is to be used primarily to identify those students who have mastered the basic facts, operations, and concepts within a subject area and who are ready to move on to more advanced subject matter, the teacher should develop a mastery test. Since the function of the test is to identify those students who have mastered the essential elements of the subject, the items selected should be relatively easy, with most students getting about 90 percent of the items correct.

However, if the purpose of the test is to measure student achievement of the instructional objectives so as to be able to order the students on the basis of the magnitude of the differences between them, a discriminatory test should be used. In constructing such a test, preference should be given to fairly difficult items. Depending on the type of item used, the average score on the test should fall somewhere between 50 percent and 75 percent. In general, the difficulty of each item should be similar to the difficulty of the test as a whole. Also, one should choose items for the test which discriminate well, that is, items which good students tend to answer correctly and which poor students tend to answer incorrectly. These topics—item and test difficulty and discrimination—are considered in greater depth in Chapter 13.

Verbal Behavior or Performance Test

After a careful analysis of the instructional objectives and the level of development of the examinees, the teacher may choose to construct a test which requires the examinee to perform activities which exhibit skills, often in producing a product (see the discussion in Chapter 10 on performance tests), or one which requires the examinee to verbalize, orally or in writing, his responses to the tasks presented. (A more thorough discussion of the oral-response type of examination is found in Chapter 6.) In tests requiring verbal responses by the examinee, the items may consist of behavioral tasks requiring cognitive activity on the knowledge, understanding, or application level or tasks requiring the examinee to express his beliefs, attitudes, or expected behavior in specified situations.

If the examinee is to respond to behavioral tasks presented to him in a written form, the teacher must still choose, from among the various selection-type and supply-type item formats available for his use, the specific format or formats which he desires to employ. The advantages, disadvantages, uses, and construction methodology of the various item formats are discussed in Chapters 4, 5, 7, 8, and 9. An example of each of the item formats discussed in these chapters is shown below.

I. Supply Items
  a) Essay—Short Answer
    In one or two sentences, explain the difference between mass and weight.

b) Essay—Extended Answer

In order for an authoritarian government to maintain its power, it must control the means of communicating ideas. Defend this statement, using a comparison between the French Revolution and the German Nazi movement.

c) Completion

Which of the cells found in the human body carries oxygen to all the other living cells?

II. Selection Items

a) Multiple Choice

Who gave colonists the same rights as other Englishmen?
A. The King
B. Local governors
C. Colonial legislatures
*D. Parliament

b) True-False

T   F   A fish is an invertebrate.

c) Matching

Some of the characteristics of vertebrates are listed in Column I. Find in Column II the vertebrate for which the description is most appropriate and record your choice on the line preceding the question number.

Column I (Structure)	Column II (Vertebrate)
___ 1. Covered with scales or shell and breathe with lungs.	A. Fish
	B. Birds
___ 2. Young breathe with gills while adults breathe with lungs.	C. Amphibians
___ 3. Fed with milk from mothers' bodies.	D. Reptiles
___ 4. Covered with scales and breathe with gills.	E. Mammals

TEST LENGTH

How long should a test be? Obviously, the test must be of sufficient length to yield reliable scores. Usually, the longer the test, the more reliable the results. If the Table of Specifications is carefully followed and the item pool is adequately sampled, the test should be valid if it is reliable. Consequently, all that is now required is to construct a test of sufficient length.

Unfortunately, administrative factors must be considered when determining the length of a test. If a test is to be administered during a class session, it should be constructed so that most of the examinees can easily finish it during the examination period. Also, particularly in the elementary school, one must consider the stamina and attention span of the pupils in determining the length of an examination period and the number of items which one can reasonably ask the examinees to answer.

How long should a test be? Long enough to be adequately reliable and short enough to be administered. If well constructed, a multiple-choice test of 35 to 45 items should be sufficiently reliable for the average end-of-unit examination. For a final examination, one might wish to use 75 or more items. However, it should be remembered that the time needed to answer test items varies with the grade level, the type of items used, the difficulty of the items, and the level of cognitive activity required. At the high school level, the typical student can usually answer about two knowledge items or one understanding or application item each minute. Allowing about ten minutes to distribute materials, explain procedures, and collect materials, the teacher can utilize about 40 minutes of a 50-minute class period and be able to administer an examination of 35 to 50 multiple-choice items with a reasonable expectation that all but the very slow will complete the test.

A time estimate can also be made for other types of items. In a minute of examination time, a high school student should be able to answer two or three well written true-false items, two or three matching items, or one or two completion items. When the examinee must furnish the answer, the amount of time required is dependent on the complexity of the mental task and the amount of writing involved in answering the question. One might be wise to schedule no more than six or seven essay questions per hour of examination time, and even fewer if the questions require extensive answers. At the elementary level one should allow more time per item, the amount of time being dependent on the test sophistication of the examinees.

These estimates are, of course, only general time estimates. The best guide for a teacher to use in determining the number of items which can be answered by his students in an examination period is his personal experience with similar examinations.

TEST INSTRUCTIONS

If the examinees do not clearly understand the question format, the test may be measuring only their understanding of item types rather than their acquisition of the instructional objectives. It is the function of test instructions to furnish the learning experiences needed in order to enable each examinee to understand clearly what he is being asked to do. Although these instructions may be oral, a combination of written and oral instructions is probably desirable, except with very young children.

The instructions should be clear, concise, and explicit. Examples of the various item types should be furnished. This is particularly important for an examination in which an item type occurs for the first time. After the examinees have read the instructions, they should be encouraged to ask questions. In most cases it is advantageous to use the instructions as a cover page, since this permits the directions to be separated from the body of the test. Table 3.3 is an example of such a cover page.

Table 3.3 Example of a test cover page

Research and Statistics Midterm Examination

Directions: This midterm examination contains 50 multiple-choice items of four or five responses each. You will mark your answers on a separate answer sheet which contains spaces for five responses per item. Be sure that you record your choice in the appropriate position. Each item will contain only one correct or best answer. Do not mark more than one response. If some items seem quite difficult to answer, it may be wise to skip them until you have attempted all the items on the test, and then to return to the skipped items if time permits.

Do Not Write on the Test: Scratch paper has been provided for use by those who need to do some figuring. Remember that this examination will be machine scored. Use the electrographic pencil which has been provided to record your answers. Be sure to print your name on the answer sheet.

To help clarify any questions regarding the procedures to be followed, a practice exercise is given below. It has been marked to indicate the correct response.

1. Why is it difficult to develop acceptable measures of ultimate goals?

   A. Because of criticism, the school is reluctant to depart from traditional methodology and measurement.

   B. Teachers adhere too firmly to textbooks and prepared curricula.

   C. Classroom instruction essentially pertains to immediate goals.

   D. Normally such goals concern behavior which is not observable in the classroom.

   E. None of the above.

TEST LAYOUT

The arrangement of the test items within the examination influences the speed and accuracy of the examinee. The best layout is one which utilizes the space available while retaining readability. In most cases it is wise to avoid a layout which results in one-line questions spanning an eight-inch-wide page. Such a page often appears cramped, makes it difficult for the examinee to keep track of his place in the examination, and, as in the case of the multiple-choice item, results in a poor utilization of available space. If the reader must make many eye shifts in reading the question, the reading rate may be reduced. A two-column page, as shown in Table 3.4, may be the best layout for multiple-choice or true-false items.

Table 3.4 Example of a test layout

1. Which of the following items is in best agreement with the accepted principles for the construction of true-false tests?
   - A. The late President F.D.R., elected to four consecutive terms, was President when Japan attacked Pearl Harbor.
   - B. A Senator of the United States is always elected to a six-year term of office.
   - C. As a candidate for the office of President, Dewey received a large number of votes.
   - *D. Douglas McArthur was Commander-In-Chief of the Allied Forces during the invasion of Normandy.

2. Presented below is a multiple-choice item. Rank the distractors in descending order of their conformity to the accepted principles of item construction.

   What is a tariff?

   - *1. A tax on imported goods
   - 2. A tax on money brought into the country by immigrants
   - 3. A tax on exported goods
   - 4. A tax on imported cats and dogs

   - A. 2,3,4
   - B. 2,4,3
   - C. 3,4,2
   - D. 4,3,2
   - *E. None of the above

3. Which one of the following statements is most applicable to the selection of distractors for multiple-choice items?
   - A. Distractors should be unequivocally false.
   - B. One should avoid tricky distractors based on misconceptions.
   - *C. Distractors should be attractive to the uninformed.
   - D. Distractors should be heterogeneous.

Questions 4–6 are based on the following item and its accompanying item analysis data.

   Why is helium used in balloons?

   - 1. It will not expand at high altitudes.
   - *2. It will not explode easily.
   - 3. It is lighter than air.
   - 4. It is lighter than hydrogen.

Item Analysis Data

	Number Right	
Response	Upper 27%	Lower 27%
1	0	5
*2	25	20
3	20	10
4	5	15

4. Place the distractors in the descending order of their contribution to item validity.
   - A. 1,3,4
   - B. 1,4,3
   - C. 3,4,1
   - D. 3,1,4
   - *E. 4,1,3

5. Which of the following values is the index of discrimination for this item?
   - A. .05
   - *B. .10
   - C. .30
   - D. .45
   - E. None of the above

6. Which of the following values is the index of difficulty for this item?
   - A. .05
   - B. .10
   - *C. .45
   - D. .90
   - E. None of the above

Sometimes the test constructor wishes to use various item types in the same examination. When this occurs, items of the same type (true-false, multiple-choice, or completion, for example) should be grouped together. Associated with each type of item are certain characteristics which result in some similarities in the mental frame of reference required to answer the majority of the items of that type. By grouping the items on the basis of type, the number of shifts in mental orientation is reduced, with a resultant saving of time and effort for the examinee. It is a good practice to use no more than two or three item types on a one-hour examination.

Some educators recommend that, as a means of reducing test anxiety, test items be arranged in order from the easiest to the most difficult items. Although this may be done, the available research on this proposition is inconclusive for achievement tests. However, as an aid to the examinee, it does seem advantageous to order the items on the basis of their content. This may result in a time order, historical order, topic order, or some other logical organization. If more than one type of item is used, the items should be ordered first by type and then by content.

As previously stated, readability is an important consideration when constructing a test. The following suggestions should aid the teacher in preparing a readable test. Each item should be completed in the column (and on the page) in which it is started. If reference material (such as a paragraph to read and interpret) is needed, it should occur on the same page as the item. If several items refer to the same reference material, try to place all the items and the material on the same page and separate them from other unrelated items by dotted lines. If the items are ordered in arabic numbers, it is wise to use letters to identify the alternatives for each item. In any case, the labels on the test should correspond with the labels on the answer sheet. Finally, the item alternatives should be arranged so that the examinee can return rapidly to the alternative of his choice after he has finished reading the item. Many of these suggestions are illustrated in Table 3.4.

REPRODUCING THE TEST

Although several methods for test reproduction are available, it is likely that most teachers will use either the ditto or the mimeograph. Both are relatively easy to use. The major consideration, other than that of obtaining legible reproductions, is to allow sufficient time for typing and reproducing the test.

SCORING THE TEST

Teachers often needlessly spend many hours of their valuable and limited time scoring examinations because they did not spend a few minutes planning scoring procedures before finalizing the layout and reproducing the test. Several factors should be considered before choosing the scoring procedure from among the large number of available methods. Will the method allow rapid and accurate scoring? What effect will the scoring method have on the examination time? Will the examinees be able to cope with the required method of recording answers? The test sophistication of the examinee is an important consideration when deciding on a response method. For example, it is not reasonable to expect primary-level children to use separate answer sheets with ease and accuracy.

Separate Answer Sheet

Methods of scoring may be classified into those which use separate answer sheets and those which do not. The former may be further subdivided into machine-scored and hand-scored. Although there is a trend toward local school district ownership and use of machines for scoring selection-type tests, it is still unlikely that the teacher at the elementary or secondary level will have a test-scoring machine available. However, many of his colleagues at the university level will be more fortunate. Many universities and colleges make test-scoring services, including item analysis data, available to the faculty member who bothers to inquire.

If an IBM Test Scoring Machine or its equivalent is not available, the teacher still may wish to use commercially manufactured answer sheets. However, teacher-made forms may be desirable because of their adaptability to various test needs and also because of their negligible cost.

In either case, the papers can be scored with a punched key prepared from a manufactured key form or an unused answer sheet. The correct answers are punched out of the key in such a way as to overlay the correct positions on the answer sheet. When the key is placed on an answer sheet, the number of unmarked positions visible is the number of errors. An example of a teacher-made punched key (prepared from an unused answer sheet) is shown in Appendix B.

If a mimeograph or ditto machine which feeds the paper with accurate alignment is available, the papers may be scored quite rapidly. All that is required is a stencil (or master) with circles drawn around the correct answer positions. When the completed answer sheets are fed through the machine, a circle will be made around each correct answer position. The teacher can then score by counting the number of circles containing a mark by the student.

The use of separate answer sheets entails a saving in scoring time, an increase in scoring accuracy, and the possibility of reuse of the test booklets. However, particularly at the elementary level, the teacher must be cognizant of the following possible disadvantages: a greater pupil error in recording answers, an increase in examinee fatigue, and a loss in administrative efficiency resulting from an increase in examination time. Another limiting factor in the use of separate answer sheets of the type described in this section is that they cannot be used with completion and essay questions and have limited application for matching items.

Overlay Key

Because of the limitations of the separate answer sheet, the teacher of young children may wish to accept a certain loss of scoring efficiency and have the examinees record their answers directly in the test booklets. Nevertheless, with a little planning, the laborious reading of each answer on each paper can be avoided. A cut-out key—an overlay with windows cut out to exhibit a pupil's responses—can be prepared for each page of the examination. The correct answer can be written or typed below the window for matching or completion items. With multiple-choice or true-false items, the window can be cut to expose only the correct answer position for the item. For example, if "T" and "F" are typed after a true-false item, the examinee can mark out the correct answer. The scorer would only need to look at the window to see whether the response is correct. An example of an overlay key is shown in Table 3.5.

Strip Key

In the strip-key method, the answers are marked in a vertical column adjacent to their respective questions. A strip key can then be used for scoring. This type of key is a strip of paper or light weight carboard on which the correct answers are printed vertically so as to line up with their respective items on the examination page. A strip key is shown in Table 3.6.

Essay Tests

The scoring time for an essay examination is obviously much greater than the scoring time for a corresponding multiple-choice test. Nevertheless, teachers can reduce scoring time by spending a few minutes considering response format before finalizing the test layout and by limiting the length of the required response. This can partially be done by supplying appropriate directions. However, regardless of the specificity of the directions, some students will insist on writing everything they think might relate to the question asked. These examinees can be limited to the desired response length by restricting the answer space provided for the item.

If the essay is of the extended-answer type, it is desirable to have the examinees start each response on a new page. Each response can then be scored with a minimum of influence carried over from the scores assigned to preceding responses.

Ideal responses to the test items should be written by the teacher before the final draft of the test is formalized. These responses can aid the teacher in discovering item defects, and they should be used during scoring as reference points. The use of such responses can aid a teacher in stabilizing scoring standards when reading a set of essays.

THE PLIGHT OF THE STUDENT

Before concluding this discussion of the factors to consider before and during test construction, it seems appropriate to draw the reader's attention to the major purpose of testing: to appraise *student* acquisition of instructional objectives. With all the various factors to keep in mind, it is possible to forget that the student is vital to the testing situation and has a stake in it.

If the test conforms to a properly constructed Table of Specifications, it will be a balanced reflection of the instructional objectives. However, unless the teacher systematically endeavors to structure the class learning experiences in keeping with the relative importance of the various instructional objectives, class learning activities may differ significantly from the pattern exhibited in the Table of Specifications, and thus from the test. Even if the instructional activities are in balance

Table 3.5 Example of an overlay answer key

Test 1: Classifying Things

1. All things found in the world may be

    classified as _____ things

    or as _____ things.

2. If anything is alive or was alive, we should be able to classify it as either

    _____ or _____ .

3. A fish may be correctly considered to be:

    A. An animal
    B. A reptile
    C. An amphibian
    D. An insect
    E. None of the above

4. How is a dog like a fish?

    A. Both are warm-blooded.
    B. Both feed their young milk.
    C. Both have backbones.
    D. Both have fur or hair.

5. A chair made from a redwood tree is not a living thing.

    TRUE or FALSE

6. All plants have seeds.

    TRUE or FALSE

Test 1: Classifying Things KEY

1. All things found in the world may

    be classified as ▓▓▓▓▓ things
    LIVING (NON LIVING)

    or as ▓▓▓▓▓ things.
    NONLIVING (LIVING)

2. If anything is alive or was alive, we should be able to classify it as either

    ▓▓▓▓▓ or ▓▓▓▓▓ .
    PLANT (ANIMAL)   ANIMAL (PLANT)

3. A fish may be correctly considered to be:

       An animal
    B. A reptile
    C. An amphibian
    D. An insect
    E. None of the above

4. How is a dog like a fish?

    A. Both are warm-blooded.
    B. Both feed their young milk.
    ▓ Both have backbones.
    D. Both have fur or hair.

5. A chair made from a redwood tree is not a living thing.

    ▓▓▓▓▓ or FALSE

6. All plants have seeds.

    TRUE or ▓▓▓▓▓

Table 3.6 Example of a strip key

Test 1: Classifying Things	KEY: Test 1
(a) _____ 1. All things found in the world may be	(a) living (nonliving) 1.
(b) _____ classified as	(b) nonliving (living)
(a) _____ things or as	
(b) _____ things.	
(a) _____ 2. If anything is alive or was alive, we	(a) plant (animal) 2.
(b) _____ should be able to classify it as either	(b) animal (plant)
(a) _____ or (b) _____ .	
3. A fish may be correctly considered to be:	
A. An animal	
B. A reptile	
C. An amphibian	
D. An insect	
_____ E. None of the above	_____ A 3.
4. How is a dog like a fish?	
A. Both are warm-blooded.	
B. Both feed their young milk.	
C. Both have backbones.	
_____ D. Both have fur or hair.	_____ C 4.
5. A chair made from a redwood tree is not a living thing.	
_____ TRUE or FALSE	_____ True 5.
6. All plants have seeds.	
_____ TRUE or FALSE	_____ False 6.

with the course objectives and even if the students were informed of or involved in the development of course objectives, there is no guarantee that students can translate this information into a meaningful expectation of what content areas and levels of the cognitive domain should occur on the test.

Consequently, in order that all the students may have an equal opportunity to understand what is to be covered on the examination and to study for it, the teacher should discuss with the class the content areas and levels of the cognitive domain to be examined. This discussion should utilize a vocabulary and a level of complexity appropriate to the developmental level of the students. The types of items to be included on the test and, if new to the students, examples of each type of item included should be presented to the class. In addition, each item should be constructed in keeping with the recommendations for its item type and in conformity with the Table of Specifications. In this way a test "fair" to the students may be constructed and administered. If the test is scored in keeping with appropriate recommendations for scoring, it should also be scored "fairly."

SUMMARY

Before a valid classroom test can be constructed, it is necessary to develop a Table of Specifications. In a Table of Specifications, content areas are shown on the vertical axis and levels of the cognitive domain are presented on the horizontal axis, with the intersection of row and column used to indicate the number of items needed to measure the instructional objectives appropriate to that content area and cognitive level. The weights assigned to the various content areas and to the levels of the cognitive domain must be carefully selected to be representative of the importance of various instructional objectives.

Before items can be selected for a test, the teacher must decide whether he wishes to have a mastery or a discriminatory test. The decision made will influence the item characteristics deemed appropriate for the test. The teacher must also decide whether to use a performance or a verbal behavior test. If the decision is to use a verbal behavior test, should it be oral or written? In the latter case, what types of items should one use—supply or selection?

Before selecting items for the test, an estimate of the number of items to use must be made, and this depends on the amount of time available for testing, the item types to be used, the test sophistication of the examinees, the amount of emphasis to be placed on higher-order mental processes, and the difficulty of the items.

During the process of constructing a test, the teacher must carefully develop his test instructions. It is the function of these instructions to furnish the learning experiences needed in order to enable each examinee to understand clearly what he is being asked to do.

The items should be carefully arranged on the test so that the available space is utilized while readability is maintained. If more than one item type is used, items of the same type should be grouped together. Items of the same type should be ordered on the basis of content, except when such an ordering will furnish clues to the correct response. The complete item must occur in the same column of the same page. If several items depend on the same qualifying material, this should be indicated.

Before laying out the test, determine how it is to be scored. If possible, use separate answer sheets. If this is inappropriate, select the easiest method for scoring the recorded answers which is compatible with the test experience of the examinees.

PROBLEMS

1. Why should a teacher develop a Table of Specifications for use in constructing a classroom test?
2. What are the components of a Table of Specifications?
3. How are the column and row weights for a Table of Specifications selected?
4. Develop a Table of Specifications for a test covering a unit of study of your own choosing. The test is to be a selection-type test with 30 to 40 items.
5. Modify the above Table of Specifications so that it is appropriate for use in constructing a supply-type test.
6. How do mastery tests differ from discriminatory tests? When should they be used?
7. What factors influence the decision concerning the number of items to be used in a test?
8. What is the major function of test instructions?
9. Discuss the factors to be considered when arranging the items on a test.
10. Why is it important to determine the scoring procedure to be used before the test is constructed?
11. Describe the situations in which a separate answer sheet is inappropriate.
12. How is a strip key constructed?

SUGGESTED READING

Adams, Georgia Sachs, *Measurement and Evaluation in Education, Psychology, and Guidance.* Holt, Rinehart, and Winston, New York, 1964, Chapter 11.

Ahmann, J. Stanley, and Marvin D. Glock, *Evaluating Pupil Growth: Principles of Tests and Measurements.* Allyn and Bacon, Boston, 1967, pp. 61–67.

Sanders, Norris M., *Classroom Questions: What Kinds?* Harper and Row, New York, 1966.

Vaughn, K. W., "Planning the Objective Test," in E. F. Lindquist (Ed.), *Educational Measurement.* American Council on Education, Washington, D.C., 1951, Chapter 6.

PART II

TYPES OF TESTS: CHARACTERISTICS,
CONSTRUCTION, AND USE

Chapter 4

Essay-Type Tests

The essay-type question requires the examinee to read the question, formulate his response, and write the response. The person scoring the response must be knowledgeable in the area being measured. This type of question can be used to measure many processes: it can require the examinee to make comparisons, to supply definitions, to make interpretations, to make evaluations, or to explain relationships.

USES

Appropriate uses for the essay test have not been clarified. One teacher may prefer to use essay tests because they emphasize the whole subject being measured; another may justify their use by the fact that they require the student to supply the response; and still another may claim that essay tests can be used to measure educational objectives which cannot otherwise be measured, such as attitudes, creativity, and the ability to organize materials. In practice, many teachers erroneously use these tests to measure knowledge of facts and principles. Such knowledge can be more effectively measured with more objective types of examinations.

Perhaps the most appropriate use of the essay examination is in assessing the quality of an examinee's higher-order mental processes: application, analysis, synthesis, and evaluation. An essay question might require the student to make comparisons, organize material, or make judgments. Selection-type examinations could be devised to measure many of these processes, but they are extremely difficult to construct. Consequently, a teacher-made essay test is often better than a teacher-made selection-type test for measuring higher-order processes.

Research indicates that the type of test expected by a student will affect his choice of study method. When preparing for multiple-choice, true-false, or completion tests, students tend to study for details and isolated ideas. When preparing for an essay test, they tend to study for general ideas and global concepts. This motivating influence of the test assignment can be useful to the classroom teacher for maximizing the learning situation.

For example, multiple-choice or completion items would probably be appropriate in a chemistry test covering the basic properties of selected elements, simply because in this case students are expected to know isolated, detailed information. A multiple-choice text might even be appropriate in determining whether or not students can apply this information in given situations. However, if a chemistry teacher wanted his students to compare, contrast and evaluate the results from two unfamiliar experiments, an essay test might be preferable. In this situation, students must organize and evaluate the given material and formulate tenable hypotheses. To do this requires general concepts and understandings in addition to specific knowledge. Therefore, a global approach to studying the chemistry material would be most advantageous.

WEAKNESSES

When measuring achievement with items prepared in the essay format, several rather complicated problems are encountered which might be thought of as "weaknesses" of this type of item. These weaknesses can be minimized, but not eliminated, by careful construction and scoring. The problems can be grouped into three broad categories: (1) lack of content validity, (2) lack of scoring economy, and (3) scorer unreliability.

Lack of Content Validity

Content validity of a classroom test may be defined as the degree to which the test conforms to the content and objectives deemed important by the teacher. Suppose that a test to measure student achievement in a teaching unit containing five content categories and five behavioral objectives is to be constructed. The test covering this unit should include measures of 25 (5 content categories × 5 objectives) aspects of student behavior. Therefore, unless content categories or behavioral objectives are combined, a valid test covering this unit should include at least 25 items, one for each category. A test of this length would allow the students less than two minutes per question in a typical 45-minute class period. It is unrealistic to expect a student to read a question, formulate his response, and write that response in less than two minutes. A test of this length would contain many more items than students could possibly answer in a regular class period. If the test were reduced to 10 items, it would still allow students only 4.5 minutes per question.

    The problem of obtaining content validity on an essay test can be somewhat alleviated by using short-answer questions rather than extended-answer questions. The former require less time per response and permit a broader coverage of content and objectives. The content validity of extended-answer essay tests can be improved by designing the test to measure a relatively small unit of material or by making a large block of time available for administration of the test. Nevertheless, because of the somewhat limited sampling of content and objectives by essay tests, the problem of content validity is seldom fully solved.

Lack of Scoring Economy

Scoring of responses to an essay examination requires the expenditure of much time by a person highly knowledgeable in the content area being measured. If a teacher carefully scores the responses of 30 students on a comprehensive essay examination, the process will probably require a minimum of ten teacher-hours (this allows 20 minutes per examination paper). However, an objective-type test can be scored by a grading assistant or teacher's aid in a short period of time, usually less than one hour. Therefore, as compared to other test formats, essay examinations lack scoring economy.

The scoring economy of an essay examination can be improved by using short-answer rather than extended-answer questions, since the former can be more rapidly read and usually contain fewer elements to be considered.

Scorer Unreliability

Because it is quite difficult to be objective when scoring essay examinations, scoring of responses has been characterized as subjective. This subjectivity may reflect reader idiosyncrasies which are extraneous to the original purpose of the examination but which can cause a score on a single examination to vary from reader to reader and from reading to reading by the same person. One teacher may be lenient while another is harsh; one may interpret the response favorably while another may interpret the response unfavorably; and one may be influenced by extraneous qualities while another may not be influenced by these qualities. The factors that influence the reader's judgment of the response can be grouped into three categories: (1) halo effect, (2) informed judgment, and (3) extraneous factors.

Cartoon No. 1

Halo effect. The halo effect occurs whenever a reader's general impression of the examinee affects the evaluation of a specific response. The effect can take numerous forms. As shown in Cartoon No. 1, the reader's evaluation of a single response is

Good? But, he is a poor student. It probably isn't that good — FAIR.

1. _____
   _____
2. _____
   _____
3. _____
   _____

Cartoon No. 2

often influenced by his evaluation of the total essay. This effect can be either positive or negative. If the reader in this illustration had evaluated the first two responses as excellent, the third response might have been evaluated as good, even though it was only of fair quality.

Previous knowledge of the student may contribute to the halo effect. As shown in Cartoon No. 2, the reader's evaluation of the essay is often influenced by his previous perception of the student who wrote the essay. If the reader perceives the student unfavorably, he may evaluate the student's essay response as being of fair quality when it is actually of good or excellent quality. Conversely, if he perceives the student favorably, he may evaluate the response as being of good quality when it is actually poor.

The halo effect can be reduced, though not eliminated, through the use of two simple techniques. In the first of these, the teacher passes to the examinees a sheet of paper containing a set of numbers. (If there are 30 students, the sheet would contain the numbers 1 to 30.) The teacher then tells the students that they are neither to write nor to print their names on the answer sheets, but that each of them is to write his name on the sheet opposite one of the numbers and place that number on each of his answer sheets. After each student has signed the signature paper, it is collected and filed. The teacher should not look at the names on the paper until after scoring all the responses. Then, in order to record the test scores, he can match the names and numbers on the signature paper with the numbers on the answer sheets. Unless the teacher is very familiar with his students' handwriting, this procedure should contribute to the reduction of errors in grading by partially eliminating the influence of the scorer's knowledge of past student achievement.

The second technique which an examiner may use to reduce the halo effect is to score all responses to a single question before reading the responses to any of the other test questions. Using this procedure, the reader would score all the responses to the first question, rearrange the examination papers in a random order, score all the responses to the second question, rearrange the examination papers, and continue until the scoring has been completed. When scoring the responses to a question, the scores for the preceding questions should not be available for scrutiny. This may be ensured by requiring that the response to each question begin on a separate page or by recording the scores on a separate sheet of paper. This procedure reduces the influence of the reader's general impression of a total examination on his assessment of a single response.

Informed judgment. Regardless of the objectivity with which a reader attempts to score an essay response, the scoring process involves some personal judgment. Two responses to an essay question may be of the same quality, but be written in different modes, using different terms. Two solutions to a mathematics problem may be of the same quality, but be approached in different ways. Two equally qualified judges may disagree as to the relative merits of the different approaches to the problem. Similarly, a single judge may perceive a response differently at different readings. These sources of variability reduce the reliability of essay examinations.

The effect of informed judgment on reliability can be partially eliminated by observing appropriate precautions when preparing and scoring essay examinations. Because of the magnitude of the relationship between the number of observations of behavior which are made and the consistency of the composite measurement, the examination should contain several questions. By increasing the number of questions on an examination, the amount of error which is made in the sampling of behavior and the net effect on the total score of the errors which are made in the scoring of the responses should be reduced.

Many judgmental errors in scoring can be prevented by properly structuring the question. Usually an unstructured question is open to a variety of interpretations and therefore, produces a variety of student responses. This situation makes it extremely difficult for a reader to judge objectively the relative merits of different responses.

The construction and use of a scoring key should improve test reliability. Such a key enables a reader or several readers to score all the responses from a single frame of reference. The use of a detailed key will reduce reader fluctuations in the scoring of responses. An additional reduction in these fluctuations can be accomplished by requiring that the reader score all the papers during one sitting.

Extraneous factors. When scoring an essay examination, the reader is often influenced by extraneous factors, that is, by intrinsic, internal factors which are not directly related to the behavior being measured. These factors include both conscious and unconscious penalties or rewards which influence the final evaluation of a response but which are not components of the content area being measured. The quality of handwriting, the use of a pen rather than a pencil, or the inclusion of spelling or grammatical errors may influence the reader's judgment of the quality of the response. When scoring essay responses, the reader should strive to assign marks which reflect students' achievement in the area being measured; he should avoid evaluating extraneous factors.

STRENGTHS

The weaknesses discussed in the previous section represent definite drawbacks to the use of the essay examination. Their effects can be minimized but not eliminated. Therefore, in order to gain a proper perspective of the importance of the essay test as a measurement instrument, consideration must be given to its strengths in light of these weaknesses.

The essay examination can be used in any paper-and-pencil testing situation. It is especially appropriate for measuring higher-order mental processes, such as analysis, synthesis, evaluation, and organization of materials. These higher-order processes are difficult, sometimes impossible, to measure with selection-type techniques. For example, if a history teacher was interested in measuring students' ability to use social, economic, and political information to generate tenable hypotheses concerning the cultural and political structure of a society, the essay test would be the most appropriate form to use, because information of this type can usually be organized in a number of ways and the hypotheses generated will depend on the organizational pattern developed. The score assigned to a response depends on the consistency between the organization of the data and the hypotheses generated, and on the pattern in which the information is organized.

Merely obtaining the correct response may not be sufficient as a measure of higher-order mental processes. The *process* by which the response was obtained is also of importance. The generation of a valid conclusion from invalid reasoning is not acceptable. One of the authors, for example, recently administered a multiple-choice test containing the following item: "What is the probability of obtaining one and only one head in four tosses of an unbiased coin?" The correct answer (.25) was obtained by most of the students. Later, when discussing the test with the class, the author discovered that several of the students had obtained the correct answer through invalid reasoning. They had reasoned that the probability of obtaining one head on four tosses would equal

$$\frac{1 \text{ (head)}}{4 \text{ (tosses)}} = .25.$$

A more valid proof is that there are 4 possible arrangements containing one head (*HTTT, THTT, TTHT*, and *TTTH*) and 16 possible arrangements in all (2 possibilities on each toss and 4 tosses $= 2^4 = 16$). The probability of obtaining one head on four tosses would equal

$$\frac{4 \text{ (arrangements containing 1 head)}}{16 \text{ (possible arrangements)}} = \tfrac{1}{4} = .25.$$

The two approaches to the problem yield the same answer, but the first procedure is not valid. An essay examination would have permitted the instructor to judge the process as well as the final product, thus enabling him to detect invalid reasoning. This particular problem could also be handled by changing the item so that no logical "wrong process" would lead to the correct response. However, this option may not be clearly available and sometimes is difficult to exercise.

As stated earlier, the type of examination expected may influence the student's mode of study. When assigned an essay examination, students tend to use a global approach in studying for the test. They tend to emphasize general understandings, comparing and relating general concepts, and the organization of ideas. But when assigned an objective examination, they tend to emphasize isolated, unrelated bits of information. *Furthermore, research indicates that the global approach to studying is more effective than the bits-and-pieces approach.* Students who have prepared for an essay examination tend to do better on all types of tests than do students who have prepared for multiple choice or true-false examinations. However, it should be remembered that most of the research in this area used multiple-choice and true-false items covering almost exclusively knowledge of facts and comprehension of facts. Mode of study for and performance on selection tests which also measure at the higher levels of the cognitive domain may be quite different.

The essay examination should be included as a vital aspect of the measurement program of most teachers. Since its major strength is in the measurement of higher-order processes, its use should be most frequent in the areas and at the grade levels in which these processes are emphasized or expected. However, it should be used sparingly in the elementary grades because of the verbal sophistication required. The relative frequency of the use of essay examinations should increase as students' verbal skills increase and as teachers' emphases on higher-order mental processes increase.

Many students have expressed a more favorable attitude toward taking essay-type tests than they do toward other types of tests. They seem to feel that essay tests are more valid as measures of higher-order mental processes. This attitudinal difference can be important to the success of any measurement or teaching program. The attitude with which students accept a teacher and his procedures can make a difference in the effectiveness of the learning process.

TYPES OF ESSAY TESTS

Short-answer

An essay question is considered to be a short-answer question when it contains only one central idea and can be answered in one or two sentences. Items requiring students to supply definitions or short explanations of concepts and relationships fall within this category.

> In your own words, define the term monopoly.
>
> There are several S-R learning theories. In one or two sentences, explain the major differences in emphasis between Thorndike's Connectionism theory and Guthrie's Conditioning theory.
>
> Briefly explain the difference between weight and mass.
>
> If X is negative, is X^3 positive or negative? Briefly explain your answer.

The desired length of the response should somehow be indicated in the question. For example, the second question contains the phrase "in one or two sentences" and the third question contains the restrictive term "briefly." The use of such phrases and terms as the sole means of limiting the length of the response will seldom be effective, because examinees will differ in their interpretations of the meaning of these phrases and terms and because a few examinees will insist on writing everything which they think might relate to the question asked. This problem can be reduced by providing the examinees with an answer sheet on which the space available for writing responses is limited. As a further precaution, the directions for the test should explicitly state that the responses are to be written in the spaces provided. The general procedures for developing and scoring short-answer questions are the same as those discussed in the following section for extended-answer questions.

Extended-Answer

The response to an extended-answer essay question may be from one-half page to several pages long. Because of the time required to respond extensively, this type of question should be used only for measuring a student's ability to deal with complex relationships, comparisons, and evaluations.

> A, a minor, was employed by the Post Office as a special delivery messenger boy. He purchased an automobile for $600 from B, an adult, for use in his employment. A wrecked the car and refused to pay B the $600. B sued A for the money. What was the decision? Why? (Be specific)

> A cannonball is fired horizontally with a muzzle velocity of 360 meters per second. The cannon is 10 meters above level ground. How far will the ball travel before it strikes the ground? (Show your work.)

> In order for an authoritarian government to maintain its power, it must control the means of communicating ideas. Defend this statement, using a comparison between the French Revolution and the German Nazi movement.

The relative importance of each question should be indicated because it helps examinees budget their time. This serves as a guard against over responding to one question at the expense of other questions. On in-class examinations, the relative importance of each question can be indicated either by stipulating the approximate length of time the examinee should allow for each question or by indicating the number of points each question is worth.

> (10 points) 1. In order for an authoritarian government to maintain its power, it must control the means of communicating ideas. Defend this statement, using a comparison between the French Revolution and the German Nazi movement.

> (15 minutes) 1. In order for an authoritarian government to maintain its power, it must control the means of communicating ideas. Defend this statement, using a comparison between the French Revolution and the German Nazi movement.

If necessary, responses can be restricted further by limiting the amount of answer space available.

On take-home examinations, the length of the response can be controlled by limiting the number of pages or the number of words which may be used in writing a response. The latter procedure is generally preferred.

> Most critics agree that Gene's confession to Finny in the hospital room is the culmination of *A Separate Peace*. Explain why this is so and why the novel could end here. Your response should be limited to no more than three double-spaced, typewritten pages.

> In 500 words or less, explain why most critics maintain that Gene's confession to Finny in the hospital room is the culmination of *A Separate Peace*. Include in your answer why the novel could end here.

The directions for an extended-answer test should explicitly state that responses are expected to be clear and concise. They should indicate that a response which contains much irrelevant information will be discriminated against on the assumption that the examinee could not associate a specific answer with the question asked and, therefore, just wrote everything he could think of that might relate to the question in the hope of obtaining some credit. This type of "verbal garbage" should be discouraged.

ITEM CONSTRUCTION[1]

The writing of good essay questions appears deceivingly simple to the novice. It is easy to construct an essay item, but it is another matter to construct a *good* one. As an illustration, read and interpret the following item as though you were given this question on an essay test.

> Was the Civil War avoidable?

An American history teacher might ask such a question with the intention of measuring the ability of students to evaluate the causes of the Civil War. However, as written, the question does not convey this purpose. It is open to a variety of interpretations. If interpreted literally, it asks for an unqualified and unsupported *yes* or *no* response. Most students would probably supply some form of extended response to the question. Even so, the variety and scope of possible answers are nearly unlimited. One student might deal with the social issues preceding the war; another might be concerned with the economic issues; and still another might consider the political issues. Furthermore, the issues and their effects are so boundless that several volumes could be written on this topic. Nevertheless, the students are expected to do justice to the question in a single class period.

---

[1] An illustration of two classroom tests (multiple-choice and essay) constructed to measure student achievement of the objectives of the same unit of study is found in Appendix B.

The variety of appropriate responses can be reduced by rewriting the question as follows:

> Was the Civil War avoidable? Take a stand. Support your stand in terms of the social, economic, and political events preceding the War Between the States as discussed in this course.

The question now conveys to the student what the teacher expects him to do, and it defines and limits the question so that it is possible for the student to do justice to the problem. Even so, it would be unreasonable to expect a student to respond effectively to this question in less than 20 minutes.

The following seven guidelines are useful in the development of good essay questions.

1. *Allow adequate time for the construction of items.* The easiest way for a teacher to fall into a trap similar to the one previously presented is to fail to allow adequate time for the construction of items. A good item does not just happen; it must be carefully developed. Before the items are ready for use in an examination, they should be carefully evaluated in order to ensure that they are subject only to single interpretations, that they contain well-defined and limited problems, and that they measure what the teacher intends to measure. It takes time to do such an extensive evaluation.

2. *An essay item should contain a problem to be solved.* The essay examination is best suited to measuring higher-order mental processes. These processes involve problem solving in its various forms.

3. *The problem should be defined explicitly.* An essay question is not valid if the students cannot interpret the question. The question must lend itself to a single interpretation so that all respondents are responding to the "same item." It is difficult to evaluate equitably the responses of several students if they have not interpreted the item in the same manner.

4. *The problem should be limited.* It is difficult for a student to respond adequately to a question which covers a large content area. Unlimited questions often elicit responses which are nothing more than broad, unsupported generalizations. Being unable to limit the problem as presented, the student may endeavor to write indiscriminately everything he knows about the topic; he may, only by accident, include some of the information sought by the teacher. An unlimited question invites guessing and thus lowers the validity of the examination.

5. *The directions for the test should be stated explicitly.* All information which is pertinent to the testing situation should be communicated to the examinees. They need to understand exactly what is expected of them: how much time to spend on each question; the type of information to be included in the responses; and the form in which the responses are to be written. The essay examination should never be the guessing game of "What does the teacher want?" This can be avoided by including a complete set of directions with the examination. A statement of the relative weight of each question should be included within the directions (or within the questions). The examinees can use this information to determine the amount of time they wish to spend on each item.

6. *Do not use optional questions.* Every question used in an examination should be important and therefore should be answered by every student. The prerequisite of a common criterion for making comparisons and discriminations among examinees does not exist when the examinees have responded to different test questions. When optional questions are used, examinees of differing abilities often respond to different questions and teachers may react more favorably to some questions than to others. Furthermore, the use of optional test items sometimes hinders the teaching process. As previously mentioned, the type of examination used by the teacher will influence the study methods employed by the students. If students know that they will have a choice of test items, they may choose to study only a portion of the material and "play the odds" on being asked questions covering the material studied.

7. *Construct a detailed key for each question.* After writing an item, the teacher should construct what he considers to be the best answer to the item. Through this procedure the teacher can often detect ambiguities and inconsistencies which may be contained in an item. Furthermore, the reliability of the examination can be improved by using this prepared answer as the standard for scoring responses.

Item: The three angles of $\triangle ABC$ are equal respectively to the three angles of $\triangle A'B'C'$: $\angle A = \angle A'$, $\angle B = \angle B'$, and $\angle C = \angle C'$. Explain why this is not a sufficient condition for proving the two triangles congruent. (Use figures in your explanation.)

Key: An infinite number of similar triangles can be constructed with the *ratio* of the sides remaining constant and the *sizes* of the angles remaining constant. For example, in the triangle below $\angle BAC = \angle B'AC'$, $\angle ABC = \angle AB'C'$, and $\angle ACB = \angle AC'B'$, and the two triangles ABC and $AB'C'$ are not congruent since the respective sides are not equal ($AB \neq AB'$, $AC \neq AC'$, and $BC \neq B'C'$). For two triangles to be congruent, both their respective angles and their respective sides must be equal.

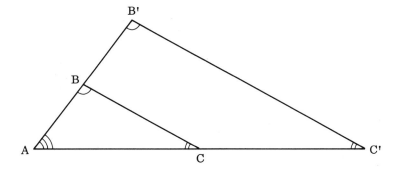

SCORING

The difficulty of scoring responses is one of the greatest weaknesses of essay examinations. Many approaches to the solution of this problem have been tried and analyzed. These have varied from skimming the response for a quick estimate of its worth to assigning points for specific bits of information included in it. Regardless of the method of scoring used, the emphasis should be on the ideas presented, relationships developed and explained, or judgments made, rather than on the factual information contained in the response. If factual information is all that is desired, it is usually more appropriate to use selection-type items, although the completion-item format offers a possible alternative.

If several questions are to be scored, one should score the first question on each paper before proceeding to the next. After all the items on all the papers are scored, the points assigned to the various questions can be summed for each paper. Furthermore, as previously discussed, the scorer reliability can be improved if the students' names are ignored while grading the papers and if the order of the papers is changed after scoring each question.

There are two basic methods of scoring essay responses which maximize scorer reliability: the sorting method and the point-score method.

Sorting Method

The sorting method of scoring consists of reading and sorting the papers into several groups, ranging from high to low. The number of groups to be utilized should be determined prior to scoring the papers. All papers are read and placed into the groups, with questionable papers assigned question marks. The border-line papers in each pair of adjacent groups are reread and as necessary resorted into the two groups, with care taken to see that the bottom papers in the "better" group are actually superior to the top papers in the "poorer" group.

When using this method, one can expect greater reliability in scoring if a predetermined number of papers are assigned to each group. In order to do this, one must first decide on the number of sorting groups to use. This is partially dependent on the size of the class, the number of points assigned to the question, and the number of gross discriminations between the papers one expects to be able to make. Then it is necessary to determine the numbers of papers which one expects to assign to each group. This process is illustrated in Table 4.1. In the

Table 4.1 Expected number in scoring groups

Group	Number expected in the group
1	2
2	4
3	8
4	4
5	2

situation represented by this table, a teacher had decided that he was going to sort the papers into five groups, and that he expected two papers to fall into the top group, four into the second group, and so on. It is important to remember that the teacher, when actually sorting the papers, is not required to conform exactly to his expected distribution. This procedure is not binding on the teacher, but it does establish an expected standard for scoring.

It is advisable to use all groupings in sorting the papers. If a nine-point scale is used, the best paper is assigned a 9 and the worst paper assigned a 1. Teachers often shy away from the extreme scores because they feel that no paper is good enough to receive the top score and no paper is bad enough to receive the bottom score. The resulting reduction in the range of scores reduces the reliability of the examination. The teacher need not feel compelled to assign an "A" to the top paper or an "F" to the bottom one. This evaluation depends not only on the score assigned to the paper but also on the teacher's judgment of its worth.

Point-Score Method

The point-score method of scoring essay responses is usually more reliable than the sorting method, because only preselected points are considered when scoring. However, there is a danger of sacrificing validity for this increase in reliability. One must avoid the pitfall of selecting "facts" as scoring points when the item is intended to measure higher-order mental processes.

In order to use this method, a grading key must be constructed that contains the responses likely to be elicited by the questions. The specific points for the reader to note must be isolated and assigned relative weights. The teacher can then read a response and assign to it the appropriate number of points. When all the questions have been scored, the points assigned to the questions can be added to determine the total score for each paper.

The point-score method is more appropriate for scoring the short-answer essay test than it is for scoring the extended-answer examination. The responses to short-answer questions are usually one or two sentences in length and deal with one central concept. Consequently, the specific points of concern can be isolated for quick, reliable scoring.

DO'S and DON'T'S

Do

1. Use essay tests to measure higher-order mental processes.
2. Include enough questions to adequately sample the material.
3. Limit the length of the response.
4. Use questions which are germane to the area being measured.
5. Use terms which will have the same meaning to all examinees.
6. Use terms which all examinees can define and understand.
7. Use questions which pose problems to be solved.

8. Explicitly state and qualify the problem so that it will be interpreted in the same manner by all examinees.

9. Make the sentence structure as simple as possible so that the problem posed will be clear to all examinees.

10. Write the question in advance so that it can be analyzed and revised if necessary before the test is given.

11. Write a comprehensive set of directions and include in these directions the weight of each question.

12. Write a model set of answers.

13. Before scoring the papers, determine the weights of the various elements expected in a complete answer.

14. Require the examinees to answer every question on the test.

15. Read a response and make a gross judgment as to its relative worth.

16. Score one question for all papers before going to the next question.

17. Score a question only on the achievement being measured.

18. Add the scores for each question to determine a paper's total worth.

19. Ignore the names of the examinees when grading.

20. Inform the examinees in advance that they will be given an essay test.

21. Analyze past questions.

Don't

1. Judge papers on extraneous factors such as handwriting, spelling, and grammar.

2. Make a general estimate of a paper's total worth as a first step in scoring.

3. Construct a test containing too few items to adequately sample the material.

4. Use optional questions.

5. Use different questions if the examinees are to be compared.

6. Use questions designed to elicit only factual information.

7. Expect the students to know the intent of the question unless it is explicitly stated.

8. Allow students to write "verbal garbage" with the hope of stumbling on the right answer.

PROBLEMS

1. What are the major limitations of the essay format? What steps can be taken to reduce these limitations?
2. Discuss the principal advantages of the essay test.
3. What are the two types of essay tests? Define both types and compare them with regard to (a) construction, (b) levels of cognitive behavior measured, and (c) mode of response.
4. Why should the essay question be limited?
5. Explain and compare the two methods for scoring essay responses.
6. Why should the teacher prepare detailed answers to the questions?
7. What steps can be taken to reduce verbiage in essay responses?
8. Develop a 10-item essay test for a unit of study. Use a Table of Specifications.

SUGGESTED READING

Adams, Georgia Sachs, *Measurement and Evaluation in Education, Psychology, and Guidance*. Holt, Rinehart and Winston, Chicago, 1964, pp. 330–334.

Ahmann, J. Stanley, and Marvin D. Glock, *Evaluating Pupil Growth: Principles of Tests and Measurement*. Allyn and Bacon, Boston, 1967, Chapter 5.

Ebel, Robert L., *Measuring Educational Achievement*. Prentice-Hall, Englewood Cliffs, N.J., 1965, Chapter 4.

Green, John A., *Teacher-Made Tests*. Harper and Row, Evanston, Ill., 1963, Chapter 5.

Horrocks, John E., *Assessment of Behavior*. Charles Merrill Books, Columbus, O., 1964, pp. 470–472.

Horrocks, John E., and Thelma I. Schoonover, *Measurement for Teachers*. Charles E. Merrill Books, Columbus, O., 1968, pp. 523–529.

Marshall, Jon C., "Composition Errors and Essay Examination Grades Re-Examined." *American Educational Research Journal*, I, 1967, 375–385.

Scannell, Dale P., and Jon C. Marshall, "Effect of Selected Composition Errors on Grades Assigned to Essay Examinations." *American Educational Research Journal*, **3**, 1966, 125–130.

Stalnaker, John M., "The Essay Type Examination," in E. F. Lindquist (Ed.), *Educational Measurement*. American Council on Education, Washington, D.C., 1951, chapter 13.

Thorndike, Robert L., and Elizabeth Hagen, *Measurement and Evaluation in Psychology and Education*. John Wiley and Sons, New York, 1969, pp. 77–87.

Chapter 5

The Completion Test

The completion item is a written statement which requires the examinee to supply the correct word or short phrase in response to an incomplete sentence, a question, or a word association. Although a supply-type item, the completion question is often classified with the more objective item types.

The completion question has been widely used in workbooks and tests accompanying textbooks. It is often found on teacher-made tests, particularly in the physical and biological sciences. Consequently, familiarity with this item type is valuable to the classroom teacher. In this chapter, the strengths and weaknesses of this item type will be considered, and guidelines for the construction and use of completion items will be developed.

WEAKNESSES

Several weaknesses are associated with the completion question. Perhaps the most serious one is found in the kinds of material for which it can be used. It is extremely difficult to construct a supply item to measure analysis, synthesis, or evaluation skills which can be answered in only one word or short phrase. Usually, if an item is designed to measure mental processes other than knowledge or comprehension, it cannot be answered in one word; thus, it becomes an essay question. This characteristic of completion items makes the validity of most completion tests suspect because they seldom measure important higher-order mental processes.

Associated with this problem is the structuring of completion items so that they have one and only one correct response. Completion items are designed to require the examinee to supply the correct word or phrase. Since the required response is very short, the correct response cannot vary much without the item becoming a guessing game of "what does the teacher want?" For example, read and react to the following completion item as though it were a question on a history test.

Who fought at Little Big Horn?

At first glance, this item might seem simple enough. An examinee might immediately write down "Custer" and go to the next item. But what about the child who responds "Sioux"?—is he not also correct? Or those students who respond "Cavalry" or "Indians," or those who give specific, but little known, names of persons in the battle—are not they also correct? How does the teacher mark these responses? Surely some answers are better than others. Or are they? This dilemma is often faced by teachers who attempt to construct completion items without careful consideration of possible item interpretations. Even when care has been exercised, students often interpret items in ways never conceived of by the teacher. When this occurs, all valid interpretations and their corresponding correct responses should be given credit. When measuring higher mental processes, this difficulty is greatly magnified because few higher-order problems have only one answer.

Even when there is just one correct response per item, completion tests lack the scoring ease associated with other objective test forms. In general, they cannot be machine-scored or hand-scored as rapidly as multiple-choice, true-false, and matching tests. Reading the written responses takes more time than checking the selected letters, as is done with multiple-choice tests. Thus, when compared to other objective test formats, the completion test lacks scoring economy.

STRENGTHS

When used to measure knowledge, the completion item has some advantages. Completion items are relatively easy to construct; while multiple-choice and matching items require alternates, completion items do not. This simplifies the item development task and reduces the amount of time needed for item construction. However, this apparent advantage is reduced somewhat by the need in completion items for establishing the entire frame of reference for answering the item in the item statement or question. With multiple-choice and matching items, part of this structuring is accomplished by the alternates.

The completion item minimizes the chance of guessing the correct answer. With selection-type items, the possibility of obtaining the correct answer by chance alone is always present. If a multiple-choice item contains four alternates, an examinee who marks the response randomly has one chance in four of selecting the keyed response. The possibility of selecting the correct response for a completion item by chance is remote.

When the items are constructed to yield only one correct response, it is simple to make a scoring key. The use of such a key makes possible a scorer agreement which approaches that of selection-type tests. Furthermore, the completion test may be scored somewhat rapidly. In contrast with other supply-type tests, the completion test has the advantage of greater scorer agreement and increased efficiency in scoring.

Completion items measure the *recall* of information rather than recognition. When it is important that the examinee recall basic facts (terms, dates, names, generalizations, etc.), these supply-type items may be more valid than selection-type items as measures of instructional objectives.

The results from several independent studies indicate that the correlation between recall and recognition is substantial. This has been misconstrued by some to mean that recall and recognition items measure the same thing. It is more likely that this relation means that good students do well on both types of tests and, similarly, poor students do poorly on both types of test. Therefore, the test form used by the teacher should reflect his behavioral objectives—recall of information or selection of information.

USES

Completion tests can be used effectively to measure the recall of terms, dates, names, and generalizations. This type of test can be used at almost all grade levels, but it seems to be especially appropriate at the intermediate level since much of the material taught at this level lends itself to the completion type of examination. At later grade levels, its importance as a testing technique decreases because of the decrease in the importance of lower-level mental skills (e.g., knowledge).

CONSTRUCTION

The completion item presents to the examinee a problem to be solved by the recall and recording of an appropriate word or phrase. In order to solve the problem, the examinee must identify the problem and recall the requisite information. The problem statement, therefore, must establish one and only one frame of reference for responding if it is to measure recall rather than skill in guessing the intent of the examiner. If too many clues are given in the attempt to establish a single frame of reference, the item will be too easy; if an insufficient number of clues are presented, the item will be ambiguous and may lend itself to several correct responses. Neither of these alternatives is desirable.

The item should be concise, unambiguous, and grammatically correct. Phrases and words not needed to present the problem or to set the frame of reference should be eliminated. Unnecessary and excessively technical words often result in hidden clues to the expected answer or in an ambiguous statement. To avoid giving hidden clues, particular care must be exercised in the use of articles and verbs. The following illustrates some of these problems:

An _____ weighs less than a pound.

The article "An" indicates that the correct response must start with a vowel, and the item fails to set a single frame of reference for responding. Both *egg* and *ounce* would be technically correct as responses. The following revision is a better statement of the problem:

What unit of measurement is exactly 1/16th of a pound? _____

The completion item can take one of three forms: the question format, the incomplete sentence format, or the association format.

Question

The best method to use in the construction of completion items is the question format. In this approach the problem is presented as a question which asks for specific, limited information.

What is the tallest mountain in the world? _____

There are several S-R learning theories. Who proposed the theory which emphasizes the formation of habits? _____

In what city was the peace treaty signed which ended Word War I? _____

Items of this type should present the problem explicitly and precisely, setting a single frame of reference for responding. If the item merely restates as a question material taken directly from the text, care should be taken to ensure that removing it from its original context does not introduce ambiguity. For example, a teacher in an introductory biology class might ask the question:

What is a red corpuscle? _____

As stated, this item lends itself to several correct responses, including: "protein," "part of blood," "a blood solid," "a cell," and "a carrier of oxygen." The item would be less ambiguous if written:

What structure in the blood carries oxygen to the cells of the human body?

_____

However, even in this form there are two correct responses: "hemoglobin" and "red corpuscles." If "red corpuscle" is the desired response, the item could be improved by substituting "cell" for "structure" in revising the above, as follows:

Which cell in the blood carries oxygen to the cells of the human body?

_____

This item contains the clue, "in the blood." This clue was included as an aid in setting the frame of reference for the question. If this clue is not needed, the item might be a better discriminator in the form:

Which of the cells found in the human body carries oxygen to all other living cells?

_____

Incomplete Sentence

The incomplete sentence format should be used sparingly because items written in this format are often either obvious or ambiguous. It is usually advisable to state the completion item as a question.

In the incomplete sentence format of the completion item, the examinee is presented with a sentence which contains one or more blanks which he must fill in with the appropriate term or terms. The sentence must contain a sufficient number of qualifiers to define explicitly the expected response without making the response obvious to the examinees. If possible, when only one piece of information is requested, the item should be constructed so that the blank occurs at the end of the sentence. Also, a sentence should not be taken verbatim from a textbook or lecture notes. This practice encourages rote learning by the students and often results in ambiguity because of presenting the statement out of its original context. Furthermore, do not mutilate a sentence so that it becomes almost impossible to answer it on the basis of the text of the question. Construct the multiresponse item so that the various responses are independent, unless, of course, the association among responses is an integral part of the content area being measured.

The following type of item should be avoided:

The (1) was fought during (2) , (3) between (4) and (5) .

The text of this item does not supply an adequate frame of reference for responding. Examinees can respond correctly only by second-guessing the teacher. Furthermore, if response (1) is incorrect, the other responses also will be incorrect. This question could be rewritten as follows:

The bloodiest engagement of the Atlanta Campaign in the American Civil War was fought about four miles north of downtown Atlanta. This battle was called (1) . It was fought during the days of (2) in the year (3) between the Union forces under (4) and Confederate forces under (5) .

Note that all blanks are the same length. This is necessary in order that the size of the space does *not* provide a clue to the correct response.

Association

The association form of the completion test consists of an introductory statement used to establish the frame of reference and a set of related words or phrases to which the examinee is to respond. The following set of items is of this type:

Listed below, under Column I, are several machines which aided in the industrial development of the United States. For each machine you are to write the name of the *inventor* on the line provided to the right of each machine under Column II.

Column I	Column II
1. Cotton gin	_____
2. Steamboat	_____
3. Gas automobile	_____
4. Airplane	_____
5. Harvester	_____

Completion items of the association type occur in clusters. The item cluster must contain an introductory statement. The function of the introductory statement is to set a general frame of reference for responding to the items in the cluster and to indicate to the examinee how he is to proceed in recording his responses. This statement should be clear, concise, and free of superfluous and technical words or phrases. The use of inappropriate vocabulary in the introductory statement can render the entire item cluster ineffective. Examine the introductory and item statements in the following set of association items.

> Some criticisms of various item types are listed in Column I. On the line to the right of each criticism (Column II), record the item type for which the criticism is most appropriate. Remember that an item type may be used more than one time.
>
> *Column I*   *Column II*
>
> 1. It tends to result in extensive sampling of comprehension in a limited number of content areas.   _____
> 2. It should be used primarily for measuring comprehension.   _____
> 3. The judgment of the scorer influences the test reliability.   _____
> 4. The items must be relatively easy to be meaningful.   _____
> 5. To write good items requires skill and time.   _____
> 6. The scorer must be an expert in the subject area.   _____

In this example, the introductory statement structures the task for the examinee. He is asked to supply the appropriate item type for each criticism listed and is told where to record his response. However, the item statements are poorly selected because it would be difficult to justify one and only one correct answer for each of the criticisms indicated. To be entirely fair, the scoring key for this item cluster would have to allow for the occurrence of more than one defensible response to some of the criticisms. This item set illustrates why completion items should rarely be used for measuring higher-order mental processes.

The item statements (premises) should be selected carefully for consistency with the introductory statement and for their ability to generate, in conjunction with the introductory statement, a single frame of reference for responding. It is the primary function of the premises to present the specific tasks to be completed. In order to accomplish this purpose effectively, they should be clear, concise, free of ambiguity, and lacking in language usage errors. It is often possible to use single words or short statements as premises.

SCORING

To facilitate scoring, the examinees should record their responses on a prepared answer sheet. In order that mistakes such as misnumbering will not enter into their scores, the answer sheet should be prepared for the examinees. The answer sheet can be designed so that the examinee's answers and the key align for ease of scoring (see Figure 5.1).

The short responses elicited by completion item tests lend them to objective scoring. An answer key containing the correct responses can be prepared by the teacher for use in scoring by para-professionals and students, as well as by teachers.

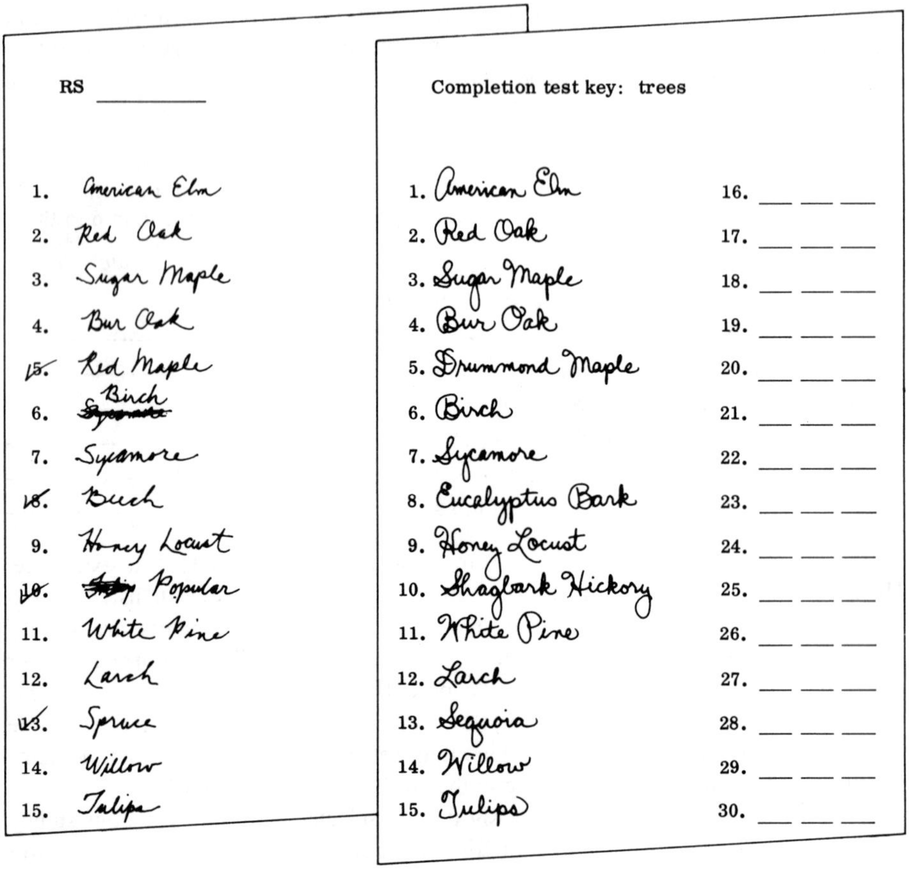

Fig. 5.1. Answer sheet for a completion test.

By matching the examinee's responses to the key, all markers should agree on the person's test score. However, to maximize this agreement among markers, there should be only one correct response per item. If this cannot be achieved, then the key should contain all possible correct responses for each item.

The scoring of the response can be on a +1 and 0 basis—one point for a correct response and zero points for an incorrect response or no response. Even though it is possible to allow partial credit for responses which are not completely correct or which contain language errors, this practice is not recommended because it tends to lower scorer agreement and scoring efficiency. Furthermore, a penalty for incorrect responses should not be used because chance plays a negligible role in completion test responses.

EXAMPLES

This section is divided into two parts. The first part consists of several *poor* completion items. Read and analyze these items; rewrite them as necessary to form well-constructed items. The second part consists of the same items presented in *rewritten, improved* form. Compare your reactions to the first set of items with your reactions to the items in the second part.

Poor Items

1. Who was president of the United States during World War II?

– –

In 1964, President Johnson appointed (2)   to important Federal positions.

– –

Hawaii is a (3)   , (4)   , and the (5)   state of the United States.

– –

The substance in human red blood cells which allows for the classification of blood into different groups is an (6)   .

– –

Who wrote each of the following books?
7. *Jane Eyre*
8. *Odes*
9. *Uncle Tom's Cabin*
10. *The Last of the Mohicans*
11. *Twice Told Tales*

– –

The life cycle of the (12)   can be separated into two distinct phases, (13)   and (14)   . This type of life cycle is called (15)   . The first phase is (16)   , (17)   , and the second phase (18)   , (19)   .

– –

20.   Why was Truman nominated the Democratic candidate for Vice-President of the United States in 1944?

---

21.   Who was one of the earliest inventors to construct a steam engine?

---

(22)   developed an early piston-and-cylinder steam engine.

---

(23)   demonstrated the usefulness of the steam engine.

The French engineer (24)   designed and built the first steam-powered vehicle constructed for use rather than for experimentation.

Lord Rutherford's classical nuclear experiment can be represented as (25)   .

Intended responses.   Listed below are the responses which were meant to be elicited by these items.

1. Roosevelt	2. ten women
3. tourist resort	4. sugar empire
5. 50th	6. agglutinogen
7. Bronte	8. Collins
9. Stowe	10. Cooper
11. Hawthorne	12. bryophytes
13. sporophyte	14. gametophyte
15. alternation of generations	16. asexual
17. parasitic	18. sexual
19. independent	20. compromise candidate
21. Branca	22. Papin
23. Newcomen	24. Cugnot
25. $_7N^{14} + {}_2He^4 \longrightarrow {}_8O^{17} + {}_1H^1$	

Improved Items

1.   Who was president of the United States during the major portion of World War II?

---

2.   How many women did President Johnson appoint to important Federal positions in 1964?

Hawaii is becoming more and more attractive to many persons as a tropical (3)   .

---

4.   What is Hawaii's major export?

---

5.   Where does Hawaii rank among the states of the United States relative to its statehood?

---

6.   What is the substance in human red blood cells called which allows for the classification of blood into different groups?

Listed below, under Column I, are several book titles. For each title write the last name of the author on the line provided to the right of the title under Column II.

Column I	Column II
7. *Jane Eyre*	_____
8. *Odes*	_____
9. *Uncle Tom's Cabin*	_____
10. *The Last of the Mohicans*	_____
11. *Twice Told Tales*	_____

----

12.   What is the plant division called which can include Mosses or Liverworts?

Many Mosses and Liverworts have a similar life history, including a regular alternation of two distinct phases in their life cycles, the (13) _____ and (14) _____ . This type of two-phase life cycle is called (15) _____ . In the dominant generation, the plants are (16) _____ in relation to other organisms. Insofar as reproduction is a part of the life cycle, this phase is the (17) _____ generation. The other phase is (18) _____ in relation to the dominant generation, and in the reproduction cycle it is the (19) _____ generation.

Because of his role in the investigation of waste and inefficiency in World War II war agencies, Truman was nominated the Democratic candidate for Vice-President in 1944 as the (20) _____ candidate.

Several developments in the evolution of the steam engine are listed in Column I. For each development, record the last name of the inventor or developer on the line provided to the right of the development under Column II.

Column I	Column II
21. The earliest turbine device in which steam was blown against vanes on a wheel.	_____
22. The earliest piston-and-cylinder steam engine resulted from the substitution of steam for gunpowder in an engine of Huygen's type.	_____
23. The first demonstration of the usefulness of the steam engine was recorded with an engine which was used to pump water from coal mines.	_____
24. The first steam-powered vehicle designed for use, rather than for experimentation, was constructed.	_____

----

25.   Write the formula which represents the classical nuclear experiment of Lord Rutherford.

DO'S AND DON'T'S

Do

1. Use completion tests to measure lower-order mental skills.
2. Limit the length of the response to a single word or short phrase.
3. Use questions which are germane to the area being measured.
4. Use terms which will have the same meaning to all examinees.
5. Use terms which all examinees can define and understand.
6. Explicitly state and qualify the question so that a single response is correct.
7. Make the sentence structure as simple as possible so that the question will be clear to all examinees.
8. Write the questions in advance so that they can be analyzed and revised if necessary before the test is given.
9. Write a comprehensive set of directions.
10. Have all examinees use a prepared answer sheet.
11. Give equal weight to all responses.
12. Construct the answer sheet so that it is easy to score.
13. If possible, use questions rather than incomplete statements.
14. For multiple-response items, have blanks of equal length.
15. Ask only for important information.
16. Inform the examinees in advance that they will be given a completion test.

Don't

1. Overmutilate sentences by leaving too many blanks.
2. Have the answers to a multiple-response item interdependent.
3. Ask for non-essentials.
4. Penalize for guessing.
5. Use items which have more than one correct answer.
6. Use questions designed to measure higher-order mental processes.
7. Pull questions verbatim from the textbook or lecture notes.

PROBLEMS

1. What are the major limitations of the completion format? What steps can be taken to reduce these limitations?
2. Discuss the principal advantages of completion tests.
3. What principal advantage do completion items have in comparison to other supply-type items?
4. What three forms can completion items take? Compare the advantages and disadvantages of each form.
5. Develop a 30-item completion test for a unit of study. Use a Table of Specifications.

SUGGESTED READING

Adams, Georgia Sachs, *Measurement and Evaluation in Education, Psychology, and Guidance*. Holt, Rinehart, and Winston, Chicago, 1964, pp. 334–336.

Ahmann, J. Stanley, and Marvin D. Glock, *Evaluating Pupil Growth: Principles of Tests and Measurement*. Allyn and Bacon, Boston, 1967, pp. 79–83.

Ebel, Robert L., "Writing the Test Item," in E. F. Lindquist (Ed.), *Educational Measurement*. American Council on Education, Washington, D.C., 1951, pp. 227–228.

Chapter 6

The Oral Test

The oral examination is a time-honored form of measurement. It is still traditional at the university level for thesis examinations, at the early childhood level for content examinations, and at the postschool level for occupational placement examinations. However, for many measurement purposes the oral examination is seldom used. Its fall from favor is a result of the many structural weaknesses in the oral examination format.

In the classical form of the oral examination, the question is presented orally to the examinee and is responded to in like manner. However, two alternative forms of response to orally presented problems (written and performance) will also be considered in this chapter because they have elements in common with the more traditional oral-response form.

ORAL-RESPONSE TEST

In the oral-response form of the oral examination, the examiner presents the questions using the spoken word and the examinee responds in the same manner. This type of test is considered by many to be the only legitimate form of oral examination.

Weaknesses

There are several severe disadvantages associated with the oral-response test. Whether the test is administered in a classroom setting or in a cubicle with only the examiner and examinee present, it is basically an individual examination restricted to the verbal interaction of examiner and examinee for any one question. Also, the administration of an oral-response test is exceedingly time-consuming, especially when it involves in-depth questioning. Of all the methods available for the collection of test data, this is the least efficient.

When an oral-response test is administered to an entire class, it is unlikely that any two students will be asked the same questions under identical conditions. Most students will be asked only two or three questions, and their responses will be judged subjectively. Since students will be asked different questions, there will be no common criterion for comparing student responses. Furthermore, the sampling of content will be too limited to yield reliable or valid results. Consequently, the oral-response test so administered is likely to lack three important characteristics: validity, reliability, and comparability of scores.

Since oral responses are generally scored at the time they are given, scorer reliability is often unacceptably low. There are several reasons why this "snap-judgment" of the scorer may be in error. For example, he may misunderstand or misinterpret the response or he may be influenced by preconceived ideas concerning the ability of the examinee. Scorer reliability, however, can be improved through careful preplanning of questions and tentative answers and through careful test administration. An additional increase in scorer reliability can be obtained by pooling several raters' judgments of responses. The use of a combination of several ratings tends to cancel out many individual errors.

Advantages

The advantages attributed to the oral-response test are due primarily to the somewhat unique characteristics of this test form: it is presented orally and responded to orally. Therefore, the reading level and writing ability of the examinee are not involved in the examination. This contributes to the overall flexibility of oral-response examinations. They can be used in many situations appropriate to other types of tests and in some unique situations where other tests are inappropriate.

The reading skills of many students are so limited as to render written examinations useless. Since the oral-response test does not require the ability to read, it can be used with such students. It can be used effectively with children at the primary school level, with students who have reading disabilities, and with foreign or culturally deprived students.

Some instructional objectives cannot be measured by written tests but are amenable to measurement by oral examinations. For example, they can be used to measure oral discrimination and oral communication skills.

The oral-response test is particularly useful for individual examinations. Its flexibility allows additional questioning in selected areas when an examiner feels that it is necessary. The oral-response test enables the examiner to probe in depth into selected areas and to restate questions which appear to be misunderstood by the examinee. Because of this flexibility, this test form is often used for examining students in advanced training.

Important psychological information often can be obtained from an individual oral examination, even when the primary purpose of the examination is to obtain data on achievement or intelligence. For example, one of the major purposes for using individual intelligence tests is to collect psychological information on the examinee. The intelligence quotient is only a portion of the information gathered through the administration of these examinations. The examiner can often obtain important and useful insights into the behavior and personality of the individual.

Construction

The practices to be followed in the construction of an oral-examination question are partially dependent on the type of question being asked. It is possible to transform any supply or selection item into an oral-response item by reading the item aloud to the examinee and requiring a verbal response to it. However, multiple-choice and matching exercises are rarely used in this format because the typical examinee finds it difficult to keep in mind all aspects of the question being presented. Except as class exercises, true-false items should not be used because they can be more efficiently employed without introducing reading or writing difficulties in the written-response form of the oral examination. Extended-answer and short-answer essay questions, as well as completion items, are often used in the oral-response test.

When writing an item to be presented orally, it is important to avoid the use of phonetically similar words unless the structure of the sentence clearly indicates the specific word being used. Although the ambiguity introduced by the use of phonetically similar words usually can be corrected by further explanation, the resulting increase in administration time reduces the efficiency of the examination. Furthermore, the examinee is likely to suffer an increase in test anxiety when faced with ambiguity in the questions asked.

The necessity of controlling the length and complexity of the question is a problem common to all types of items. This is a particularly significant concern in oral examinations because the examinee does not have an opportunity to review the critical portions of the item without asking the examiner to repeat it. When achievement, other than auditory comprehension *per se*, is to be assessed, the question should be sufficiently long to allow each student to understand exactly what is being asked, but not so long as to make it difficult for the examinee to recall the item in composing his response.

As an aid in refining the oral-response item, one should prepare an acceptable response to the item during the process of item construction. If the items being developed are to be used in a discriminatory instrument, the prepared answers should contain both "good" and "minimal" responses. On the other hand, if the examination is to be used to test mastery, only the minimal response is necessary.

With the exceptions noted, the practices to be followed in the construction of oral-response items mirror the practices which should be followed in writing comparable essay or completion items. In the stiuation where an orally presented problem is to be solved by the recall and verbal statement of an appropriate word or phrase (comparable to the completion item), the item should set one and only one frame of reference for responding to the task presented. The item should be concise, clear, grammatically correct, and unencumbered by superfluous words and phrases. After the item has been written, it should be carefully studied for hidden clues and ambiguity. It is a good practice to present the problem as a question, although it is possible to use an incomplete sentence.

Who was the King of England during the American Revolution?

In what city did the First Continental Congress meet?

To whom did the Second Continental Congress give command of the Colonial Army?

In developing an oral-response item containing only one central idea and answerable in one or two sentences, one should follow the guidelines for the construction of short-answer essay questions. The desired length of the response should be indicated in the question. The item should be brief and concise, should contain only one central idea, should be open to one and only one interpretation, and should explicitly state the problem to be solved.

What were two of the economic causes of the U.S. Civil War?

Briefly define the term *set*.

Name two ways that police help people.

If you were using operant conditioning to train a retarded child, on what aspect of the procedure would you be placing the greatest importance?

The oral-response item may require an extended answer. When this is so, the item is comparable to the extended-answer essay question and should be developed in accordance with the guidelines for constructing essay questions. This type should be used only to measure higher-order mental processes; they are generally inappropriate for class examinations. The question should briefly and clearly convey to the student the problem, indicate the scope of the question, and limit the content to be covered in the response.

Questions of this type obviously require more time to answer than short-answer or completion items; therefore, an examination comprised of extended-answer, oral-response questions should contain fewer items than an examination of the short-answer or completion oral-response type.

What was the political attitude prevalent in the South immediately preceding the Civil War and what effect did this attitude have on the outbreak of the war?

What basic changes have occurred in transportation during the past 60 years and what influence have these changes had on society?

Administration

The oral response test is essentially a structured interview. It is an encounter between two human beings, between two personalities. Both the teacher and the student are subject to the same kinds of stress. In an attempt to be objective in the examination, the teacher may become stilted or impersonal in manner. He may overidentify with examinees' problems or feel pangs of guilt because of examinees' test anxieties. The examinee, being somewhat uncomfortable, will respond in the manner least threatening to himself.

Even though these conflicts reflect some of the problems associated with oral tests, the testing situation is much more complex than this. Each role-incumbent has a set of roles to play, and these roles will vary from time to time. The examinee may fluctuate among his roles as a youth leader, a subordinate in the home, a boyfriend, a buddy, an athlete, and a student. The examiner may play the roles of a husband, a father, a teacher, a club leader, and a tester. Society defines all of these roles by assigning expected role behaviors. The effectiveness of personal interaction depends on the efficiency of the communication of these expected role behaviors. Understanding between role-incumbents is dependent on the similarity of interpersonal perceptions of expectations. Misunderstanding or conflict between persons emerges from the lack of congruence of these perceptions.

Thus there are many possibilities in the role interactions between the teacher-examiner and the examinee. These possibilities include interactions with actual roles, perceived expectations, and expectations of others for both role-incumbents. Even in the most permissive schools, the teacher usually maintains a role of authority. He is expected to provide leadership, make decisions, and give structure to the learning situation. The role of examiner enhances these authoritative expectations. In an information-giving oral test, the roles of the teacher-examiner and examinee are relatively clear-cut. Even though there is often stress in these situations, roles can be clearly delineated through careful planning and testing. However, in testing higher mental processes involving problem-solving tasks, the roles often become confused. The examinee is required to make judgments and decisions which generally are considered to be in the domain of the examiner. If the examiner perceives his role as that of advising or prescribing, or if his personality is domineering or aggressive, he will probably arouse anxiety and conflict in the oral-testing situation.

The examiner is under pressure during the entire testing period—asking questions, rewording items, and recording or evaluating responses. Of paramount importance to the success of the examination is the poise of the examiner in resolving role conflicts and reducing test anxiety. He must always be alert, watching every reaction of the examinee. Also, he must be able to communicate to the examinee in a clear, distinct, unthreatening manner.

Scoring

The scoring of oral responses is a major liability of the oral examination. It is very difficult to obtain acceptable scorer reliability and objectivity. When possible, it is best to develop and use a record sheet for recording the actual response of the examinee. After the examination is completed, the responses on the record sheet can be carefully compared with those on a prepared answer key. This is the basic procedure followed in scoring most individual intelligence tests. Unfortunately, however, it is rather difficult to employ this procedure with the extended-answer, oral-response test. The alternative procedure of tape-recording the responses for future playback and scoring has been successfully used by some examiners.

The scoring of oral-response examinations can be improved through the use

Fig. 6.1. Rating scale for oral response tests

Question	Rating
1. — — — — — — — —	5 4 3 2 1
2. — — — — — — — —	5 4 3 2 1
3. — — — — — — — —	5 4 3 2 1
4. — — — — — — — —	5 4 3 2 1
5. — — — — — — — —	5 4 3 2 1
6. — — — — — — — —	5 4 3 2 1
7. — — — — — — — —	5 4 3 2 1
– — — — — — — — —	5 4 3 2 1
– — — — — — — — —	5 4 3 2 1
– — — — — — — — —	5 4 3 2 1
– — — — — — — — —	5 4 3 2 1

of rating scales and check-lists. The rating scale is better suited for extended-answer items; the check-list, for short-answer and completion questions. An example of a rating scale is shown in Figure 6.1. When this scale is used, each question is read to each examinee and each of his responses is given a 5 if it is outstanding, a 4 if it is good, and so on. In order to use this scale accurately, the examiner must develop guidelines for each question according to what he considers a 5-response, a 4-response, etc. By using a rating scale instead of recording the actual responses, one can administer more items during an examination period but the scoring will usually be more subjective.

Fig. 6.2. Check-list for oral response test

Question	Yes	No
1. — — — — — — — — —	— — — —	— — — —
2. — — — — — — — — —	— — — —	— — — —
3. — — — — — — — — —	— — — —	— — — —
4. — — — — — — — — —	— — — —	— — — —
5. — — — — — — — — —	— — — —	— — — —
6. — — — — — — — — —	— — — —	— — — —
– — — — — — — — — —	— — — —	— — — —
– — — — — — — — — —	— — — —	— — — —

The check-list is similar to the rating scale (see Figure 6.2). Instead of assigning a rating to the examinee's performance, the examiner checks "YES" if the response is acceptable and "NO" if it is unacceptable. By subdividing each question into its various components, this type of check sheet can be more detailed, thus improving the measurements. The examiner can check each of the components that is included in the examinee's response.

WRITTEN-RESPONSE TEST

In the written-response form of the oral examination, the questions are presented by the examiner by the use of the spoken word and are answered in writing by the examinee. The written-response test can be thought of as falling somewhere between the classical oral examination (oral-response) and the written examination. Whether it is closer to the oral-response test or the written test depends primarily on the purpose for using this particular test form.

Weaknesses

In the written-response form of the oral examination, many of the advantages of the oral-response test do not apply. Since the examinees must be able to write, skill in writing tends to become a part of the score given to a response. It is seldom appropriate for use with the young child or with the physically handicapped who lack writing skills. Furthermore, the opportunity to probe in depth in selected areas at the discretion of the examiner is lost. In addition, it is of little value in measuring oral communication skills. The written-response form lacks most of the unique advantages of the more traditional oral examination except for a few instructional objectives which are amenable to written tests.

In contrast with written examinations composed of comparable items, this form of the oral examination is less efficient in its use of testing time, requires the oral repetition of items during test administration, increases the possibility of ambiguity because of similarity in word sounds, and reduces the length and complexity of questions because of the need for the examinee to keep in mind all pertinent information during the presentation of the problem and the formulation of the response.

The items constructed for use in the written-response form of the oral examination may be similar in format to extended-answer or short-answer essay questions, question-type completion items, or true-false items. In general, the weaknesses associated with its counterpart in the supply-type question or the true-false item are applicable to the written-response form of the oral examination. The various weaknesses associated with specific item types are covered in their respective chapters.

Advantages

The written-response form of the oral examination is used by the classroom teacher more often than the oral-response form. Since it can be used to examine several students simultaneously, rather than only one at a time, many of the liabilities of the oral-response test are less significant for this test form. For example, all examinees have the opportunity to respond to every item, thus providing a common criterion for comparing responses. Furthermore, unless the examinees are privately quizzed, in a given amount of testing time each examinee can be asked more questions in the written-response test than in the oral-response test.

There are three situations in which this form of the oral examination may prove to be more appropriate than its written examination counterpart: (1) where there is a shortage of supplies needed to reproduce the tests; (2) when auditory comprehension is an integral part of the test; and (3) when it is extremely difficult to write questions to measure instructional objectives that can be measured by oral examination items. For example, spelling skill can be measured by the teacher pronouncing the words and the students writing them on a sheet of paper.

Construction

Avoid the use of words which are phonetically similar to other words. Although the ambiguity introduced by the use of phonetically similar words usually can be corrected by further explanation, the necessity of doing so is likely to increase test anxiety and reduce the number of items which can be administered in a specified length of time.

The length and complexity of each item must be carefully controlled. If the question is too long or too complicated, the examinee will find it difficult to remember the salient portions of the item while formulating his response. When this occurs, test efficiency is reduced as a result of the repetition of questions and test anxiety is increased. Also, the immediate recall ability of the examinee (in this case the recall of the test item) will become a factor in the score received. On the other hand, the question must be long enough to set a frame of reference for responding and to present clearly the problem to the examinee.

During the process of writing and revising the written-response item, an acceptable response for the item should be prepared. Unless the items are to be used in a mastery test, the prepared answers should contain "good" and "minimal" responses. By endeavoring to answer the question, one can often discover alternative interpretations of the question. When this happens, the item should be revised before it is used in a test.

With the exceptions noted, the practices to be followed in the construction of written-response questions are similar to the practices which should be followed in constructing comparable supply-type and true-false items. When the problem is read to the examinee and he is expected to respond by writing an appropriate word or phrase, the procedures for the construction of the question-type completion item are appropriate to the construction of the written-response question.

If one internal angle of a triangle is obtuse, what term would describe the sizes of the remaining internal angles?

What term best describes the process by which sunlight is used in green plants to convert carbon dioxide and water to plant food?

When was the Declaration of Independence signed?

Which amendment to the U.S. Constitution grants to an accused the right to refuse to answer questions asked by an arresting officer?

What were the names of the first three men who traveled around the moon?

A written-response item constructed in the completion format should be clear and concise, grammatically correct, free from ambiguity, void of hidden clues, and open to only one interpretation of the meaning of the question. Usually the item should present the problem as a question. Unnecessary or irrelevant technical words should be eliminated.

It is possible to construct written-response items which can be answered "true" or "false." However, unless there are compelling reasons for using an oral examination (such as a lack of duplicating materials or inadequate reading skills on the part of the examinees), it is advantageous for the students to have copies of the test in front of them.

If items of this type are to be used, each item should be concise, unambiguous, explicit, and free of irrelevant clues. The item should be either absolutely true or completely false: it is unfair to expect the examinee to guess the degree of error required by the examiner before he considers the correct answer to be false. Finally, the item should contain one and only one central idea.

> In some triangles all internal angles are acute angles.
>
> It is possible for a triangle to have two obtuse internal angles.
>
> The number of U.S. Senators which a state may have is determined by how populous the state is.
>
> Carbon dioxide is a by-product of photosynthesis.

If a written-response item contains only one central idea and can be answered in one or two sentences, it is analogous to the short-answer essay question. The guidelines for the construction of items of the latter sort should, in general, be followed in the construction of comparable written-response items. The expected length of the response should be indicated in the question. The item should be concise, contain only one central idea, be open to one and only one interpretation, and state the problem to be solved explicitly.

> Define photosynthesis.
>
> In one or two sentences, describe the physical appearance of a hydrocephalic child.
>
> List the symptoms of acute appendicitis.
>
> What is the difference between a number and a numeral?

When a written-response item requires a somewhat extensive answer, it is comparable to the extended-answer essay question and should be constructed in keeping with the guidelines of the latter item type. It should convey briefly and clearly the problem to be solved, indicate the scope of the question, and limit the content to be covered in making an adequate response. Since only a small number of these items can be asked during an examination period, they should be used only to measure higher-order mental processes.

Describe the process by which green plants manufacture their food. Include in your response the role in this process of each of the following: water, carbon dioxide, oxygen, carbohydrates, and chlorophyll. You have 20 minutes in which to respond.

Briefly list the various types of neuroses and their major symptoms. This question is worth 15 points.

What are the major factors contributing to the balance-of-payments problem of the United States? This question is worth 20 points.

It should be apparent that only a few items of this type can be administered during a typical 45-minute examination period. Even if duplicating supplies are unavailable, it should be no great chore for the teacher to write the questions on the board. Consequently, this form of the written-response test is generally inappropriate for examination purposes.

Administration

The administration of a written-response oral examination is slightly more difficult than that of comparable supply or selection tests. The administration of this type of test should correspond to that of other types of tests. In addition, the examiner must communicate to the examinee in a clear, distinct voice. The examinee must be able to hear and understand every word spoken by the examiner.

Scoring

The scoring of written-response items should follow the guidelines for scoring their counterparts in the supply-type and selection-type tests. If the question is of the extended-answer type, it should be scored by using either the sorting method or the point-score method. If the written-response item is of the short-answer variety, the point-score method of scoring is preferable. If the question is of the completion type, it can be easily scored by using a prepared key, allowing one point for a correct response and none for an incorrect response. The scoring of the written-response test of the true-false variety is readily accomplished by use of an overlay key, providing an appropriate answer sheet was prepared for use by the examinees.

ORAL-PERFORMANCE TEST

In the oral-performance test, the student is orally presented with a task to carry out, and his skill in executing it is assessed. A more detailed discussion of performance tests is presented in Chapter 10. Since it is one kind of performance test, the principles developed in that chapter will apply to the oral-performance test. This special type of test is presented here because of the special characteristics it has in common with other oral tests.

If any distinction can be made between the performance test to be discussed here and performance tests described in Chapter 10, it is in regard to the importance of the oral statement of the examiner to the tasks to be performed. If the oral statement consists only of directions concerning these tasks, the test is not an oral examination. On the other hand, it would be an oral examination if the examiner's statement were an integral part of the tasks to be performed. An example of this type of oral-response test is an examination in which the teacher dictates a letter to be recorded in shorthand by the examinees.

Weaknesses

There are several disadvantages inherent to the oral-performance test. In an examination setting it is difficult to identify tasks to be performed which truly reflect the student's ability to perform in a real-life situation. The tasks selected must be pertinent to performance in the natural setting and must be subject to reliable measurement. Usually the tasks are selected to allow measurement of skills thought to be essential in producing the final product. It is often very difficult and time-consuming to obtain an adequate sampling of such tasks.

Scorer reliability is often unacceptably low when oral-performance tests are scored at the same time they are given. It is difficult to avoid the halo effect in scoring these tests. It is difficult for the examiner to avoid being influenced by his general impression of the examinee and by his generalized view of the performance. When the product being judged cannot be marked in the right-wrong dichotomy, the assessment of the performance becomes even more subjective. Even when the performance test can be scored at some time after the completion of the examination, it is difficult to obtain good scorer reliability.

The oral-performance test is often inefficient in its use of examinee and examiner time. Since appropriate tasks often require time to perform, it is difficult to obtain an adequate sampling of behavior. It is not unusual for a performance test to require only one or two samples of behavior in an examination period. Also, when these tests are given individually or in small groups, there is a loss of time in test repetition and an increase in the possibility of test compromise.

The scoring of oral-performance tests is often difficult and time-consuming. If a manufactured or created product is to be scored, the expenditure of time needed to score the products of an entire class may be measured in hours or even days.

Advantages

Many instructional objectives which cannot be measured by written tests are amenable to measurement by oral examinations of the performance variety. If an instructor of drama wished to assess the ability of his students to express different emotions, he would probably find written tests inappropriate. These objectives are better measured with an oral-performance test, since examinees could be required individually to verbally and physically express emotions appropriate to situations presented by the examiner.

Oral-performance tests are particularly well suited to the languages and related areas. For example, students may be required to translate a passage read to them in a foreign language, carry on a brief and controlled conversation in a foreign language with an examiner, or transcribe in shorthand a letter dictated to them.

Construction

The construction of an oral-performance test consists primarily of choosing tasks to assign to the examinees—tasks which are of appropriate difficulty and which are germane to the instructional objectives being considered. In selecting appropriate tasks, the instructor must identify the specific skills needed and the operations to be performed in reaching the instructional objective, and then select tasks of appropriate difficulty to represent these skills. As much as possible, only those tasks which are essential to the activity, sufficiently difficult to differentiate among students, and relatively quick to perform should be selected.

The construction of an oral-performance test may appear deceptively easy. To measure the students' ability to take dictation, all that is necessary is to dictate a letter to them. However, the rate of dictation, the pronunciation, and the vocabulary of the examiner are vital factors in the performance of the examinees and should be carefully considered in constructing the test.

When selecting specific tasks to be performed, it is important that the elements of the tasks selected are either new to the students or equally available to them. For example, the results of an oral-performance test in which statements in German are read to the students may be meaningless if the students are differentially familiar with the passages used. If the passages are written specifically for the test, this problem is avoided.

Administration

The proper administration of a performance test of the oral-examination variety is essential if the results are to be meaningful. The examiner must speak in a clear and distinct voice. If the speed with which he speaks is a factor, he must carefully pace his delivery. The tasks must be presented in a uniform and consistent manner, especially if examinees are to be tested at different times. Again, the directions for the test must be clear, concise, and complete.

Scoring

The format for scoring an oral-performance test must be carefully thought out during the construction of the examination, and it often is more difficult to prepare than the test itself. If it is necessary to assess aspects of the examinee's performance during the administration of the examination, and if the examiner needs to interact verbally with the examinee during the performance, scorer reliability is likely to be low. However, it may be improved by the use of an appropriate rating scale or check-list. (See Figs. 6.3 and 6.4).

In constructing a rating scale, the teacher must identify the crucial elements of the performance, select the criteria to be used in assessing the quality of the performance on each element, and determine the number of measurement units to use in the scale.

Fig. 6.3 Assessing skill in demonstrating emotions

Directions: The scales to be used in rating each emotion are shown below. For the emotion demonstrated, check the position in each scale that represents the effectiveness of that aspect of the performance in demonstrating the requisite emotion. Comments may be added in the space provided.

Emotions	Ratings:	Poor (1)	Average (2)	Good (3)

I. Fear
  A. Facial expression
  B. Use of voice
  C. Use of hands
  D. Body stance
  Comments:

II. Humor
  A. Facial expression
  B. Use of voice
  C. Use of hands
  D. Body stance
  Comments:

III. Hate
  A. Facial expression
  B. Use of voice
  C. Use of hands
  D. Body stance
  Comments:

IV. Love (maternal/paternal)
  A. Facial expression
  B. Use of voice
  C. Use of hands
  D. Body stance
  Comments:

V. Love (sensual)
  A. Facial expressions
  B. Use of voice
  C. Use of hands
  D. Body stance
  Comments:

VI. Anxiety
  A. Facial expressions
  B. Use of voice
  C. Use of hands
  D. Body stance
  Comments:

(cont.)

VII. Exhaustion
    A. Facial expressions
    B. Use of voice
    C. Use of hands
    D. Body stance
    Comments:

Fig. 6.4 Check-list for assessing skill in expressing emotions

Directions: This check-list is to be used for assessing the various aspects of the performance demonstrated. Check "YES" if appropriate to the emotion and "NO" if not used or inappropriate. Comments may be added in the space provided.

Emotion	Yes	No

I. Fear
    A. Face expresses fear
    1. eyes
    2. brow
    3. mouth

    B. Voice expresses fear
    1. timbre
    2. rhythm
    3. pitch
    4. loudness

    C. Body expresses fear
    1. head position
    2. posture
    3. use of hands

    D. Comments:

II. Humor
    A. Face expresses humor
    1. eyes
    2. brow
    3. mouth

    B. Voice expresses humor
    1. timbre
    2. rhythm
    3. pitch
    4. loudness

    C. Body expresses humor
    1. head position
    2. posture
    3. use of hands

    D. Comments:

The rating scale in Figure 6.3 is an example of the scale that an instructor in drama might use to measure the skill of his students in expressing various emotions. For each emotion to be measured, the instructor should create an appropriate situation for the expression of the emotion by the student. If the examinee is to employ specific lines in his performance, the material should be no more than two or three lines long. Otherwise, the examinee's skill in memorizing the lines could become a factor in his score.

If an examiner suspects, as a result of time limitations or the complexity of the performance, that he will be unable to use several categories in assessing the quality of performance, he may wish to use a check-list. The check-list is similar to the rating scale except that the examiner checks "YES" if the response is acceptable and "NO" if the response is unacceptable. For example, instead of the rating scale illustrated in Figure 6.3, a drama instructor might prefer to use a check-list similar to the one in Figure 6.4. The check-list in Figure 6.4 contains entries for only two of the seven emotions shown in Figure 6.3. This partial check-list could be easily expanded to provide entries for all of the emotions which the examiner wished to assess with this performance test.

In many classroom oral-performance tests the examinee records his response (e.g. letter dictation). When this occurs, the examiner can score the product after the examination is completed. Consequently, scorer reliability can be improved by using the sorting method or point-score method, as discussed for scoring essay tests. However, the criteria employed in scoring the product should be decided while constructing the test. For example, the criteria for scoring a shorthand oral-performance test may be the number of misused or misformed symbols.

DO'S AND DONT'S

Do

1. Include enough questions to adequately sample the material.
2. Limit the length of the response.
3. Limit the length of the question.
4. Use questions which are germane to the area of skill being measured.
5. If applicable, use unfamiliar material in performance tests.
6. Use terms that all examinees can define and understand.
7. Use terms that will have the same meaning to all examinees.
8. Explicitly state and qualify the question so that it will be interpreted in the same manner by all examinees.
9. Make the sentence structure as simple as possible so that the questions will be clear to all examinees.
10. Prepare the questions in advance so that they can be analyzed and revised if necessary before the test is given.
11. Write a comprehensive set of directions.
12. Write a model set of answers.
13. Read the directions and questions to the examinees using a clear, distinct voice.
14. Use an oral-response test primarily with individuals.
15. Use a rating-scale or check-list for scoring an oral-response test.

16. Use the sorting method or point-score method for scoring a written-response test.

17. Inform the examinees in advance that they will be given an oral test.

18. Use the same questions if the examinees' performances are to be compared.

Don't

1. Judge responses on extraneous factors.
2. Evaluate a student by his responses to just a few questions.
3. Use different questions if the examinees are to be compared.
4. Allow students to respond with "verbal garbage" hoping to stumble on the right answer.
5. Ask for nonessentials.
6. Use an oral-response test for measuring individual achievement in a large group.
7. Assign grades to the responses if using an oral-response test as a review.

PROBLEMS

1. What are the major limitations of the oral format? What steps can be taken to reduce these limitations?
2. Discuss the principal advantages of the oral test.
3. What are the three types of oral tests? Define each type and compare them in regard to: (a) advantages and disadvantages, (b) construction, (c) administration, and (d) scoring.
4. Why is the oral-response test *not* recommended as a method of classroom measurement?
5. Develop a 10-item oral test for a unit of study. Use a Table of Specifications.

SUGGESTED READING

Brody, William, and Neal J. Powell, "A New Approach to Oral Testing." *Educational and Psychological Measurement*, **7**, 1947, 289–298.

Gerberich, Raymond J., Harry A. Greene, and A. N. Jorgensen, *Measurement and Evaluation in the Modern School*. David McKay Co., New York, 1962, Chapter 9.

Household, Henry L. M., "Examining Oral English: Brighton Experiment." *Times Educational Supplement*, No. 2521, September 1963, 295.

Lopez, Felix M., *Evaluating Employee Performance*. Public Personnel Association, Chicago, Ill., 1968, Chapter 11.

Remmers, H. H., N. L. Gage, and Francis J. Rummel, *A Practical Introduction to Measurement and Evaluation*. Harper and Brothers, New York, 1960, Chapter 8.

Chapter 7

The Multiple-Choice Test

The multiple-choice type of test item has gained considerable popularity among constructors of standardized tests. It is also widely used by classroom teachers. Extensive research has been conducted to determine if the multiple-choice test is more effective than supply-type tests and how best to employ items of this type. It has been damned and praised, blamed for the ignorance of children, and credited with the improvement of instruction. Both critics and proponents have often taken the mantle of the evangelist, seeking to save the soul of education. In this chapter, the weaknesses and strengths of this type of item will be considered and guidelines for the construction of the multiple-choice item will be developed.

WEAKNESSES

The multiple-choice item has few inherent weaknesses. Although critics claim that it can be used only to measure factual knowledge, many items have been developed to measure understanding, application of principles, analysis, synthesis, and evaluation. It is claimed that these tests penalize the "creative" student, but the results of the limited research in this area have failed to support this supposition. In fact, because of the greater objectivity involved, the creative student may actually be better off with selection-type tests, rather than supply-type tests. Similarly, selection-type tests are criticized for not being adaptable to measuring creativity. Even though this is quite true, it is unlikely that items can be written in any test format which will accurately measure this dimension and also measure the acquisition of instructional objectives. To be effective in ranking students on the basis of their achievement, test questions must provide the examinee with a frame of reference. This structuring is likely to suppress creativity; there is no reason to believe that creativity can be turned on or off at the command of a test question. In any event, it does not seem appropriate to try to stimulate creativity with classroom tests.

Although one might question the validity of most criticisms of this item form, the multiple-choice item is not without drawbacks. In order to develop good items, the writer must have a thorough knowledge of the course content, an awareness of the methodology of item writing, skill in the use of language, and a thorough knowledge of the level of development of his students. This suggests that item writing is difficult and can be done successfully only by the skillful individual. Although this is true, the capable teacher should be skillful enough to acquire considerable facility in item writing. In any case, good item writing is not easy. Considerable time and effort are needed, particularly when writing items measuring higher-order mental processes. Consequently, unless one expects some reuse of the items which prove to be good, it may not be advisable to write multiple-choice items for the purpose of examining small groups of students on only one occasion.

Compared with true-false items, multiple-choice items require more time to answer. Since fewer multiple-choice items can be asked in a given period of time, a less thorough sampling of content may result. Considering this along with the greater difficulty encountered in constructing these items and the smaller number of items which can be placed on a given page, we are likely to judge true-false items as preferable—at least for testing knowledge. The apparent advantage of true-false items partially disappears, however, when one considers their lack of usefulness in testing higher-order mental processes and their relatively lower discriminatory power.

Another limitation of the multiple-choice item is that it cannot be used to measure an examinee's ability to organize materials or to clearly express his answers according to acceptable language usage rules. If either of these dimensions is an objective of the examination, the essay-type examination is the only available item format in which there is any hope of measuring these skills.

STRENGTHS

The multiple-choice test is the most flexible and versatile of all selection-type examinations. It may be used to measure instructional objectives at all levels of the cognitive domain: knowledge, comprehension, application, analysis, synthesis, and evaluation. The following items are presented as examples of multiple-choice items written to measure instructional objectives at the various levels of the cognitive domain. The teacher may find it useful to consider application, analysis, synthesis, and evaluation levels as parts of one general category—application.

Knowledge. Which of the following publications contains useful information about published standardized tests?

A. *Comparative Educational Research Yearbook*
B. *Journal of Experimental Testing*
C. *New Test Yearbook*
D. *Educational and Psychological Handbook*
*E. *The Mental Measurements Yearbook*

Comprehension. Which of the following correlation coefficients would indicate the greatest usefulness for predicting one trait from another?

*A. $-.82$
B. $-.31$
C.   .00
D. $+.20$
E. $+.74$

Application. Miss Higglebottom, the history teacher, felt that Tommy should be doing better than he was in her class. In order to check the accuracy of her conclusion about Tommy, she could:

A. Compare his score on the social science section of the TAP with his history grade.
B. Compare his score on an intelligence measure with his history grade.
C. Compare his score on the social science section of the TAP with his history test scores using standard scores.
D. Compare his score on an intelligence measure with his history test scores using standard scores.
*E. Compare his score on the social science section of the TAP with his history test scores using a scattergram of the class.

Analysis.† As a ninth-grade biology teacher you are interested in obtaining a standardized achievement test which you can give to your class at both the beginning and end of the course. This test has to be given in your regular 50-minute class period and must be able to be scored by machine as well as by hand. Which of the following tests would probably fit these demands?

A. *California Tests in Social and Related Sciences, Part III*
B. *Cooperative Biology Test*
*C. *Nelson Biology Test*
D. *Survey Test in Biological Sciences*

---

† This item is based on a set of tables available to the examinee.

Synthesis. Items 50–56. Presented below is a case study. Analyze the material presented and then answer questions 50–56.

Bill is 8 years old and is in the third grade. He is tall and makes a good appearance. He is well-behaved, quiet, interested in outside activities, and does not read well. Bill's father is a salesman and both parents are high school graduates.

School Data	Second Grade	Third Grade
Reading	Fair	Poor
Language Arts	Fair	Poor
Social Studies	Fair	Fair
Mathematics	Excellent	Excellent
General Science	Fair	Good
Physical Education	Average	Average

(Range: Excellent, Good, Average, Fair, Poor)

Test Data	Third Grade
Lorge-Thorndike Intelligence Test	IQ 120
WISC (Verbal)	IQ 90
WISC (Performance)	IQ 125
WISC (Total)	IQ 115

Sociometric Testing (30 children, 1st, 2nd, 3rd choices)

Received 0 first choices
Received 0 second choices
Received 2 third choices
He chose the 3 most popular boys in the class.

50. Based on the above information, what should be your next step as his teacher in dealing with Bill's personal behavior?

   A. No particular action is indicated.
   B. Watch for critical incidences which might indicate emotional adjustment difficulties.
   *C. Initiate further inquiry into Bill's behavior, possibly involving the school counselor.
   D. Refer Bill to the school counselor for immediate counseling.
   E. It is impossible to make decisions concerning personal behavior on this kind of information.

Evaluation. Rank the following three essay items from best to worst.

   I. List the major factors present in modern America which make for greater economic stability. Discuss each factor.
   II. Discuss the stability of the Italian political situation today as compared to 25 years ago.
   III. Compare and contrast the policies of the Jacobins in the French Revolution with those of the Bolsheviks in the Russian Revolution.

   A. I, II, III
   B. II, I, III
   C. II, III, I
   *D. III, II, I
   E. III, I, II

The versatility of the multiple-choice item is further apparent in its adaptability for use in essentially all subject matter areas and with examinees at all grade levels.

Since a large number of items can be answered during a normal examination period, it is possible to include items covering several instructional objectives in many content areas. If a Table of Specifications is carefully prepared and used in the construction of the test, the examination is likely to have a relatively small content sampling error.

When contrasted with supply-type items, scoring errors are of small concern in multiple-choice tests. They may be scored rapidly, accurately, and objectively by individuals who are unqualified to teach in the subject area being examined; thus secretaries, teacher's aids, or student assistants may be used without jeopardizing the accuracy of the results. Furthermore, the scoring of these examinations is not influenced by the previous performance, mode of dress, mannerisms, or general neatness of the examinees.

Although the scoring is completely objective, it should be remembered that expert judgement must be exercised during the process of item construction. However, if the item is clear, concise, and without ambiguity, the well-prepared student generally will be capable of determining the "correct response," even if he does not always agree with the teacher as to the correctness of the keyed response.

Because ambiguity is a problem common to all test questions, the test developer must continually attempt to eliminate, or at least reduce, ambiguity. However, when contrasted with other item types, ambiguity is relatively less difficult to control in the multiple-choice item.

CONSTRUCTION[1]

General

When the teacher is preparing to write a multiple-choice item, he should consider the purpose of the test—mastery or discrimination—and the item's specific instructional objective. This will aid in developing valid items which will contribute to the reliability of the total test.

When writing an item, a number of changes in the item will probably be necessary. To facilitate the revision of tentative items, it is wise to prepare the original draft in pencil, using a separate piece of paper for each item. It is advisable to have someone read these tentative items before preparing them in final form for the examination. If a teacher in the same academic area is not available, a teacher from a different area, a friend, or a spouse may be able to help identify weaknesses in items.

The multiple-choice item is composed of a stem, foils or distractors, and a keyed response. The various components of an item are labeled in the following example.

---

[1] An illustration of two classroom tests (multiple-choice and essay) constructed to measure student achievement of the objectives of the same unit of study is found in Appendix B.

Where is water found?   ] STEM

A. It is found in the air.
B. It is found on the earth's   FOILS (OR DISTRACTORS)   ALTERNATES
   surface.
C. It is found in the ground.
*D. All of the above.   ] KEYED RESPONSE

Before examining the components of the item individually, look at the item as a total unit. To paraphrase a construct of the field psychologist, the whole item is greater than the sum of its parts. The item should contain a central theme or idea. It should establish only one frame of reference for responding. Consequently, no foil should combine with the stem to offer a second, defensible frame of reference which would justify that foil being considered an acceptable answer. In the original form of the item below, both "B" and "D" are acceptable answers, depending on the frame of reference used.

Original

Colonists were given the same rights as other Englishmen by:

A. Local governors.
B. 1542.
C. Charters.
*D. Parliament.

Revised

Who gave the Colonists the same rights as other Englishmen?

A. The King
B. Local governors
C. Colonial legislatures
*D. Parliament

The item should be concise, unambiguous, and grammatically correct. Phrases and words not required to express the question or to set an appropriate frame of reference should be eliminated. Unless they are a vital part of the achievement to be measured by that specific item, difficult and technical words and phrases should be avoided. Also, the item should be presented in a simple and clear writing style, avoiding, whenever possible, figurative language and complex sentences. Proper language usage is essential and particular care should be taken not to provide clues through tense conflicts, misuse of articles, and singular-plural conflicts between verbs and nouns. Each alternate must linguistically fit the stem.

In its original form, the item in the following illustration exhibits extensive superfluous information in stem and distractors, contains a few difficult words which are unimportant to the intent of the item, contains figurative language, and is ambiguous.

Original

President Abraham Lincoln, who was once told by a little girl that he should wear a beard, was President during the Civil War. Once having written a speech to be delivered at Gettysburg on the back of an envelope, why did he make the Emancipation Proclamation in 1862?

A. There were a large number of slaves in the U.S. and Abraham Lincoln, coming from a frontier region, did not believe in the institution of slavery.

B. Believing that man is his "brother's keeper," he was trying to keep the slaves happy.

C. Being Commander-in-Chief of the Confederacy, he wanted to gain support for his cause among the church leaders of the South.

D. He wanted to entice slaves to revolt against their masters.

*E. Unless he emancipated the slaves, he would alienate the majority of his party.

Revised

From the statements below, select the most compelling reason for President Lincoln's decision to issue the Emancipation Proclamation.

A. He was opposed to slavery.

B. He wanted to gain support from church leaders in the South.

C. He was trying to encourage slaves to run away from their masters.

*D. He was in danger of losing the support of his party.

E. He was trying to unify the people in the North.

The Stem

The stem serves two primary functions: it presents the problem and it sets an appropriate frame of reference. After reading the stem, but before looking at the alternates, an informed examinee should be able to formulate some broad answer to the central question. Since the stem sets the stage for answering the question, it must include all the conditions and limitations needed in order to respond. When qualifying material is required, it is wise to incorporate this material in an introductory statement preceding, but separate from, the stem. In items designed to measure higher-order thought processes, it is not uncommon to find in an introductory statement some data to be analyzed, synthesized, or evaluated.

In the first of the three items which follow, the stem of the original item fails to present the problem or to set a frame of reference for responding. If the item is to determine whether or not the examinees know when World War II occurred, the revised form of the item is a definite improvement. In the last two examples, the qualifying material is intermixed with the presentation of the problem, resulting in some difficulty in defining the problem itself. The revised forms of the items correct this deficiency.

Original

1. World War II was:

   A. The result of the failure of the League of Nations.
   B. Horrible.
   C. Fought in Europe, Asia, and Africa.
   *D. Fought during the period 1939–1945.

2. What fact is overlooked when one concludes that, from the actions of England and the reactions of the colonies, the colonies wanted to be independent from England because of trade laws and taxes?

   *A. The colonists wanted representation, not independence.
   B. The tax laws were generally fair.
   C. The trade regulations helped colonial business.
   D. The colonists wanted the right to elect colonial legislatures.

3. According to the 1940 amendment to the Hatch Act, which one of the following would be the lowest illegal, individual contribution?

   A. $4000
   B. $4999
   C. $5000
   *D. $5500
   E $6000

Revised

1. In which of these time periods was World War II fought?

   A. 1914–1917
   B. 1929–1934
   *C. 1939–1945
   D. 1951–1955
   E. 1961–1969

2. From the actions of England and the reactions of the colonies, one might conclude that the colonists wanted to be independent from England because of the trade laws and taxes. This conclusion overlooks the fact that the colonists:

   *A. Were requesting representation in Parliament.
   B. Thought that the tax laws were generally fair.
   C. Felt that the trade laws helped colonial business.
   D. Wanted the right to elect colonial legislatures.

3. The 1940 amendment to the Hatch Act regulated contributions to national campaigns. Which one of the following would be the lowest illegal, individual contribution?

   A. $4000
   B. $4999
   C. $5000
   *D. $5500
   E. $6000

Sometimes extensive qualifying material must be furnished for the examinee to answer the item. For example, a poem may be presented for interpretation, a table of data for analysis, or a short written document for evaluation. Such extensive qualifying data should be clearly differentiated from the stem, perhaps by placing it in a separate paragraph. The following items illustrate this point. It should be noted that the qualifying data requires considerable space and will result in more time spent in reading than would be the case with most items. Consequently, it is a common practice to present to the examinees several items developed to use the same introductory statement.

Questions 1–3 are based on the following statement.
The Pueblo, a poorly armed U.S. naval intelligence ship, was captured in international waters, near the coast of North Korea, on January 28, 1968. It was captured by North Korean gun boats. The ship was surrendered to the aggressors without firing a shot in defense. However, the crew attempted to destroy all classified materials before the ship was boarded. The captain and his crew were imprisoned for approximately one year by their captors, during which time the captain signed a statement in which he confessed to being in Korean waters on a spying mission. He signed after being told that his crew would be executed, one by one, in front of him if he did not confess.

---

1. Assuming that the above statements are true, according to International Law the U.S. should consider this to be:

   A. A serious breach of etiquette but not a cause for war.

   *B. An act of such serious magnitude as to justify a declaration of war.

   C. Justified because the Pueblo was a spy ship.

   D. Justified because the two countries were on unfriendly terms.

2. If the Commanding Officer is tried by Court Martial for his act of surrender, his best defense would probably be that:

   A. He did not surrender, he was seized by force.

   B. He acted only out of concern for the safety of his crew.

   C. He had destroyed all materials of value to the enemy before surrendering.

   *D. He surrendered only after he no longer had the power to resist.

3. The treatment of the Commanding Officer of the ship by his captors violated the Geneva Convention. What valid argument could be given by North Korea for its failure to abide by this Convention?

   A. The prisoners would not cooperate.

   B. The crew should not have destroyed the classified materials.

   *C. North Korea is not a member of the Convention.

   D. All of the above could be used as valid arguments.

The central problem may be expressed as a question, a complete statement, or an incomplete statement. It is usually possible to express the same problem in each of these ways. Thus one could say: "What is the primary advantage of the multiple-choice test?" or "The primary advantage of the multiple-choice test is. . . ." or "From the following list of purported advantages of the multiple-choice test, select the most important one." Clarity, simplicity, and efficiency should be the determinants in selecting the form to be used. Most beginning item constructors find it easier to ask a question. Notice how the original item is improved when the incomplete statement is turned into a question.

Original

1. When Gene told Finny that he (Finny) would make a "mess, a terrible mess out of the war" even if his leg were not injured, Gene meant:

    A. Finny lacked the discipline necessary for a good soldier.
    *B. Finny lacked the capacity for hatred necessary for war.
    C. Finny lacked the courage necessary for a good soldier.
    D. Finny had too much sympathy for the enemy in wartime.

Revised

1. What did Gene mean when he told Finny that he (Finny) would make a "mess, a terrible mess out of the war" even if his leg were not injured?

    A. Finny lacked the discipline necessary for a good soldier.
    *B. Finny lacked the capacity for hatred necessary for war.
    C. Finny lacked the courage necessary for a good solider.
    D. Finny had too much sympathy for the enemy in wartime.

There are several varieties of multiple-choice items, each requiring a slightly different behavioral pattern in responding to the central problem. The stem alone, or in conjunction with some preceding set of instructions, determines the appropriate behavioral pattern. The examinee may be required to select the "correct" answer. For example, "Which of the following is an advantage of the multiple-choice item?" In this situation all alternates except one must be clearly incorrect. On the other hand, the examinee may be expected to select the "best" answer; for example, "What is the primary advantage of the multiple-choice test?" With this stem, each alternate could be correct if considered alone, but, when the alternates are considered together, only one is clearly better than any of the others.

Correct Answer

1. Which of the following is an advantage of the essay test?

    A. It may be rapidly scored.
    *B. It is adaptable to testing higher-order mental processes.
    C. The scoring results are usually reliable.
    D. It usually includes an adequate and representative sample of behaviors.

Best Answer

1. What is the primary advantage of the essay test?

    A. It is relatively easy to construct.
    B. It is adaptable to testing higher-order mental processes.
    *C. It is adaptable to testing the ability to organize information.
    D. It is adaptable to nearly all testing situations.

It is possible to ask the examinee to select from the alternates the only one which can *not* be considered a correct answer to the central question; for example, "Which of the following is *not* an advantage of the multiple-choice test?" Unless this form is clearly needed in order to efficiently measure the desired behavior, it should be avoided. Research indicates that questions so phrased tend to be more difficult and thus are less likely to adequately discriminate between good and poor students. When using this form, never include negative statements or words in the alternates. Otherwise, the item is likely to be no more than a trick question containing double and triple negatives, and as such it would have little relevance to the actual content being measured. The following two items illustrate the "correct answer" and the "not a correct answer" forms as applied to the same content area.

Correct Answer	*Not a Correct Answer*
1. Which of the following is a part of the structure of an insect?	1. Which of the following is *not* a part of the structure of an insect?
A. A backbone with vertebrae	A. Body divided into 3 parts
B. Four legs	B. Two feelers
C. Body divided into 2 parts	C. Six legs
*D. Two-chamber heart	*D. A backbone with vertebrae

It is sometimes desirable to require students to order a list of statements according to some explicit criterion. A multiple-choice item designed to do this would contain the question, a list of statements to be ordered, and a set of alternates containing the statements in varying order. In the following example, it should be noted that the alternates do not provide all possible combinations.

1. In order, from most to least important, rank the following advantages of the multiple-choice test.
  I. Rapid Scoring
  II. Objectivity in Scoring
  III. Good Content Sampling
  A. I, II, III
  B. I, III, II
  C. II, III, I
  D. II, I, III
  *E. III, II, I

It is possible to instruct the examinee that any number of the responses of an item may be correct and that he should mark each alternate which correctly answers the question. This multiple-response item is actually a cluster of true-false questions and should be treated as such, with each alternate acting as a separate true-false item. A test composed of multiple-response items should rarely be used because it is difficult to set an adequate frame of reference for responding to these items except when measuring factual knowledge. In addition, it is virtually impossible to obtain an acceptable weighting of the various parts of the test.

Some additional ideas to keep in mind when writing item stems are: it is best to incorporate in the stem all words which otherwise would have to be repeated in each alternate; the item should never require the examinee to express an opinion; and the general discussion of item construction should be carefully considered in selecting and revising item stems.

In the first of the two following illustrations, all of the alternates in the original item contain "a fish is an animal" but, in the revised form, these words are placed in the stem. In the original form of the second illustration, all alternates must be considered correct.

Original	*Revised*
1. What is a fish?	1. A fish is an animal which has:
*A. A fish is an animal with gills.	*A. Gills
B. A fish is an animal with a four-chamber heart.	B. A four-chamber heart
C. A fish is an animal with hair.	C. Hair
D. A fish is an animal with an external skeleton.	D. An external skeleton
2. Which of the following acts of delinquency by female juveniles do you consider to be most serious?	2. Below are some common acts of delinquency by female juveniles. Which act would be considered most serious by psychologists?
*A. Running away from home	*A. Running away from home
B. Truancy	B. Truancy
C. Shoplifting	C. Shoplifting
D. Illegal drinking	D. Illegal drinking

The Alternates

Although one function of the stem is to establish a general frame of reference for responding, the alternates must serve to refine and delimit this frame of reference so that, in a well-constructed item, one and only one alternate will appeal to the well informed individual.

The alternates of an item perform as a team, each member of which must be grammatically consistent with and appropriate to the stem. Linguistically, they all should be equally attractive. Also, they should be of about the same length and complexity. When this is true, the alternates appear as an attractive set of options for answering the problem presented in the stem.

In the original form of the following item, the article "a" in the stem is grammatically in conflict with two of the alternates (A and B). Consequently, an examinee may eliminate them because of the conflict and, since they are foils, increase his chance of marking the correct response. However, if the stem were "Alexander Goldenweiser was a," the correct response (A) would be incompatible with the stem. In the revised form of the item this conflict is resolved.

Original	*Revised*
1. Albert Einstein was a:	1. Who was Albert Einstein?
A. Anthropologist.	A. An anthropologist
B. Astronomer.	B. An astronomer
C. Chemist.	C. A chemist
*D. Mathematician.	*D. A mathematician

If "none of these" and "all of these" are to be employed as alternates, they should appear early in the test as keyed responses for relatively easy items. This early appearance in the test of "none of these" and "all of these" responses is necessary to deter an avoidance response-set to them as correct responses. Also, they should not be used with "best answer" questions because "all of these" is inconsistent with the "best answer" concept and "none of these" will nearly always be defensible as an answer. If another response is intended to be keyed as correct, one should be very sure that the stem does not join with the "none of these" response to form a defensible answer. This problem is particularly acute when the alternates are possible answers to a calculation and in this situation, the amount of accuracy required in the answer must be specified.

The following item is of the "best answer" variety. As can be seen in the first version of the item, the response "all of the above" is inconsistent with the basic problem presented in the stem. The examinee must decide whether the item is intended to be of the "best answer" variety or of the "correct answer" variety. The deletion of the "E" response strengthens the item. Similarly, in the second version of the item, the alternate "none of the above" is inappropriate as a distractor and the elimination of the "E" response improves the item.

All of the above	*None of the above*
1. The federal government under the Articles of Confederation had a number of weaknesses. The major weakness was its lack of power to:	1. The federal government under the Articles of Confederation had a number of weaknesses. The major weakness was its lack of power to:
*A. Tax citizens directly.	*A. Tax citizens directly.
B. Regulate interstate commerce.	B. Regulate interstate commerce.
C. Regulate commerce with foreign powers.	C. Regulate commerce with foreign powers.
D. Enforce its laws.	D. Enforce its laws.
E. All of the above.	E. None of the above.

When selecting alternates for a multiple-choice item, be alert for overlapping alternates. If alternates do overlap, the item will have more than one correct answer or the examinee will be able to improve his chance of choosing the correct response by eliminating from consideration the overlapping alternates. In the original form of the following item, if either of the first two alternates is correct, "C" is also correct.

Original	*Revised*
1. During what age period is thumb-sucking likely to produce the greatest psychological trauma?	1. During what age period is thumb-sucking likely to produce the greatest psychological trauma?
A. Infancy	A. From birth to 2 years old
B. Preschool period	B. From 2 years to 5 years old
*C. Before adolescence	*C. From 5 years to 12 years old
D. During adolescence	D. From 12 years to 20 years old
E. After adolescence	E. 20 years of age or older

The alternates should be arranged for clarity and ease of reading. If there is a numerical or logical order among the alternates, they should be so ordered in the choice positions of the item. Also, it is often helpful to place the alternates in a column below the stem. The alternates in the following two items are ordered logically and appear in a column below their respective stems.

1. The 1940 amendment to the Hatch Act regulated contributions to national campaigns. Which one of the following would be the lowest illegal, individual contribution?

  A. $4000
  B. $4999
  C. $5000
  *D. $5500
  E. $6000

2. Who was President of the United States during the Spanish-American War?

  A. Grover Cleveland
  B. Benjamin Harrison
  *C. William B. McKinley
  D. Theodore Roosevelt
  E. William H. Taft

The Keyed Response

The keyed response must be a better answer to the question than any other alternate. It is not necessary that the keyed response be the best of all possible answers, but it must be the best of the offered responses. As an answer, it should be fully acceptable to competent authorities. In the original form, the following item has two correct responses (D and E). This problem is eliminated by modifying the stem to include "lowest." The elimination of response "E" would have removed the problem of two correct responses, but not the problem of overlapping alternates. The first three alternates may be eliminated from consideration by the test-wise student because, if one of them is true, "D" is also true.

Original

1. The 1940 amendment to the Hatch Act regulated contributions to national campaigns. Which one of the following individual contributions would be illegal?

  A. $4000
  B. $4999
  C. $5000
  *D. $5500
  E. $6000

Revised

1. The 1940 amendment to the Hatch Act regulated contributions to national campaigns. Which one of the following would be the lowest illegal, individual contribution?

  A. $4000
  B. $4999
  C. $5000
  *D. $5500
  E. $6000

To eliminate irrelevant clues, the keyed response should not be a synonym of any word in the stem nor should it have a clang[2] association with the stem. In addition, it should be about the same length as the other alternates and possess similar grammatical characteristics. The words "declared" and "independence" in the stem of the original form of the following item serve as direct clues to the correct response.

---

[2] Two words have a clang association if they sound as if they belong together; for example, short and fat, exerted and pressure, and Southern and fried chicken.

Original	*Revised*
1. The members of the Second Continental Congress declared the independence of the colonies from England. The document which they signed is known as: A. The Articles of Confederation. B. The Document of Secession. C. The Bill of Rights. *D. The Declaration of Independence.	1. The members of the Second Continental Congress proclaimed the secession of the colonies from England. The document which they signed is known as: A. The Articles of Confederation. B. The Document of Secession. C. The Bill of Rights. *D. The Declaration of Independence.

If the keyed response is frequently found in the same particular choice position, this can serve as a clue to the correct answer. On most teacher-made tests, the old rule of thumb, "when in doubt, mark 'B' or 'C'," may pay large dividends to the test-wise student. Most teachers are reluctant to place the correct response in the first alternate position because of the desire to have the students consider at least some of the foils before answering. From past experience, the test-sophisticated examinee may believe that, on five-choice items, the keyed response is more likely to appear in the "C" position than in any other choice position and that it is less likely to appear in the "A" or "E" positions than in the "B" or "D" positions. His beliefs are supported by research.

After all the items for the test have been selected, the teacher should count the number of times the keyed response occurs in each choice position. Generally, the keyed response should appear in each position about the same number of times. Thus, on a test of 100 five-choice, multiple-choice items, the keyed response should be found in each choice position about 20 times. To eliminate the bias for choice position "C" and against positions "A" and "E," it may be necessary to reorder the alternates within several items, carefully avoiding the introduction of a rotational pattern for the occurrence of the keyed responses. Should such a pattern occur in the test, it is probable that some test-wise student will discover the pattern and improve his score accordingly.

The Distractors

The primary purpose of distractors is to offer the examinee lacking in requisite knowledge plausible choices which he may choose in preference to the keyed response. In presenting foils which appeal to the poorly prepared examinee, it is often advantageous to use common misconceptions, common errors, logical but false clues, and terms which are synonyms of words in the stem or have clang association with the stem.

Since it is not easy to devise appropriate and discriminating alternates, the wise teacher makes a mental note of misconceptions and errors as they occur in class exercises and recitations. Many of these classroom misconceptions and errors eventually can be incorporated in test items. Nevertheless, sometimes it may be necessary to use some completion type items simply because acceptable distractors cannot be devised. The students' common errors and misconceptions shown in their responses to completion items can be incorporated in future tests as distractors on multiple-choice items.

In the following item, alternate "B" illustrates a logical but erroneous response while alternate "C" illustrates what may be a common misconception among children.

1. You are preparing to cross the street and you notice that the traffic light is red. What should you do?
   A. Run across to get out of the way.
   B. Look both ways for cars before crossing.
   C. Wait for the light to turn green, but as soon as it turns green, run across.
   *D. Wait for a green light and then look both ways for moving cars before crossing.

When developing the foils for a multiple-choice item, remember that the distractors must be grammatically consistent with the stem because many students eliminate from consideration alternates which clash grammatically with the stem solely on the basis of the grammatical error. The revised form of the following item is preferred because grammatical conflicts have been resolved.

Original

1. What are the major structural characteristics of adult amphibians?

   *A. They breathe with lungs, are cold-blooded, and are covered with skin.
   B. They breathe with gills.
   C. They have fins with which to move themselves through the water.
   D. They are covered with scales and have two wings.

Revised

1. Which of the following are structural characteristics of adult amphibians?

   I. breathe with lungs
   II. covered with scales
   III. cold-blooded
   IV. have fins

   A. I and II
   *B. I and III
   C. II and III
   D. II and IV
   E. III and IV

The purpose of the distractor is not to trick the examinee but to offer him a plausible choice if he does not know the answer. The distractors should not introduce ambiguity. To avoid ambiguity, avoid being overly specific in regard to such factors as dates, places and people. It is unlikely that the writer of the following item really believes that the exact year of publication of the book is important, but that information is required of the examinee in answering the original item.

Original	Revised
1. When was *Leaves of Grass* first published?	1. When was *Leaves of Grass* first published?
A. 1854	A. 1825
*B. 1855	*B. 1855
C. 1856	C. 1895
D. 1857	D. 1925

The difficulty of the item is determined by the effectiveness of the foils and the degree of homogeneity exhibited by the alternates. The greater the similarity among all alternates, the more difficult the item. This is illustrated in the following items.

Easy

1. Which of the following publications contains useful information about published standardized tests?
   - A. *Adult Leadership*
   - B. *Elementary School*
   - C. *Journal of Educational Research*
   - D. *School and Society*
   - *E. *The Mental Measurement Yearbook*

2. Which of the following are structures of arachnids?
   - A. Backbone
   - B. Fins
   - C. Three-chamber heart
   - *D. Four pairs of legs

3. Who was President of the U.S. during the War of 1812?
   - A. Grover Cleveland
   - B. Abraham Lincoln
   - *C. James Madison
   - D. Harry Truman
   - E. George Washington

Difficult

1. Which of the following publications contains useful information about published standardized tests?
   - A. *Comparative Educational Research Yearbook*
   - B. *Educational and Psychological Handbook*
   - C. *Journal of Experimental Research*
   - D. *New Testing Yearbook*
   - *E. *The Mental Measurement Yearbook*

2. Which of the following are structures of arachnids?
   - A. Wings
   - B. Two feelers
   - C. Three-part body
   - *D. Four pairs of legs

3. Who was President of the U.S. during the War of 1812?
   - A. John Q. Adams
   - B. Andrew Jackson
   - C. Thomas Jefferson
   - *D. James Madison
   - E. George Washington

Most multiple-choice items contain either four or five alternates. Research indicates, however, that it is better to construct an item with only one good foil than it is to construct an item with more than one foil if the additional ones are poor. Unless a given foil is attractive to poor students, its inclusion in the test may not only be a waste of the item writer's time but may also be a deterrent to test reliability and validity. Occasionally, it is desirable to have an item with more than five responses. Even though such an item is seldom appropriate, it can be used when symmetry is needed among the alternates.

In no instance should an item contain more than the logical alternates. If an item consists of the alternatives "increase," "decrease," or "remain constant," for example, it would be ridiculous to include the fourth alternative "none of the above," because the first three responses are exhaustive. (An exception to this rule occurs when "cannot be determined from the data furnished" is a logical possibility.) Therefore, the number of alternatives in an item should depend on the type of responses used, the content of the responses, and the ability of the item writer to construct good foils.

The Answer Sheet

Because it greatly improves scoring efficiency, a separate answer sheet should be used when examining students who are capable of handling the extra sheet accurately and efficiently. There are almost as many possible formats for answer sheets as there are item writers. However, there are two basic formats appropriate for the teacher-made answer sheet which have been found to be a convenience to the examinee in recording his responses and to the teacher in accurate and rapid scoring. These are: (1) typed letters corresponding to the item responses after the item number; and (2) typed 0's after the item numbers under appropriate column headings as shown here.

		A B C D E	
1. A B C D E		1. 0 0 0 0 0	
2. A B C D E		2. 0 0 0 0 0	
3. A B C D E		3. 0 0 0 0 0	
4. A B C D E		4. 0 0 0 0 0	
5. A B C D E		5. 0 0 0 0 0	

Using either of these formats, answer spaces for 100 five-choice, multiple-choice items can be placed on each side of legal-sized paper without crowding the spaces. However, if either of these is to be used, students should be instructed to either shade over the appropriate letter or shade in the appropriate circle, depending upon the format. Scoring can then be easily accomplished with a punched-out key. (Types of answer sheets and their uses for various types of items are discussed in Chapter 3.)

Other Multiple-Choice Formats

The main focus of this chapter has been on the multiple-choice item in which the stem is immediately followed by written alternates. However, other formats for presenting the item may sometimes be more efficient, may better structure the behavioral tasks presented, or may permit measuring instructional objectives with less ambiguity. The following three examples illustrate variations of the basic multiple-choice item format.

Item Formats

1. You are the left forward (LF) on the volleyball team. You are in the correct position to spike the ball using the direct approach. Which diagram indicates your position?

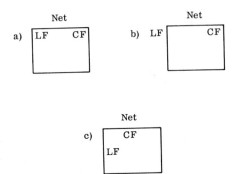

DIRECTIONS FOR ITEMS 2–7. The next six questions are statements concerning views which might have been held by the English and/or the Colonist, 1763–1775. Read each statement carefully and answer as follows:

If view was widely held by A. The Colonists
                             B. The English
                             C. Both the English and the Colonists
                             D. Neither the English nor the Colonists

2. Parliament should have full power to pass laws for governing the colonies.
3. Taxes to be paid by Colonists should be voted by the colonial legislature.
4. The Intolerable Acts were passed to punish Massachusetts.

DIRECTIONS FOR ITEMS 8–13. The following sentences contain some words which are underlined and numbered. From the corresponding choices on the right, determine which word should be in the underlined position.

The student know the answer to every question,
                8

The robins sang early this morning.
             9

We were real glad to hear the final score.
           10

George thompson lives in horse heaven, Washington.
       11   12   13   14

8. A. know
   B. knew
9. A. sing
   B. sang
   C. sung
10. A. real
    B. very
11. A. thompson
    B. Thompson
12. A. lives
    B. Lives
13. A. horse
    B. Horse
14. A. heaven
    B. Heaven

DO'S AND DON'T'S

Do	Don't

Do

1. Use multiple-choice tests to measure higher-order mental processes.

2. Include enough items to adequately sample the material.

3. Use a Table of Specifications to ensure adequate sampling.

4. Establish a frame of reference for answering the item in the stem.

5. Express the problem in the stem.

6. Write concise, unambiguous, and grammatically correct items.

7. Use questions which are germane to the area being measured.

8. Incorporate in the stem all words which would otherwise need to appear in each alternate.

9. Adhere to any logical ordering of the alternates which might exist.

10. Provide about the same number of keyed responses in each choice position on the total test.

11. Control the difficulty of the item by the homogeneity of the reponses.

12. Make every foil appealing to the students who do not know the correct answer.

Don't

1. Use multiple-choice tests to measure writing skill or creativity.

2. Have conflicting frames of reference embedded in the same item.

3. Have grammatical errors in the item.

4. Be ambiguous.

5. Provide superfluous information in the item.

6. Have clang associations between keyed response and the stem.

7. Have long keyed responses and short foils or the reverse.

8. Have a pattern in the rotation of the keyed responses among the choice positions.

9. Use unnecessary, technical terminology.

10. Include poor foils in an item.

11. Use "none of the above" or "all of the above" as alternatives in "best" answer items.

PROBLEMS

1. What are the major limitations of the multiple-choice format? What steps can be taken to eliminate or reduce these limitations?

2. Discuss the principal advantages of the multiple-choice test.

3. What are the components of the multiple-choice item?

4. Why must each alternate be linguistically compatible with the stem?

5. Why should superfluous information in an item be eliminated?

6. How can one reduce ambiguity in an item?

7. The central problem of an item may be presented in three ways. Discuss and define them.

8. Discuss the two major functions of the item stem.

9. What is the function of the distractor in a multiple-choice item?

10. Is it necessary for the keyed response to be the best of all possible answers? Defend your answer.

11. Using a Table of Specifications, develop a 30-item, multiple-choice test for a unit of study.

SUGGESTED READING

Dizney, H., "Characteristics of Classroom Test Items Identified by Students as 'Unfair'." *Journal of Educational Measurement*, **2**, 1965, 119–121.

Dressel, Paul L., and others, *Evaluation in Higher Education*. Houghton Mifflin, Boston, 1961, Chapters 4, 5, 6, and 7.

Dressel, Paul L., and Clarence Nelson, *Questions and Problems in Science, Test Item Folio No. 1*. Educational Testing Service, Princeton, N.J., 1956.

Ebel, Robert L., "Writing the Test Item," in E. F. Lindquist (Ed.), *Educational Measurement*. American Council on Education, Washington, D.C., 1951, pp. 229–249.

Ebel, Robert L., *Measuring Educational Achievement*. Prentice-Hall, Englewood Cliffs, N.J., 1965, Chapter 5.

Gerberich, J. Raymond, *Specimen Objective Test Items*. Longmans, Green, New York, 1956, Parts I and II.

Hughes, H. H., and W. E. Trimble, "The Use of Complex Alternatives in Multiple-Choice Items." *Educational and Psychological Measurement*, **25**, 1965, 117–126.

Mosier, C. L., M. Claire Myers, and Helen G. Price, "Suggestions for the Construction of Multiple Choice Test Items." *Educational and Psychological Measurement*, **5**, 1945, 261–271.

Williams, B. J., and R. L. Ebel, "The Effect of Varying the Number of Alternates per Item on Multiple Choice Vocabulary Test Items," in *Fourteenth Yearbook*. National Council on Measurement in Education, New York, 1958.

Chapter 8

The True-False Test

Among the selection-type examinations, the true-false test may hold the questionable distinction of being the most popular with classroom teachers. It is entirely possible that these tests have been misused more often than any other type. Certainly, they have been subject to considerable criticism regarding their construction and the significance of what they apparently measure. A statement with some prescribed method of registering agreement or disagreement comprises what is commonly known as the true-false question. In this chapter we will consider the weaknesses and strengths of the true-false item and will develop some guidelines for its construction.

WEAKNESSES

It has been suggested by some educators that teachers should not use true-false items because of their inherent weaknesses and because of the widespread use of poorly constructed items. Others have suggested that this type of item should be reserved for use only as an instructional aid and should not be employed in pupil evaluation. Nevertheless, it does continue to be popular. Hence, the teacher should be cognizant of its weaknesses and endeavor to control or overcome them when using true-false items in his own tests.

It has been argued that the true-false test, with its fifty-fifty chance of guessing the correct response, encourages students to guess wildly. Although one may doubt the importance of guessing and question the validity of the various penalties suggested to discourage it, the possibility of getting one-half of the items correct by chance alone presents some problems. The pattern of responses to a true-false test is generally of little value in locating gaps in a student's knowledge. Even an analysis of the pattern of responses of the class would be of only limited assistance in identifying specific instructional objectives not achieved by the class. Also, since it is desirable for the lowest scores on the test to fall above the chance-score region, the average test difficulty must be approximately 75 percent. This results in items which generally do not discriminate well between those examinees receiving the highest scores on the total test and those receiving the lowest scores. Consequently, because of the relatively greater influence of chance on the scores received and the likelihood that a properly constructed true-false item will not discriminate as well as a properly constructed multiple-choice item, a test composed of true-false items will rarely be as reliable as a multiple-choice test of equal length.

In order to be fair to the examinee, the statement requiring a true-false response must be either absolutely true or completely false. When this condition is not met, the student is required to judge the relative trueness or falseness of the item and relate this to his perception of the intent of the item writer. Such a feat should not be required of any individual. It is quite difficult to develop statements which can be answered absolutely true or false, and such statements tend to be concerned with the measurement of factual knowledge. This item type is seldom applicable to the measurement of complex understandings and other higher-order mental processes. Consequently, it is virtually impossible to construct a true-false test which conforms to the Table of Specifications unless the instructional objectives exist only at the factual and comprehension levels of the cognitive domain.

STRENGTHS

The true-false test may be rapidly and accurately scored by individuals unqualified to teach in the subject matter area being examined. The scoring is completely objective. Such extraneous factors as dress, neatness, politeness, and writing style have no influence on test scoring. It can also be administered relatively quickly since less time per item is required to answer true-false questions in comparison with any other item-type.

When compared with other selection-type items, the true-false item exhibits greater efficiency in the utilization of time expended in construction and refinement of items. The structure of this item-type is less complex than the structures of other selection-type items. For example, because this item-type has no distractors, the time normally expended in developing distractors is saved. Since the response choices are always the same and inherent to the item, the item statement need not include instructions on how to respond. Consequently, it is less difficult to write and requires less time to develop and refine acceptable items. Nevertheless, it does require more skill and a greater expenditure of time to develop good items than most teachers would suspect.

The true-false item is adaptable for use in situations where the measurement of the acquisition of factual, noninterpretive information is desired—for example, vocabulary, technical terms, formulae, dates, and proper names. A comprehensive sampling of content corresponding to such instructional objectives may be rapidly obtained with the true-false test.

CONSTRUCTION

Before undertaking to develop true-false items, the instructor should carefully consider the limitations of this item format and select from among his instructional objectives those which are amenable to measurement with items of this type. The achievement of instructional objectives which are not appropriate to assessment with items of this type can be relegated to measurement by other item types. This should contribute to the construction of a test which better conforms to the Table of Specifications and this results in a more valid test.

Before an item is actually ready for use, it will probably undergo a number of revisions. The revision should be simplified if each item is originally written in pencil on a separate 3 × 5 card (or piece of paper). Also, with each item on a separate card, it is easier to place the items in the desired order on the test.

The true-false item consists of a statement and a prescribed method of registering agreement or disagreement with the statement. In the most widely used form of this item type, the examinee is instructed to mark the statement "true" or "false," "right" or "wrong," or "yes" or "no." Usually, the general instructions for registering agreement or disagreement are a part of the test directions which appear in a separate paragraph (often on a cover page) at the beginning of the test or in an introductory statement preceding all of the true-false items on the test. As shown in the following example, instructions specific to a cluster of true-false items may also appear within the test as an introductory statement for the item cluster.

The following items are True-False questions. If the statement is *true*, blacken out the circle under A on your answer sheet; if the statement is *false*, blacken out the circle under B on your answer sheet. Be sure that the item number that you are marking on the answer sheet corresponds to the item number of the question you are answering.

1. According to cognitive theorists, a learner will learn by rote if he lacks a cognitive structure.
2. According to the cognitive theorists, learning something new is a matter of seeing where it "fits in."
3. Bypassing less abstract stages of learning is sometimes desirable for the improvement of understanding without memorization.
4. The *Readers' Guide to Periodical Literature* is the oldest indexing periodical which includes educational items.

The following sentences may (or may not) contain grammatical errors. In front of each item are a "T" and a "F." If the sentence is *grammatically correct*, thoroughly mark out the "T." If it is *not grammatically correct*, mark out the "F."

T F 1. I heard you was at the bowling party.
T F 2. He don't plan to study engineering at college.
T F 3. Are you calling us?
T F 4. The rear tires had wore out.

Some teachers are not satisfied with simply asking the examinee for a true or false (correct/incorrect) answer to the item, but want him to identify the false or incorrect element in the statement and correct it. The addition of this activity to the behavioral tasks of the examinee modifies the characteristics of the true-false item and creates some problems for the test developer. A major drawback to this type of item is that a false item can usually be changed to a true statement in any of several ways. For example, the false item "Abraham Lincoln was the first President of the U.S.," could be corrected to read "George Washington was the first President of the U.S." It would also be correct to say: "Abraham Lincoln was the first Republican President of the U.S.," "Abraham Lincoln was the 16th President of the U.S.," or "Abraham Lincoln was the President of the U.S. during the Civil War." It is apparent that an element of subjectivity is introduced into the scoring, and if an examinee offers a correction to the item not anticipated by the teacher, it may be scored as incorrect even though it is a defensible answer.

When the student is expected to identify the incorrect element in the statement and correct it, the speed of responding is reduced, and thus fewer items can be answered in a given period of time. Also, it will take longer to score a test of this type than it will the more traditional true-false test. Furthermore, scoring machines cannot be used.

If the examinee is required to correct the error in a true-false test, the examiner is faced with the problem of assigning scoring weights to the various items of the test. This problem may be solved by scoring one point for correctly responding "true" or "false" and one point for satisfactorily revising the false statement. The danger in this approach is that certain content areas may be heavily weighted as a result of the double scoring of false responses.

The format for this variation of the true-false item generally consists of: (1) the typical true-false statement, (2) a space provided to write the incorrect portion of the statement, and (3) a space provided to write the corrected portion of the statement. This is illustrated in the following examples. It should be noted that this type of item is really a set of three interdependent items: one true-false item and two completion items, the latter items being scored only when they are not left blank.

The following items are True-False questions. If the statement is *true*, circle *T* and go to the next item. If the statement is *false*, circle *F*, write the portion of the statement that makes it false in *space A*, and rewrite the incorrect portion so that it is true in *space B*.

T F 1. An achievement test is designed to measure a pupil's ability to perform in school subjects.
A _____   B _____

T F 2. A profile is a graphic method for representing an examinee's scores on several tests.
A _____   B _____

T F 3. Intelligence is defined as innate ability.
A _____   B _____

T F 4. Individual intelligence tests are more reliable than group intelligence tests.
A _____   B _____

This format could be modified slightly by instructing the examinee to under-line the false portion of the statement rather than writing it out. This type of item can be made more objective by: (1) underlining the portion of the statement that the examinee is to change if the item is false and/or (2) providing a list of alterna-tives from which the examinee can select a change-response if the item is false.

The following items are True-False statements. If the statement is correct, *place an X through T* and go on to the next item. If the statement is *incorrect, place an X through F*, underline the portion of the statement that makes it false, and rewrite the incorrect portion so that it is true in the space provided.

1. The lake had frozen hard.   T F _____
2. I have rode that horse.   T F _____
3. He begun the fight.   T F _____
4. He has drove.   T F _____
5. They had fallen.   T F _____
6. They had went.   T F _____
7. She drove the car.   T F _____
8. I went home.   T F _____
9. He seen her.   T F _____

When three or four true-false statements are clearly related, it is often possible to organize them in an item cluster somewhat comparable in form to a multiple-choice item. However, each alternate is scored separately. When this can be accomplished, three advantages are realized: a better utilization of space in the examination; a reduction in the time needed by the examinees to respond to the items because of the reduction in the amount of material which must be read; and the establishment of a general frame of reference for responding to the set of related items.

Consider each statement below. If it is characteristic of multiple-choice items mark it true; otherwise, mark it false.

1. It may be rapidly scored.
2. Scoring is subjective.
3. It requires the examinee to choose from among offered alternates.
4. It may be used to measure higher-order mental processes.
5. It is likely to have a large sampling error.
6. Items are usually easy to write.
7. It is adaptable to measuring creativity.
8. It may be scored by a student aide.
9. It is a supply type test.

It is possible to construct a set of related true-false items which can be answered correctly only when related to data presented in the examination as shown in the following example. When this is to be done, it is often possible to construct the items so that they measure at the higher levels of the cognitive domain.

Items 50–56 are true-false items. If the item is *true, mark A*, and if it is *false, mark B*. Analyze the material presented in the case study below and, on the basis of your analysis, answer questions 50–56.

Bill is 8 years old and is in the third grade. He is tall and makes a good appearance. He is well-behaved, quiet, interested in outside activities, and does not read very well. Bill's father is a salesman; both parents are high school graduates.

School Data:

	Second Grade	Third Grade
Reading	Fair	Poor
Language Arts	Fair	Fair
Social Studies	Fair	Fair
Mathematics	Excellent	Excellent
General Science	Fair	Good
Physical Education	Average	Average

(Range: Excellent – Good – Average – Fair – Poor.)

Test Data	Third Grade
Lorge-Thorndike Intelligence Test	IQ 120
WISC (Verbal)	IQ 90
WISC (Performance)	IQ 125
WISC (Total)	IQ 115

Sociometric Testing (30 children, 1st, 2nd, 3rd choices)

Received 0 first choices
Received 0 second choices
Received 2 third choices
He chose the 3 most popular boys in the class.

---

50. Bill's ability scores and his achievement are in agreement.
51. Bill is probably having emotional difficulty.
52. The difference between Bill's verbal IQ and performance IQ is probably nothing more than a chance difference.
53. The teacher should remove him from the classroom setting so that she can teach him on an individual basis.
54. Bill needs special help in reading. If this help cannot be provided in the regular classroom, he should be referred to a class for the retarded so that he can obtain special help.
55. The teacher should have Bill work in group situations with selected children in the class.
56. Bill's father probably cannot read.

In another variety of this item type, the statement may be true, it may be false, or it may be either true or false (T—F—TF). This variety is most applicable when qualifying data is being presented or when working with mathematical concepts. Approach this variety with great caution because it often results in even greater ambiguity than does the true-false variety. The "TF" category is not to be used to cover degrees of truth. It should be used only if the statement may be true under some circumstances and false under other circumstances.

> Consider each statement below. If it is *true*, place an *X through T*, and, if it is *false*, place an *X through F*, but if it is sometimes true and other times false, place an *X through TF*.
>
> T F TF 1. A triangle has two acute angles.
>
> T F TF 2. All sides of a square are equal.
>
> T F TF 3. The sides of a triangle are equal.
>
> T F TF 4. The sides of a rectangle are equal.
>
> T F TF 5. A triangle has two obtuse angles.
>
> T F TF 6. All sides of an equilateral triangle are of the same length.

In writing true-false questions, be very sure that the item is absolutely true or completely false, except when using the "TF" category. However, this third category cannot be used to cover degrees of correctness; it is appropriate only when the statement may be true under certain identifiable circumstances and false under other conditions. It is unfair to expect the examinee to guess the amount of error you will tolerate in a statement before considering the statement to be incorrect. The original forms of the following items exemplify the partially true statement that should not occur in true-false items.

Original	*Revised*
T F 1. The underdeveloped nations are poorer today than they were fifty years ago.	T F 1. In most underdeveloped nations, the per capita income is less today than it was fifty years ago.
T F 2. The Vice President of the United States is a member of the Senate.	T F 2. The Vice President of the United States is permitted to vote on all bills coming before the Senate.

The true-false statement should possess one and only one central theme. If part of the item is true and part of it false, it is difficult to know how to respond.

For example the statement, "Abraham Lincoln, the 23rd President of the U.S., was in office during the trying days of the Civil War," contains two themes and is, consequently, a poor item. If a student marks this item false, is it because he knows that Lincoln was not the 23rd President or is it because he does not know when Lincoln was in office?

It is important that the true-false statement be free from ambiguity. Unlike the multiple-choice item, it does not involve any structuring outside of the problem statement. Consequently, it is doubly important that the statement be concise, unambiguous, grammatically correct, and explicit. Unnecessary words and phrases tend to create ambiguity in an item. In the following examples, ambiguous statements are improved in the revised forms.

Original	*Revised*
T F 1. Freezing is a method of preserving in which food is placed at the freezing point.	T F 1. One method of preserving food is to reduce its temperature to below 32° F.
T F 2. All one needs to make jelly is pectin, acid, and sugar.	T F 2. In order to produce jelly, one must have the following ingredients: pectin, acid, sugar and fruit.
T F 3. Crane can give hope to young writers because he was young himself.	T F 3. Young writers should be encouraged by Crane's literary success during his twenties.

Negative statements should be avoided. The use of a double negative may muddle the intent of the question. Also, examinees often miss the negative connotation. The revisions of the following negative statements are clearer in meaning and less likely to be misinterpreted by examinees.

Original	*Revised*
T F 1. Crane was not influenced by Social Darwinism.	T F 1. Crane was influenced by Social Darwinism.
T F 2. It is correct to say that Crane was not a Romanticist.	T F 2. In his literary work, occasionally Crane was a Romanticist.
T F 3. Spoilage in canned food is not caused by minute plants present in the air, soil, and water and on all foods.	T F 3. Minute plants present in the air, soil and water cause spoilage in canned foods.

Words such as "some," "few," and "many" should rarely be used because these qualifying terms generally introduce true statements and often render a statement partially true and partially false. The examinee is forced to guess how many "some" is or how many "few" is.

Original	*Revised*
T F 1. Only a few men have been elected President of the U.S. after having been defeated for that office in a preceding general election.	T F 1. Only three men have been elected President of the U.S. after having been defeated for that office in a preceding general election.
T F 2. Few American astronauts have died as a result of the space program.	T F 2. Less than five American astronauts have died as a result of the space program.

In preparing a true-false examination one should avoid irrelevant clues. "All" and "none" and similar words should be used with caution since they are indicative of a false statement. However, they can be used occasionally in true statements. For example, "No American astronaut lost his life in space during the first eight years of the space program," is a true statement and the word "no" does not function as a clue to the correct response. However, the following item contains the word "never," and this acts as a clue to the correct response of false. "It is correct to say that Crane never indulged in Romanticism."

It should be remembered that the need to make true statements always true may result in many qualifying clues. For example, a long sentence may be a clue that the statement is correct. Try to make false statements about as long as true statements.

An examination should contain approximately the same number of true and false statements. This is the easiest way to avoid establishing a reputation of constructing tests on which most items are true (or on which most items are false). Also, the examiner must be careful not to establish a pattern among the responses of the occurrence of true statements. The best way to avoid patterning the responses is to randomly order the statements within each content area of the examination.

It should be remembered that items do not exist in isolation on a test. The characteristics of an item may be influenced by the existence of other items on the test. In the following example, the presence of the first item serves as a clue to the second item.

T F 1. Naturalism often leads to a lack of economy in writing.

T F 2. Crane differs some from naturalists in that he does have economy in his writing.

The statement used in a true-false item should not be taken directly from the text because this leads to memorization on the part of the examinees. It is likely to produce ambiguous items—ambiguous after being removed from the structuring influence of the textual content surrounding it in its original form.

The Answer Sheet

When examining students who are capable of handling the added task accurately and efficiently, a separate answer sheet should be used. The following examples illustrate two of the many possible answer sheet arrangements for true-false tests.

					T	F	TF
1.	T	F		1.	0	0	
2.	T	F		2.	0	0	
3.	T	F		3.	0	0	
4.	T	F		4.	0	0	
5.	T	F	TF	5.	0	0	0
6.	T	F		6.	0	0	
7.	T	F	TF	7.	0	0	0
8.	T	F		8.	0	0	
9.	T	F	TF	9.	0	0	0
10.	T	F	TF	10.	0	0	0

Either of these formats should serve the need for accurate and efficient scoring. Notice that a third option (TF) occurs only for those items where this is a realistic third choice. If the answer sheet is being prepared for a specific examination, recording errors by examinees are reduced. Of course, if a third option is to be used with some items and if the answer sheet is to be used for a number of different tests, the third option position must occur for each item. (Types of answer sheets and their uses for various types of items are discussed in Chapter 3.)

DO'S AND DON'T'S

Do

1. Include enough items to adequately sample the material.
2. Use a Table of Specifications to assure adequate sampling.
3. Establish a frame of reference for answering the item.
4. Write concise, unambiguous, and grammatically correct statements.
5. Use questions which are germane to the area being tested.
6. Have approximately the same number of true and false statements.

Don't

1. Use questions which are partially true or partially false.
2. Use unnecessary words and phrases.
3. Have more than one theme in the item.
4. Have irrelevant clues.
5. Have a pattern in the order of the responses.
6. Use negative statements.
7. Use the qualifying terms: all, none, some, few, or many.
8. Pull statements directly from the textbook or class notes.

PROBLEMS

1. Why may it be said that a true-false test will be unlikely to exhibit the same reliability as a multiple-choice test of the same length?
2. Why should a true-false item be either absolutely true or completely false?
3. Defend the use of true-false items on classroom tests.
4. Using a Table of Specifications, prepare a 40-item, true-false test for a unit of study.
5. What are the advantages in using true-false item clusters?
6. Why is it difficult to avoid ambiguity in true-false items?

SUGGESTED READING

Ahmann, J. Stanley, and Marvin D. Glock, *Evaluating Pupil Growth: Principles of Tests and Measurement*. Allyn and Bacon, Boston, 1967, pp. 84–89.

Ebel, Robert L., *Measuring Educational Achievement*. Prentice-Hall, Englewood Cliffs, N.J., 1965, Chapter 5.

Chapter 9

Matching Tests

The matching item is a specialized form of the multiple-choice item type in which a set of related stems (premises) share the same set of alternates. It is not widely used in standardized achievement test batteries but often occurs in tests prepared to accompany text books. When used, it is most likely to appear in conjunction with multiple-choice items. In this chapter we will consider the limitations and strengths of this item type and develop some guidelines for its construction. The following is an example of the matching test.

The statements under Column I describe various types of clouds. For each statement, find the type of cloud in Column II for which the statement is most appropriate and record your choice on the line preceding the question number. Do *not* use an answer more than one time.

Column I	*Column II*
___ 1. A white, filmy cloud of ice crystals formed at high altitudes.	A. Altocumulus
___ 2. Massive, puffy, white cloud with flat base and rounded sides and top.	B. Altostratus
	C. Cirro-cumulus
___ 3. A low altitude cloud of great width, covering most of sky.	D. Cirro-stratus
___ 4. Fleecy, whitish, globular cloudlets at high altitudes.	E. Cirrus
	F. Cumulo-nimbus
___ 5. Massive, darkish, mountainous cloud with flat base and usually discharging precipitation.	G. Cumulus
___ 6. A gray cloud at low altitude of great width from which rain is falling.	H. Nimbo-stratus
	I. Stratus

STRENGTHS

Matching items may be used to measure the lower levels of the cognitive domain. Vocabulary, dates, events, formulae, and simple relationships can be efficiently and effectively measured with these items. They are particularly adaptable to who, what, when, or where situations. Although it is not easy to develop matching items which measure at the higher levels of the cognitive domain, it is possible to do so, particularly when qualifying material is presented and the matching exercise is based on this material. Furthermore, they may be scored rapidly, accurately, and objectively by individuals who are unqualified to teach in the subject area being examined.

WEAKNESSES

The matching type of item is not particularly applicable to measurement at the higher levels of the cognitive domain. It is extremely difficult to develop a set of premises for a matching exercise that will measure at the higher levels of the cognitive domain and can, at the same time, share alternates. Unless reserve is exercised in the use of these items, the resultant test may be justifiably subject to the charge of measuring the irrelevant and insignificant.

In order for a set of matching items to function properly, it must contain homogeneous premises. Otherwise, the differences among premises will provide clues to the correct responses. It is often difficult to find enough important and homogeneous ideas to form a matching set. Moreover, the construction of a homogeneous set of matching items often places an overemphasis on a rather small portion of the content area to be tested. This may result in failure to conform to the Table of Specifications and, thus, cause a bias in content sampling.

The items of a set are interdependent. How the examinee responds to one premise of a set influences how he will respond to all other premises. Although there are techniques which can be employed to reduce this interdependence, it cannot be removed. Because of this, it is difficult to improve a set through the revision or replacement of some of its premises. Whatever is done to one premise might well influence the performance of all the other items in the set.

CONSTRUCTION

Matching items occur in clusters. A cluster of matching items must contain an introductory statement, a set of related premises, and a list of alternates to be shared by all the premises in the cluster. This item cluster functions as a total unit. Any modification or change in one premise or in one alternate may affect the operation of the remainder of the cluster. Consequently, the test constructor should endeavor to establish harmony among the various parts of the cluster and ensure that each premise and alternate carries its weight in the test.

When preparing a matching exercise, a teacher should keep clearly in mind his instructional objectives and carefully select his premises to conform to the Table of Specifications. If this is done, and if the exercise is developed with the intent of obtaining the item statistics appropriate to the purpose of the test (mastery or discrimination), the matching exercise should be valid and its items should contribute to the achievement of adequate test reliability.

The matching exercise is a cluster of items and is therefore somewhat complex. It is unlikely that one could develop such an exercise without making a number of revisions during the process. To facilitate these revisions, it is wise to prepare the original draft in pencil on a separate sheet of paper or 5 × 7 card. Furthermore, before preparing the final form of the examination, it is advisable to have someone read and react to the exercise.

The Introductory Statement

The introductory statement must set a general frame of reference for responding to the items of the cluster and clearly indicate to the examinee how he is to proceed in selecting his responses. It should be either a clear and concise declarative sentence or set of such sentences. Unnecessary words and phrases should be eliminated. The language used should be appropriate to the level of development of the examinees—this is not the place to measure the student's vocabulary. The use of technical terms which some students might not understand can render the item cluster ineffective. Awkward sentence structures introduce ambiguity and should be avoided.

In the example which follows, the introductory statement fails to set a general frame of reference for responding. An examinee would be unable, on the basis of this statement, to anticipate in any way the topic covered by the premises to follow. Also, the statement is quite wordy, primarily as a result of stating the premises as incomplete statements. The revised form of the item eliminates some of these problems.

ORIGINAL

Directions—The following is a list of incomplete sentences numbered 1 to 5. You are to select the word or words from the list on the right which best describes or completes the phrase. Put the letter corresponding to your choice next to the number of the phrase on the answer sheet. *Answers may be used more than once.*

1. The belt of calm air nearest the equator is called the . . .
2. Climate characterized by clear skies, dry air, and little rainfall is found in the area of the . . .
3. The wind belt immediately north or south of the doldrums is called the . . .
4. Most of the United States lies in the belt of winds known as the . . .
5. The best of calm air at latitudes 30° N and 30° S is called the . . .

A. Trade winds
B. Horse latitudes
C. Doldrums
D. Prevailing westerlies
E. Prevailing easterlies
F. Polar easterlies

REVISED

The statements in Column I are descriptions or geographic characteristics of wind belts. For each statement find the appropriate wind belt in Column II. Record your answer in the appropriate space on the answer sheet. *Answers may be used more than one time.*

Column I	*Column II*
1. Region of high pressure, calm and light baffling winds.	A. Doldrums
2. The belt of calm air nearest the equator.	B. Horse latitudes
3. A wind belt in the northern hemisphere typified by a continual drying wind.	
4. Region of clear skies, dry air and little rainfall.	C. Polar easterlies
5. A region typified by rapid raising hot and moist air.	D. Prevailing easterlies
6. Most of the United States is found in this belt.	E. Prevailing westerlies
7. Panama Canal is found in this region.	

The introductory statement in the following exercise sets a general frame of reference for responding, but it is misleading. After reading the introductory statement, one would expect Column II to contain types of precipitation and Column I to contain statements pertinent to these. However, the second premise does not refer to a type of precipitation and alternate "A" is not a precipitate.

The statements in Column I describe various types of precipitation. For each statement, find the type of precipitation for which the statement is most appropriate in Column II and record your choice on the line preceding the question number. Do not use an answer more than one time.

Column I	Column II
___ 1. Formed by large drops of water being carried from a lower, warmer portion of a cloud to an upper, below freezing portion of the cloud.	A. fog B. hail
___ 2. Water vapor in the air condensed to form visible droplets suspended in the air near the surface of the earth.	C. rain
___ 3. Small, suspended crystals in the air combined to form larger crystals which fall to the earth.	D. sleet
___ 4. Small drops of suspended water in upper layers of the air combined to form larger drops which are no longer suspended.	E. snow

Besides setting a general frame of reference for responding, the introductory statement commonly includes information concerning how to respond. If an alternate can be used more than one time, some reference to this fact should appear in the introductory statement. Either here or in more general directions, the examinee must be told how and where to record his responses. This is generally done on lines preceding the premises or on a separate answer sheet similar to that used for multiple-choice tests. The introductory statement in the illustration which follows is brief; nevertheless, it sets a general frame of reference and indicates where and how the responses are to be recorded.

ORIGINAL

For each item-type in Column I select the criticism from Column II which is most appropriate to it. Record your choice on the line preceding the question number. Do not use an answer more than one time.

Column I	Column II
___ 1. Multiple-choice	A. It tends to result in extensive sampling of comprehension in a limited number of content areas.
___ 2. True-false	B. It should be used primarily for measuring comprehension.
___ 3. Matching	C. Judgment of scorer influences test reliability.
___ 4. Essay	D. The items must be relatively easy to be meaningful.
___ 5. Short answer	E. To write good items requires skill and the expenditure of considerable time.
	F. It cannot measure creativity.

In this example, the introductory statement structures the task for the examinee. He is asked to select for each item type the appropriate statement from Column II. He is given a general orientation to the task and is told what to do. Note, however, that the statements in Column II are rather long. Unless he disregards the instructions, the examinee must read this list of long statements for each premise in Column I. A saving of time, without a loss in the effectiveness of the measuring instrument, could be achieved by reversing the two columns.

REVISED

Some criticisms of various item types are listed in Column I. Find in Column II the item type for which the criticism is *most* appropriate and record your choice on the line preceding the question number. Remember that an item type may be used more than one time.

Column I	*Column II*
___ 1. It tends to result in extensive sampling of comprehension in a limited number of content areas.	A. extended-answers
___ 2. It should be used primarily for measuring comprehension	B. matching
___ 3. The judgment of the scorer influences the test reliability	C. multiple-choice
___ 4. The items must be relatively easy to be meaningful.	D. short-answer
___ 5. To write good items requires skill and time.	E. true-false
___ 6. The scorer must be an expert in the subject area.	

The Premise

In function and in its characteristics, the premise is similar to the stem of the multiple-choice item. It serves to specify in more detail the frame of reference suggested in the introductory statement. The specific problem to be solved is presented in the premise, and it should be expressed clearly and concisely. Errors of language usage should be avoided. All superfluous and unnecessarily difficult words should be eliminated. Unless essential to the concept being measured, highly technical terms should be excluded. Certainly, it is not advisable to use figurative language and complex sentences. If the premise is written as a complete declarative sentence, ambiguity is less likely to occur. This latter point is illustrated in the revised item on page 129.

Each premise in the original example contains several words which are not needed to establish a specific frame of reference for the item or to present the problem to be solved. The introductory statement establishes that the statements comprising the premises refer to structures in the conduction system of the heart; it is not necessary to repeat this in each premise. Also, the first premise is grammatically incorrect and stated in question form. Correction of the grammar and reformulation as a declarative statement would improve this premise.

ORIGINAL

The statements in Column I pertain to the structures which comprise the conduction system of the human heart. For each statement, find the appropriate structure in Column II and record your answer on the separate answer sheet. Remember that a structure may be used more than one time.

Column I

1. Which of the structures on the left is commonly referred to as "pacemakers"?
2. This structure is responsible for producing the contraction of the ventricle by innervation of the papillary muscle and lateral walls of the ventricle.
3. This structure is responsible for the regularity of the heartbeat.
4. This structure is responsible for initiating the impulse which is then carried to its destination by the Purkinje fibers.
5. It is the responsibility of this structure to transmit the impulses to the Purkinje fibers.

Column II

A. Atrio-ventricular bundle
B. Atrio-ventricular node
C. Purkinje fibers
D. Sinoatrial node

A revised form of this matching exercise is illustrated in the following item cluster.

REVISED

The statements in Column I pertain to the structures which comprise the conduction system of the human heart. For each statement, find the appropriate structure in Column II and record your answer on the separate answer sheet. Remember that a structure may be used more than one time.

Column I

1. It is commonly called a pacemaker.
2. It produces the contraction of the ventricle by innervation of the papillary muscle and lateral walls of the ventricle.
3. It is responsible for the regularity of the heartbeat.
4. It initiates the impulse which is carried to its destination by the Purkinje fibers.
5. It transmits impulses to the Purkinje fibers.

Column II

A. Atrio-ventricular bundle
B. Atrio-ventricular node
C. Purkinje fibers
D. Sinoatrial node

Even after revision, this matching exercise is not entirely free from justifiable criticism. Items 1 and 3 are basically the same. Unless it is important to know that the sinoatrial node is called a "pacemaker," it is not necessary to have both items. Also, alternate "C" and the last two premises contain the phrase "Purkinje fibres." An uninformed examinee should be able to eliminate "C" as a possible answer for these two items and, as a result, improve his likelihood of guessing a correct answer. If he assumes that a phrase used so often must be a correct response, he might mark this response for items 1 through 3. If he does this, he will answer item 2 correctly.

The number of premises in a cluster should rarely exceed six or seven. It is difficult to find even this many homogeneous ideas which are worthy of measuring, and even more difficult to avoid sampling bias. Finally, remember that the total cluster—statement, premises, and alternates—must appear on the same page of the test.

ORIGINAL

The following items refer to the Pre-Revolutionary period in United States history (1763–1775). Match the information given under I with the appropriate information given under II. An answer may be used only one time.

Column I	Column II
1. Regulated colonial trade.	A. Parliament
2. Frontier closed by proclamation.	B. Navigation Acts
3. English legislative body.	C. 1763
4. British troops raided Lexington and Concord.	D. Stamp Act
5. Taxed newspapers, legal papers, calendars.	E. 1768
	F. 1775

The major weaknesses in the previous item cluster arise from the attempt to use premises which are not homogeneous. In order to use such items, it was necessary to be somewhat ambiguous in the introductory statement. After reading the introductory statement, an examinee can know only that the items which follow are related to the period extending from 1763 to 1775. Also, the heterogeneity of the items gives a number of clues to the test-sophisticate. For example, without any knowledge of British government, item 3 should be correctly answered; alternates "A," "C," "E," and "F" would likely be eliminated from consideration for items 1, 2, and 5; and item 4 is likely to be answered by one of three alternates (C, E, F). The following revision corrects many of these shortcomings.

REVISED

Listed below under I are the basic provisions of several acts enacted during the Colonial Period (1763–1775) of the United States. Match these provisions with the names of the acts listed under II. Remember that the name of an act may be used more than once.

Column I	Column II
1. Taxed newspapers, legal papers, calendars.	A. Intolerable Acts
2. Taxed imported goods.	B. Navigation Acts
3. Regulated Colonial trade.	C. Stamp Act
4. Called for enforcement of the Navigation Acts.	D. Townshend Acts
5. Took right of self-government away from Massachusetts.	

The Alternates

The list of available solutions to the problems presented in the premises are placed in Column II. Each of the alternates must be grammatically appropriate to each premise of the cluster. Linguistically, they all should be equally appealing. The alternates must furnish each premise with one and only one best answer to its central problem. They should be somewhat homogeneous in content since the degree of homogeneity influences the difficulty of the set.

It is important that the number of alternates be greater than the number of premises or that the instructions state that an alternate may be used more than one time. In the latter situation, alternates must occasionally be used two or more times to make this instruction plausible. If ambiguity is not introduced, it is advantageous to have both an excess of alternates and alternates used more than one time. This decreases the likelihood of marking the correct response by eliminating previously used alternates from consideration.

The number of alternates should be somewhat limited since the examinee must read the list of alternates each time he answers a premise. The use of more than ten to twelve alternates will result in a loss of testing efficiency and create for the examinee the problem of remembering the earlier members of the list when he has finished reading the last alternates.

What is wrong with the following item cluster?

ORIGINAL

Select from Column II the name or date which is associated with the statement in Column I. Remember that each answer may be used only one time.

Column I	Column II
1. The year in which the Declaration of Independence was signed.	A. George Washington
2. The first President of the United States.	B. Benjamin Franklin
3. The year in which the Civil War began.	C. Babe Ruth
4. The baseball player who holds the home run record.	D. 1777
5. The inventor of bifocals.	E. 1861

The primary weakness in this set is found in the alternates. They are not homogeneous. Since dates and names are mixed, premises 1 and 3 have only two alternates available for consideration (D and E). Likewise, for premises 2, 4, and 5, only three alternates are available for consideration. Another weakness is found in the premises. They are not homogeneous in content, spreading nearly two centuries in time and covering several unrelated topics (sports, politics, and inventions). Also, the item cluster has the same number of alternates as it has items. Finally, the introductory statement fails to offer an adequate frame of reference for responding. The following item cluster is not subject to these criticisms.

REVISED

Several inventions of historical significance are listed in Column I. For each item, select the name in Column II which is associated with that event. Record your choice on the line preceding the question number. Remember that an answer may be used only one time.

Column I

___ 1. airplane
___ 2. steamboat
___ 3. automobile
___ 4. radio
___ 5. iron stoves
___ 6. television

Column II

A. John Baird
B. Sir Frederick Banting
C. Henry Ford
D. Benjamin Franklin
E. Robert Fulton
F. Marchese Marconi
G. Orville Wright

If there is some logical order suggested by the alternates, this order should be followed. Thus, dates should be listed in chronological order and names alphabetically. Also, in order to reduce patterning clues, the correct alternates should be somewhat randomly rotated in relation to their respective premises. However, only rarely should premise and keyed response appear directly opposite each other.

Examples

It is possible to use the matching format with recognition and identification tasks. In geography, for example, one might reproduce a map of Europe but with letters used instead of the names of countries. The premises could consist of the names of the countries to be located. Another example of this use of the matching exercise may be seen in the following item cluster.

The various structures associated with the heart are listed below. For each question, locate the structure on the diagram and record the letter identifying its location in the appropriate blank on your answer sheet.

1. descending aorta
2. mitral valve
3. left ventricle
4. myocardium
5. pulmonary vein
6. inferior vena cava
7. right atrium
8. aortic arch
9. semilunar valves
10. tricuspid valve

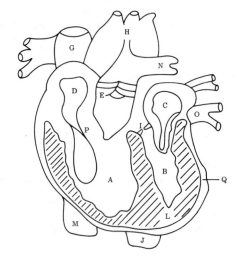

The following matching exercise illustrates how careful planning can produce a very efficient set of items to measure certain instructional objectives—efficient in terms of utilization of examination booklet space and examinee time.

Directions: Listed below are British and American actions between 1763 and 1775. On the chart following the lists, some actions have been omitted. For Questions 41 to 50, you are to choose the appropriate actions from the list and complete the chart, matching the action to the appropriate date. Place all answers on the answer sheet.

British actions

A. Stamp Act passed
B. Intolerable Acts passed
C. Townshend Acts repealed
D. Navigation Acts are strictly enforced
E. Stamp Act repealed
F. British seize American ships

American actions

A. Boston Tea Party
B. Settlers ignore the law
C. Minutemen resist
D. British goods boycotted
E. First Continental Congress protests
F. Colonists form an army

	British actions	*American actions*
1763	Frontier closed by proclamation	41
1764	42	
1765	43	Stamp Act Congress protests
1766	44	
1767	Townshend Acts passed	45
1770	46	
1773	Cheap tea supplied to colonies	47
1774	48	49
1775	Troops raid Lexington and Concord	50

DO'S AND DON'T'S

Do

1. Use a Table of Specifications to insure adequate sampling.
2. Establish a frame of reference for answering the item in the premise.
3. Establish a general orientation in the introductory statement.
4. Be clear and concise.
5. Use correct grammar.
6. Adhere to a logical ordering of alternates if one exists.
7. Control the difficulty of the item by the homogeneity of the alternates.
8. Have homogeneous premises and homogeneous alternates.

9. Inform the examinees if an alternate may be used more than once.

10. Use for who, what, when, or where situations.

Don't

1. Expect to measure higher-order mental processes.
2. Have errors of grammar in premises or alternates.
3. Provide superfluous information.
4. Have clang associations between keyed responses and premises.
5. Have a pattern between the order of appearance of premises and keyed responses.

6. Use unnecessary, technical terminology.
7. Have more than twelve alternatives.
8. Have an equal number of premises and alternatives.

PROBLEMS

1. Discuss the major limitations of the matching exercise format.
2. Why might it be said that the premises of a matching exercise should conform to the principles for constructing multiple-choice stems?
3. What is the function of the introductory statement in a matching exercise?
4. Why is it recommended that the number of alternates exceed the number of premises?
5. It has been suggested that alternates should be homogeneous. Why? Discuss.
6. Construct two matching exercises for a test.

SUGGESTED READING

Adams, Georgia Sachs, *Measurement and Evaluation in Education, Psychology, and Guidance.* Holt, Rinehart and Winston, New York, 1965, pp. 342–345.

Ahmann, J. Stanley, and Marvin D. Glock, *Evaluating Pupil Growth: Principles of Tests and Measurement.* Allyn and Bacon, Boston, 1967, pp. 96–103.

Ebel, Robert L., "Writing the Test Item," in E. F. Lindquist (Ed.), *Educational Measurement.* American Council on Education, Washington, D.C., 1951, pp. 200–201 and 239–241.

Chapter 10

The Performance Test

Performance tests are tests of skill—the skill with which students can identify objects, manipulate objects, perform assigned tasks, or react to real or simulated situations. Tests of performance are quite often found in areas involving physical skills. For example, typing teachers use this technique in tests of typing speed, in simulated situation tests (the typing of business letters, personal letters, and narratives), and in identification tests of typing equipment. Similarly, teachers of vocational and physical education courses continually use tests of performance. Furthermore, this technique is often used to assess laboratory skills in areas such as chemistry, physics, and foreign language.

THE NEED FOR AND USE OF PERFORMANCE TESTS

Performance testing has long been a neglected form of classroom testing. A survey of testing practices would indicate to the most casual observer that teachers are preoccupied with tests of verbal behavior. These verbal tests should not be discounted because they afford valuable information for the classroom teacher, as well as for students, parents, and administrators. In many areas, though, performance testing can significantly enhance a teacher's measurement program. In still others, performance testing may comprise the entire measurement program.

For a person to function at such a level that his behavior is adaptable to new and continually changing situations, he must obtain a relatively high level of learning. This implies the integration of the understanding of general concepts supported by basic facts and information in a manner that the learning can be applied in life situations. This behavior complex is illustrated in Fig. 10.1.

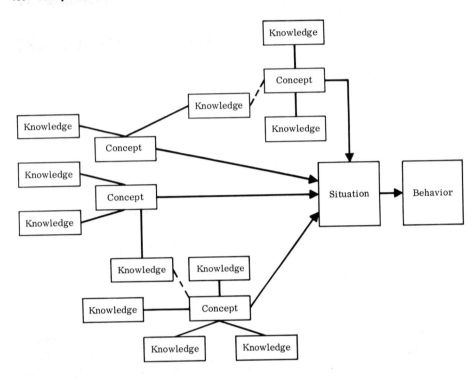

Fig. 10.1. The behavior complex.

The *understanding* of a concept is dependent on supporting knowledge, and certain facts may contribute to the understanding of more than one concept. If the person understands the necessary concepts and can appropriately apply them to new and continually changing situations, he demonstrates *effective* behavior. If, on the other hand, he does not understand the necessary concepts, or if he cannot appropriately apply them to life situations, he will demonstrate *ineffective* behavior. Thus, if the person demonstrates effective behavior, he probably understands the concepts and can apply them in appropriate situations, but if the behavior demonstrated is ineffective, he has failed either to understand the basic concepts or to develop the skills necessary to apply these concepts. The role of performance testing is to measure the effectiveness of the final behavior whereas the role of verbal testing is to measure the understanding of basic concepts and knowledge associated with these concepts. When examinees lack the verbal skills needed to cope with verbal examinations, performance tests can be used to measure the levels of the examinees' understanding of basic concepts.

EARLY CHILDHOOD: NURSERY SCHOOL THROUGH GRADE TWO

Performance tests are particularly useful in the early elementary grades. During these early educational years, most children do not have the reading skills necessary to take most paper-and-pencil tests. Nevertheless, controlled measures of the skills taught during these years are needed. Too often, early childhood teachers depend solely on subjective opinions formed under uncontrolled conditions. In addition to the lack of comparability among scores, these evaluations contain all the possible errors which may be found in essay examinations. Consequently, they are generally unreliable and invalid.

One of the cardinal principles of teaching at the early childhood level is that the teacher be sensitive to individual differences. Children entering a typical first grade class will demonstrate a wide range in social and academic readiness, and will also exhibit a wide range of achievement. The teacher cannot effectively teach these children by treating them as one homogeneous group. However, the effectiveness of her instruction is not necessarily improved by separating them into three or four general achievement groups. Such grouping tends to "peg" children in ability groups which carry social connotations, to overemphasize general differences through the establishment of relatively static groups, and to ignore individual problems within the content area which do not conform to the group boundaries.

Grouping should be a continuing process. It should be based on specific problems rather than on gross ability differences. Although ability differences do somewhat define problem differences, they are inadequate when used as the sole criterion for establishing working groups. For example, children are often assigned to reading groups on the basis of their differences in reading achievement. This procedure is as it should be, but if the process stops at this point, it is insufficient. This general procedure is not sensitive to the differences in oral and silent reading, problems with word pronunciation, and problems with syllabication. Such problems are often overshadowed by the children's general levels of achievement.

Teaching within the framework of individual differences necessitates an effective use of the process of developing continually changing and meaningful groups. This process is dependent on the availability of reliable and valid measures of pupil achievement. Consequently, teachers at this early-education level need to utilize good classroom examinations. They are handicapped because they cannot use written examinations. This handicap can be minimized through the effective use of performance tests.

LATER EDUCATION: GRADE THREE AND HIGHER

The correlation between knowledge and performance in the field is often relatively low. Factors other than the subject matter correlates are generally influential in successful performance. Some of the most obvious areas in which this is apparent are: driver education, swimming, sewing, cooking, and manual training. Performance tests are not limited to these "skill" areas. They can be and are used in many academic areas, such as science, language, and mathematics.

Teachers often neglect the use of performance tests on the assumption that a substantial relation between knowledge and performance must exist. This is one of the more serious measurement errors made by teachers. Because of this erroneous assumption, verbal tests are often mistakenly substituted for measures of performance.

Furthermore, teachers neglect to use performance tests to measure higher levels of achievement because: (1) it is often difficult to construct an instrument which measures an adequate sample of behavior; (2) it is difficult to score a performance test with an adequate degree of objectivity; and (3) it is often difficult to administer performance tests in a reasonable period of time. Nevertheless, it is the teacher's responsibility to measure the behavior that is germane to the course of instruction. If the teacher's objectives include performance behavior, then the teacher is obliged to measure the levels of performance obtained by the students.

Verbal tests are not suited to the measurement of work success. A supervisor can use a verbal test to measure the prospective teacher's knowledge and understanding of the teaching process, but high scores on such a test will not guarantee that the teacher will do a good job in the classroom. This can only be measured by the use of a performance instrument. Since this is the only instrument designed to measure work success, the performance test should be used whenever applicable.

THE PROCESS OR FINAL PRODUCT

Before a performance test can be constructed, decide whether skills exhibited during the performance of the activity are to be measured or if the quality of the final product is to be assessed. It may be decided that both should be assessed separately, that only the process can be assessed, that only the product should be judged, or that process and product cannot be separated and, therefore, the measures will reflect both. This decision has a considerable impact on the construction of the measuring instrument and even influences the selection of appropriate tasks.

When measuring performance, the teacher should not be deceived by the convenience of scoring the final product if, as is often true, the process is also important. For example, during the first few weeks of an introductory typing course, a student may be able to type, using the "hunt and peck" system with accuracy and reasonable speed. If the process is disregarded and he is scored only on the final product, he may obtain a good grade. However, at this stage in training, process is more important than output. The typing speed which he is capable of achieving, while maintaining reasonable accuracy, with adequate training and experience is much less for the "hunt and peck" system than it is for the "touch" system. Measurement of performance often includes both process and product, but placement of the primary emphasis should depend on the skill being assessed.

TYPES OF PERFORMANCE TESTS

Tests have been classified on the basis of the similarity of the test-tasks to those likely to be encountered in a natural course of events. If the purpose of a test is to determine how effectively one would perform in a natural setting, the greater the similarity of the behavioral tasks of the test to those encountered in a natural setting, the more confidence we would have that test performance indicates the ability to perform in a natural setting. A study of a random selection of examinations normally considered to be performance tests would reveal a considerable variation among them on this dimension. Using as the basis for classification this variation among tests, we will consider three types of performance tests: Identification, Simulated Situations, and Work Sample.

Identification Tests

The purpose of the identification test is to measure the examinee's ability to identify an object or set of objects, to distinguish between correct and incorrect procedures and practices, to identify the basic elements of a process, or to recognize the components of a product. Its object is to draw inferences about the examinee's ability to perform the activity under investigation. This type of test is comparatively easy to construct, and such a test is applicable to a number of school testing situations.

The distinction between the identification form of the performance test and verbal tests is sometimes unclear. If students are requested to name and point to the various parts of a typewriter, we would have what is commonly called a performance test. However, the fact that he can correctly identify all of the parts of a typewriter does not guarantee that the student can type, clean the typewriter, or change a ribbon. Identification tests do not measure the effectiveness of an individual's final behavior because neither skill in performing a task nor quality of the final product are directly measured. Supply and selection tests are sometimes used to measure an examinee's knowledge and understanding of selected portions of an academic field (historical events, mathematical functions, biological laws, governmental organizations, etc.). Similarly, identification tests are used to measure an examinee's knowledge and understanding of selected aspects of performance. Although the identification test has been classified historically as a performance test, it is difficult to contend that it differs significantly from its format counterparts in the supply-type or selection-type test.

An identification test, if it really is a performance test, must involve more than a mere repetition of specific facts memorized by examinees. The identification task should reflect an integration of skills and mental processes, where the integration, as well as the processes and skills, is important in the educative process or where it is quite difficult, if not impossible, to separate and measure the individual skills and processes involved in performing the identification task. For example, an examination in biology might consist of a set of displays placed on laboratory tables for the examinees to identify. Thirty microscopes, each containing a different slide, are set up at different stations. The examinees are assigned to these stations and they are given one minute to examine the slide and to identify its contents. Then, on cue from the examiner, the students rotate to a new station. This procedure continues until the examinees have had an opportunity to react to all 30 displays. In this example, to correctly identify the contents of the slides (the product being measured) requires that the examinee know and recognize the organisms on the slides, differentiate between the various organisms studied, and skillfully manipulate the microscopes.

Simulated Situations Test

In the simulated situations test, the examinee is presented with isolated but essential activities of a task which might be encountered in a life situation. Sometimes the examinee is required to use equipment which is specifically designed for training and testing purposes. In driver education, for example, a simulator may be used to assess an examinee's skill in handling an automobile.

A vocal music teacher, in order to assess one aspect of singing performance, could present to each student in his class, one note at a time, a series of notes appropriate to the student's range and require him to vocally duplicate the notes. If this were done, the teacher would have isolated one aspect of singing performance for measurement in a simulated situations performance test.

Work Sample

If the tasks to be performed by the examinee elicit essentially the same behavior as that exhibited in a natural setting, the performance test is of the work sample variety. In this type of test, the examinee is required to produce an actual sample of work under standard and carefully controlled conditions. The tasks performed may include only selected, crucial portions of the total behavior expected in a natural situation. It is sometimes difficult to distinguish between the simulated situations test and the work sample.

The work sample is no stranger to the school. The music teacher who has each of her students sing a few selections and who judges each performance is using a work sample test. The shorthand teacher employs a work sample test when she dictates a letter and then counts the number of errors made by each student in the transcription. In order to obtain measures of physical strength, the number of pushups completed by each student is counted by a coach. He has given a work sample test. When the driver education teacher has a student drive over a specified course and records the errors made, he uses a work sample test. These are but a few examples of work sample tests.

If a woodworking instructor wishes to measure the skills of his students in performing certain woodworking activities, he could construct a work sample performance test. In one such test, each student is given a four-inch cube of wood, a wood chisel, a drill, a box of appropriate bits, a wood screw, two finishing nails, a screw driver, a hammer, and a ruler. The students are given the following instructions:

On the table in front of you are all the materials which you will need to perform the tasks described in 1 through 6. Do each task as accurately and rapidly as possible. You have 30 minutes to complete the test.

1. Cut a groove $\frac{1}{2}$ in. deep, 2 in. long and $1\frac{1}{2}$ in. wide on side A of the block of wood. Make the sides of the groove perpendicular to the surface of side A. Center the groove.

2. At right angle to the first groove, place a second groove. Use the same dimensions as before. Center the groove and make the sides of the cut perpendicular to the surface.

3. Using appropriate tools, place the wood screw in the center of side B and screw it into the wood until it is flush with the surface of the wood.

4. On side C, drill three 1 in. deep holes of the following diameters: $\frac{1}{16}$ in., $\frac{1}{8}$ in., and $\frac{1}{4}$ in.

5. Hammer one of the finishing nails into side D at a spot 2 in. from the middle. The nail should be at right angle to the surface of the board. The head of the nail should be sufficiently below the surface to enable one to woodfill and sand.

6. At a spot on side D which is one inch from the first nail, insert the second nail at a 45-degree angle. The head of the nail should be below the surface of the wood.

CONSTRUCTION[1]

General Procedures

Construction of a performance test is not excessively difficult for many school situations. The difficulty increases rapidly, though, when the emphasis of the test shifts from simple physical skills to complex integration of physical skills and cognitive processes. Although this technique may be used to assess personal characteristics, such as attitude and personal relations, the development of testing instruments for these purposes is even more difficult.

The basic principles for constructing performance tests are similar to those principles outlined for constructing other measuring instruments. Nevertheless, the following special precautions should be taken.

Select an important sample of behavior. The administration of a performance test is often time-consuming for both the student and the examiner. The examinee is expected to demonstrate a skill, and this measurement requires more of the examinee's time than does a question on a verbal test. In many instances, the examinee is required to furnish a finished product, such as a typed paper or a woodworking project. These products are often difficult to score, and the scoring of the projects requires a considerable amount of the examiner's time. Also, in many examining situations, only one student can be examined at a time. Conse-

---

[1] An illustration of two classroom performance tests (identification and simulated situations) constructed to measure student achievement of the objectives of the same unit of study is found in Appendix C.

quently, it is often impossible to measure all or even a large portion of the examinee's behavior.

The examiner must be highly selective in the particular behaviors he attempts to measure. The tasks selected should be essential in measuring the extent to which the instructional goals are being met, be able to differentiate effectively between students (unless a mastery test is utilized), and result in the minimum of repetitive motions from one task to another. Within the limitations imposed by time and other practical considerations, the tasks selected should sample as many of the activities involved in the nonschool behavior as possible.

If the sample of behavior is valid, the results of the performance test can be generalized to evaluate the examinee's expected behavior when confronted with similar tasks in a nonschool setting. The selection of appropriate tasks is, therefore, particularly crucial to the construction of a performance test because usually only a small sample of behavior can be obtained.

Control the situation.   The conditions under which the test is administered should be carefully controlled. Whenever possible, all examinees should be required to demonstrate their skills under the same conditions; however, this is difficult to achieve with the individual performance test. Nevertheless, the teacher should be aware that the time of day, the teacher's mental attitude, the student's physical condition, the noise level in the room, the temperature of the room, and other factors can affect test results.

Since it is important that all examinees be presented the same tasks in a performance test which must be administered to one student at a time, the teacher must be aware of the possibility that the test may be compromised. When it is important that the tasks not be a topic of discussion among the students before all have been examined, the teacher should try to discourage such discussions.

If a performance test is to be administered to one student at a time, it is essential that the directions for the administration of the test be followed carefully. Unless every student is given unlimited time for the completion of the examination, the time limits must be observed strictly. Otherwise, the students are not actually presented the same tasks since, under timed conditions, time is an important aspect of the task.

Assign measurements to the tasks.   It is not always possible to separate measurement and evaluation. In judging the quality of a musical selection performed, for example, it would be essentially impossible for the examiner to obtain objective measures with which he can make an evaluation. In this case, the scoring of the performance depends on his subjective judgment. Nevertheless, whenever possible, measurement and evaluation should not be confused in the scoring of performance tests.

A task should be broken down into its several parts. The parts can be scored, and these scores can be added to formulate a composite score for the task. The final scores can be recorded in the form of measurements or evaluations, depending upon the situation. If the latter is to be recorded, a standard for evaluation should be determined before scoring is attempted.

Determine the scoring procedure. Performance tests may be scored in a variety of ways. One may score process, product, or both. One may obtain objective measures, somewhat subjective measures, or evaluations. The method chosen will limit the number of possible formats which may be used in the construction of the test and, therefore, should be determined in the initial stages of test construction.

Construction of Identification Tests

A number of item formats have been used with the identification test. Tasks have been presented orally (identification of musical selections), visually (identification of the contents of a slide on a microscope), and visually from a reproduction on the examination paper (identification of parts of a sketch of a typewriter). Examinees have been required to respond orally and in writing. In the latter case, responses have been short-answer, completion, multiple-choice, and matching. In examining a sufficiently large sample of performance tests, it is likely that one would discover that every item format has been used. However, the most common form for response is the completion item.

In developing the identification test, give careful consideration to the procedures followed in the construction of its item-type counterpart among the selection and supply tests. In addition, in constructing these tests ensure: that the problem statement clearly establishes one and only one frame of reference for responding to the item; that the item is concise, unambiguous, and grammatically correct; and that superfluous and unnecessarily technical words and phrases are not used. Finally, the directions for the test should state explicitly the general procedures for responding to the tasks presented and for recording the responses.

The tasks of an identification test can be presented to students in a number of ways. For example, if a typewriter is placed on a desk and if the students are requested to name and point to the various parts of it, we would have one form of an identification test. However, this individual test could be converted to a group test by labeling the parts to be named, and having the students record their responses on a sheet of paper. Rather than using an actual typewriter, one could present the examinees a scaled drawing of a typewriter on an examination paper (as illustrated in Fig. 10.2). Selected parts of the object are numbered, and the examinees are requested to name the parts indicated. Items covering specific parts of the typewriter could be presented in the completion, multiple-choice, true-false, or matching formats. The test illustrated is in the completion format.

In the example shown in Fig. 10.2, notice that the directions are clear and explicit, that only one frame of reference is possible, that the examinees are told where to record their responses, and that the response spaces are arranged for ease of scoring with a strip key.

On the right is a scale drawing of part of a typewriter. Identify the numbered parts. *Write only the name of the part* in the space provided below.

1. _____

2. _____

3. _____

4. _____

5. _____

6. _____

7. _____

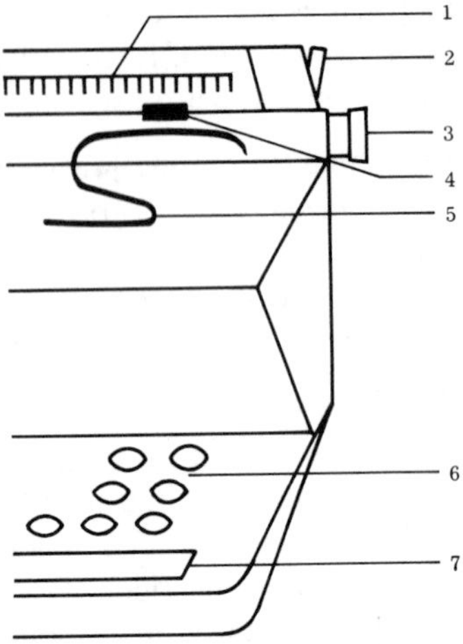

Fig. 10.2. Identification performance test of typewriter parts.

Simulated Situation and Work Sample Tests

It was suggested previously that it is not always possible to determine readily whether a performance test should be classified as the simulated-situation type or as the work-sample type. These two types of performance tests share so many factors to be considered in test construction that it is not practical to treat them separately. In the section on General Procedures we have already considered some of these shared factors: the selection of appropriate behavioral tasks; the control of the testing situation; the assignment of measures to tasks; and the importance of selecting an appropriate scoring procedure.

Some of the major decisions made in developing performance tests concern process and product. The instructor must determine what is to be scored: process, product, or both. If process is to be scored, he must decide whether the scoring emphasis shall be on quality and accuracy of performance or on speed of performance. After these decisions are made, he must select those elements of process or product which are to be considered in developing the scoring procedure. In making these decisions it is important to keep in mind the practical consideration of efficiency in administration and scoring, the need for tasks which will differentiate between students and which have a minimum of repetitive motions, and the need to establish the relation of the tasks to the desired nonschool behavior.

The tasks should be presented to the examinees in a clear, understandable manner. Since performance of skills is the point of interest, avoid superfluous or unduly technical words and phrases in the descriptions of the tasks to be performed. The statements structuring the activity to be performed should be subject to only one valid interpretation.

SCORING

In discussing the procedures to be followed in scoring performance tests, it is advantageous to elaborate on the distinctions made in discussing the construction of tests and consider the identification test separately. But first, some general comments seem in order.

The selection of the scoring format should be made before the test is organized in its final form, with careful thought given to improving scoring efficiency, scorer reliability, and administrative efficiency. All other things being equal, the most desirable format is one which will permit group rather than individual test administration, objective rather than subjective scoring, scoring after the examination rather than scoring during the testing period, and rapid scoring by machine or overlay key.

Identification Test

The scoring procedures to be followed with identification tests parallel closely the procedures used in scoring their item counterpart in the supply or selection type of test. With very young examinees or with those who cannot write, it may be necessary to use an oral response format. In this situation, the examiner may decide to tally the errors as the test proceeds, but it is often useful to have a record of the specific items missed. If so, one can record on a prepared answer sheet the responses given or check the items missed on a duplicated answer key.

If the examinees are to record their responses to each task in one or two sentences, the discussion of scoring procedures for the short-answer essay question (Chapter 4) is generally appropriate. Under most circumstances, the items can be scored 1, 0 or 2, 1, 0. The point-score method is appropriate.

If the examinee is to respond to each of the identification tasks with a word or short phrase, the scoring can be facilitated by scoring each response "1" or "0" and by requiring the examinees to record their responses on an answer sheet prepared by the teacher. The answer sheet should have the responses on the answer key align with the responses of the examinee (Fig. 10.3).

John Doe 10/9/69	Test 1: Physical Geography
Physical Geography I	10/9/69
MWF 10	
1. *quartz*	1. quartz
2. *slate*	2. slate
3. *sandstone*	3. limestone

Fig. 10.3. An answer sheet and answer key for the identification test.

The scoring efficiency of the test can be further improved by providing the examinees a list of options from which to select the appropriate response to an identification item. Figure 10.4 illustrates an answer sheet developed for this purpose.

DIRECTIONS: You are to identify each of the displays on the table. Find in Column II the name of the rock which is displayed and record your choice on the line preceding the appropriate display number in Column I. Some of the rocks in Column II occur in more than one display.

Column I   *Column II*

_____ 1.	A. coal
_____ 2.	B. conglomerate
_____ 3.	C. flint
_____ 4.	D. geode
_____ 5.	E. granite
_____ 6.	F. limestone
_____ 7.	G. quartz
_____ 8.	H. sandstone
_____ 9.	I. shale
_____ 10.	J. slate
_____ 11.	
_____ 12.	Name _____
_____ 13.	Physical Geography
_____ 14.	Hour _____ Days _____
_____ 15.	Date _____

Fig. 10.4. Answer sheet with options for an identification performance test.

In Fig. 10.4, note that the directions clearly indicate the tasks to be performed by the examinees, that the options in Column II are listed in logical (in this case, alphabetical) order, that the options are similar in nature, that there are only ten options to be read by the examinees, and that any option may be used more than one time. These are desirable characteristics of tests of this type.

Simulated Situation and Work Sample Tests

The methodology to be followed in measuring or evaluating a process or product is of major importance to the meaningful interpretation of performance tests. The careful selection or construction of the measuring instrument is vital and should be developed with consideration for the reliability of its measures, its practicality in use, and its appropriateness for the intended performance test. In many cases, the construction of this instrument is more difficult than the selection of the behavioral tasks for the test.

A number of different scales are available for use in the measuring instrument. The scale used should be selected on the basis of the intended use of the results, what behavioral tasks are involved, and whether process or product is measured. Most of these scales may be adapted for use in assessing process and product. There are five types of scales: quantitative, qualitative, status, product, and descriptive.

Quantitative scales. The quantitative type of scale is scored in terms of the frequency of occurrence of some specified behavior. The scorer observes the behavior or product of the examinee and records the relative frequency with which selected behaviors or product characteristics occur on a scale designed for this purpose. Since the characteristic or behavior under examination is normally considered to be distributed on a continuum on which the scale is superimposed, theoretically the scale can be as finely divided as the examiner desires. Because of practical considerations, such as time limitations on observing behavior, and because of the limits imposed by the ability of the observer to distinguish behavioral differences between adjacent categories, it is unlikely that one would use more than ten categories. Most quantitative scales have between two and five categories.

The check-list, as a quantitative scale, contains two categories for marking: "YES" and "NO"; or, "check (✓) only if the behavior is observed." In developing a check-list the teacher must identify all essential aspects of the behavior to be marked. When a check-list is used with a process, before attempting to construct the instrument, it is wise to carefully observe the process unfold in a natural setting and to study the literature for help in identifying critical aspects of the behavior. The following is a portion of a check-list scale which could be used in the supervision of student teaching.

Directions: This is a check-list of the activities which might be used in the classroom. If the teacher uses the activity stated, place a check (✓) in the blank to the left of the statement. Otherwise, do not mark the statement.

_____ Uses community resources and real-life situations in the classroom.

_____ Subdivides the class so that groups of students can work together on common problems.

The check-list used in the example can be developed into a quantitative rating scale of three or four categories (as shown in the next two examples). In order that the desired distinctions can actually be made, be careful to restrict the number of categories used in constructing the rating scale.

Three-point Scale:

Directions: This is a rating scale of activities which might be used in the class-room.

Shade over A, if the teacher generally uses the activity.
Shade over B, if the teacher sometimes uses the activity.
Shade over C, if the teacher never uses the activity.

A B C   Uses community resources and real-life situations in the classroom.

A B C   Subdivides the class so that groups of students can work together on common problems.

Four-point Scale:

Directions: This is a rating scale of activities which might be used in the class-room.

Shade over A, if the teacher always or almost always uses the activity.
Shade over B, if the teacher often uses the activity.
Shade over C, if the teacher seldom uses the activity.
Shade over D, if the teacher never uses the activity.

A B C D   Uses community resources and real-life situations in the classroom.

A B C D   Subdivides the class so that groups of students can work together on common problems.

Composite scores for quantitative scales can be determined by adding all the weighted responses of all the statements. The following weights might be assigned to the first statement in the previous example: $A = 4$, $B = 3$, $C = 2$, and $D = 1$. If a teacher received a rating of C on the statement, he would be assigned a score of 2 for the item. The sum of the scores for all the statements would yield his composite score.

Quantitative scales are difficult to construct and score. In constructing them, endeavor to use words with unequivocal meaning. A typical error in the construction of rating scales is to use descriptive words which are open to several interpretations. If scorer reliability is to be obtained, the statements must be worded in such a manner that all raters assign the same meaning to a statement. Another difficulty encountered by the scorer is that of deciding between adjacent categories—such as, "Does he almost always use the activity?" or, "Does he often use it?"

Qualitative scales. The qualitative type of scale is scored in terms of the absolute "goodness" of the given behavior. Because the scorer is required to observe the behavior of the examinee, evaluate this behavior, and record his decision concerning the degree of excellence of the behavior observed, this type of scale should rarely be used. It is open to considerable ambiguity as to what constitutes "excellent," etc. Unless an identifiable criterion for judging the absolute "goodness" of the behavior can be established, preference should be given to other types of scales. Nevertheless, it can be used to judge process or product.

The qualitative scale is similar to the quantitative scale and is often used in the same types of situations. The scale is usually divided into three or five rating categories. The following examples illustrate the use of the three-category and the five-category organization.

Three-point Scale:

Directions: This is a rating scale of activities which might be used in the classroom. Rate each activity according to the behavior exhibited by the teacher.

Shade over A, if you consider the teacher's performance to be *good.*
Shade over B, if you consider the teacher's performance to be *fair.*
Shade over C, if you consider the teacher's performance to be *poor.*

A B C Use of community resources and real-life situations in the classroom·

A B C Use of subgroups of students so that students with common problems can work together.

Five-point Scale:

Directions: This is a rating scale of activities which might be used in the classroom. Check (✓) each activity according to the quality of behavior exhibited by the teacher.

Activity	Performance				
	Excellent	Good	Fair	Poor	Unsatisfactory
Use of community resources and real-life situations in the classroom	( )	( )	( )	( )	( )
Use of subgroups of students so that students with common problems can work together	( )	( )	( )	( )	( )

In Fig. 10.5, an example of a qualitative scale illustrates how an art teacher could approach the problem of evaluating the products of art students.

Name:		Date:			
Class:		Product:			
Aspect to be Judged	Performance				
	Excellent	Good	Fair	Poor	Unsatisfactory
Blending of colors	( )	( )	( )	( )	( )
Appropriateness of color selections	( )	( )	( )	( )	( )
Shading	( )	( )	( )	( )	( )
Style	( )	( )	( )	( )	( )
Form	( )	( )	( )	( )	( )
Brush strokes	( )	( )	( )	( )	( )
COMMENTS:					

Fig. 10.5. A portion of a qualitative scale for evaluating art products.

Status scales. The status type of scale is scored in terms of the "goodness" of the given behavior in relation to a specified reference group. The scorer is required to observe the behavior of the examinee, evaluate the behavior relative to a reference group, and record his decision concerning the degree of excellence of the behavior observed. This scale differs from a qualitative scale in that an external reference group is required. The qualitative scale is scored on the basis of the rater's perception of "good" and "poor," while the status scale is scored according to the rater's perception of the typical performance of the reference group.

As with the qualitative scale, this scale is commonly divided into three or five rating categories. The former would consist of categories such as *above average*, *average*, and *below average*, while the latter would consist of categories such as *excellent*, *above average*, *average*, *below average*, and *poor*. These scales can be formulated in much the same manner as illustrated in the previous section on qualitative scales.

Descriptive scales. The descriptive type of scale is scored by checking the statements which best characterize the behavior of the examinee. These statements are grouped according to the characteristic they describe. The rater is required to check the statement in each set that best describes the examinee's performance. For example, a rating scale for teacher effectiveness might contain the items in Fig. 10.6.

TEACHER RATING SCALE

Directions: This is a rating scale designed to measure teacher effectiveness. Below you will find several sets of descriptive terms. In each set, check (✓) the term which best describes the teacher's behavior.

1. Use of Examinations:
   a) _____   _____   _____
      Stressed understanding   Stressed both understanding and knowledge   Stressed knowledge

   b) _____   _____   _____
      Selection type questions only   Both selection and supply type questions   Supply type questions only

   c) _____   _____   _____
      Items easily understood   Some items not understood   Most items not clear

2. Class presentation:
   a) _____   _____   _____
      Mostly discussion   Both discussion and lecture   Mostly lecture

   b) _____   _____   _____
      Highly stimulating   Sometimes stimulating   Usually boring

Fig. 10.6. A portion of a descriptive scale for rating teachers.

Product scales. When a student's product is to be assessed in scoring a performance test, the ease and reliability of scoring can often be improved by using a product scale as the scoring criterion. Product scales are not new to performance tests. E. L. Thorndike, in 1909, employed what is basically a product scale in a test which he developed to assess handwriting (*Thorndike Handwriting Scale*).[2] His version of the product scale was not the first.

In developing a product scale for classroom testing, a teacher usually constructs or selects from products of previous students a series of products distributed along a quality continuum ranging from very poor to very good. As far as possible, these samples should be evenly spaced along the quality continuum. Although it is not impossible to use ten or more product samples to represent varying points along the scale, most teachers find it easier to develop an adequate scale if the scale is restricted to only five levels of quality.

EXAMPLES

Early Childhood

Most kindergarten teachers would consider the following to be some of the major objectives of kindergarten for the young child: to develop greater independence from mother and mother surrogates; to participate freely in cooperative play activities; and to acquire the social graces of the school—raising hand to speak, waiting quietly for a turn to speak, remaining seated when this is appropriate for the ongoing activity. A check-list along the lines of the example (Fig. 10.7) could be constructed to furnish somewhat objective measures of the development of children in these areas.

It should be noted that this combination rating scale and check-list is not designed to be used with a structured performance test. However, with some difficulty in controlling pertinent factors, a check-list similar to the one shown in Fig. 10.7 could be used in situations where the behavioral responses are to specific situations created by the teacher for measurement purposes.

Elementary Drafting

Figure 10.8 offers an example of a product performance test which could be used in an elementary drafting course at the high school level. The test was constructed by Mr. Richard Matteson, a student at Ohio University, during the spring of 1968.

The tasks which the students are expected to perform for this test are often encountered as rather elementary and basic aspects of more complicated activities of a draftsman. By selecting key elements of tasks involved in preparing a drawing

---

[2] Thorndike, E. L. "Handwriting," *Teacher College Record*, 11: 83–175, 1910.

SOCIAL BEHAVIOR SCALE

Name: _____   Date: _____

Class: _____

Three areas of social behavior are listed below. Contained within each area are five statements. Read each statement carefully and place a check in the appropriate space provided at the right of the statement.

Independence

Did he cry or protest when his mother left?

Yes	No

Estimate the amount of time that the child remained within an arm's reach of the teacher.

Less $\frac{1}{2}$ hr	$\frac{1}{2}$–1 hr	1–1$\frac{1}{2}$ hr	1$\frac{1}{2}$–2 hr	over 2 hr

Number of appeals for comfort or assurance.

0	1–2	3–4	5–6	7 or more

Number of requests for help directed toward teacher.

0	1–3	4–6	7–9	10 or more

Number of requests for help directed toward class-mates.

0	1–3	4–6	7–9	10 or more

Cooperative Play

Number of self-initiated attempts at cooperative play.

0	1–2	3–4	5–6	7 or more

Estimate the duration of cooperative play.

Less than 10 min	10–19 min	20–29 min	30–39 min	Over 40 min

Number of rejections of other children's attempts to involve him in cooperative play.

0	1	2	3	4 or more

Number of refusals to attempt cooperative play suggested by his teacher.

0	1	2	3	4 or more

Number of times he shared toys with others during play period.

0	1	2	3	4 or more

School Social Graces

Number of times he had to be reminded to raise his hand for permission before speaking.

0	1–2	3–4	5–6	7 or more

Number of times he spoke without permission.

0	1–2	3–4	5–6	7 or more

Number of times he was reminded that someone else was speaking and he should wait quietly for his turn.

0	1–2	3–4	5–6	7 or more

Number of times he was reprimanded for being out of his seat.

0	1–2	3–4	5–6	7 or more

Number of times he was out of his seat without spoken or tacit permission.

0	1–2	3–4	5–6	7 or more

Fig. 10.7. Social behavior scale.

of a three dimensional object and presenting them in a carefully structured setting, the examiner hopes to measure reliably the drafting skills of his students within acceptable time limitations for administering and scoring the products.

The procedures for scoring this examination could take many forms. One possibility is shown in Fig. 10.9.

ELEMENTARY DRAFTING EXAMINATION

You will have fifty (50) minutes to complete this exam. You may use a drawing board, T-square, triangles, scale, etc.

Use the paper included in the test booklet to solve the problems.

You will be graded for neatness, so be careful with your test booklet.

Problem 1: Draw the number of views necessary to describe the object below. Make your drawing double size.

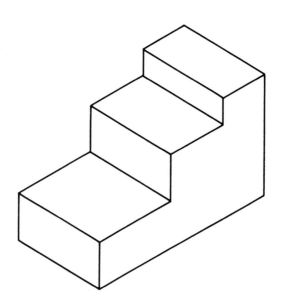

Problem 2: Complete the two unfinished views and dimension the drawing.

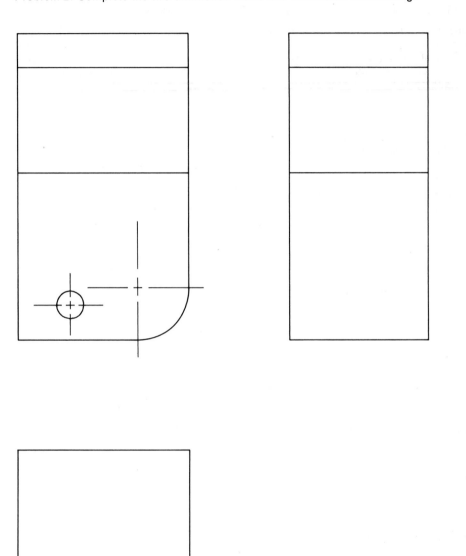

Fig. 10.8. Elementary drafting performance test.

RATING SCALE FOR ELEMENTARY DRAFTING PERFORMANCE TEST

Directions: This rating scale is to be used in scoring the elementary drafting test. For each characteristic, check the position on the scale which best represents the quality of the student's work. The number in parentheses below the position marked on the scale is the student's score on that scale. The total score is found by summing the scores of the individual scales.

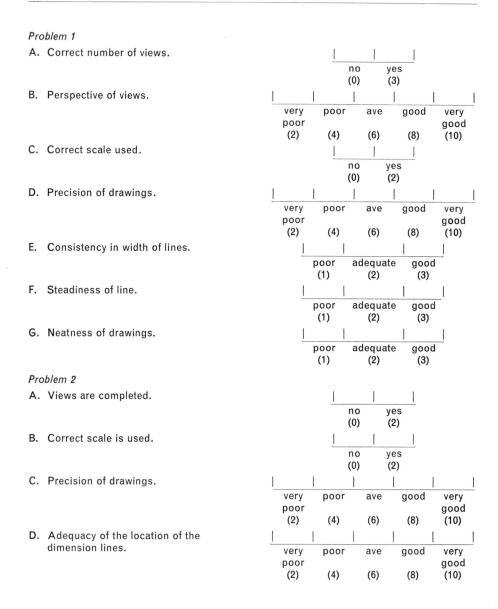

Problem 1

A. Correct number of views.

B. Perspective of views.

C. Correct scale used.

D. Precision of drawings.

E. Consistency in width of lines.

F. Steadiness of line.

G. Neatness of drawings.

Problem 2

A. Views are completed.

B. Correct scale is used.

C. Precision of drawings.

D. Adequacy of the location of the dimension lines.

E.   Accuracy of measured dimensions.

| | | | |
poor   adequate   good
(1)   (2)   (3)

F.   Consistency in width of lines.

| | | | |
poor   adequate   good
(1)   (2)   (3)

G.   Steadiness of lines.

| | | | |
poor   adequate   good
(1)   (2)   (3)

H.   Neatness of drawings.

| | | | |
poor   adequate   good
(1)   (2)   (3)

Name: _____   Total Score: _____

Class: _____   Date: _____

Fig. 10.9. Rating Scale for Elementary Drafting Examination.

Primary Grades

A teacher of first or second grade youngsters, wishing to evaluate the development of her pupils' penmanship, could look at their written work. The product scale offers her the opportunity to do so under somewhat controlled conditions. The product scales shown in Figs. 10.10 and 10.11 were constructed from work samples of first grade pupils in the College of Education Laboratory School at Ohio University. Since these samples were obtained about the middle of January, they represent a grade level of about 1.5 *for this school*. Mrs. Lee Kliesch, the first grade teacher at the Laboratory School, collaborated with the authors in the construction of these product scales.

The products used in constructing the scale in Fig. 10.10 were obtained by furnishing the pupils with lined paper, asking them to use their best writing, and reading them the sentence to be written. The scale in Fig. 10.11 was constructed from products obtained from the same pupils a few days later, but this time they were given the sentence to copy. The performance test used in the latter case is shown in Fig. 10.12. (The examples were reduced to two-thirds size.)

Looking at the two scales, we can see that the copying exercise resulted in better performance by the poorer students—that is, the product samples on the scale scored 10 and 20 in Fig. 10.11 resemble the product samples on the scale scored 20 and 30, respectively, in Fig. 10.10 more clearly than they do their numerical counterparts. This emphasizes the point that, in constructing a product scale, the teacher must be aware that the method used in presenting the task influences the quality of the resultant products.

HANDWRITING PRODUCT SCALE—LEVEL 1.5

Directions; (1) Hand out the performance test. (2) Read to the pupils the following statement:

I would like to have a sample of your best handwriting. First, I want you to write your names at the top of your papers. (Pause.) Have you written your names? Good. I have written a sentence on the papers which you now have in front of you. Carefully copy this sentence on the lines directly below the words of the sentence. You may write now.

(3) Allow enough time for all to complete. Collect the papers.

Scoring: To score, slide each student sample down the scale until you find a scale sample of the same quality. The number beside this scale indicates the numerical value of the sample.

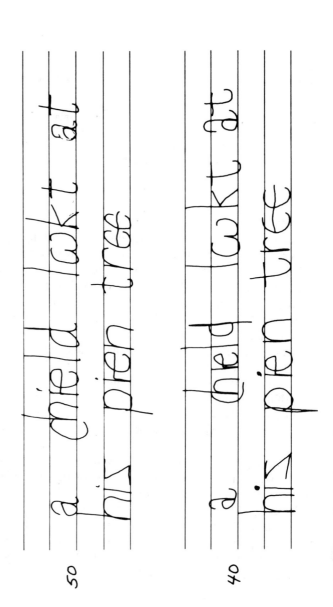

50

40

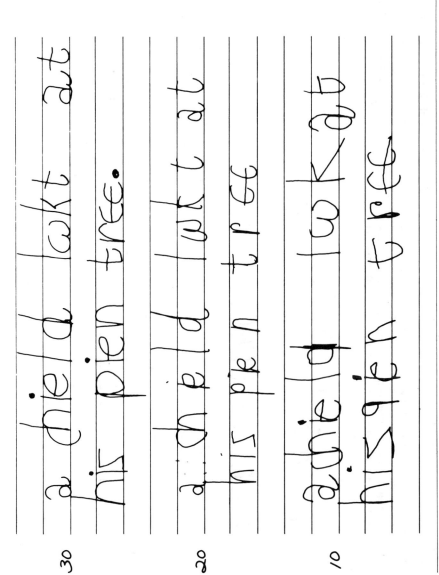

Fig. 10.11. Handwriting product scale based on samples from first grade pupils who are learning to read by I.T.A.; copied sentence.

HANDWRITING PRODUCT SCALE—LEVEL 1.5

Directions: (1) Hand out the lined paper. (2) Read to the pupils the following statement:

I would like to have a sample of your best handwriting. I will tell you the sentence I want you to write after you have written your names at the top of your papers. Write your names on the paper. (Pause.) Have you written your names? Good. The sentence is: "A child looked at his pine tree." (Pause.) I will repeat it more slowly. "A child looked at his pine tree."

(3) Allow enough time for all to complete. Collect the papers.

Scoring: To score, place page two directly below this page. Slide each student sample down the scale until you find a scale sample of the same quality. The number beside this scale sample indicates the numerical value of the sample.

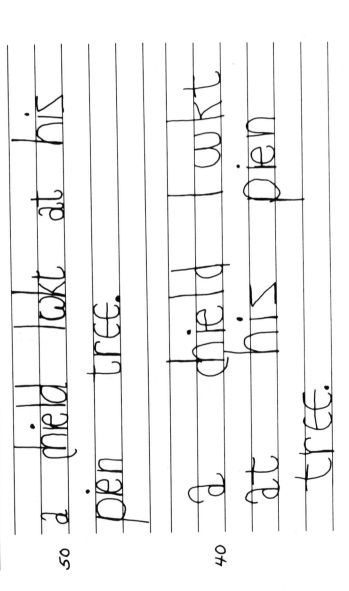

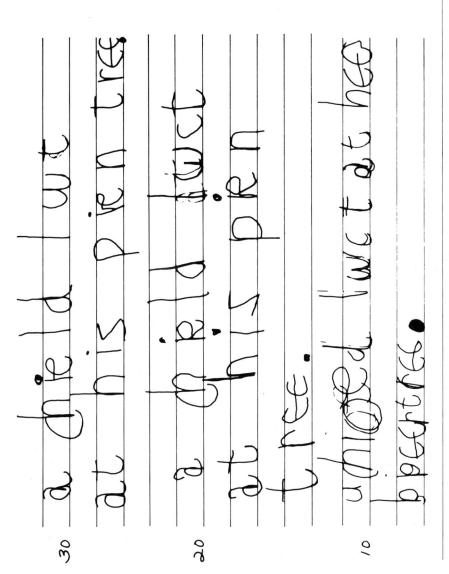

Fig. 10.10. Handwriting product scale based on samples from first grade pupils who are learning to read by I.T.A.; read sentence.

HANDWRITING PERFORMANCE TEST FOR GRADE ONE

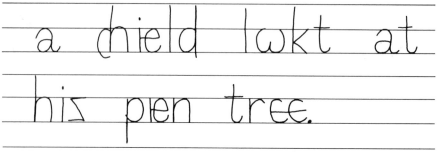

Fig. 10.12. Handwriting performance test; sentence to be copied.

If a teacher wants to improve the reliability of her measures of handwriting at this grade level, she could construct two additional sentences of about the same length for administration as two separate tests. The three tests should be administered on separate days, but within a span of one week. In constructing these tests, an attempt should be made to use each important sound combination somewhere within the three sentences. The average score obtained on the three tests can be used as a measure of the pupils' handwriting development.

Higher Education

The format of the evaluation instrument illustrated in this section is unique. It combines the formats of both a rating scale and a check-list. The scale* (see Fig. 10.13) is designed to rate the clinical performance of student nurses in five areas: personal characteristics; technical performance; relation to patient and family; relation to the health team; and relation to administrative and teaching staff.

Ten representative statements of behavior are identified for each of the areas. Five of the statements are positive, and five are negative. The supervisor is instructed to check (✓) the statements which correspond to the behavior exhibited by the trainees. A total score for each area is determined by totaling the number of behavioral characteristics checked: one point is given for each positive characteristic checked; and one point is given for each negative characteristic not checked (left blank). The total score for each area can range from 0 to 10, an 11-point scale.

This procedure offers several advantages over traditional scales. The marking of the scale is easier and more objective than the traditional scale since it requires only that the clinical supervisor check the behavior observed. Furthermore, it yields a composite score for each of the five behavioral areas, a score which is not overly muddled with supervisor evaluations. Unlike many scales, it allows the separation of measurement and evaluation. The measurements obtained (composite scores) can be evaluated in the form of a letter grade at the supervisor's discretion. Furthermore, evaluative standards can be established for the measures at the discretion of the teaching and administrative staffs.

---

* This scale is currently being used at the School of Nursing, St. Louis City Hospital.

Fig. 10.13. Performance scale for evaluating student nurses.

CLINICAL PERFORMANCE SCALE

NAME OF STUDENT _____ CLASS _____ RATING: F P
(Miss, Mrs., Mr.)

SCHOOL OF NURSING _____ CLINICAL EXPERIENCE DATE: From ___ To ___

Directions: Five areas of performance are listed below. Contained within each area are ten statements. Read each statement carefully. If the statement describes a characteristic of the student being evaluated, place a check (√) in the space provided at the left of the statement. If the statement does not describe a characteristic of the student being evaluated, leave the provided space blank—*do not mark the statement.* (Spaces are provided for *three sets of observations.* Score each set independently.)

Scoring: The five areas of performance are assigned scores ranging from 0 to 10. The score is determined using the following steps:

1. For statements 1–5, add the number of *checks.*
2. For statements 6–10, add the number of *blanks.*
3. Add the sums from 1 and 2.
4. Record the score obtained in 3 by circling the appropriate number corresponding to the problem area.

I. *Personal Characteristics*

        1st — 0 1 2 3 4 5 6 7 8 9 10
        2nd — 0 1 2 3 4 5 6 7 8 9 10   Grade _____
        3rd — 0 1 2 3 4 5 6 7 8 9 10

  1st   2nd   3rd

____ ____ ____ 1. Displays friendliness (e.g., communicates in a pleasing manner, meets people with ease, courtesy).
____ ____ ____ 2. Is appropriately groomed for duty (e.g., hair groomed, nails manicured, clothes clean, make-up applied with discretion, neat).
____ ____ ____ 3. Is thoughtful and considerate of the feelings of others.
____ ____ ____ 4. Displays good work habits under all conditions (e.g., working alone, with coworkers, or under observation).
____ ____ ____ 5. Remains calm under stress; is not overly excitable.
____ ____ ____ 6. Lacks self-confidence.
____ ____ ____ 7. Rigid; is not adaptable to new and different situations.
____ ____ ____ 8. Immature; dependent upon others.
____ ____ ____ 9. Shows poor judgment; does not follow instructions.
____ ____ ____ 10. Overly sympathetic; too easily involved with patients.

DATE ____ ____ ____

II. *Technical Performance*

        1st — 0 1 2 3 4 5 6 7 8 9 10
        2nd — 0 1 2 3 4 5 6 7 8 9 10   Grade _____
        3rd — 0 1 2 3 4 5 6 7 8 9 10

  1st   2nd   3rd

____ ____ ____ 1. Uses proper (or correctly improvised) equipment when carrying out nursing procedures at least 90% of the time.
____ ____ ____ 2. Reports significant changes in patient's condition.
____ ____ ____ 3. Written communications are neat, clear, concise, complete, up to date.
____ ____ ____ 4. Adjusts procedures to meet emotional and physical needs of patients.
____ ____ ____ 5. Verbal communications are audible, concise, and clearly understood by patients.
____ ____ ____ 6. More than 20% of the student's reports do not indicate changes in the patient's condition as reported by supervisory nurse.

(cont.)

1st	2nd	3rd		
——	——	——	7.	Carries out procedures without regard to patient's needs.
——	——	——	8.	Does not utilize resources (physical therapy, social service, dietary, VNA, occupational therapy) available for rehabilitative needs of patient.
——	——	——	9.	Does not prepare all necessary equipment before carrying out nursing procedure.
——	——	——	10.	More than 20% of the time, clinical assignment is not completed.

DATE —— —— ——

III. *Relation to Patient and Family*

1st — 0 1 2 3 4 5 6 7 8 9 10
2nd — 0 1 2 3 4 5 6 7 8 9 10   Grade ————
3rd — 0 1 2 3 4 5 6 7 8 9 10

1st	2nd	3rd		
——	——	——	1.	Is courteous and tactful in approach (displays appropriate behavior) to patient at least 90% of the time.
——	——	——	2.	Is courteous and tactful in approach to patient's family at least 90% of the time.
——	——	——	3.	Can communicate necessary information to patient in patient's own language (using demonstrations when appropriate); patient must be able to communicate back the correct information.
——	——	——	4.	Succeeds in obtaining the cooperation of most patients.
——	——	——	5.	Usually succeeds in obtaining cooperation from the patient's family, when necessary.
——	——	——	6.	Judges patient's values according to his own standards.
——	——	——	7.	Reacts to patient's values according to his own standards.
——	——	——	8.	Shows partiality in care of patients.
——	——	——	9.	Fails to provide assurance when necessary.
——	——	——	10.	Impatient with the lack of cooperation and understanding on part of the patient and his family.

DATE —— —— ——

IV. *Relation to the Health Team*

1st — 0 1 2 3 4 5 6 7 8 9 10
2nd — 0 1 2 3 4 5 6 7 8 9 10   Grade ————
3rd — 0 1 2 3 4 5 6 7 8 9 10

1st	2nd	3rd		
——	——	——	1.	Courteous; is considerate and respectful of co-workers.
——	——	——	2.	Tactful; gracefully handles unusual situations and avoids offending coworkers.
——	——	——	3.	Cooperative; willing to assist coworkers when requested.
——	——	——	4.	Asks for assistance when needed.
——	——	——	5.	Carries her own load; does not expect others to do her work for her.
——	——	——	6.	Often unsure; changes her mind according to the person with whom she talks.
——	——	——	7.	Unreliable; cannot be depended upon to complete her work.
——	——	——	8.	Overly sensitive; critical of most of her coworkers.
——	——	——	9.	Displays a feeling of superiority over her coworkers; thinks that she knows more about nursing than her coworkers.
——	——	——	10.	Often disrespectful to coworkers; belligerent; often in a bad mood.

DATE —— —— ——

V. *Relation to Administrative and Teaching Staff*

1st — 0 1 2 3 4 5 6 7 8 9 10
2nd — 0 1 2 3 4 5 6 7 8 9 10   Grade ————
3rd — 0 1 2 3 4 5 6 7 8 9 10

1st	2nd	3rd		
——	——	——	1.	Reports nursing care accurately (e.g., type of patients, diagnosis, therapy plan, nursing care plans).

```
       1st    2nd    3rd
      ————  ————  ————   2.  Submits written assignments on time, in proper form, and
                              completed.
      ————  ————  ————   3.  Seeks assistance from proper sources.
      ————  ————  ————   4.  Utilizes criticism constructively.
      ————  ————  ————   5.  Uses courtesy and tact when dealing with authority.
      ————  ————  ————   6.  Does not know names and titles of authorities.
      ————  ————  ————   7.  Indifferent to the completion of written or clinical assign-
                              ments; voices disapproval of such assignments.
      ————  ————  ————   8.  Lacks insight into own limitations.
      ————  ————  ————   9.  Disregards rules of professional conduct.
      ————  ————  ————  10.  Does not use proper lines of authority.
DATE  ————  ————  ————
```

Signature: Clinical Instructor _____

Student _____

DO'S AND DON'T'S

Do

1. Use performance tests to measure the effectiveness of final behavior.

2. Use at early grade levels, before paper-and-pencil tests can be effectively used.

3. Use at higher grade levels to measure performance behavior.

4. Measure both process and final product.

5. Select important samples of behavior.

6. Control the situation.

7. Assign measurements to the tasks.

8. Predetermine scoring procedure.

9. Score after the examination period, if possible.

10. For identification test, follow procedures for construction of the selection- or supply-type item counterpart.

11. Present task in a clear, understandable manner.

12. Write a comprehensive set of directions.

13. Explicitly state and qualify the instructions so that a single interpretation is correct.

14. Use terms which all examinees can define and understand.

15. If examinees are to be compared, use the same tasks.

16. If identification test, score using the methods for the supply or selection-type item counterpart.

17. If simulated situation or work sample test, score using one of the following types of scales: quantitative, qualitative, status, product, or descriptive.

18. Inform the examinees in advance that they will be given a performance test.

Don't

1. Use superfluous or unduly technical words or phrases.

2. Present statements structuring the activity which can be interpreted in more than one way.

3. Use different tasks if the examinees are to be compared.

4. Expect the students to know the intention of the task unless it is explicitly specified.

5. Use the performance test to measure verbal knowledge or concepts.

PROBLEMS

1. What are the major limitations of the performance test? What steps can be taken to reduce these limitations?
2. Why should a teacher include performance tests in the measurement program?
3. What are the three types of performance tests? Define each type and compare them in regard to: (a) purpose, (b) construction, (c) administration, and (d) scoring.
4. Define and compare the following methods of scoring performance tests: (a) quantitative scale, (b) qualitative scale, (c) status scale, (d) product scale, and (e) descriptive scale.
5. Develop a 10-item identification test for a unit of study. Use a Table of Specifications.
6. Develop a simulated situation test for a unit of study. Use a Table of Specifications.
7. Develop a work sample test for a unit of study. Use a Table of Specifications.

SUGGESTED READING

Adams, Georgia Sachs, *Measurement and Evaluation in Education, Psychology, and Guidance*. Holt, Rinehart, and Winston, New York, 1964, Chapter 12.

Adkins, Dorothy C., *Construction and Analysis of Achievement Tests*. U.S. Civil Service Commission, Washington, D.C., 1947, Chapter 5.

Ahmann, J. Stanley, and Marvin D. Glock, *Evaluating Pupil Growth: Principles of Tests and Measurement*. Allyn and Bacon, Boston, 1967, Chapter 8.

Ahmann, J. Stanley, Marvin D. Glock, and Helen L. Wardenberg, *Evaluating Elementary School Pupils*. Allyn and Bacon, Boston, 1960, Chapters 11, 12, and 13.

Arny, Clara M., *Evaluation in Home Economics*. Appleton-Century-Crofts, New York, 1953, Chapter 7.

Bean, Kenneth L., *Construction of Educational and Personnel Tests*. McGraw-Hill Book Co., New York, 1953, Chapter 6.

Cooper, A., and E. L. Cowen, "The Social Desirability of Trait Descriptive Terms: a Study of Feeling Reactions to Adjective Descriptions." *Journal of Social Psychology*, **56**, 1962, 207–215.

Dressel, Paul L., and others, *Evaluation in Higher Education*. Houghton Mifflin, Boston, 1961, Chapter 7.

Freyd, M., "The Graphic Rating Scale." *Journal of Educational Psychology*, **14**, 1923, 83–102.

Horrocks, John E., and Thelma I. Schoonover, *Measurement for Teachers*. Charles E. Merrill Books, Columbus, O., 1968, Chapter 18.

McPherson, Marion W., "A Method of Objectively Measuring Shop Performance." *Journal of Applied Psychology*, **29**, 1945, 22–26.

Miner, J. B., "The Evaluation of a Method for Finely Graduated Estimates of Abilities." *Journal of Applied Psychology*, **1**, 1917, 123–133.

Ryans, David G., and Norman Frederiksen, "Performance Tests of Educational Achievement," in E. F. Lindquist (Ed.), *Educational Measurement*. American Council on Education, Washington, D.C., 1951, Chapter 12.

Siro, Einar E., "Performance Tests and Objective Observation." *Industrial Arts and Vocational Education*, **32**, 1943, 162–165.

Wall, Clifford N., H. Kruglak, and L. E. H. Trainer, "Laboratory Performance Tests at the University of Minnesota." *American Journal of Physics*, **19**, 1951, 546–555.

PART III

TEST SCORES:
DESCRIPTION AND EVALUATION

Chapter 11

Describing Test Scores

After a test is administered and scored, how can the students' scores be meaningfully presented? Suppose, for example, that Mrs. Beasley administered a mathematics test with a possible 57 points to her sixth grade class. The scores shown in Table 11.1 are the results of this test for the 30 students in her class.

Table 11.1 Test results for 30 students

Name	Score	Name	Score
Alda	39	Irene	45
Andrea	47	Laura	43
Arden	44	Lawrence	42
Bernard	43	Lyle	48
Blythe	41	Lynn	45
Burke	38	Marie	36
Cherie	49	Maximilian	50
Cynthia	43	Natalie	41
Emil	45	Nicole	39
Fabian	40	Quillon	35
Floyd	44	Reginald	43
Gwendolyn	36	Roberta	48
Henry	36	Siegfried	44
Herman	49	Trixie	41
Ingrid	40	Zelda	43

What do these scores indicate about individuals or about the group? Examination of the results indicates that Maximilian obtained the highest score on the mathematics test; further analysis of the data shows that Quillon obtained the lowest score; and, after further assiduous study of the data, one might suspect that Bernard, Emil, and Trixie obtained scores somewhere in the middle of the class. Nevertheless, the data in their present form are quite cumbersome to interpret.

How can the scores be more meaningfully displayed? One way to bring order to this chaos is to list the scores from the highest to the lowest. This is illustrated for Mrs. Beasley's mathematics test in Table 11.2. Even though it is easier to locate specific scores in this ordered distribution than in the original list, the data remain cumbersome to interpret. The first step in analyzing Mrs. Beasley's test scores is to reorganize them into a frequency distribution.

Table 11.2 Ordered test results for 30 students

Name	Score	Name	Score
Maximilian	50	Reginald	43
Cherie	49	Zelda	43
Herman	49	Lawrence	42
Lyle	48	Blythe	41
Roberta	48	Natalie	41
Andrea	47	Trixie	41
Emil	45	Fabian	40
Irene	45	Ingrid	40
Lynn	45	Alda	39
Arden	44	Nicole	39
Floyd	44	Burke	38
Siegfried	44	Gwendolyn	36
Bernard	43	Henry	36
Cynthia	43	Marie	36
Laura	43	Quillon	35

FREQUENCY DISTRIBUTION

In its simplest form, a frequency distribution is a record of the number of times (*frequency*) each score occurs in the distribution. The mathematics test scores for Mrs. Beasley's class form the frequency distribution presented in Table 11.3.

Table 11.3 Frequency distribution for 30 scores

Score	Frequency	Score	Frequency
50	1	42	1
49	2	41	3
48	2	40	2
47	1	39	2
46	0	38	1
45	3	37	0
44	3	36	3
43	5	35	1

By comparing this frequency distribution with the alphabetically arranged test results presented in Table 11.1, we can see that using a frequency distribution greatly increases the clarity of the form of the distribution of scores. As illustrated in Table 11.3, we usually drop the names of individual students when setting up a frequency distribution. If it is desirable to maintain name identification for the scores on the same sheet as the frequency distribution, it would be easy to group the students' names in the left-hand margin opposite the distribution of scores.

CENTRAL TENDENCY

Mean

One way to represent a set of test scores is to determine a value which describes the most typical scores. The *mean*, or arithmetic average, is often used for this purpose. Suppose that one wished to determine the typical salary a person might *expect* to earn if he were in a specific occupation. In order to determine this *expected value* he might ask three workers in this occupation what they earn a week: worker A might earn $75; worker B, $100; and worker C, $200. The average salary of these three workers is

$$\frac{75 + 100 + 200}{3} = \frac{375}{3} = 125,$$

that is, $125 a week. The expected value is the arithmetic average or *mean* of the scores.

The formula for calculating the *mean* is

$$\bar{X} = \frac{\Sigma X}{N},$$

where $\bar{X}$ = mean, Σ = sum of, X = score, N = number of scores.

The *mean* score is determined by adding all the scores and dividing the sum by the number of scores. For Mrs. Beasley's mathematics test, the number of scores is 30 and their sum is 1277. The mean score is $1277/30 = 42.6$. This mean score can be determined from the frequency distribution. Remembering that multiplication is a shortcut for addition (e.g. $20 + 20 + 20 = 3 \times 20 = 60$), the scores can be multiplied by their respective frequencies and the products added to obtain the sum of the scores. The calculation of the mean from the frequency distribution for Mrs. Beasley's test (as shown in Table 11.3) is illustrated in Table 11.4.

Table 11.4 Calculation of mean from frequency distribution

Score (X)	Frequency (f)	Frequency times score (fX)
50	1	50
49	2	98
48	2	96
47	1	47
46	0	0
45	3	135
44	3	132
43	5	215
42	1	42
41	3	123
40	2	80
39	2	78
38	1	38
37	0	0
36	3	108
35	1	35
	$N = 30$	$\Sigma X = 1277$

$$\bar{X} = \frac{\Sigma X}{N} = \frac{1277}{30} = 42.6$$

Median

Another method of describing the most typical scores is to determine the middle or *median* score. This scorepoint partitions the distribution into two equal parts so that one half of the frequencies fall on either side of it. Since the median is the middle score, it is determined through a simple counting procedure.

The median for Mrs. Beasley's test can be found by determining that scorepoint above which 15 frequencies fall and below which 15 frequencies fall. Using the ordered distribution in Table 11.2, the median can be determined by finding that scorepoint midway between the fifteenth and sixteenth student. Counting from the bottom, Reginald is the fifteenth student with a score of 43 and Laura is the sixteenth with a score of 43. Since these values are the same, the median is

$$\frac{43 + 43}{2} = 43.$$

The number of frequencies to count from the end of the distribution can be determined by $(N + 1)/2$. In this case,

$$\frac{N + 1}{2} = \frac{30 + 1}{2} = 15.5$$

or midway between the fifteenth and sixteenth frequencies.

The median score can be estimated from a frequency distribution. In order to do this, each score in the distribution has to be considered to represent an interval of scores. In the frequency distribution we have been considering, the scorepoint 50 would represent the one point interval from 49.5 to 50.5; 49, 48.5 to 49.5; 48, 47.5 to 48.5; and so on. The highest point in each interval is called the *upper real limit* of that interval and the lowest point is called the *lower real limit*.

The procedure for determining the median from a frequency distribution is similar to the counting process previously mentioned. It is illustrated in Table 11.5 for Mrs. Beasley's mathematics test. The similarity between the two medians should be noted. The estimated value is only one-tenth of a point different from the directly determined value. Even though error is introduced when using a frequency distribution in estimating the median, its magnitude is generally too small to be of significant consequence.

Comparison of Mean and Median

The mean reflects in its calculation every score in the distribution. It is the "balance point" of the distribution in that the sum of the distances of the scores above the mean is equal to the sum of the distances of the scores below the mean. This is reflected in the sum of difference between the scores and the mean; for all scores, $\Sigma(X - \bar{X}) = 0$.

The median is based on the one scorepoint corresponding to the middle frequency. Therefore, the calculation of the median does not reflect the other scores in the distribution. Since it is based on only one score, it is more liable to chance fluctuations when one tests several groups of similar students than is the

Table 11.5 Calculation of the median from a frequency distribution

	X	f	cf*	Steps
	50	1	30	1. $\frac{1}{2} N = \frac{1}{2} \times 30 = 15$ frequencies
	49	2	29	
	48	2	27	2. Count up the of column to
	47	1	25	interval containing the 15th
	46	0	24	frequency.
	45	3	24	
	44	3	21	3. There are thirteen frequencies below scorepoint
43.5	43	5	18	42.5.
42.5	42	1	13	
	41	3	12	4. Hence two of five, or two-fifths, of the frequencies
	40	2	9	in interval 42.5–43.5 are needed.
	39	2	7	
	38	1	5	5. Therefore need $\frac{2}{5}$ or .40 of the
	37	0	4	interval.
	36	3	4	
	35	1	1	6. Median $= 42.5 + \frac{2}{5}$
				$= 42.5 + .4$
				$= 42.9$

* cf, or cumulative frequency, represents the number of frequencies at or below a given score; e.g., there are $1+3+0+1+2=7$ frequencies below scorepoint 39.5.

mean, and thus the median is a less stable measure of central tendency than the mean.

Either of these measures can be used to indicate the norm for the group taking the test. Individual students can be compared to this norm to determine relative levels of achievement or to compare the relative achievement levels of different classes taking the same test.

Since the mean reflects all the test scores, it can be used in other algebraic calculations. For example, the mean for a set of composite scores determined by adding the scores for each student on several tests can be calculated by adding the means on the tests being combined. Medians cannot be combined in this manner. The median of a set of composite scores would have to be determined in exactly the same manner as it would for any of the individual tests in the combination.

For the purpose of describing the group norm, the median is, in general, preferred over the mean if the distribution contains a few extreme scores. Suppose that five men are eating lunch at the same table. During the course of conversation it is discovered that one man is a large corporation executive with an annual income of $100,000. The other four men are teachers with annual incomes of $9000, $8000, $7000, and $6000, respectively. The mean salary of these five men is $130,000/5 = $26,000. Is this value typical of the group of men? Obviously, this figure is not adequate if the purpose of reporting this scorepoint is to reflect the general magnitude of salaries for these men. The median ($8000) more adequately describes their general income level.

VARIABILITY

It is highly unlikely that all the scores on an examination will be identical. Generally, they will vary over several scorepoints. This dispersion of scores is referred to as the *variability* of the scores.

The variability in scores for Mrs. Beasley's mathematics test has been noted: Maximilian obtained the highest score; Quillon obtained the lowest score; and students such as Emil, Floyd, and Laura obtained middle scores. The "center" of the score distribution was described by the mean (42.6) and the median (43). However, no index of the variability among the scores has been defined.

Before we consider specific indices of variability, it might be advantageous to visualize the dispersion of scores. This may be done by placing the scorepoints of the distribution on the horizontal axis, plotting the frequency of occurrence of each score, and connecting the plots. A graph so constructed is called a frequency polygon. A frequency polygon of Mrs. Beasley's mathematics scores is shown in Figure 11.1.

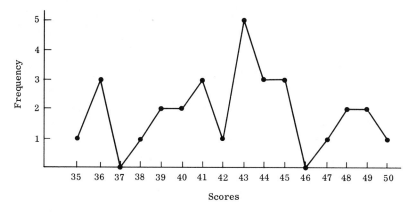

Figure 11.1. Frequency polygon of Mrs. Beasley's mathematics test scores

Range

The *range* is the weakest measure of variability since it is based only on the highest and lowest scores. It is the distance between these extreme scorepoints:

$$R = H - L, \quad \text{where } R = \text{range}, H = \text{highest score}, L = \text{lowest score}.$$

For Mrs. Beasley's test, the highest score is 50 and the lowest is 35. The range of scores is $50 - 35 = 15$. This score defines the distance over which the scores are spread.

The range is a very unstable measure since the extreme scores often change considerably from one administration of a test to another administration of the same test. Furthermore, two distributions of scores can be very similar, yet the extreme scores may differ by several points. Even though the range describes the overall spread of scores, it does not necessarily reflect the variability of the majority of the test scores.

Nevertheless, the range can be used by teachers to describe the variability of a set of test scores. It is a particularly useful measure when the number of scores is so small that more precise measures are not warranted.

Quartile Deviation

Many of the weaknesses inherent in the range can be avoided by using a measure of variability which describes the spread of the middle one-half of the scores. This measure is the *interquartile range.*

A set of scores can be divided into four equal parts or quarters; that is, they can be so partitioned that one fourth of the frequencies are in each part. These parts are defined as *quartiles:* Q_1, the point below which one-fourth of the frequencies fall; Q_2, the point below which one-half of the frequencies fall; Q_3, the point below which three-fourths of the frequencies fall; and Q_4, the point below which all of the frequencies fall. Since the interquartile range (IQR) is the spread of scores which includes the middle one-half of the frequencies, it is the difference between Q_3 and Q_1.

The second quartile, Q_2, is the median. For Mrs. Beasley's test, $Q_2 = 42.9$, and is calculated in the manner illustrated in Table 11.5. The other quartiles are calculated in this same manner except that in the initial calculation one-fourth N is used for Q_1, three-fourths N is used for Q_3, and N is used for Q_4. For Mrs. Beasley's test the quartiles are calculated as follows:

$$Q_4 = 50.5 + 0 \quad = 50.5 \qquad (N = 30).$$

$$Q_3 = 44.5 + \frac{1.5}{3} = 45.0 \qquad (\tfrac{3}{4} N = 22.5),$$

$$Q_2 = 42.5 + \frac{2}{5} = 42.9 \qquad (\tfrac{1}{2} N = 15),$$

$$Q_1 = 39.5 + \frac{.5}{2} = 39.75 \qquad (\tfrac{1}{4} N = 7.5),$$

The interquartile range is equal to 5.25.

$$\text{IQR} = Q_3 - Q_1 = 45.00 - 39.75 = 5.25.$$

Thus the middle half of the frequencies is spread over a distance of 5.25 score-points.

When quartiles are used to describe the variability of a set of scores, the *quartile deviation* is often the value reported. It is one-half of the interquartile range:

$$Q = \frac{Q_3 - Q_1}{2}.$$

The quartile deviation for the distribution of scores for Mrs. Beasley's test is 2.62.

$$Q = \frac{45.00 - 39.75}{2} = \frac{5.25}{2} = 2.62.$$

This method of describing the variability of scores is more stable than the range since it is based on two scores toward the center of the distribution which are more stable than the extreme scores used for determining the range. Furthermore, since the quartile deviation provides an index of the spread of the most typical scores in the distribution, it is more meaningful than the range as a description of the variability of the scores.

Since both the quartiles and median are determined by calculating the score-points below which given proportions of frequencies fall, the quartile deviation and the median are companion measures of variability and central tendency. Since the median always partitions the distribution into two equal parts and since $2Q$ is always the range of scores for the middle 50 percent of the frequencies, these statistics should be used to describe the central tendency and variability of score distributions which are markedly nonsymmetrical.

For Mrs. Beasley's test, these values indicate that the norm is about 43 points and that one-half of the students obtained scores within a spread of 5.25 points in the total of 57 points possible.

Standard Deviation

The measure of variability which reflects all the scores in the distribution is the *standard deviation* (S). It is based on the average of the squared distance of the test scores from the mean. The standard deviation is defined by the formula

$$S = \sqrt{\frac{\Sigma (X - \bar{X})^2}{N}}.$$

Calculation of the standard deviation from this formula is illustrated in Table 11.6.

Table 11.6 Calculation of standard deviation: method 1

X	$X - \bar{X}$	$(X - \bar{X})^2$	Calculation
9	4	16	
7	2	4	$S = \sqrt{\dfrac{\Sigma(X - \bar{X})^2}{N}}$
5	0	0	
3	−2	4	
1	−4	16	
		—	$S = \sqrt{\frac{40}{5}}$
		40	
$\Sigma X = 25, \ \bar{X} = \dfrac{25}{5} = 5$			$S = \sqrt{8} = 2.83$

This statistical concept can be illustrated by using the relation between the length of the side of a square and its area. The length of the side of a square is a distance and the area of the square is the square of this distance. The values in the column "$X - \bar{X}$" of Table 11.6 are the distances of each score from the mean (the highest score is 4 points above the mean, the next score is 2 points above the mean, etc.). The corresponding values in the third column are the squares of these distances, or the areas of squares 4 units, 2 units, 0 units, 2 units, and 4 units, respectively, on a side. The first square has an area of 16 units, the second square of 4 units, and so on. The sum of the areas (or sum of squares) is 40 units. The average area is determined as any mean would be by dividing by the number of scores; in this case, 5 squares. The mean square area is $\frac{40}{5} = 8$ units and the length of the side of the square is $\sqrt{8} = 2.83$ units.

$$\left.\begin{array}{c}\\\\\end{array}\right\}\ 2.83$$

The area of the mean square is called the *variance*. The length of the sides of the mean square is called the *standard deviation*.

$$S = \sqrt{\text{area of mean square}} = \sqrt{\text{variance}}.$$

The variance is used as the measure of variability for most advanced statistical computations. The standard deviation, on the other hand, is used often for descriptive statistical computations.

The standard deviation can be calculated using the formula

$$S = \sqrt{\frac{N\Sigma X^2 - (\Sigma X)^2}{N^2}}.$$

This formula is equivalent to the one used to define the standard deviation, and it usually simplifies computations because it does not require the manipulation of as many difference scores. (The difference scores $X - \bar{X}$ usually contain decimals and are therefore cumbersome to work with.) The calculation of the standard deviation of the five scores presented previously is illustrated in Table 11.7.

The standard deviation can be determined from a frequency distribution. Remembering that multiplication is a shortcut for addition, the scores and the squares of the scores could be multiplied by their respective frequencies and the products added to obtain the sums of the scores and the scores squared. The calculation of the standard deviation from the frequency distribution for Mrs. Beasley's mathematics test (as shown in Table 11.3) is illustrated in Table 11.8.

Several shortcut methods for calculating the standard deviation have been devised, but most of them have proved to be too unreliable for general use. How-

Table 11.7 Calculation of standard deviation: method 2

X	X^2	Calculation
9	81	
7	49	$S = \sqrt{\dfrac{5 \times 165 - (25)^2}{(5)^2}}$
5	25	
3	9	
1	1	$S = \sqrt{\dfrac{825 - 625}{25}}$
—	—	
25	165	
		$S = \sqrt{\dfrac{200}{25}}$
		$S = \sqrt{8} = 2.83$

Table 11.8 Calculation of standard deviation from a frequency distribution

Score (X)	f	fX	fX^2	Calculation
50	1	50	2500	$S = \sqrt{\dfrac{N\Sigma X^2 - (\Sigma X)^2}{N^2}}$
49	2	98	4802	
48	2	96	4608	
47	1	47	2209	
46	0	0	0	$S = \sqrt{\dfrac{30 \times 54853 - (1277)^2}{(30)^2}}$
45	3	135	6075	
44	3	132	5808	
43	5	215	9245	
42	1	42	1764	$S = \sqrt{\dfrac{1645590 - 1630729}{900}}$
41	3	123	5043	
40	2	80	3200	
39	2	78	3042	
38	1	38	1444	$S = \sqrt{\dfrac{14861}{900}}$
37	0	0	0	
36	3	108	3888	
35	1	35	1225	$S = \sqrt{16.512}$
Total		1277	54853	$S = 4.06$

fX = frequency × score
fX^2 = frequency × (score × score) = (frequency × score) × score

ever, the following approximation formula for the standard deviation will yield adequate results for use with classroom tests.[1]

$$S = \frac{\Sigma \text{ highest } 1/6 \text{ of the scores} - \Sigma \text{ lowest } 1/6 \text{ of the scores}}{(1/2) \, N}$$

Table 11.9 illustrates this method of approximation of the standard deviation using a set of 69 scores.

---

[1] Robert L. Lathrop, "A Quick but Accurate Approximation to the Standard Deviation of a Distribution." *Journal of Experimental Education*, **29**, 1961, 319–321.

Table 11.9 Approximation of standard deviation

X	f	f'	f'X		
50	1	1	50		$N = 69$
49	1	1	49		$(\frac{1}{6}) N = 11.5$
48	1	1	48	Σupper $(\frac{1}{6})X = 539.5$	$(\frac{1}{2}) N = 34.5$
47	3	3	141		
46	4	4	184		
45	8	1.5	67.5		
44	9				
43	11			$S = \dfrac{539.5 - 446.0}{34.5} = 2.71$	
42	9				
41	8				
40	7	4.5	180		
39	4	4	156		
38	0	0	0	Σlower $(\frac{1}{6})X = 446$	
37	2	2	74		
36	1	1	36		

This same process could be used to estimate the standard deviation of Mrs. Beasley's 30 mathematics test scores. The process would be as follows (using information presented in Table 11.8):

$$\frac{1}{6}N = \frac{1}{6} \times 30 = 5,$$

$$\frac{1}{2}N = \frac{1}{2} \times 30 = 15,$$

Σ highest 5 scores $= 50 + 49 + 49 + 48 + 48 = 244,$
Σ lowest 5 scores $= 35 + 36 + 36 + 36 + 38 = 181,$

$$S = \frac{244 - 181}{15} = \frac{63}{15} = 4.2.$$

Note that the estimated value of 4.2 differs only .14 point from the actual value of 4.06 (Table 11.8). Yet, the estimated standard deviation is based on only ten scores. When using a larger number of scores, the error will seldom be over 1 or 2 percent (.1 of a point when $S = 5$).

The quartile deviation and the standard deviation are analogous to the mean in that they represent averages. While the mean represents the *average position* in a distribution of scores, Q represents the average distance of Q_1 and Q_3 from the median, and S^2 represents the average squared distance of each score from the mean. However, remember that the *measures of central tendency are points on a score line while Q and S are distances along a score line.*

Just what does a standard deviation of 8 on a test mean? By itself, it does not mean much. But if you know that the standard deviations for the other classes on the same test are less than 5 points, you can begin making meaningful interpretations. (Two distributions with the same means but divergent standard

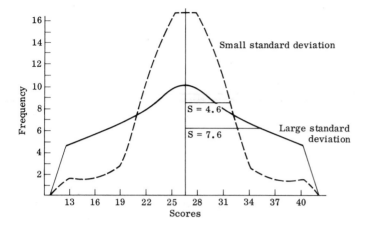

Fig. 11.2. Frequency polygons of distributions with large and small standard deviations

deviations are illustrated in Fig. 11.2.) At this time, you can infer that this class is more heterogeneous than the other classes in the behavior being measured. Extreme differences in variability (as well as means) might indicate the need for employing varying teaching strategies in the different classes.

Measures of variability can be used to reflect the distance of test scores with respect to the mean. If the scores form a symmetric bell-shaped distribution, the standard deviation can aid teachers in making individual test interpretations relative to the group administered the test. If the frequency distribution is *normal*, exact percentages of frequencies within any interval of scores can be determined. Roughly, 68 percent of the frequencies will fall within one standard deviation of the mean; over 95 percent will fall within two standard deviations of the mean; and less than 1 percent will fall more than three standard deviations from the mean (Fig. 11.3). Consequently, the range of scores for the normal distribution is usually considered to be the six standard deviations. Of course, in any symmetrical distribution (or whenever Q_2 is equally distant from Q_1 and Q_3), 50 percent of the frequencies fall within one quartile of the median. However, very few actual score distributions will be symmetrical, much less normal. Therefore, extreme caution must be taken in using these characteristics for test interpretations.

The concept of the normal distribution is overused and often misinterpreted. The normal distribution is a mathematical concept. This use of the term "normal" should not be confused with the psychological use of the term as representing typical or adjustive behavior. The normal curve is a bell-shaped, symmetrical curve which can be mathematically identified according to the relative height of the curve at any given distance from the mean. For example, the height of the curve at one standard deviation away from the mean is .607 of the height of the

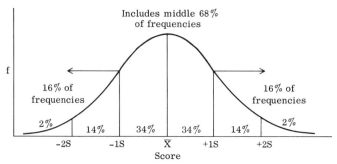

Fig. 11.3. Normal distribution

curve at the mean. If the curve forms a normal distribution and there are 100 frequencies at the mean, there would be 60.7 frequencies (.607 × 100) at the scorepoints one standard deviation above and below the mean.

The height of a normal curve could be similarly determined for any given scorepoint in the distribution. Tables for determining the height of a normal curve at selected points are available in many educational or psychological statistics books. It should be noted that one cannot identify a normal distribution simply by looking at it. A normal distribution can appear extremely peaked or extremely flat, depending on the size of the score units or frequency units used to graph the distribution. Holding the frequency units constant, the distribution can be made to look more and more peaked by continually narrowing the width of the units on the score scale or more and more flat by continually widening the width of the units on the score scale. Similar changes in the appearance of the distribution can be accomplished by manipulating the width of the units on the frequency scale.

It should be re-emphasized that the normal distribution is a mathematical concept, not a psychological one. Many measurement, psychology, and statistics texts suggest that there is an underlying law of normality for psychological traits. This simply is not true. *There is no underlying law of normality*. In fact, an examination of the research literature and a classification of types of distributions found, would result in a large number of classifications. Some of the distributions would be positively skewed, some U-shaped, some J-shaped, some rectangular, and some normal. Moreover, those distributions which would be identified as normal would probably constitute a small minority of all the distributions classified.

One of the reasons that education and psychology students overuse the normal distribution may be that the norm distributions for most standardized achievement and aptitude tests are normal. However, this is an artifact of the scoring and reporting practices of test constructors and does not necessarily reflect the form of the distributions for the traits being measured. The nature of many of the distributions of human traits is unknown in the general population or varies according to the specific population under consideration. Many of our measurement instruments are designed to gather data to describe hypothetical traits such as personality factors, interests, and intelligence. Even with achievement measures, the instrument contains only a sampling of the seemingly infinite number of possible behaviors which could be utilized. Consequently, the actual nature of most of these distributions is unknown and often assumed to be normal. The specification of the shape of any distribution of human traits is meaningless unless the population is also specified.

The foregoing remarks should be regarded as a warning against the over-interpretation of test results on the assumption that the trait is normally distributed. However, the normal curve is a useful concept in that: (1) many educational and psychological traits seem to be *approximately* normally distributed; and (2) *measurement errors are normally distributed.* This characteristic associated with random errors in test scores allows much greater precision than would otherwise be possible in interpreting and determining the reliability of test scores.

Measures of variability can be effectively used for making individual as well as group interpretations. They can be used to reflect distance with respect to the mean. For example, they can be used to compare an individual student's relative achievement on successive tests to spot dramatic shifts in achievement levels (e.g., a student might obtain a score 1.5 standard deviations above the mean on one test and .5 standard deviations below the mean on another for a relative change of 2 standard deviations).

The number of standard deviations the score is from the mean can be determined by subtracting the mean from the score and dividing by the standard deviation. For example, Maximilian obtained a score of 50 on Mrs. Beasley's mathematics test. His score is 7.4 (50–42.6) points above the mean, or 1.8 (7.4/4.06) standard deviations above the mean. When a raw score is converted to the number of standard deviations it is away from the mean, this new score is called a *z-score.*

$$z = \frac{X - \bar{X}}{S}.$$

If all the raw scores for a test are transformed into *z*-scores, the mean of this new distribution of scores will equal 0, and the standard deviation will equal 1. This can be seen in that a 0 *z*-score indicates that the obtained score is 0 standard deviations away from the mean or it is equal to the mean; a $+1.0$ *z*-score indicates that the obtained score is 1 standard deviation above the mean; and a -1.0 *z*-score indicates that the obtained score is 1 standard deviation below the mean (Fig. 11.4).

The range of scores on a test will seldom be more than 6 standard deviations (in *z*-scores, a range from -3.0 to $+3.0$). A good teacher-made test designed to discriminate among students will generally have a range of between 4 and 5 standard deviations, or 2.0 to 2.5 standard deviations on either side of the mean.

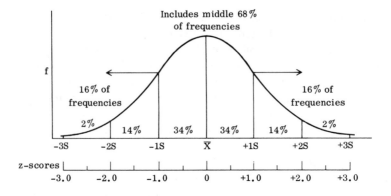

Fig. 11.4. Distribution of z-scores in relation to the normal curve

PERCENT CORRECT SCORES

The *percent correct score* is probably used by classroom teachers more than any other type of converted score. This score is the percent of the items on a test which were answered correctly (or percent of total points obtained). For example, if a student answered 30 questions correctly on a 50-item test, his percent correct score is $\frac{30}{50} \times 100 = 60$.

This type of score has the same basic interpretative value as the raw score. The mean and standard deviation (or median and quartile deviation) must be calculated and used as reference points (as is also true of the raw score distribution).

Nevertheless, students seem to feel comfortable with percent correct scores because they indicate the percent of items answered correctly. In a few instances, this type of score may provide a basis for conclusions concerning a student's performance on the test content. For example, if a valid spelling test is constructed from a defined universe of spelling words and a student achieves a percent correct score of 75, it can be inferred that he knows how to spell correctly about 75 percent of the words in the universe.

STANINE SCORES

Stanine scores form a nine-point score system in which the scores range from 1 to 9, $\bar{X} = 5$, $S = 2$, and the scores form a normal "bell-shaped" distribution. They are determined by sorting the answer sheets into nine piles according to a predetermined distribution. Table 11.10 contains the percent of papers which would be assigned to each of the nine categories to form the theoretical stanine distribution. The lower 4 percent of the scores would be assigned a stanine of 1, the next 7 percent would be assigned a stanine of 2, and so on.

Table 11.10 Stanine distribution

Percent of frequencies at each scorepoint	4%	7%	12%	17%	20%	17%	12%	7%	4%
Stanine Score	1	2	3	4	5	6	7	8	9

For example, if 50 papers are to be assigned stanine scores, the bottom two would be assigned a score of 1 (.04 × 50 = 2). In the classroom situation, the number of papers will not usually fit evenly into a stanine distribution. In the previous example of 50 papers, theoretically $3\frac{1}{2}$ papers would be assigned a score of 2 (.07 × 50 = 3.5). In actuality, the teacher would have to round off the frequency down to 3 or up to 4. Consequently, the distribution of scores obtained by the classroom teacher will only approximate the stanine distribution. Since in most classroom situations the exact stanine distribution cannot be realized, the approximate percentages given in Table 11.11 can be used. These approximate percentages will ease calculation since they are all multiples of 4.

Table 11.11 Approximate stanine distribution

Percent of frequencies at each scorepoint	4%	8%	12%	16%	20%	16%	12%	8%	4%
Stanine Score	1	2	3	4	5	6	7	8	9

Stanine scores lend themselves to the sorting method of scoring essay examinations. The responses can be sorted into the nine predetermined categories. Stanines can be easily interpreted, particularly to parents. The limited range of scores reduces the likelihood of overinterpretation of differences between scores. This limited range of scores also serves as a disadvantage for stanines. The units of measurement are coarse and thus limit the possible discriminations among students. A further disadvantage is that the levels of achievement represented by differences between scores and within scores may not be equal. The difference in achievement represented by the scores 2 and 3 and the difference in achievement represented by the scores 6 and 7 may not be the same. Stanines reflect the ranks of the papers but not the relative levels of achievement. The top paper may be of excellent quality and the second paper of only good quality, but since they received the ranks of 1 and 2, both may be given a stanine score of 9.

CORRELATION

The concepts of reliability and validity were introduced in Chapter 1. These concepts are generally expressed in terms of statistical correlation. Before discussing them further, we must consider the meaning of correlation. In measurements, the intention is often to describe the relation[2] between two variables. The correlation coefficient is a useful tool for describing the "going-togetherness" of two variables because it expresses the relation in terms of a single decimal fraction.

If two variables vary directly, they are said to be *positively* correlated. For example, when students who obtain high scores on an intelligence test tend also to obtain high scores on a reading test and when those who obtain low scores on the intelligence test tend also to obtain low scores on the reading test, the tests are said to be positively correlated.

When two variables vary inversely, they are said to be *negatively* correlated. If the students who obtain high scores on a school adjustment test tend to obtain low scores on an achievement test and if those who obtain low scores on the school adjustment test tend to obtain high scores on the achievement test, the tests are negatively correlated.

If two variables do not vary together, they are said to be *uncorrelated*. Tall students obtain the full range of intelligence test scores and the same is true for students who are short. Thus, height and intelligence test scores are uncorrelated.

The relation between two sets of scores is statistically described by determining the *coefficient of correlation*. There are several methods for calculating coefficients of correlation. The method most common in testing situations is the Pearson product-moment coefficient (r). The correlation coefficient can range from -1.00 to $+1.00$. The coefficient of -1.00 represents a perfect negative correlation; $+1.00$ represents a perfect positive correlation; and 0.00 represents no correlation. These are illustrated in Tables 11.12, 11.13, and 11.14.

Table 11.12 Illustration of $r = +1.00$

Student	Arithmetic test	Reading test
Billy	90	25
Mary	83	23
Jo	71	19
Sam	36	10
Sally	15	4

Table 11.12 represents a perfect positive ($+1.00$) correlation. There is a direct correspondence between the scores: Billy obtained the highest score on both tests; Mary the second highest; etc.

---

[2] The term "relation" is used here in preference to the term relationship, although the latter term is the one commonly used in behavioral measurements and statistics books. Since the term relationship (relation + ship) refers to the quality of the relation, it implies known characteristics (often causal quality) concerning the relation. However, the correlation coefficient does *not* indicate causal quality. Therefore, the term "relation" is used here in the mathematical sense as a ratio, proportion, or something in common by which two quantities can be compared. This use of the term relation is more consistent with the concept of correlation than is the term relationship.

Table 11.13 Illustration of $r = -1.00$

Student	History test	Spelling test
Billy	75	5
Mary	71	8
Jo	63	14
Sam	47	26
Sally	29	32

Table 11.14 Illustration of $r = 0.00$

Student	Science test	English test
Billy	82	45
Mary	73	60
Jo	68	29
Sam	46	66
Sally	41	32

Table 11.13 represents a perfect negative (-1.00) correlation. There is an inverse correspondence between the scores: Billy obtained the highest score on the first test and the lowest score on the second test; Mary, the second highest and next to lowest; etc.

Table 11.14 represents no (0.00) correlation. There is neither direct nor inverse correspondence between scores: Billy obtained the highest score on the first test and the middle score on the second test; Mary, second highest on both tests; etc.

The concept of correlation can also be visualized by using *scattergrams*. The scattergram (Fig. 11.5) is a two-way plot of scores. The first set of scores (variable X) is represented on the horizontal axis and the second set of scores (variable Y) is represented on the vertical axis.

Student	First test	Second test
Billy	5	4
Mary	4	5
Jo	3	2
Sam	2	3
Sally	1	1

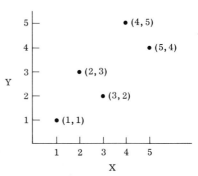

Fig. 11.5. Scattergram plots and scores on two spelling tests for five students

The scores on the X-axis increase from left to right, and the scores on the Y-axis increase from bottom to top. A single point on the scattergram represents a pair of scores (X, Y) determined by the place where the column containing the X-score and the row containing the Y-score intersect. The procedure for plotting is shown in Fig. 11.5. Billy has a score of 5 on the first spelling test (X) and a score of 4 on the second spelling test (Y). The plot of his scores (5, 4) is 5 units across on the horizontal axis and 4 units up on the vertical axis. Mary has a score of 4 on the first test and a score of 5 on the second test. The plot of her scores (4, 5) is 4 units to the right of the vertical axis and 5 units above the horizontal axis. Similarly, the plots of Jo, Sam, and Sally are: (3, 2) (2, 3) and (1, 1), respectively

The plots in Fig. 11.6 represent several selected degrees of relation. If all the plots fall on a straight line, the relation is perfect; if the plots are evenly spread

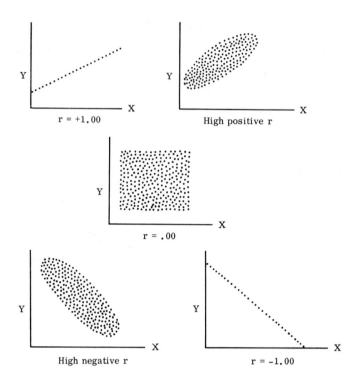

Fig. 11.6. Scattergram plots representing selected correlation coefficients

over the scattergram, there is no relation between the variables. The closer the plots come to forming a straight line the greater the relation exhibited. The plot of the scores in Fig. 11.5 suggests that a moderately high relation exists between scores on the two spelling tests.

The calculation of the *coefficient of correlation* involves the determination of three variances: the variance of the X-scores; the variance of the Y-scores; and the covariance of the two sets of scores. The raw score method for calculating variance, as previously described, can be used to obtain each of these variances.

$$\text{Variance of } X = \frac{N\Sigma X^2 - (\Sigma X)^2}{N^2},$$

$$\text{Variance of } Y = \frac{N\Sigma Y^2 - (\Sigma Y)^2}{N^2},$$

$$\text{Covariance of } X, Y = \frac{N\Sigma XY - (\Sigma X)(\Sigma Y)}{N^2}.$$

The coefficient of correlation is the ratio of the covariance to the geometric average of the individual variances. The formula can be written as follows:

$$r = \frac{\text{Covar } X\,Y}{\sqrt{(\text{Var } X)(\text{Var } Y)}},$$

$$r = \frac{\dfrac{N\Sigma XY - (\Sigma X)(\Sigma Y)}{N^2}}{\sqrt{\left(\dfrac{N\Sigma X^2 - (\Sigma X)^2}{N^2}\right)\left(\dfrac{N\Sigma Y^2 - (\Sigma Y)^2}{N^2}\right)}}.$$

The denominator of this equation contains $1/N^2$ within both bracketed terms; the square root of the natural square is $1/N^2$. Thus, $1/N^2$ appears in both the numerator and the denominator and can be divided out. The simplified equation for the correlation coefficient is:

$$r = \frac{N\Sigma X^2 - (\Sigma X)(\Sigma Y)}{\sqrt{[N\Sigma X^2 - (\Sigma X)^2][N\Sigma Y^2 - (\Sigma Y)^2]}}.$$

Calculation of the coefficient of correlation is illustrated in Table 11.15. The specific values needed in order to use this formula are: the sum of the test scores

Table 11.15 Calculation of Pearson Product-Moment Correlation Coefficient

Student	X	Y	X^2	Y^2	XY	Calculation
1	5	7	25	49	35	
2	9	9	81	81	81	
3	10	9	100	81	90	
4	7	8	49	64	56	
5	2	4	4	16	8	
6	5	9	25	81	45	
7	7	6	49	36	42	
8	2	1	4	1	2	
9	1	1	1	1	1	
10	6	8	36	64	48	
	$\Sigma 54$	62	374	474	408	

$$r = \frac{N\Sigma XY - (\Sigma X)(\Sigma Y)}{\sqrt{[N\Sigma X^2 - (\Sigma X)^2][N\Sigma Y^2 - (\Sigma Y)^2]}}$$

$$= \frac{10\,(408) - (54)\,(62)}{\sqrt{[10(374) - (54)^2][10(474) - (62)^2]}}$$

$$= \frac{4080 - 3348}{\sqrt{[3740 - 2916][4740 - 3844]}}$$

$$= \frac{+732}{\sqrt{(824) \times (896)}} = \frac{+732}{\sqrt{738304}}$$

$$= \frac{+732}{859.2} = +.852$$

PLOTS OF X, Y

(ΣX and ΣY); the sum of the squared test scores (ΣX^2 and ΣY^2); the sum of the products of the test scores (ΣXY); and the number of test scores. To simplify, only 10 pairs of scores are used in the illustration. Usually, correlations are not calculated with less than 30 cases. Below this number, the correlation coefficient tends to be unstable.

MARKING AND REPORTING

One of the duties of the teacher is to inform the student, his parents, and the school administrators of the student's progress toward the goals of the educational program. There are two general procedures for reporting students' evaluations: (1) written reports, and (2) standard quantitative-qualitative indices.

The Informal Letter

Written reports usually take the form of personal letters written to students' parents. The *informal letter* can be used to report pupil progress. This letter can be individualized and personalized to convey effectively to parents their child's strengths and weaknesses. The child's progress toward the mastery of skills can be spelled out and his interpersonal relations with the other children can be communicated. In addition, careful preparation of these letters can aid the teacher in establishing rapport with parents, and effective letters can be a good beginning for teacher-parent conferences.

The teacher should present the information contained in the informal letter as objectively as possible, maintaining an air of individuality. Exact scores (IQ's, performance test scores, etc.) should not be reported in the letter. Many of the recipients of these reports would not know how to interpret them. What would a test score of 25 or even an IQ of 125 mean to most parents? The interpretations made of these scores would likely be based on incomplete data or misinformation. Furthermore, most sets of test scores are not sufficiently reliable to allow *highly specific*, individual reporting.

An informal letter should be relatively short. It should indicate a child's strengths and weaknesses with brief explanations of them. If problems arise, making it impossible to maintain brevity, then a teacher-parent conference may be in order. In this situation, the letter should indicate the general nature of the problem and offer the parent an invitation to a conference to consider the problem in greater depth.

Quantitative–Qualitative Indices

Quantitative–qualitative indices usually take the form of letter or number marks. Many somewhat standard marking systems have been developed. Several of these systems are illustrated in Table 11.16.

The similarities and differences among the systems can be readily noted from the table. The qualitative descriptions corresponding to the letter and number marks are presented in the left-hand column of the table.

The use of letter marks presupposes that they are valid. In order for this criterion to be realized, marks must relate levels of performance to some important

Table 11.16 Examples of marking systems

Qualitative description	Nine-point number scale	Modified conventional letter scale	Seven-point number scale	Conventional five-letter scale	Conventional percent scale	Four-category, five-letter scale	Two-category letter scale
Excellent	9	A	1	A	90+	H	P
	8	$\frac{A+B}{2}$	2			S	
Good	7	B	3	B	80–89	G	
	6	$\frac{B+C}{2}$					
Fair (or average)	5	C	4	C	70–79		
	4	$\frac{C+D}{2}$				P	
Poor	3	D	5	D	60–69		
	2	$\frac{D+F}{2}$	6				
Unsatisfactory	1	F	7	F	59–	X	F

behaviors and should be translatable in terms of these behaviors. This signifies that the behaviors must be defined and that they must not consist of subbehaviors which are independent and, for some individuals, inversely related, thus confounding interpretation of evaluations.

Teachers' evaluations cannot reflect all possible student behaviors. For a summary mark to be interpretable it must represent selected important behaviors. These behaviors should not be so inclusive as to embrace all possible behavioral areas. Rather, they should include those areas which are directly related to the domain being studied. In this manner, marks can be interpreted according to the appropriate measurement objectives for a course, even though the total learning objectives may be even more inclusive.

The improvement in the validity, reliability, and comparability of teachers' marks is essential to the improvement of pupil evaluation. Assuming that the measurements collected are otherwise valid and properly combined into composite scores, the following guidelines are offered to help teachers avoid foppery in their classroom evaluation.[3]

1. Clarify behavioral objectives.
2. Differentiate between teaching objectives and evaluation objectives.
3. Predetermine a realistic and somewhat flexible standard for evaluation.
4. Report your judgment as to a student's achievement in the content area *per se*; other judgments should be reported, but not as part of the letter grade.

The marking systems presented in Table 11.16 can be grouped according to two major classifications: *absolute* and *relative systems*.

Absolute marking systems are those where absolute qualities in learning are preassigned to each marking category. The preassignment of quality often takes the form of absolute percentages of items correct on classroom exams. Percentage scales (such as 90 percent correct for an "A," 80 percent to 89 percent for a "B," 70 percent for a "C," and so on) are still used in many schools. This method appeals to academically oriented teachers, because it supposedly indicates only the student's proficiency in the area of instruction and does not reflect his relative standing in a group of students.

The fallacies of an absolute marking system should be somewhat obvious. The fixed percentage method of assigning marks is based on the underlying assumption that the measurement instruments used are infallible; there is no room for error. If the test is difficult, it is generally assumed that the students have achieved poorly, or if the test is easy, that the students have achieved well. However, such assumptions are often unwarranted, because the relative difficulty of a test is as much an artifact of test construction as of achievement level of the students. Measurement instruments may be too difficult because the teacher expects too much from the level of students he is teaching. For example, it is quite common for the "new" assistant professor to expect college freshmen to be doing graduate level work; the "new" high school teacher to expect students to be doing

[3] Jon C. Marshall, "Evaluation: Does it Mean Anything?" *The Clearing House*, **42**, 1968, 535–538.

college level work; or the "new" elementary teacher to expect students to be doing junior high school work. The beginning teacher may be overly demanding in evaluating students' achievements. A teacher's judgments of the levels of quality of students' learning may periodically change. This inconsistency in expectations can be seen among different schools. Many universities which have highly selective admittance requirements have as high a "flunk out rate" as similar institutions which do not have selective admission. However, those teachers who support an absolute marking system have to assume that all persons knowledgeable in an area would define varying degrees of quality in the same way. This system of marking would seem illogical since the basic assumptions—(1) infallibility of measurement, (2) agreement among specialists as to the levels of quality, and, (3) consistency of expectations of students—cannot be supported.

Relative marking systems are those in which the students are assigned grades according to their relative positions in a group. One of the most common methods is to assume that the classroom measurements should form a normal distribution with the mean being equal to a C. The following distribution is the one usually recommended for the assignment of marks using this system: A—top 7 percent of the students, B—next 24 percent of the students, C—middle 38 percent of the students, D—next 24 percent of the students, and F—lowest 7 percent of the students. In a classroom of 30 students, using this procedure, the assignment of marks would be: two A's, seven B's, twelve C's, seven D's, and two F's.

A similar system uses the mean and standard deviation as criteria for assigning marks. In this system, the marks are assigned according to the distance the score is from the mean. One method is to assign the marks as follows: A—students with scores 1.58 or more standard deviations above the mean; B—students with scores between .50 and 1.57 standard deviations above the mean; C—students with scores between .49 standard deviation above the mean and .49 standard deviation below the mean; D—students with scores between .50 and 1.57 standard deviations below the mean; and F—students with scores 1.58 or more standard deviations below the mean. This procedure would be equivalent to that of assigning 7 percent each to A's and F's, 24 percent each to B's and D's, and 38 percent to C's, when the distribution of scores is normal. However, in actual classroom practice this method will, in general, yield fewer A's and F's and more middle marks than will the percentage method because the results of classroom tests usually form distributions which are only 4 or 5 standard deviations wide instead of the 6+ standard deviations for the normal distribution.

The use of the same standard curve for all classes does not adequately improve the assignment of marks. If the class or school is largely composed of high-ability students, the average and average-plus students are penalized since they are compared with "high-ability" groups. In another class or school these same students might be in the upper portion of the group and receive top marks. The use of the standard deviation in determining cutting points for assigning marks does allow some flexibility in that the middle C can be adjusted by shifting the point of reference (generally the mean score) up or down in the marking scale relative to the teacher's perception of the achievement level of the typical student in the class.

The purpose of the preceding discussion is to help the classroom teacher avoid some of the many pitfalls when assigning marks. A paper written by Scannell[4] and reported by Adams[5] presents a proposal for a method of making marks more meaningful. The interested teacher is referred to these sources.

COMBINING MEASURES

Course evaluations are made on the basis of such material as classroom tests, papers, and reports. In order to determine a common base for comparison, the separate measures must be combined before final marks are assigned.

Composite scores for most teachers will be made up of the tests administered during the marking period. The separate tests can be combined in a number of ways, but this poses the problem of choosing the best method of pooling scores.

Teachers usually indicate to students the relative weight for each test. For example, a teacher may state that the final exam will count double that of any one unit test. Without further consideration, the teacher may double the scores on the final exam and add them to the sums of the scores on the unit tests. However, this procedure does not necessarily yield the desired combination of scores. In fact, it may yield results which are very different from those desired by the teacher.

Various methods of weighting test scores have been tried: equating means, equating numbers of items, making variabilities equal, or multiplying by pre-assigned relative weights. Most of these methods have an effect similar to that of multiplying the scores by random numbers; that is, they may increase or decrease the disparity among the tests. The characteristic which will affect a test's weight relative to other tests is the test variability. If the standard deviations of two tests are 10 and 5, respectively, the first test will count twice as much as the second one in the composite. This weighting of the two tests is independent of the number of items in them and of their means.

When combining several tests, the determination of the best weights is not as easy as equating standard deviations. The general procedure would necessitate the determination of the interrelations (i.e. intercorrelations) among all the tests. The time required to do this is so great as to make it prohibitive for most classroom teachers. Therefore, the authors recommend that the individual standard deviations be checked to ensure that no one measure overshadows the rest. For example, suppose that the points given for homework amount to a sizable sum. The standard deviation of these points might be very large, say 100 points, as compared to a unit test with a standard deviation of about 5 to 10 points. Without adjustment, when directly combined with tests to form a composite, the homework points could count for more than all the other measures put together. This could be

---

[4] Dale P. Scannell, "Making Grades Meaningful: a Proposal," *University of Kansas Bulletin of Education*, **15,** 1960, 26–35.
[5] Georgia Sachs Adams, *Measurement and Evaluation in Education, Psychology and Guidance*, Holt, Rinehart and Winston, Chicago, 1964, Chapter 16.

guarded against by dividing every student's homework points by 10, thus decreasing the standard deviation to 10.

After the standard deviations have been equalized, the scores can be further manipulated to reflect any relative weight desired by the teacher. If one test is to count double, it would be an easy matter to multiply each score by two before adding them to the other ones.

Marks assigned to individual tests should not be averaged to form the composite. One weakness of this procedure is the continual regression of the marks toward the center mark. If a large number of tests are administered, all "A's" and "F's" may drop out because of the interchanges of scores on tests. Suppose that on three tests a student obtains an A, C, and A, respectively. Using a four-point numbering system would give him $4 + 2 + 4 = 10$ grade points for an average of 3.3, a letter mark of B. However, this student may be the best in the class; he may have obtained points for top A's and a high C. Thus, in terms of letters, if his score is the highest, it follows that averaging letter marks would result in *zero* A's in the class.

Another serious problem of averaging marks is the grossness of the scales. On a given test, the B-range may run from 40 scorepoints to 50 scorepoints. By averaging marks, the 50 would be treated as being equal to the 40 and quite different from the 51; the scores in an interval of 11 scorepoints would be treated equally while scores only one point apart would be treated very differently.

SUMMARY

Several methods of describing test scores have been presented in this chapter. The first step in examining test scores is to organize them into a meaningful display. This can be accomplished by developing a *frequency distribution*, which is a record of the number of times each score occurs.

One aspect of describing test scores is to determine the central location of the distribution along a continuum. The two methods generally used to determine the norm are the mean and median. Both are measures of central tendency, but each describes this location in a different way. The *mean* is the arithmetic average of the scores; the *median* is the scorepoint below which half of the frequencies fall. The mean is usually the preferred measure because, being based on all the scores, it is the most stable, and can be used in other statistical computations. However, if the distribution departs markedly from being a normal "bell-shaped" one, the median is generally preferred because it is more likely to reflect the "typical" scores of the distribution.

Another aspect of describing test scores is to determine the *variability* of the distribution. The three methods generally used for this are the standard deviation, quartile deviation, and range. All three are indices of the dispersion of the scores, but each describes this variability differently. The *standard deviation* is based on the average square of the differences between each score and the mean. This statistic utilizes in its computation all the scores in the distribution. The *quartile deviation* is based on two scorepoints in the distribution—the point below which

25 percent of the frequencies fall and the one below which 75 percent of them fall. The *interquartile range* is the difference between these scorepoints and is the spread of the middle 50 percent of the frequencies. The quartile deviation is one-half the interquartile range. The *range*, like the quartile deviation, is based on two score-points—the highest score and the lowest score.

The standard deviation is usually the preferred index of variability. It is the most stable measure because it is based on all the scores; it can be used for additional statistical computations; and it is the companion measure of the mean. If the distribution departs markedly from a normal "bell-shaped" curve, the quartile deviation is usually preferred because $2Q$ (interquartile range) always represents the spread of the middle 50 percent of the frequencies, and it is the companion measure of the median. The range is the least preferred index since it represents only the distance between the two extreme scores.

z-scores are derived scores which can be used to express students' test scores in terms of the number of standard deviations the test scores are away from the mean.

Percent correct scores are derived scores which express students' test scores as the percent of items they answered correctly. These scores are usually interpreted in the same manner as raw scores.

Stanines are derived scores which are determined by sorting test papers into predetermined categories with score values from 1 to 9. The mean stanine is 5 and the standard deviation is 2. Stanines are particularly useful for scoring essays, using the sorting method.

The relation between two variables can be described in gross terms such as a high positive correlation, high negative correlation, or a low correlation. The Pearson product-moment correlation coefficient (r) is an excellent method for determining the degree of relation between two variables. However, this index of relation reflects only the degree of association between the variables and *not* cause and effect.

The correlation coefficient is a mathematical index of the relation between two variables. This index is based on the ratio of the covariance of two variables and the geometric mean of the variances of each variable. The size of the coefficient indicates the degree of relation between the two variables, with ± 1.00 being a perfect relation and 0.00 being no relation. The sign of the coefficient indicates the direction of the relation, with $+$ reflecting a direct relation and $-$ reflecting an inverse relation.

The data collected on students should be meaningfully translated and reported. This is generally done using either an *informal letter* or *quantitative/qualitative indices*. The informal letter is usually preferable at the primary grades and the quantitative/qualitative indices above that level.

Quantitative/qualitative indices usually take the form of letter or number marks. Many somewhat standard systems have been developed: nine-point number scale; modified conventional letter scale; seven-point number scale;

conventional five-letter scale; conventional percent scale; four-category, five-letter scale; and two-category letter scale.

When combining measures, the *test scores* should be added to form the composite. This is preferred to the combining of letter marks. The weight of a single test in the composite is a function of its variability of scores. Therefore, the standard deviations should be equalized (by multiplying or dividing each score by the appropriate constant) when the tests are to count equally in the composite.

PROBLEMS

Use the following test scores for Problems 1–8.

29	35	37	36	33
32	33	36	32	30
30	32	34	28	31
31	35	33	32	27
33	34	30	33	34

1. Set up the frequency distribution for the above scores.
2. Calculate the mean of the above scores:
   a) from raw scores
   b) from the frequency distribution
3. Determine the median score from the frequency distribution.
4. Determine the range of scores.
5. Determine each of the following values:
   (a) Q_1 (b) Q_2 (c) Q_3 (d) Q_4 (e) interquartile range   (f) quartile deviation
6. Determine the standard deviation using:
   a) raw scores from frequency distribution
   b) the approximation procedure
7. The range of scores includes how many standard deviations?
8. What is the z-score corresponding to 30?
9. Which measure of central tendency should be used to describe the following scores: 50, 41, 39, 38, 37? Why?
10. If a quick and fairly reliable calculation is needed, which measure of central tendency would probably be used?
11. Listed below are spelling test and reading test scores for 10 students:

Students	A	B	C	D	E	F	G	H	I	J
Spelling	8	10	6	1	7	3	4	6	4	1
Reading	14	16	9	4	14	7	10	4	6	6

   a) Calculate the variance of the spelling scores.
   b) Calculate the variance of the reading scores.
   c) Calculate the covariance of the spelling and reading scores.

d) Determine the correlation between spelling and reading from the two variances and covariance.

e) Determine the correlation between spelling and reading from the raw scores.

f) Interpret the obtained coefficient of correlation.

12. Compare the strengths, weaknesses, and assumptions of absolute and relative marking systems.

ANSWERS TO PROBLEMS

1.

Score	37	36	35	34	33	32	31	30	29	28	27
f	1	2	2	3	5	4	2	3	1	1	1

2. (a) 32.4, (b) 32.4.   3. 32.6.   4. 10.

5. (a) 30.62, (b) 32.6, (c) 34.08, (d) 37.5, (e) 3.46, (f) 1.73.   6. (a) 2.47, (b) 2.47.

7. Approximately 4.1.   8. −0.98.   11. (a) 7.8, (b) 17.2, (c) 9.3, (d) .80, (e) .80.

LIST OF SYMBOLS USED IN CHAPTER 11

Symbols	Verbal Equivalents
cf	Cumulative frequency
f	Frequency
fX	Frequency of occurrence times the score value
fX^2	Frequency of occurrence times the square of the score value
IQR	Interquartile range
L	Lowest score in a set of test scores
$M, \bar{X}$	Mean, arithmetic average
N	Number of examinees
Q	Quartile deviation; semi-interquartile range
Q_1	First quartile
Q_2	Second quartile
Q_3	Third quartile
Q_4	Fourth quartile
r	Pearson product-moment correlation coefficient
X	Score
X^2	Score squared; midpoint squared
z	z-score
Σ	Sum of; add the indicated scores
ΣX	Sum of the scores
ΣfX	Sum of the frequencies times scores
ΣX^2	Sum of the squared scores
ΣfX^2	Sum of the frequencies times squared scores
$(\Sigma X)^2$	Sum of the scores, quantity squared
$(\Sigma fX)^2$	Sum of the frequencies times scores, quantity squared
ΣXY	Sum of products

SUGGESTED READING

Blommers, Paul, and E. F. Lindquist, *Elementary Statistical Methods in Psychology and Education*. Houghton Mifflin, Boston, 1960.

Chase, Clinton I., *Elementary Statistical Procedures*. McGraw-Hill Book Company, New York, 1967.

Clark, Robert B., Arthur P. Coladarci, and John Gaffrey, *Statistical Reasoning and Procedures*. Charles E. Merrill Books, Columbus, O., 1965.

Ebel, Robert L., *Measuring Educational Achievement*. Prentice-Hall, Englewood Cliffs, N.J., 1965, Chapters 8 and 13.

Green, John A., *Teacher-Made Tests*. Harper and Row, Evanston, Ill., 1963, Chapter 8.

Lien, Arnold J., *Measurement and Evaluation of Learning*. William C. Brown Company, Dubuque, Ia., 1967, Chapter 9.

Lindvall, C. M., *Measuring Pupil Achievement and Aptitude*. Harcourt, Brace, and World, Chicago, 1967, Chapter 9.

Nunnally, Jum C., *Educational Measurement and Evaluation*. McGraw-Hill Book Company, New York, 1964, Chapter 7.

Remmers, H. H., N. L. Gage, and J. Francis Rummel, *A Practical Introduction to Measurement and Evaluation*. Harper and Brothers, New York, 1960, Chapter 9.

Thorndike, Robert L., and Elizabeth Hagen, *Measurement and Evaluation in Psychology and Education* (3rd ed.). John Wiley and Sons, New York, 1969, Chapter 17.

Walker, Helen M., and Joseph Lev, *Elementary Statistical Methods* (2nd ed.). Holt, Rinehart, and Winston, New York, 1958.

PART IV

TEST QUALITY
ASSESSMENT AND IMPROVEMENT

Chapter 12

Reliability and Validity

Before a teacher, counselor, or administrator uses test information, he should be confident that the test actually measures something and that what it measures is relevant to the use he intends to make of the information. To be relevant, a test must first consistently measure something. Therefore, a test user must examine both the consistency and relevancy of an instrument before he uses the resulting information.

Consistency of test results refers to the reproducibility of test scores. A test is internally consistent when students who obtain high scores on one set of items also obtain high scores on other sets of presumably equivalent items, and those who obtain low scores on one set of items also obtain low scores on other sets of items. Similarly, a test is consistent over a period of time when students retain their same relative ranks on two separate testings with the same instrument. The degree of consistency among test scores is called *reliability* (r_{11}).

A test may be highly reliable and yet not be relevant to the behavior one is attempting to measure. An English grammar test, for example, may be reliable but would not be relevant for testing mathematical ability. Similarly, a history teacher could not use the results of a mathematics definition test to determine the problem-solving ability of his students, no matter how reliable it might be.

A classroom test should be both consistent and relevant. This combination of characteristics is called *validity*.

ESTIMATING RELIABILITY

To understand the concept of reliability, consider a hypothetical pool of all possible items that might be written to measure whatever is to be measured. If we were to carefully select two sets of items from this item pool in order to obtain equal test statistics, the degree of correctness of the responses of a student on one set should be similar to the degree of correctness of his responses on the other set of items. If we were to administer these two tests to a group of students, we could compute a coefficient of correlation between the two sets of scores. This calculated value is called the *reliability coefficient* (r_{11}) of the test.

Errors of Measurement

If it were possible to construct two tests from the hypothetical item pool with identical test statistics, the coefficient of reliability would not be 1.00. Errors of measurement would be present and would contribute to the failure to achieve perfect agreement between the two sets of scores. The function of the coefficient of reliability is to express the confidence which one may have in the consistency of the scores. Consequently, it should be influenced by all of the possible sources of error which can contribute to a test's lack of reliability.

What are the sources of error which can contribute to a reduction in test reliability? First, error may arise from the failure of the instrument to reflect adequately this hypothetical pool of items—such as sampling errors in the instrument.

A second source of error may be in the test administration. On the day that the test was administered the room may have been hot or noisy; there may have been distractions outside the classroom; or the test instructions may not have been followed. If the test were readministered on a different day, under different circumstances, the results might be different. Variations in the testing environment contribute to the lack of consistency in test scores.

A third source of error is found within the examinee. He may have been ill or recovering from illness; he may have been anxious; or he may have been distracted by family plans for the weekend. In these situations, his score would not be a good indicator of what he might be expected to do when feeling differently. These variations in the mood and physical well-being of the individual contribute to the failure of test data to be perfectly reliable.

A final source of error is found in the variable being measured. The variable itself may not be consistent. Theoretically, if the variable is consistent, the individual who is poor in one aspect will be poor in all aspects. However, this is not always true. Consequently, the measuring instrument constructed to assess this variable may lack reliability as a result of inconsistency in the variable.

There are several different methods of determining reliability, each reflecting a different emphasis on sources of error in measurement. This results in varying estimates of the actual test reliability, depending on the methods of estimation used. However, the several sources of error will be present and operating to reduce the consistency of the test scores, whether or not the index calculated reflects them.

Internal Consistency Method

This method describes the consistency with which students react to the items in the test. If the test is reliable, students who respond correctly to one set of items in the test will tend to respond correctly to other equivalent sets of items in it.

Odd-even formula. This measure of reliability is usually determined by use of the odd-even method of calculation. The test is divided into two subtests; one subtest consists of the odd-numbered items and the other subtest consists of the even-numbered items. Thus, every student obtains two scores: the number of odd-numbered items answered correctly and the number of even-numbered items answered correctly. The reliability of the half-test ($r_{\frac{1}{2}\frac{1}{2}}$) is determined by calculating the Pearson product-moment correlation between these subtests. Since this reliability coefficient corresponds to the subtests (one-half the total test) rather than the actual test, it is corrected for total test length by means of the Spearman-Brown Prophecy formula:

$$r_{tt} = \frac{2r_{\frac{1}{2}\frac{1}{2}}}{1 + r_{\frac{1}{2}\frac{1}{2}}}.$$

The reliability coefficient is an indicator of the confidence a teacher can place in a set of test results. If the calculation of the test reliability yields a high positive correlation coefficient, the teacher can be reasonably confident that a student's score on the test is a consistent measure of the behavior elicited by the test. However, if the correlation coefficient is near zero, it is likely that the score represents little more than a chance result. It is difficult to say how large a coefficient of reliability should be—other than as high as possible. We believe that classroom tests with split-half reliabilities of at least $+.60$ can be constructed by concerned teachers. For most standardized test batteries, the reliability coefficients are greater than $+.90$.

Kuder-Richardson Formula 21. Determination of the odd-even correlation coefficient of a large number of students will take more time than most teachers have available. The Kuder-Richardson Formula 21 offers a quicker method of calculation. The coefficient obtained with this method will usually be an underestimate of the "true" internal consistency correlation (that is, it is a "lower bound"), but the time saved in its calculation makes it worthwhile to consider here. The formula[1] is:

$$r_{\text{KR21}} = \frac{k}{k-1}\left[1 - \frac{\bar{X}(k - \bar{X})}{kS^2}\right],$$

where k = number of items, $\bar{X}$ = mean score, S = standard deviation.

For example, for a 50-item algebra test with a mean of 30 and standard deviation of 5, the calculation is as follows:

$$r_{\text{KR21}} = \left(\frac{50}{50-1}\right)\left(1 - \frac{30\,(50 - 30)}{50(5)^2}\right) = \left(\frac{50}{49}\right)\left(1 - \frac{30\,(20)}{50\,(25)}\right)$$

$$r_{\text{KR21}} = (1.02)\,(1 - .48) = (1.02)\,(.52) = +.53.$$

This short-cut procedure should be used only with objective tests in which each item is scored $+1$ and 0 and in which only one type of item is used. Parenthetically speaking, a reliability coefficient of .53 indicates that the test scores are barely worth recording and should not be used for critical decisions unless it is impossible to obtain better information.

---

[1] Appendix D contains a chart for estimating internal consistency reliability using Kuder-Richardson Formula 21.

Generalized internal consistency equation. When endeavoring to estimate the reliability of tests appearing in some item formats (for example, essay tests), odd-even and KR21 methods cannot be used. However, the following more generalized equation for calculating the internal consistency reliability coefficient of a test, from which KR21 may be derived, can be used:

$$r_{kk} = \frac{k}{k-1}\left[1 - \frac{\Sigma S_j^2}{S_X^2}\right],$$

where k = number of test items,

S_j^2 = variance of scores on an item,

S_X^2 = variance of total scores for the set of papers.

The derivation and a thorough explanation of this equation, which under special restriction is called the Kuder-Richardson Formula 20 (KR20), are presented by Nunnally.[2]

This equation presented above cannot be readily used in determining the reliability of a test. However, the following equation can be derived from it without the addition of a single assumption and can be used with fair efficiency in calculating test reliability.

$$r_{kk} = \frac{k}{k-1}\left(1 - \frac{n\Sigma X_{ji}^2 - \Sigma X_{j\cdot}^2}{n\Sigma X_{\cdot i}^2 - X_{\cdot\cdot}^2}\right)$$

where k = the number of items,

n = the number of examinees,

X_{ji}^2 = the square of the score on item j by examinee i,

ΣX_{ji}^2 = the sum of the squares of each item score by each individual,

$X_{j\cdot}^2$ = the square of the sum of the scores received by all examinees on item j,

$\Sigma X_{j\cdot}^2$ = the sum for all items of the square of the sum of the scores received by all examinees on each item,

$X_{\cdot i}^2$ = the square of the total score received by examinee i,

$\Sigma X_{\cdot i}^2$ = the sum of the squares of the total scores received by all examinees,

$X_{\cdot\cdot}^2$ = the square of the sum of all the scores received.

Nevertheless, if either the KR21 or odd-even method is appropriate, it would be better to use one of them because both are easier to employ than the generalized equation described in this section.

The following schematic illustration (Table 12.1) should help clarify the meaning of the various components of this equation. This schematic representation is based on five examinees and four test items. In most situations, there will be

---

2 The equation given by Nunnally in Jum C. Nunnally: *Psychometric Theory*, McGraw-Hill Book Co., New York, 1967, p. 196, appears to be slightly different because of subscript variations.

many more examinees; for each examinee there will be a row. Also, the number of columns under Test Item depends on the number of questions on the examination; if six questions, there will be six columns.

Table 12.1 Schematic illustration for internal consistency equation

Examinee	Test item (j)				$X_{\cdot i}$
(i)	X_1	X_2	X_3	X_4	
a	X_{1a}	X_{2a}	X_{3a}	X_{4a}	$X_{\cdot a}$
b	X_{1b}	X_{2b}	X_{3b}	X_{4b}	$X_{\cdot b}$
c	X_{1c}	X_{2c}	X_{3c}	X_{4c}	$X_{\cdot c}$
d	X_{1d}	X_{2d}	X_{3d}	X_{4d}	$X_{\cdot d}$
e	X_{1e}	X_{2e}	X_{3e}	X_{4e}	$X_{\cdot e}$
Total	$X_{1\cdot}$	$X_{2\cdot}$	$X_{3\cdot}$	$X_{4\cdot}$	$X_{\cdot\cdot}$

This approach to the estimation of test reliability is illustrated in Tables 12.2 and 12.3. The values shown in Table 12.2 are the scores received by five examinees on four essay questions. Thus, Charlie had a score of 3 on the first question, a score of 4 on the second question, a score of 6 on the third, and a score of 2 on the last question, giving him a total score of 15.

The scores for any one item can also be found in Table 12.2. Thus, for item four, the scores are 4 for Adam, 2 for Barbara, 2 for Charlie, 0 for Dee, and 1 for Ellen, giving a total of 9 points assigned to question four. Finally, the square of each score for a test question is indicated in the table. Thus, for item four, the square of the scores are 16 for Adam, 4 for Barbara, 4 for Charlie, 0 for Dee, and 1 for Ellen, giving the total of the squares of the scores as 25.

The calculation of the reliability coefficient for the test scores in Table 12.2 is shown in Table 12.3. Since there are four questions and five examinees, k and n are 4 and 5, respectively. In order to obtain r_{kk} it is necessary to add together the square of each score for all students on all questions (ΣX_{ji}^2), and this value is 313. Also needed is $\Sigma X_{j\cdot}^2$ (the sum of the squares of the total score assigned to each item), and this value is 1331. Furthermore, it is necessary to obtain the sum of the square of the score received by each student on the test ($\Sigma X_{\cdot i}^2$), and this value is 1013. Finally, the square of the total of all the scores assigned ($X_{\cdot\cdot}^2$) is needed and this value is 4761. The calculations of $\Sigma X_{ji}^2, \Sigma X_{j\cdot}^2, \Sigma X_{\cdot i}^2$, and $X_{\cdot\cdot}^2$ are shown in Table 12.3. The reliability of this test example is .31.

Test-Retest Method

This method describes the consistency of examinees' scores on two administrations of the same test. The time lapse permitted between the two administrations of the test depends upon the intended use of the test. The longer the time lapse, the lower the expected reliability coefficient since more irrelevant factors are likely to occur between the two administrations and affect an examinee's performance.

The test-retest method of determining reliability is more appropriate for speed tests than the internal consistency method. The fact that many students will not

Table 12.2 Estimating test reliability on an essay examination; test data

Examinee	Test Question				$X_{.i}$ (Test Score)
	X_1 X_1^2	X_2 X_2^2	X_3 X_3^2	X_4 X_4^2	
Adam	1	2	3	4	$10 = X_{.a}$
	1	4	9	16	
Barbara	2	3	5	2	$12 = X_{.b}$
	4	9	25	4	
Charlie	3	4	6	2	$15 = X_{.c}$
	9	16	36	4	
Dee	4	5	3	0	$12 = X_{.d}$
	16	25	9	0	
Ellen	5	6	8	1	$20 = X_{.e}$
	25	36	64	1	
$X_{j.}$	15	20	25	9	69 $X_{..}$
X_{ji}^2	55	90	143	25	
	$X_{1.}$ ΣX_{1i}^2	$X_{2.}$ ΣX_{2i}^2	$X_{3.}$ ΣX_{3i}^2	$X_{4.}$ ΣX_{4i}^2	

Table 12.3 Estimating test reliability on an essay examination; calculation

$\Sigma X_{ji}^2 = \Sigma X_{1i}^2 + \Sigma X_{2i}^2 + \Sigma X_{3i}^2 + \Sigma X_{4i}^2 = 55 + 90 + 143 + 25 = 313,$

$\Sigma X_{j.}^2 = X_{1.}^2 + X_{2.}^2 + X_{3.}^2 + X_{4.}^2 = 15^2 + 20^2 + 25^2 + 9^2 = 1331,$

$\Sigma X_{.i}^2 = X_{.a}^2 + X_{.b}^2 + X_{.c}^2 + X_{.d}^2 + X_{.e}^2 = 10^2 + 12^2 + 15^2 + 12^2 + 20^2 = 1013,$

$X_{..}^2 = 69^2 = 4761.$

$k = 4, n = 5$

$$r_{kk} = \frac{k}{k-1}\left(1 - \frac{n \Sigma X_{ji}^2 - \Sigma X_{j.}^2}{n \Sigma X_{.i}^2 - \Sigma X_{..}^2}\right) = \frac{4}{3}\left(1 - \frac{5(313) - 1331}{5(1013) - 4761}\right)$$

$$r_{kk} = \frac{4}{3}\left(1 - \frac{234}{304}\right) = \frac{4}{3}(1 - .77)$$

$$r_{kk} = .31$$

finish the test and, with perfect consistency, will miss all those items not reached will inflate the internal consistency coefficient.

If the test is reliable, the students who obtain high scores on the first administration will tend to obtain high scores on the second administration of the same test, and vice versa. This measure of reliability is determined by calculating the Pearson product-moment correlation between the scores obtained by the examinees on the two administrations of the test.

Equivalent Forms Method

This method measures the consistency of examinees' scores between two administrations of equivalent tests. The tests generally are administered on two different days. It is usually preferred for school-wide standardized tests because equivalent forms of the same test will be needed for periodic administration. This measure of reliability is determined by calculating the Pearson product-moment correlation between the scores obtained by the examinees on the two forms of the test.

Comparisons of Methods

Three methods for estimating test reliability have been considered: internal consistency (odd-even, Kuder-Richardson Formula 21, and the generalized equation), test-retest, and equivalent forms. The "reliabilities" estimated by these three methods are not equivalent in meaning because they differ in the types of errors reflected in their indices. In the internal consistency method, errors resulting from inadequate sampling of material reduce the size of the coefficient. However, errors arising from the variations in the test administration environment or from day-to-day variations in the individual have no direct influence on the index calculated by this method. Nevertheless, the internal consistency method offers a practical and reasonable way for a teacher to judge the reliability of his test. He usually does not have equivalent forms available and cannot afford to use extra class periods for retest purposes.

The test-retest method permits errors arising from variations in the individual from day to day and errors resulting from variations in the test administration environment to reduce the size of the coefficient. Since the test contains only one sampling of the hypothetical item pool, the index obtained by use of the test-retest method does not reflect sampling inconsistency.

The equivalent forms approach to reliability estimation is probably the most complete method. Day-to-day variations in the individual, inadequacy of sampling, and variations in the test administration environment are reflected in the index calculated.

Interpretation

The coefficient of reliability reflects the proportion of the total test variance which is associated with "true" scores on the instrument. The remaining portion of test variance is the result of error. For example, if the reliability of a test is .53, about 53 percent of the test variance could be accounted for by differences in "true" scores and about 47 percent $(1.00 - .53)$ of the variance would be error.

It is important to remember that actual "true" scores will not contain error from any source. Hence, if the method used to calculate the coefficient of reliability does not permit all sources of error to influence the size of the coefficient, the proportion of test variance attributed to differences in "true" scores will contain error from those sources *not* permitted to influence the reliability coefficient.

Standard Error of Measurement

Because of the presence of errors of measurement, the score which an individual receives on a test will seldom be exactly equal to the score which he should have received (his *true score* in the achievement being measured). Thus, each examinee's test score can be partitioned into true score and error score. If one could determine the amount of error in each examinee's test score, it would be possible to calculate the standard deviation of these error scores for the group. This value is called the *standard error of measurement* (SE_{meas}).[3]

It is not possible to determine for an individual that portion of his obtained score which resulted from errors of measurement. Consequently, it is not possible to calculate the standard error of measurement directly. However, one can estimate the SE_{meas} if the standard deviation of the test and the reliability of the test are known. The SE_{meas} may be found by

$$SE_{meas} = S_x \sqrt{1 - r_{11}},$$

where S_x is the standard deviation of the test and r_{11} is the reliability[3] of the test. The table in Appendix F can be used to obtain the $\sqrt{1 - r}$.

The SE_{meas} can be used to define *confidence intervals* for the students' true scores based on their obtained scores. A confidence interval is defined as a *range of scores which can be assigned a specific probability of containing the student's true score*. This score range is analogous to the percentile band which is often reported by test publishers instead of the actual percentile rank of a student's score on a test. The 95 percent confidence interval, then, is that range of scores which 95 out of 100 times will contain the student's true score.

This concept may be best understood in terms of a couple of examples. If Bill received a score of 28 on a science test and if the test had a SE_{meas} of 5, one could say that Bill's true score is in the range 23–33 (± 1 SE_{meas}), accepting the risk of being wrong 32 percent of the time. Thus, one would expect to be correct 68 percent of the time in making this assumption. If one wised to be correct more often (say, 95 percent of the time), the range needed is ± 2 SE_{meas}. For Bill, on this test, one could assume that his true score will be somewhere in the range 18–38, accepting a risk of being wrong 5 percent of the time.

---

[3] In calculating the SE_{meas} for a test, any method for calculating the reliability coefficient may be used for r_{11} in the equation, but it should be kept firmly in mind that the method used determines the errors protected against.

The most commonly used confidence intervals are:

1. 68 percent confidence interval—obtained score $\pm 1.0 \times SE_{meas}$
2. 95 percent confidence interval—obtained score $\pm 2.0 \times SE_{meas}$
3. 99 percent confidence interval—obtained score $\pm 2.6 \times SE_{meas}$.

Increasing Test Reliability

If a teacher administers a test and discovers that the coefficient of reliability is too small, as is true of the .53 value of the algebra test previously mentioned, what can be done to improve the measurement instrument? First, he should improve the individual items. Some of the techniques for doing this have been presented in the preceding chapters on test construction and others will be considered in the subsequent chapter on item analysis. However, since the test has already been administered, these techniques will not help the teacher solve his immediate problem of obtaining reliable information on the current group of students.

Another way of improving the reliability of a test, if the reliability coefficient is not too low initially, is to increase the length of the test. The following formula applies:

$$\frac{(\text{Reliability desired}) \times (1 - \text{Reliability obtained})}{(\text{Reliability obtained}) \times (1 - \text{Reliability desired})} = \text{increased length of test.}$$

In the earlier example ($r_{KR21} = .53$), if the teacher desired a reliability of at least .75, the test would have to be increased 2.66 times:

$$\frac{(.75) \times (1 - .53)}{(.53) \times (1 - .75)} = 2.66 \text{ (times as long as the first test).}$$

Since the original test containing 50 items had reliability equal to .53, a comparable test of 133 (2.66×50) similar items could be expected to have a reliability of about .75. Therefore, an additional test of 83 ($133 - 50$) similar items could be administered to the class to bring the overall reliability up to .75.

This relationship of reliability to the number of test items may seem inconsistent with the definition of reliability. However, we would usually have more assurance that a child can solve arithmetic problems if he demonstrates his achievement level by working ten assigned problems rather than only one. Furthermore, the dependence of reliability upon the number of test items assumes that the additional test items are drawn from the same hypothetical item pool. If this assumption can be reasonably satisfied, the illustrated procedure will yield a good estimate of the desired length for the test.

The calculation of the desired length of a test can also be interpreted as the number of similar tests needed to reach the desired level of reliability. In the previous example, the 2.66 could be interpreted to mean that 2.66 50-item tests (with each test having a coefficient of reliability of .53) are needed to reach a composite reliability of .75. Therefore, a teacher might expect to approach this level of reliability by administering two 50-item tests and one 33-item test (each having about .53 reliability) during the marking period, if all three are to be treated as one in the composite.

Reliability of Teacher-made Tests

Generally speaking, teacher-made tests are infamous for their lack of reliability. Many classroom tests have coefficients of reliability approaching zero. Probably most fall in the range .20–.40. Only a small percent of teacher-made tests have reliabilities above .60. Tests constructed in the multiple-choice format usually are among the most reliable of classroom tests, while those constructed in the essay format usually are among the least reliable. Nevertheless, the experienced and knowledgeable teacher with training in the construction of classroom tests should become sufficiently skillful in test development to produce selection-type examinations (multiple-choice, true-false, matching) which usually yield reliabilities above .60 and supply-type examinations (essay, short-answer, completion) with reliabilities above .45.

Selection-type tests. The various methods of calculating reliability are not equally applicable to all item formats. With selection-type tests, any of the methods described could be employed. However, because of the need for efficient use of teacher and student time and effort, neither equivalent-form nor test-retest methods are appropriate as measures of reliability for classroom tests. Also, if a set of items on the test pertains to one passage to be read and responded to by the examinee, it is possible that an odd-even reliability coefficient will be inflated as a result. If a test contains more than one type of selection item, Kuder-Richardson Formula 21 may considerably underestimate the reliability. Since most selection-type, teacher-made examinations are power tests, the limitation in appropriateness of KR21 and odd-even methods for speeded tests should rarely be a detriment to their use by teachers. Consequently, an internal consistency method should be appropriate for use with a selection test. However, if the tests are to be scored by hand, KR21 is preferable and should yield an acceptable estimate of test reliability while maintaining an efficient use of teacher time. Under appropriate conditions, this method should serve the teacher well.

Supply-type tests. Supply-type examinations typically are less reliable than selection-type examinations. This decrease in reliability can be attributed primarily to two factors: less adequate sampling and increased error in scoring (due to variation in scoring standards and variation in interpretation of responses). Although error in scoring can exist in selection-type examinations, it should be relatively small—more the result of decisions made during the construction of items than of errors made in scoring the papers.

Even in tests which have been constructed, administered, and scored with equal care and skill, the previously discussed factors (difficulty in obtaining an adequate-sized sample of behavioral tasks and error in scoring) will still exist and exhibit differential influence on the various types of supply tests. Because of these factors, essay examinations composed of extended-answer questions will typically be less reliable than essay examinations composed of short-answer questions, and both can be expected to be less reliable than examinations containing only completion items.

Since the essay examination is likely to lack reliability, it would appear that a mandate exists for determining the reliability of these tests. Unfortunately, mandate or no mandate, the task of determining the reliability of essay tests is both difficult and time-consuming. Because of the inherent nature of the examination, neither the Kuder-Richardson Formula 21 method nor the odd-even correlational approach can be appropriately used. The test-retest method could be used except that the coefficient is likely to be inflated as a result of the student's memory of previous responses to items. If the first administration results are discussed with the examinees, the correlation coefficient will be influenced by this learning experience. However, equivalent forms can be constructed and administered, if test reliability is to be estimated. Since this introduces inefficiency in the use of student time and effort, it should be used with discretion—perhaps restricted to occasional use with end-of-term examinations.

In terms of efficient utilization of teacher and student time and effort, the generalized internal consistency equation provides the preferred method for estimating test reliability of essay examinations. It requires only one test, administered once, and scored just once. However, the calculation procedure is complex and slow. The teacher who does not have access to a computer or desk calculator will most likely find it necessary to restrict the use of this method to major tests.

Fortunately, it is possible to consider the influence of one of the factors which contributes to poor reliability of essay tests—errors of scoring—without the necessity of administering equivalent forms of the examination or using the generalized internal consistency equation. The teacher can obtain an estimate of scorer reliability. Although it is possible to estimate scorer reliability by obtaining the coefficient of correlation between the scores assigned the same set of papers by two separate teachers, it is more practical in most teaching situations for the regular classroom teacher to score the papers twice. In either case, the procedures for scoring essay examinations discussed in Chapter 4 are appropriate.

When scorer reliability is to be calculated by correlating the scores assigned to a set of papers by the same teacher at two different scoring sessions, some precautions should be taken to reduce as much as possible the influence of teacher's memory and other extraneous factors on the scores assigned. Most of these precautions are described in Chapter 4 and will be summarized here. Before administering the examination, vertically print the numbers 1 through N on a sheet of paper, where N is the number of students in the class. Instruct the examinees that each is to select a number, print his name beside the selected number, and print this number on each of his answer sheets. Emphasize that they are not to use their names on their answer sheets. Circulate the numbered paper to collect the names, pick up the paper, and store it. Then you can give the test.

In scoring the examination, score each question for all examinees before proceeding to the next question. Record the scores assigned on a separate page: do *not* write on the answer sheets. After all questions for all students have been graded, obtain the total score for each student by summing his item scores. Put the papers aside for a few days. Then, using the same scoring procedure but with a different recording sheet, rescore the examinations. Calculate the product-moment coefficient of scorer reliability. The teacher should keep in mind that *this is only an index of scorer reliability*. It does not reflect the other factors which contribute to the failure to achieve perfect reliability.

A coefficient of scorer reliability for completion tests may be obtained by using this same procedure. A student identifying number still should be used to obtain impartial scoring. However, scoring all the responses to one question before proceeding to the next rarely improves scorer reliability sufficiently to justify the increased scoring time. If the papers are to be scored twice, a separate recording sheet should be used for the first scoring. Marks made on the answer sheets will influence the second scoring of the papers. After a few days, the second scoring can be made, this time directly on the students' papers.

A teacher may occasionally wish to obtain an index of scorer reliability with completion tests as a check on the objectivity of his scoring. However, if completion tests are carefully constructed and scored, the problem of scorer reliability is only slightly greater for this test form than it is for selection-type tests. Furthermore, when the responses are scored 1 if right and 0 if wrong, an estimate of test reliability can be obtained by either the KR21 or the odd-even (stepped-up for half scores) method. The limitations we considered when discussing methods of estimating the reliability of selection-type tests also apply to completion tests.

The reliability of the oral response form of the oral examination is rarely calculated. In the case of a group oral response test, no acceptable method exists. However, since such a test lacks validity—whether or not it is reliable is an academic question—the answer is that it is not.

When the oral response test is administered individually, it is sometimes possible to obtain an estimate of test reliability or of scorer reliability. In the case of the oral examination before a committee (common in doctoral programs), the deviation from the average score on each question given by each member of the committee can be used in calculating scorer reliability. However, the procedures to be used are beyond the scope of this text; furthermore, an acceptable measure of test reliability is not available.

If only one examiner (the teacher) is involved and if the responses are scored 1 and 0, it is possible to estimate test reliability. In order to do so, the examiner must either record the exact response of each examinee to each question (preferred method) or score each question on an answer sheet during the examination. KR21 reliability can then be calculated. In any case, for the classroom teacher, test-retest and equivalent forms are too inefficient and should not be used. If the responses elicited are scored other than 1 and 0, the generalized internal consistency equation can be used, but it is a time-consuming process.

Sometimes the oral examination is given to several examinees simultaneously, with the examinees writing their responses to each question. The classical spelling test is an example. Except that the problems are presented to the examinees orally, a test of this type will be similar in format to one of the selection- or supply-type tests. Likewise, the problems associated with test reliability will be the same as those associated with its selection or supply test counterpart, except that variations in verbal delivery by the examiner will influence the responses made by the examinees. The methods suggested for estimating test reliability and scorer reliability for the various supply- and selection-type tests are appropriate to their written response, oral examination counterparts.

Performance tests. The factors that influence the reliability of supply and selection tests also affect the reliability of performance tests. Thus reliability reflects the adequacy of content sampling, changes in the individual from day to day, variations in test administration, and accuracy of scoring. However, when considering carefully constructed performance tests, we find that these factors do not contribute equally to the lack of perfect test reliability nor will they maintain the same relative contribution to error variance for different types of performance tests.

The identification type of performance test can be presented in a number of item formats (e.g., orally with oral response, orally with written response, visually with written response, and visually with oral response). The mode of response is the major factor in determining the procedures to be used in estimating test reliability. Also, in most cases, an examination in the oral response form will be less reliable than a test in the written response form because scorer reliability is likely to be a more serious problem for the oral response test. For the test requiring an oral response, the discussion of the reliability of oral examinations (oral response form) is apropos. The written response form can occur in any of the selection or supply item formats; however, the completion format is the most common. The methods suggested for the various supply- and selection-type tests are appropriate to their written response, identification test counterpart.

In considering the problems associated with the estimation of scorer and test reliability of simulated situation and work sample tests of performance, it is necessary to distinguish between product and process, and in considering these two factors to focus primarily on methods of scoring. When the examinee is expected to produce some sort of product (a typed page, a dress pattern, a scaled drawing, etc.), the examination usually can be administered to several examinees at one time. When this can be done, it may be appropriate to use test-retest or equivalent forms to obtain an estimate of reliability. Whether or not either is appropriate depends on the ease of construction of an equivalent form, the possible value of a repeat or second test as a learning experience, the likelihood that an examinee will change as a result of the first administration of the test, and the extent to which this would result in an inefficient use of teacher and student time and effort. It should be appropriate, for example, to estimate the reliability of a test of typing skill or accuracy of handwriting by the test-retest or equivalent forms method.

In the event that the examination has a number of problems which are scored separately, a gain in efficiency may be possible by treating each portion of the examination as a separate question. The generalized internal consistency equation could then be used to estimate test reliability. For example, the various test activities in the woodworking work sample performance test presented in Chapter 10 could be separately scored and these subscores for each examinee used to calculate the internal consistency reliability.

In order to score a process or, to a lesser extent, a product test of performance, it is often necessary to devise and use a check list or a rating scale. The reliability of such an instrument can be estimated by test-retest or equivalent forms. Unfortunately two separate test administrations are often prohibitively inefficient in their utilization of teacher and student time and effort. This is particularly true if the test must be individually administered. However, when a check list is used, each item can be scored 1 or 0, and if summing these item scores produces a meaningful total score, KR21 may be appropriate. Where a rating scale is used, it is often possible to estimate reliability with the more complex and time-consuming generalized internal consistency equation.

The lack of scorer reliability is often a major problem for simulated situation and work sample tests. When process is being assessed, the only method available for determining scorer reliability is the use of two or more scorers (unless the examination is recorded on a video tape). In this case, scorer reliability is the correlation between the scores assigned by different scorers to the examinees. Unless team teaching is being used, the availability of two or more qualified judges for scoring the examination is unlikely. However, the teacher occasionally may wish to have various students rate the process at the same time as the teacher is rating it. The correlation between the average student's rating and the teacher's rating should yield a basement value below which the reliability of the teacher's assessment should not fall. Also, the activity of rating could be a valuable learning experience for the students.

When scoring student products, it is possible to obtain a measure of scorer reliability. All one needs is two separate scorings of the products. A discussion of the safeguards used in scoring essay examinations is appropriate here. Have the students write their names on a numbered sheet of paper and record the number on the product. If the test has two or more distinct components, score for all examinees one component before moving on to the scoring of the next component. Record the scores on a separate sheet of paper. Use a new recording sheet for the second scoring. The correlation of the scores received on one scoring of the papers with the scores received on the second will yield an estimate of the reliability of scoring.

ESTIMATING VALIDITY

If a test is to be useful in a given situation, the scores obtained by examinees must be consistent and relevant to the particular situation. An English test might yield consistent scores and thus be highly reliable as a test, yet the same test is useless to the algebra teacher since it is not applicable to his needs. If a test reliably measures what is relevant, it is said to be *valid*. If the test is not reliable, it cannot be valid since an unreliable test provides useless data. Validity, therefore, can be thought of as a function of the reliability of the test and its relevance to the behavior of interest to the tester. According to the classical model in measurement theory, the *maximum* value which the coefficient of validity can reach is the square root of the reliability coefficient. In practice, the validity coefficient rarely approaches this value.

Since a test is valid to the extent that it is relevant to the purpose for which it is to be used, and since there are different purposes for testing, it follows that there are several ways of estimating the validity of a test. Some methods are based predominately on logical thought and careful analysis of the relation between the variables to be measured and the behaviors elicited by the test items. The study of opinions of experts, the analysis of books and courses of study, and the comparative analysis of the concepts contained in the test are all logical attempts to establish the validity of the measuring instrument.

Other methods are concerned primarily with establishing the empirical relation between the test scores and other pertinent measures. If results of a test are used to help students determine whether or not they should go to college, the empirical (measured) relation between test scores and college success is required as an indicator of the validity of the test. An easily and rapidly administered test can be used in lieu of a more time-consuming and costly test. In this case, the correlation between the scores received by a sample of individuals on the two tests may be an appropriate indicator of the test's validity. To measure a single, pure factor or trait, a factor analysis[4] of the items should yield information about the validity of the test. As a final example of the relation between test validity and the purpose of the test, given a set of hypothetical constructs[4] for explaining some aspects of human behavior, the validity of the test could be established by showing that these constructs partially explain the scores received on the test.

In general, validity should indicate the relevance of a test for a specific purpose. Since this book is concerned primarily with classroom testing procedures, only three types of validity will be presented: *predictive validity, concurrent validity*, and *curricular validity*.

Predictive validity. In many school situations the dominant question is whether the test is relevant to some future event—one week, one year, or five years hence. Suppose that we want to ascertain whether or not a math test will predict success

---

[4] The use of factor analysis and construct validity is beyond the scope of this textbook. The interested reader is referred to standard advanced textbooks in measurement.

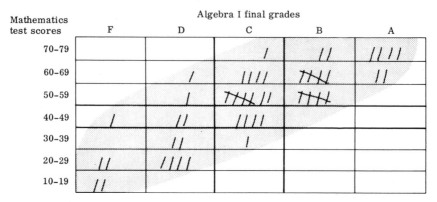

Fig. 12.1. Scattergram showing math scores and final grades.

in first year algebra. To provide the necessary test data, we administer the test to 30 freshmen before the beginning of Algebra I. At the end of the school year, we construct a scattergram, using the test scores (in 10-point intervals) and the Algebra I final grades (Fig. 12.1).

Analysis of the scattergram suggests that a student who scores below 30 on the mathematics test will probably do poorly in Algebra I. Further analysis of the scattergram indicates that the test scores and final grades are positively correlated. The tally marks in the scattergram form a slope increasing from lower left to upper right. This reflects a positive correlation (Fig. 11.6).

The predictive validity coefficient is a Pearson product-moment correlation between the scores on the test and an appropriate criterion, where the criterion measure is obtained after the desired lapse of time. In Fig. 12.1, this coefficient is the correlation between the mathematics test scores and the Algebra I final grades obtained after a time lapse of one term.

The major obstacle in endeavoring to establish the predictive validity of a test is the identification and selection of an adequate criterion and criterion measure. If we have constructed a test of academic aptitude, what should we use as *the* criterion? Should we use grades? Since there are many factors other than academic aptitude which contribute to grades, the correlation between grades and aptitude scores would be influenced by factors not pertinent to the purpose of the test. Should we use some standardized test of academic ability? The failure to achieve a high correlation in this case may be partially the fault of an imperfect criterion and partly the result of the two tests measuring slightly different aspects of academic aptitude. The difficulty of selecting the criterion measure is a major problem in statistical validity studies.

Concurrent validity. If a test correlates highly with important present behavior, it is said to have *concurrent validity*. This concept is identical to predictive validity except that there is little or no time lapse between administrations of the two tests.

There are two particular instances when classroom teachers might be concerned with concurrent validity. A classroom teacher might ask, "Are my tests actually discriminating between the better and poorer students?" The concurrent validity of the composite test results (as well as for a single test) could be obtained by calculating the product-moment coefficient of correlation between the results of his tests and those of a reputable standardized test in the same content area. However, the teacher could estimate the relation between the two sets of scores by using a scattergram of the type illustrated in Fig. 12.1, with the standardized test scores on one axis and the classroom test scores on the other. The darker lines divide the scattergram into four quadrants. Most of the tallies should be in the lower left-hand quadrant and the upper right-hand quadrant. The former corresponds to those persons who did poorly on both the standardized test and the classroom tests, the latter corresponds to those persons who did well on both sets of tests. The teacher would expect some students to fall into the other two quadrants, but the general trend of tallies should be from lower left to upper right in the scattergram. If the scattergram analysis does not indicate a positive trend between the two achievement measures, the teacher should seriously consider the possibility that his classroom testing procedures are poor or that the standardized test is an inadequate measure of what he is attempting to teach. Either factor could account for the lack of concurrent validity when it is determined in the preceding manner.

Concurrent validity might also be of interest to teachers whenever it is not feasible to determine the predictive validity of a testing instrument. An ultimate concern of most teachers is the preparation of a child for situations which he will encounter in the future. Since a classroom teacher rarely has the opportunity to conduct long-term follow-up studies on his teaching procedures, he might instead validate his procedure on some pertinent current behavior. It is commonly understood that the degree of relation between two variables decreases over time. Aptitude tests scores, for example, will be more highly related to current achievement than they will be to the same individual's achievement ten years from now. The academic achievement of a ninth-grade student can be predicted with greater accuracy from an aptitude test administered at the beginning of the ninth grade than can his academic achievement in the twelfth grade from the same ninth-grade aptitude test. Consequently, the predictive validity of a test would be expected to be somewhat lower than its concurrent validity. On the other hand, if the concurrent validity of a test is zero, you may expect the validity for predicting the same behavior at a future time to be zero also. Therefore, concurrent validity can aid teachers in detecting tests which are likely to lack relevance to their ultimate concerns.

Curricular validity. One of the most important questions asked by the classroom teacher is, "Does this test conform to the content and the goals my pupils and I have for this class?" This question involves both concurrent and predictive validity since the immediate goals of the class are current criterion behaviors and these immediate goals are generally related to the ultimate aims of the teacher.[5] However, the estimation of curricular validity is somewhat complicated because the only measure of the criterion behavior is the test to be analyzed and because there is no second measure with which to compare the test.

It is usually impossible to construct a test which will include the total universe of behavior with which the teacher is concerned. Therefore, a random or representative sample of behavior from this universe must be selected for the test. Suppose, for example, that a teacher has assigned a total of 400 vocabulary words to his class during an academic year. It is impractical to administer to this class a vocabulary final examination containing all 400 words. Therefore, the teacher may select randomly 40 of the words for inclusion in the final examination. Inferences about the universe of 400 words can be made on the basis of the students' results on this shorter test. Such a test would contain content validity because the test items were selected randomly from a distinct universe of behavior. Furthermore, if it were possible to calculate the coefficient of curricular validity, the maximum value it could reach would depend on the reliability of the test, and is estimated by "$\sqrt{\text{reliability}}$." If the reliability of the vocabulary test, for example, is .70, its maximum validity will be the square root of .70, or .84.

In most classroom situations, teachers will not encounter such clear-cut universes of behavior. In these instances, curricular validity should be determined by comparing the test items with the content and goals established by the teacher. When determining whether a standardized test can be used to measure classroom achievement, the teacher should ask, "Does this test measure the behavior I think is important?" This question can be answered by determining whether the test items sample the content and the goals deemed important by the teacher. One can avoid such an "after-the-fact" analysis on teacher-constructed tests through appropriate planning before the items are written. A two-way Table of Specifications[6] should be constructed as an initial stage in test construction. One dimension is the course content; the other dimension is the cognitive-affective performance domain. A single cell in the table corresponds to a specific content category at a specific level of the cognitive-affective performance domain as it relates to a specific instructional objective. The use of such a table aids the classroom teacher in constructing a test which is representative of the determined content and goals. If the test is consistent with these emphases determined by the teacher, it is said to have curricular validity.

---

[5] A discussion on the writing of classroom objectives is presented in Chapter 2.

[6] Chapter 3 contains a discussion on test planning which includes an illustration of a Table of Specifications.

Validating Classroom Tests

The key to validity is relevance. The test must be relevant to its intended use. Since the purpose of most teacher-constructed tests is to measure the extent of student acquisition of instructional objectives, relevance is the extent to which the test measures achievement cogent to these objectives. Obviously, if a test is to achieve this goal, instructional objectives must be identified, clarified, and stated in terms of observable student behavior, and content and levels of cognitive domain and/or physical skills must be selected and related to these instructional objectives.

If the items on a test measure the attainment of instructional objectives, the items are relevant. However, it is not sufficient for the items to be relevant. The items comprising the test must also reflect the desired balance among the various instructional objectives. The proper utilization of a Table of Specifications should contribute significantly to the construction of a relevant test—a test containing relevant items and exhibiting the desired balance among the various instructional objectives. The extent to which a test conforms to the Table of Specifications is an indication of its curricular validity.

Most teacher-made tests are composed of selection-type or supply-type items. Tables of Specifications for such tests usually have content categories on the vertical axis and levels of the cognitive domain on the horizontal. Specific difficulties encountered in constructing the various selection- and supply-type tests have been considered in earlier chapters and will not be repeated here. Many of these have a direct bearing on test validity. In general, one may say that supply-type examinations are less likely to exhibit balance (that is, to conform to the Table of Specifications) because only a few questions can be asked and these, of necessity, cover more than one content area and cognitive domain level. On the other hand, it is more difficult to devise selection-type items which measure at the higher levels of the cognitive domain.

An oral examination may require a performance response, a verbal response, or a written response. The problems in developing a valid verbal response test are comparable to those encountered in performance tests. To construct a valid oral response test is always difficult. If the examination is to be used as an individual test for an advanced degree or diploma, the questions must require the examinee to integrate in his responses, concepts, understandings, and knowledge drawn from a number of courses and experiences. The responses to the various components of the test should, as a whole, indicate the strength and weaknesses of the examinee's qualifications for entering his chosen field. If the test achieves this end, it is valid.

If the oral response test is used as a substitute for a written test, a more formal Table of Specifications, with content on one axis and levels of the cognitive domain on the other axis, can be used in test construction. The extent to which the test conforms to this table reflects its validity. Likewise, if a written response is required, validity is dependent on the adequacy of the Table of Specifications and the test's relationship to it. The validity factors to be considered, in this case, must also include the factors associated with the examination's format counterpart among the selection and supply examinations.

With the identification test of performance, one encounters a test emphasizing some performance activity but at what is primarily a cognitive level. The Table of Specifications will likely resemble that of a verbal behavior test. Validity depends on the balance of the test, the relationship between test items and instructional objectives, and the adequacy of the Table of Specifications.

The typical Table of Specifications for a work sample or simulated situations performance test is likely to differ somewhat from that for the written examination. On the vertical axis are indicated the situations under which some skill or skills are to be exhibited, and on the horizontal axis the specific skills to be shown. Usually the tasks are selected to be lifelike and the curricular validity of the test depends on its logical relationship with similar behavioral tasks in a life situation. Many of the factors discussed in Chapter 10 are pertinent to the development of valid performance tests.

SUMMARY

Reliability is the degree of consistency among test scores. When all sources of error in measurement are permitted to operate upon the coefficient of reliability, it is the proportion of test variance which can be attributed to variations in true scores. However, various methods of estimating test reliability differ in the sources of error permitted to influence the size of the coefficient; thus all methods for determining test reliability are not measuring the same phenomena.

The internal consistency method of estimating reliability is based on the assumption that students who respond correctly to one set of items on a reliable test will respond correctly to other equivalent sets of items on the test. The KR21 formula and the odd-even formula yield estimates of internal consistency. The consistency of test scores between two administrations of a test is described by the test-retest method for expressing test reliability. If two equivalent forms of a test are administered to a class on two separate days, the coefficient of correlation between the two sets of scores is the equivalent-forms reliability of the test.

In Fig. 12.2 some sources of error which could reduce the consistency of test scores are contrasted with some of the methods for estimating reliability. A check mark ($\sqrt{}$) indicates that the method on that row permits the error in that column to operate on the coefficient.

The standard error of measurement is the standard deviation of the error components in test scores. If the test reliability and the test standard deviation are known, it may be rapidly calculated. The standard error of measurement helps the teacher interpret a student's score by permitting him to establish a range of scores which can be assigned a specific probability of including the student's true score.

Validity is a function of the reliability of a test and its relevance to the behavior of interest to the examiner. The validity of a test may be established by correlating

Method of estimate	Sources of Error			
	Sampling of content	Administrative variations	Test environment variations	Changes in examinee from day to day
Generalized internal consistency	√			
Odd-even	√			
KR21	√			
Test-retest		√	√	√
Equivalent forms	√	√	√	√

Fig. 12.2. Sources of error reflected in various methods of estimating reliability.

the scores on a test with relevant behavioral measures obtained at some future time (predictive) or by correlating the scores with measures of relevant behavior obtained at about the same time the test was administered (concurrent). However, for classroom tests curricular validity is more often used. If a Table of Specifications is carefully constructed and followed in the selection of items for a test, it is quite likely that the test will exhibit curricular validity.

PROBLEMS

1. What is the influence of the errors of measurement on test reliability?
2. What is the impact of errors of measurement arising from the testing environment and the administration of the test on the KR21 coefficient of reliability?
3. What sources of error are controlled by the test-retest method for calculating the coefficient of reliability?
4. How effective is the equivalent forms method in controlling errors of measurement?
5. What is the relationship between the standard error of measurement and test reliability?
6. A teacher administered a 40-item test to his class and obtained a mean of 25 and a standard deviation of 5. What is the test reliability (KR21)? What is the standard error of measurement?

7. Bill had a score of 27 on a test with a standard error of measurement of 7. If you wanted to be sure that the confidence interval would contain his true score 95 percent of the time, what confidence interval would you use?

8. A 35-item classroom test yielded a reliability coefficient of .65. The teacher wants to have a reliability of .90 on his test composite. How many times as long as the original test must the composite be? (Assume that he is adding equivalent items.)

9. Define curricular validity.

10. Why would a classroom teacher be more likely to use curricular validity than predictive validity?

11. A teacher validates his test by calculating the coefficient of correlation between scores on a standardized test in history and his final examination in American History. Both tests are given the same week. What kind of validity is this? Of what use would this coefficient be?

12. Describe the relationship between validity and reliability.

LIST OF SYMBOLS USED IN CHAPTER 12

Symbols	Verbal Equivalents
k	Number of items on a test
n	Number of examinees
r	Pearson Product-Moment Correlation Coefficient
r_{11}	Reliability coefficient
r_{kk}	Reliability coefficient estimated from generalized internal consistency formula
r_{KR21}	Reliability coefficient estimated from Kuder-Richardson Formula 21
r_{tt}	Reliability coefficient for total test estimated from the stepped-up Pearson r between odd and even items
S	Standard deviation
$\bar{X}$	Mean
X_{ji}^2	Square of the score on item j by examinee i
ΣX_{ji}^2	Sum of the squares of each item score by each individual
$X_{j.}^2$	Square of the sum of the scores received by all examinees on item j
$\Sigma X_{j.}^2$	Sum for all items of the square of the sum of the scores received by all examinees on each item
$X_{.i}^2$	Square of the total score received by examinee i
$\Sigma X_{.i}^2$	Sum of the squares of the total scores received by all examinees

$X^2_{..}$ Square of the sum of all the scores received

SE_{meas} Standard Error of Measurement

ΣS_j^2 Sum of the Variances of the scores on each item

S_X^2 Variance of the total scores for a set of papers

SUGGESTED READING

Adams, Georgia Sachs, *Measurement and Evaluation in Education, Psychology, and Guidance*. Holt, Rinehart and Winston, Chicago, 1964, Chapters 4 and 5.

Anastasi, Ann, *Psychological Testing* (3rd ed.). Macmillan Company, New York, 1968, Chapters 4, 5, and 6.

Cureton, Edward E., "Validity," in E. F. Linquist (Ed.), *Educational Measurement*. American Council on Education, Washington, D.C., 1951, Chapter 16.

Ebel, Robert L., *Measuring Educational Achievement*. Prentice-Hall, Englewood Cliffs, N.J., 1965, Chapters 10 and 12.

Horrocks, John E., *Assessment of Behavior*. Charles E. Merrill Books, Columbus, O., 1964, Chapter 3.

Horrocks, John E., and Thelma I. Schoonover, *Measurement for Teachers*. Charles E. Merrill Books, Columbus, O., 1968, Chapter 4.

Nunnally, Jum C., *Educational Measurement and Evaluation*. McGraw-Hill Book Company, New York, 1964, Chapters 2 and 4.

Nunnally, Jum C., *Psychometric Theory*. McGraw-Hill Book Company, New York, 1967, Chapters 3, 6, and 7.

Thorndike, Robert L., "Reliability," in E. F. Lindquist (Ed.), *Educational Measurement*. American Council on Education, Washington, D.C., 1951, Chapter 15.

Thorndike, Robert L., and Elizabeth Hagen, *Measurement and Evaluation in Psychology and Education* (3rd ed.). John Wiley and Sons, New York, 1969, Chapter 6.

Chapter 13

Item Quality: Difficulty and Discrimination

The test has been administered and scored. Pupils have been assigned grades on the basis of the test measures. The job is done, or is it? In the comfort of the arm chair in front of the fire, the wise teacher might begin to think, "But was it a good test? It must have been. Before constructing the test, the objectives of the unit of study were carefully considered. Items were constructed to measure these objectives at various levels—knowledge, understanding, application. Each item was carefully constructed in accordance with the accepted practices for that type of item. But *was* it a good test?"

Perhaps at this point the teacher computes the coefficient of reliability of the test. "It is a fairly reliable test—.70. But, how could I improve the test? If I wanted to use some of the items again, which items should I use? Certainly I would question the item which my better pupils missed and my poorer pupils got right. In fact, unless my better pupils tended to do better on the item than my poorer pupils, I would question the value of that item. Also, if the item is so difficult that nearly all of my pupils missed the item or so easy that nearly all got it right, would the item help me to discriminate between pupils on the basis of their knowledge in the area tested?"

Two questions could now be asked about each item on the test: (1) How difficult was each item for the class? and (2) To what extent did each item discriminate between the better and the poorer pupils? The answer to the first question is usually sought through the computation of an index of difficulty. An index of discrimination would be of aid in answering the second. These two indices are used in what is commonly called an item analysis. Item analysis data are used to eliminate weak items, to find weaknesses in other items, and to aid in the selection of items for a test. Most of the discussion in this chapter is based on the discriminatory multiple-choice type item, but application can be made to other item formats.

DIFFICULTY
Index of Difficulty

The difficulty of an item on a classroom test may be expressed as the proportion of the class who answered the item correctly. This proportion is called the *index of difficulty*. It should be emphasized that the larger the proportion getting the item correct (that is, the larger the index of difficulty), the easier the item.

If R is used to represent the number of individuals who answered the item correctly and N is used to represent the number of individuals who took the test, and if a correct answer is scored 1 and an incorrect response is scored 0, then the item difficulty, D, can be determined using the formula

$$D = \frac{R}{N}.$$

If 21 out of 30 examinees respond correctly to an item, then the item difficulty equals $21/30 = .70$. It should be noted that this index can range from a minimum value of 0.00 to a maximum value of 1.00.

For reasons to be considered later, the index of discrimination for an item is often obtained from the test papers remaining after the middle 46 percent have been excluded. If the members of a class are ranked from the highest to the lowest on the basis of the total score on a test, the test papers for the upper 27 percent of the class can be called the upper group and the test papers for the lower 27 percent can be identified as the lower group. These two groups may then be used to compute an index of discrimination. If this is done, it may be advantageous to use the same two groups to estimate the index of difficulty. This approach would permit a more efficient use of time and provide an index of difficulty based on the same individuals used in computing the index of discrimination. The values obtained in this manner are usually quite similar to those obtained from the total group. If the subscripts U and L are used to represent the upper group and the lower group, respectively, item difficulty is determined using the formula

$$D = \frac{R_U + R_L}{N_U + N_L}.$$

Test Difficulty

A test designed to obtain maximum differentiation among the examinees theoretically should be of 50 percent difficulty; thus a test containing 100 items should have a mean of 50. Without exception, this is true for supply-type tests. However, on selection-type tests, chance is a factor in the score obtained. If the answer sheet for a five-choice, 100-item, multiple-choice test were randomly marked, one would expect to receive a score of 20.[1] Although there is evidence to suggest that scores below chance are relatively stable for power tests, indicating that incorrect knowledge is a contributing factor, it is reasonable to exclude the chance portion of the range from primary consideration. Consequently, the average difficulty of most achievement tests should be about midway between chance score and 100 percent of the items.

The Item Difficulty Debate

There is considerable debate concerning the optimal distribution of item indices of difficulty for a test. Test authorities seem to be distributed at various points

---

[1] Chance score on a selection-type test is determined using the formula: Chance Score = number of items/number of choices per item. (For a five-choice, 100-item test, chance score = 100/5 = 20.)

along the continuum extending from requiring all items on a test to be of approximately 50 percent difficulty to having the indices distributed somewhat evenly within the range .15 to .85. Those who support the latter position usually contend that easy items are needed to discriminate among the poorer students and difficult items are needed to discriminate among the better ones. Some supporters also add a motivational factor and state that some easy items are needed to motivate the poorer students while some difficult items are needed to motivate the better ones.

Item Intercorrelation

Although the maximum number of discriminations which an item can make occurs at .50 difficulty, the selection of items of 50 percent difficulty will not necessarily result in the most discriminating test. The extent of item intercorrelation must also be considered. In the theoretical case where all the intercorrelations between the items on a test are 1.00, a test composed of 100 perfectly discriminating items of 50 percent difficulty would be no better than a test composed of one item of .50 difficulty; one-half of the examinees would respond correctly to all the items and one-half would miss all the items. However, if the indices of difficulty were spread evenly along the scale from very difficult to very easy items of perfect discrimination, the test would be a quite effective tool in discriminating among students. On the other hand, if the item intercorrelations for the test were zero, the maximum number of discriminations would be made by a test containing only items of .50 difficulty and perfect discrimination. In this case, if the indices of difficulty were evenly spread along the difficulty scale, the test would be a poor discriminator.

Tests vary considerably in the extent to which their items are intercorrelated. When the items on a test are quite similar in content, high item intercorrelation is to be expected and the distribution of item difficulties should extend somewhat evenly throughout the range of difficulty. An example of a test of this type is an arithmetic test measuring only the ability to add series of one- and two-digit numbers. However, when the items on a test cover a wide range of concepts and factual information, low item intercorrelation is to be expected and the distribution of item difficulties should cluster closely around the .50 level. Since most achievement tests attempt to measure a variety of facts and understandings, it is generally best to select items of approximately 50 percent difficulty.

Test and Item Difficulty

As has been suggested previously, the difficulty of a test should fall approximately midway between chance score and 100 percent. Similarly, the mean of the indices of item difficulty should fall approximately midway between chance score and 100 percent. Items difficulties, therefore, should cluster around this midpoint even though items of 50 percent difficulty have the greatest potential for discrimination. Since low item intercorrelation is to be expected for most achievement tests, on a five-choice, multiple-choice test, item difficulties should fall in the range .40–.75, clustering around a mean of near .60.

Correcting for Chance

With the introduction of test items which offer the examinee the correct response among one or more incorrect alternatives, there exists the possibility that the correct response might be chosen entirely by accident. This produces a dilemma. Should the number of correct responses which an individual makes to a test be treated as his score or should a correction factor be applied to remove that portion of his total score which is equivalent to those scores which supposedly resulted from chance selection when the answer was not known? To correct for chance, the classical solution is to use the formula

$$S = R - \frac{W}{k - 1},$$

where S is the "true" score, R is the number of correct responses by an individual, W is the number of incorrect responses by the individual, and k is the number of item alternatives.

Perhaps the primary reason given for the use of the "correction for guessing" formula is to keep those who have a tendency to guess from having the advantage over those who do not guess. Other reasons are: to discourage guessing by pupils, to make the scores more meaningful, and to make comparable the indices of difficulty obtained on items varying in the number of foils presented. If the test scores are to be corrected for chance, it might be wise to also correct the proportion of correct responses for the upper group and for the lower group before calculating the indices of difficulty and discrimination.

However, there are many reasons why a correction for chance formula should *not* be applied to the scores.

1. The ranking of the students in a class is *not* changed by the use of the correction formula.

2. Those students who choose an incorrect response as a result of misinformation are penalized twice by this formula.

3. Those who are poor guessers are penalized by having their scores reduced while those who are good guessers (test sophisticates) are not penalized.

4. Since it is usually possible for the examinee to eliminate one or two of the foils on those items which are not known, the student who disregards instructions is rewarded by this "correction," while the student who follows the instruction not to guess is penalized.

5. An assumption of the correction formula is that the answer is either known or is not known, but partial knowledge is not considered.

6. The use of the correction formula tends to lead to the erroneous assumption that the corrected scores are somehow "true" scores.

Factors Influencing Item Difficulty

The difficulty of an item is the function of the learning experience of the examinees, the question asked, and the responses offered. The complexity of the item stem, as well as the extent of ambiguity in the stem, influences item difficulty. Perhaps even more influential, however, are the alternatives offered. If the alternatives are quite homogeneous, the item will be more difficult than if the choices are relatively heterogeneous. Consider these two items:

Heterogeneous alternatives	*Homogeneous alternatives*
The second President of the United States was:	The second President of the United States was:
*A. John Adams	*A. John Adams
B. Winston Churchill	B. John Q. Adams
C. Lyndon Johnson	C. Thomas Jefferson
D. Abraham Lincoln	D. Zachary Taylor
E. George Washington	E. George Washington

Obviously the first item is less difficult than the second. An item which is too easy might be improved by making the alternatives more homogeneous. If the foils are common misconceptions, the item will tend to be more difficult than if the foils are reasonable but not common misconceptions. Consider these two items:

Without common misconceptions	*With common misconceptions*
The concept of "born equal" in a democracy means that all citizens have equal	The concept of "born equal" in a democracy means that all citizens have equal
*A. Rights before the law.	*A. Rights before the law.
B. Physical strength.	B. Educational opportunities.
C. Height and weight at birth.	C. Economic opportunities.
D. Appearance at birth (i.e. nude).	D. Mental potential.

The items with common misconceptions as foils are obviously more difficult than the items which do not contain such common misconceptions.

ITEM DISCRIMINATION

In the selection of the best items for a test it is desirable to have some criterion external to the examination against which to validate the items. This is often done in the construction of tests of interest, manual dexterity, and mental health. For example, in the construction of the Strong Vocational Interest Blank, members of various occupations were used as criterion groups for the validation of the items of its various scales; that is, items which differentiated between a specific occupational group and men in general were considered to be valid for inclusion in the scale for that occupation. However, although various criteria have been suggested (for example, teachers' grades and the ratings of experts), in the construction of achievement tests it is seldom possible to find an adequate external criterion for item validation. Consequently, in the construction of teacher-made and standardized achievement tests, it is common practice to use the internal measure of total test score as the criterion. If the examinees who did well on the total test also did well on the item and if the examinees who did poorly on the total test also did poorly on the item, the validity of the item may be assumed to have been established.

Of course, before the item was originally included in the test, it should have been examined for content validity. The ability of the item to discriminate between the better and the poorer examinees, as established by total test score, is measured by computing an index of discrimination. The validity (V) or discriminating power of the item may then be defined as the extent to which success or failure on that item indicates the possession of the trait or achievement being measured.

Although total test score is most often used as the criterion against which to validate the items to be used in a test (that is, to be used in obtaining indices of discrimination), there is a lack of agreement as to which method of obtaining an index of discrimination yields the best results with acceptable expenditure of time. The majority of the nearly a hundred methods suggested for computing indices of discrimination are correlational techniques for expressing the relation between a score on an item and the total test score. Many of these correlational techniques can be classified as: techniques which treat the total score as a continuous variable; techniques which divide the total score criterion into two equal parts; or techniques which divide the total score criterion into three parts and compare the two extreme groups. To some extent each of these categories could be subdivided into techniques based on the assumption that the score on an item is an artificial dichotomy imposed on a continuous variable, and those based on the assumption that the score on an item is a true dichotomy. The most commonly used correlational methods are: Flanagan's r, Davis' index, and the tetrachoric r. These three methods will be considered later in the chapter.

On the other hand, many approaches to item analysis have been used which are based on the differences in the *percentages* or number of cases in different groups and are not dependent on the assumptions underlying correlational techniques. These include such diverse techniques as chi square, probit analysis, sequential sampling, upper-lower ratios, and net D. Because of certain advantages inherent in this index, net D also will be considered later.

Upper-Lower 27 Percent Groups

In the computation of a coefficient of correlation, one normally has two measures for each person in the sample, and these two measures are compared through the use of the coefficient for the total group.[2] In correlational methods of computing the index of discrimination, the score on the item is one measure and the total score is the other. The coefficient may be obtained from the data for the total group, making use of the information available concerning the differences between the various members of the group on each measure. The calculation of such a measure, however, is very time-consuming. Consequently, it is common practice to dichotomize the group on total score and thus treat the sample as two groups— an upper group and a lower group.

---

[2] Procedures for calculating a coefficient of correlation are presented in Chapter 11.

Assuming that the criterion variable (total score) is a continuous, normally distributed variable which is to be dichotomized for the convenience of item analysis, Kelley[3] algebraically evolved the percentage of cases which should be included in each group for the most efficient study of items. After regressing the continuous criterion scores for systematic error and thus obtaining estimates of true scores, he obtained the function which must be maximized. The percentage obtained when the function was maximized was 27.02678. On the basis of his study, Kelley recommended the use of extreme groups of 27 percent in item analysis.

Although he accepted the general procedure followed by Kelley, Cureton[4] did not fully accept the assumption that the distribution of criterion scores is normal. Saying that platykurtosis (flattening of the distribution) is usually found in the distribution of scores on experimental tests, he used a unit-rectangular distribution in evolving the optimal percentage to be included in each group. Finding this value to be $\frac{1}{3}$ for the unit-rectangular distribution, he recommended that both the upper group and the lower group contain 29 or 30 percent of the total distribution for distributions which are usually platykurtic.

After scoring classroom examinations, if item analysis data are to be computed, it is suggested that the papers be ordered from highest score to lowest score. The top 27 percent of the papers should be set aside and designated the upper group, and likewise, the lower 27 percent of the papers should be set aside, designated the lower group. (The percent could vary between 27 percent and 30 percent, but the same number of papers must be placed in both groups.)

Flanagan's r

Based on the 27 percent who scored the highest on the test and the 27 percent who scored the lowest on the test, Flanagan's r expresses the relation between success on an item and the total test score as an estimated product moment coefficient of correlation. It assumes that item score and total score are both artificially dichotomized, continuous, normal variables. This index of discrimination is relatively easy to compute, gives a good estimate of the product moment coefficient when the assumptions are met, and is supposedly uninfluenced by item difficulty.

However, several limitations are associated with the use of this index. Flanagan's r might be said to reflect difficulty as well as discrimination, in that, for the same absolute difference in the number of discriminations made, Flanagan's r is biased in favor of the very easy items and the very hard ones. Another disadvantage of this method is that the scale is not interval in nature. That is, if the index of discrimination were increased from .50 to .70, the increase in discriminatory power

---

[3] Truman L. Kelley, "The Selection of Upper and Lower Groups for the Validation of Test Items." *Journal of Educational Psychology*, **30**, 1939, 17–19.

[4] Edward E. Cureton, "The Upper and Lower Twenty-Seven Per Cent Rule." *Psychometrika*, **22**, 1957, 293–296.

would not be equal to the increase in discriminatory power resulting from increasing the index from .70 to .90, yet both differences represent changes of .20 on the correlational scale.[5] The index of discrimination is inflated by the inclusion of the item in the total score criterion; however, it would be extremely time-consuming to rescore the test for each item. Furthermore, it is difficult to meet the assumptions of the index in practical test situations. Finally, it is relatively difficult to compute as compared to some other methods.

Flanagan[6] developed a chart which gives the *r* values. This table, reproduced in *Statistical Inference*,[7] is entered with the proportion getting the item correct in the upper group and the proportion getting the item correct in the lower group.

Davis' Indices

For each value of the biserial *r* in Flanagan's table, Davis obtained its corresponding *z'*-value.[8] Then he multiplied each *z'* value by the constant 60.241, producing an index of discrimination with a range from 0 to 100. Thus, the Davis index is based on the assumptions of the biserial coefficient, and has all the advantages and disadvantages of Flanagan's *r* with the following exceptions: it has an interval scale of values, and all indices based on samples of the same size will have the same error of measurement. In a publication by Davis[9] one can find both a thorough discussion of his index and a copy of his table.

Tetrachoric Coefficients of Correlation

The tetrachoric coefficient of correlation yields an estimate of the product-moment coefficient. Its assumptions are similar to those of Flanagan's *r*. The advantages and disadvantages attributed to Flanagan's *r* are also applicable here, with the possible exception that it is even less influenced by item difficulty. The total score criterion is normally dichotomized at the median, although quite reliable estimates of this index may be obtained from the upper and lower 27 percent groups. Additional information concerning this index and a chart for the computation of the tetrachoric *r* are found in a book by Wood.[10]

---

[5] This characteristic of correlation is discussed in Chapter 11.

[6] John C. Flanagan, "General Considerations in the Selection of Test Items and a Short Method of Estimating the Product-Moment coefficient from Data at the Tails of the Distribution." *Journal of Educational Psychology*, **30**, 1939, 679.

[7] Helen M. Walker and Josph Lev, *Statistical Inference*. Holt, Rinehart, and Winston, New York, 1953, pp. 472–475.

[8] Distributions of correlation coefficients are not normally distributed. The *z'* value is a mathematical transformation from the non-normal distribution of *r* values to a normal distribution of *z* values. (See Chapter II for a discussion of *z*-scores.)

[9] Frederick B. Davis, "Item-Analysis Data: their Computation, Interpretation, and Use in Test Construction." *Havard Educational Papers*, **2**, 1949, 1–42.

[10] Dorothy Adkins Wood, *Test Construction*. Charles E. Merrill Books, Columbus, O., 1961, pp. 84–88.

Net D Index of Discrimination

Net D is based on the difference between the *proportions of success* on an item in the 27 percent scoring highest on the test and the 27 percent scoring lowest on the test. Net D is an unbiased index of the absolute difference in the number of discriminations made between the upper group and the lower group—it is proportional to the net discriminations made by the item between the two groups.[11] The only assumption of this index is that those who possess more of a trait will receive a higher total score on a test than will those who possess less of a trait, an assumption common to any internal criterion measure of item validity. Although useful, assumptions that the criterion and item score distributions are continuous are not necessary.

Many advantages have been claimed for this index. Perhaps the most important advantage is the ease with which it can be computed. The general shape of the distribution of net D, with a range from $+1$ through 0 to -1, is another advantage. The standard error can be easily derived and is relatively small, the largest error occurring when the true discrimination is zero and the item difficulty is .50.

Net D has been criticized for not being a correlational technique and for tending to select items of .50 difficulty when contrasted to Flanagan's r. For reasons to be considered later, the maximum number of correct discriminations an item can make is directly related to the difficulty of the item. Therefore, it should be anticipated that net D, being directly proportional to the net discrimination made by the item, would tend to select items of 50 percent difficulty.

Considering the assumptions, advantages, and disadvantages of the various indices of discrimination discussed in this chapter, *it is recommended that net D be used in item analysis* of classroom tests. The instructor or teacher should not be apologetic for employing this index of discrimination because of its computational ease. The strengths of this index certainly offset its weaknesses.

Since net D is directly proportional to the net discriminations made, one might suspect that tests containing items with high indices of discrimination would be reliable. In a study by Hales,[12] it was found that items selected from an item pool containing 605 social studies items on the basis of the magnitude of their net D indices did, in fact, produce reliable tests. Through the use of the Kuder-Richardson Formula 20 (KR20), which is a special form of the generalized internal consistency equation, the index of reliability of a tenth grade social studies test was calculated as .904. The net D values of the 50 items selected for this test had a range of .47 to .76, and a median of .60. The KR20 index of reliability of an eleventh grade social studies test was .925. The net D values of these 50 items had a range of .59 to .79, with a median of .66. The KR20 index of a social

---

[11] Warren G. Findley, "A Rationale for Evaluation of Item Statistics." *Educational and Psychological Measurement*, **16**, 1956, 176–177.

[12] Loyde W. Hales, "An Empirical Study of Selected Test Characteristics as Functions of Three Item Selection Techniques." Unpublished doctoral dissertation, University of Kansas, 1964.

studies test for both the tenth and the eleventh grades was .917. The net D values had a range of .54 to .73, with a median of .60. In the same study, comparable grade level tests were constructed on the basis of the magnitude of the Flanagan's r indices and on the basis of the magnitude of the Flanagan's r indices computed from proportions which had been corrected for chance success. The reliabilities of the tests constructed on the basis of net D tended to be higher than the reliabilities of the comparable grade level tests constructed on the basis of Flanagan's r, or Flanagan's r corrected for chance success. The differences were not statistically significant.

Computing Net D

Net D may be found by using the following equation, with V representing item validity:

$$V = \frac{R_U}{N_U} - \frac{R_L}{N_L},$$

and since $N_U = N_L$,

$$V = \frac{R_U - R_L}{N_U},$$

where R_U is the number of correct responses on the item by the upper group, R_L is the number of correct responses on the item by the lower group, N_U is the number of examinees in the upper group, and N_L is the number of examinees in the lower group.

However, it is not necessary to perform all of the steps involved in the calculation of net D from this equation. In order to reduce the computation time, Fig. E.1 in Appendix E was developed. When the number in the upper group is between 0 and 45, this graph gives the index of discrimination associated with each absolute $R_U - R_L$ difference. To find net D, determine the number of papers in the upper group (N_U), the number of correct responses to the item by the upper group (R_U), and the number of correct responses to the item by the lower group (R_L). Find the $R_U - R_L$ value for this item. Enter the first (outside) column of numbers on the diagonal axis (the column labeled "$R_U - R_L$") with this value. Proceed in a horizontal direction as far as the column for the value of N_U. This column is located by entering the first (upper) row of numbers on the horizontal axis with the N_U-value. From this point proceed along the diagonal line to the right-hand axis and read net D from that scale.

For example, if the upper group and the lower group each contained 20 examinees, if 15 examinees got the item correct in the upper group and if 5 examinees got the item correct in the lower group, then $R_U - R_L = 15 - 5 = 10$. Entering the diagonal column of the graph $R_U - R_L$ with 10 and going across the row to the column corresponding to $N_U = 20$, we find a net D value of .50.

Note: If R_L is larger than R_U, the net D obtained is negative. If, in the example above, $R_U = 5$ and $R_L = 15$, then $R_U - R_L = 5 - 15 = -10$ and net D would then be $-.50$.

Obtaining the Index of Difficulty

Item difficulty may be found by using the following equation:

$$D = \frac{R_U + R_L}{N_U + N_L}.$$

It is not necessary, however, to perform all the steps involved in the calculation of D from this equation. Figure E.1 may be used to reduce computational time. This figure gives the index of difficulty associated with each $R_U + R_L$ value. To find D, enter the second (inside) column of numbers on the diagonal axis (the column labeled $R_U + R_L$) with the sum of the number of correct responses to the item by both groups ($R_U + R_L$). Proceed in a horizontal direction as far as the column containing the total in both groups. This column is located by entering the second (lower) row of numbers on the horizontal axis with the $N_U + N_L$ value. From this point, proceed along the diagonal line to the right-hand axis and read D from that scale. For example, if the upper group and the lower group each contained 20 examinees, if 15 examinees got the item correct in the upper group and if 5 examinees got the item correct in the lower group, then $R_U + R_L = 15 + 5 = 20$. Entering the $R_U + R_L$ diagonal column of the table with 20 and going across the row to the column corresponding to 40, we find the index of difficulty to be .50.

Interpretation of Net D

The interpretation of net D is somewhat comparable to that of a coefficient of correlation. Whenever the value is negative, the item exhibits negative discrimination; thus, it reduces the discrimination of the test. When the value is less than .20, the discriminatory power is so small as to be considered negligible. Items with indices between .20 and .40 are of some value in discriminating between examinees. Items with indices between .40 and .60 are good discriminators. Those with indices above .60 are unusually good.

Factors Influencing Discrimination

The discriminatory power of the item is influenced by a number of factors, including: the previous learning experiences of the examinees; the ability of the stem (aided by the choices offered) to structure the question for the examinee; the extent of ambiguity in the item; the ability of the foils to appeal to those with incorrect or lack of knowledge; the presentation of only one best or correct answer which will appeal to the upper group; and the difficulty of the item.

The maximum number of discriminations which an item can make between two groups occurs when all the members of one group get the item correct and all the members of the second group miss the item.

$N_U = N_L = 10,$

$R_U = 10, \qquad R_L = 0,$

$D = \dfrac{10 + 0}{10 + 10} = .50,$

$V = \dfrac{10}{10} - \dfrac{0}{10} = +1.0.$

The number of discriminations made (NDM) can be determined by the formula:

$$\text{NDM} = R_U \times (N_L - R_L).$$

For example, if 10 pupils in one group passed the item and 0 pupil in the other group passed it, 100 discriminations would be made.

$N_U = N_L = 10,$

$R_U = 10, \qquad R_L = 0,$

$\text{NDM} = 10 \times (10 - 0) = 10 \times 10 = 100.$

The process involved is that of counting the total number of pupils in one group which were differentiated from pupils in the other group. In the previous example (NDM = 100), the first student in the upper group was differentiated from 10 students in the lower group, thus providing 10 discriminations. The second student in the upper group was also differentiated from 10 students in the lower group, thus providing another 10 discriminations. The same number of discriminations is made for each member of the upper group who got the item correct. Since 10 pupils in the upper group got the item correct, the number of discriminations made would be 100.

$\text{NDM} = 10 + 10 + 10 + 10 + 10 + 10 + 10 + 10 + 10 + 10,$

or

$\text{NDM} = 10 \times 10$ (since multiplication is a shortcut for addition),

$\text{NDM} = 100.$

The relationship between item difficulty and optimum discrimination is illustrated in Table 13.1. It can be noted that as the index of difficulty departs from .50, the absolute number of discriminations which can be made by that item decreases.

Table 13.1 Optimal discrimination and the index of difficulty

Item difficulty	Number correct		Number of discriminations made (NDM)
	Upper group	Lower group	
1.00	10	10	$10 \times 0 = 0$
.90	10	8	$10 \times 2 = 20$
.80	10	6	$10 \times 4 = 40$
.70	10	4	$10 \times 6 = 60$
.60	10	2	$10 \times 8 = 80$
.50	10	0	$10 \times 10 = 100$
.40	8	0	$8 \times 10 = 80$
.30	6	0	$6 \times 10 = 60$
.20	4	0	$4 \times 10 = 40$
.10	2	0	$2 \times 10 = 20$
.00	0	0	$0 \times 10 = 0$

$$N_U = N_L = 10$$

USING ITEM ANALYSIS DATA

In the preceding portions of this chapter, the rationale for the use of item analysis data was developed, consideration was given to selected issues in the field, and methods for obtaining indices of difficulty and discrimination were presented. In the remainder of the chapter, the focus will be on the acquisition and use of item analysis data. The procedures for computing item analysis data will be presented in a step-by-step, sequential order. The application of item analysis to the rejection, selection, and revision of items will be demonstrated. Although the primary emphasis is on multiple-choice tests developed for maximum discrimination among pupils, the application of these procedures to other formats and the use of this information in the construction of mastery tests will be considered.

The Item Analysis Card

An item analysis card can be used to keep an accurate account of information obtained from several test administrations of a test question. Information so recorded is readily available for use in the selection and revision of items for a new classroom test. By recording the topic and level (knowledge, understanding, application) of the item at the top of the card, the effectiveness of the item analysis card system is enhanced because the cards can be scanned in a file for items appropriate to the topic without reading each item completely.

Item analysis cards can be reproduced on 5 × 8 cards. A line should be drawn down the middle of the card, dividing it into two 5 × 4 sections. The left-hand portion of the card can be used for recording the item, with the item topic and level. The right-hand portion can be used for reporting the item analysis data (see sample in Fig. 13.1). For each item choice, the number of correct responses

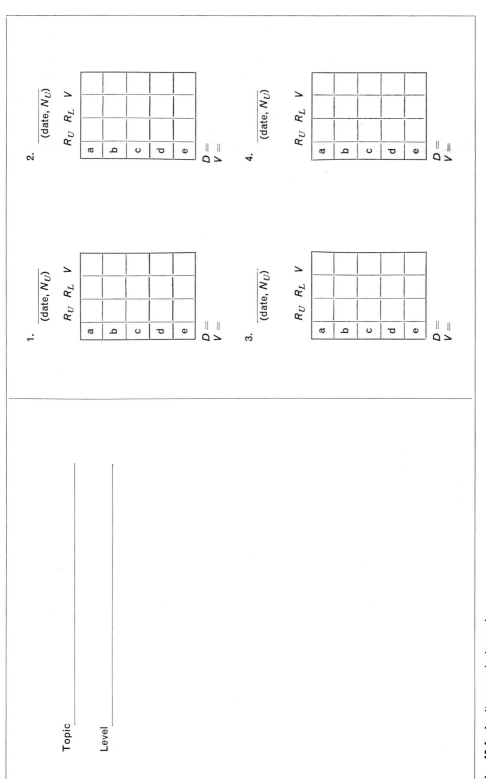

Fig. 13.1. An item analysis card.

by the upper group (R_U) and the number of correct responses by the lower group (R_L) should be recorded in the appropriate columns. If the class size is near 75, one might also wish to record the V-values for each foil in the appropriate column. Below these columns the index of difficulty and the index of discrimination should be reported for the correct response. Also, the correct response should be indicated on the card. Item analysis cards can be mimeographed to reduce recording time. The item can be typed or cut out from the test and pasted on the card.

Steps in Obtaining Item Analysis Data

The use of the following procedures should be helpful in obtaining item analysis data for recording on the analysis cards.

1. Prepare an item analysis card for each item. Paste or record the item on the left-hand portion of the card.
2. Arrange the cards in the same order as the items on the test.
3. Score the papers.
4. Order the examination papers from the highest to the lowest score.
5. Select the top 27 percent of the papers and designate these as the upper group.
6. Select the lowest 27 percent of the papers and designate these as the lower group.
7. Obtain the number of responses for each choice for each item by the upper group and record on the item analysis cards.
8. Obtain the number of responses for each choice for each item by the lower group and record on the item analysis cards.
9. Use Fig. E.1 to obtain the indices of discrimination and difficulty for each item. (Figure E.1 can be used to find the V values for each foil.)

Although the general procedures for the calculation of item analysis data have been presented, it might be worthwhile to consider in more detail various methods for determining the frequencies of choices of item alternates for the upper group and for the lower group. When the answers are recorded on separate answer sheets which are then machine scored, it is often possible to use the same machine to tally the number of choices for each item alternate for both groups separately. These tallies can then be transferred to the item analysis cards.

If it is inconvenient to machine-score the papers, it may be necessary to tally by hand the frequencies for each alternate. This can be accomplished by placing all the papers in the upper group side by side, with the first item of each paper visible. Then it is a relatively simple matter to count the number of pupils in the upper group who chose the first alternate, the number who chose the second alternate, and so on, for all alternates for this item. The same procedure can be followed for each item for each group.

A typewriter can be used to prepare a master list of responses to each item alternate for each group separately. Any keys on the keyboard can be used to represent the alternates. Thus, for a five-choice item numbered 1–5, "a" might be used for alternate 1, "s" for alternate 2, "d" for alternate 3, "f" for alternate 4, and "g" for alternate 5 (see Fig. 13.2). The master list shows for each item all

UPPER GROUP: $N = 15$

Item number

```
[000000000011111111112222222222233333333334444444444 5]
[123456789012345678901234567890123456789012345678 90]
```

Responses

```
aasgaddgffsadfagfdsaasgsfafffasgfgfasfdsasgfsafdds
adsgaadgfdsffgagfdssasgsfafffaggfgfasfdsssgfsaddds
ddsgasdgffsadgagfdfaasgsfafffasgfgffagdaasgfssfdda
adsgfddgffsgdfagfdsasssaaafffasgfgfasfdsasgfaaddds
adagadddffsadfagfdsaasgafafffassfgfasfdaasgfafddds
aasgaddgffsgdfagfdsaasgsfafffasgfgssffdsasggfadddf
ddsgaddgffsfdfagsassssgssafffafffgfasfdsasgfsaddds
adagaddgffsfdfagsdsassgafafffafgfggfafdassffsaddds
adsggddgffsfagagfdsafagagafffasgfgfgffdsasgfsaddds
afsgaddgffsfdfagfdssasgssaagfasgfgfasgdsaagfasddss
dasgaddggfsfdfagadsaasgsfaaffasgfgfgsfdfasggsadada
dgfafgdfggsfdfagfdssasgafafffasgfgfasffssagfsaddds
adsgaddgffsfdfagagsaaagsfaaffaggfgfssadfasgasadgds
adsgaddgsfsfdfagfdsagsasfssffasgfgaasfdgasffaaddfg
agagaddggfafdfagddsassgsfaaffasgggfasadsaaggssadfg
```

LOWER GROUP: $N = 15$

Item number

```
[000000000011111111112222222222233333333334444444444 5]
[123456789012345678901234567890123456789012345678 90]
```

Responses

```
gaagaddgffsfsfdfagsssagsfafffasgfgfasfdsasgfaaddds
gdsgadaaffsfadgaassssasggdfasddagafadgdfdsffsadfdd
fdfgadfsffsfddfagafffagfaggsfddasgfdfgddsadfsgdads
sdssfggsfggfggaaasgfgdgffdfsssfdsdgagfssassasadffd
gassdadffgasgddafagffasffdgsfsfdfdgfsadsaaggfaadas
ddfgddgffsfadfggagsgasgsafgsadsdfffgfddsasddsffssa
sdgssasdaaadffagfgaasffgfsgfaggffsfaaafdsadfsafsdf
dadgasdgadgsagffddssssfgadsgffsadsagssfdsssgdsaggds
fgsfagedffagdaggdfgdfsagfafggagsgagsfdsagfgdasfdfa
ffsaffaffdasadssdsssagssfagaagffgafsafsaafadaafsss
aadddfsfafdaggagdfagaaggagaaagasaagasfdafgfadsfgag
gsffaddsfafsdfafasafsafagafggdgdgssafgaadgfgadffsa
afggssdfssggdsgsadfaggfagasgasddssagasgsadgfdgdfgs
gassgaddfasgfsafadassdgaagaddgdasffaagadadfgasfssa
agsfdasdfgaafdssgaadffgaddagfssfaddsgafdsgadfsafdd
```

Correct
response

```
adsgaddgffsfdfagfdsassgsfafffasgfgfasfdsasgfsaddds
```

Frequency of responses for item 1

	Responses							Responses				
Group	a	s	d	f	g		Group	1	2	3	4	5
Upper	11	0	4	0	0	or	Upper	11	0	4	0	0
Lower	3	2	2	3	5		Lower	3	2	2	3	5

Fig. 13.2. Example of typewritten master list of responses for a 50-item test.

the choices made for that item by all the members of that group. Each row on the master list represents a different person and each column a different item. The advantage of this method is the speed with which one can obtain the number of selections of each item alternate.

If this method is to be employed the following steps should be taken:

1. Insert a piece of paper in the typewriter and number sequentially across the top of the page the number of items on the test, returning the carriage to the space under item number 1.

2. Select the keys which will represent the various item responses.

3. To prepare the master list for the upper group, take the first paper for that group and type the answer to item 1 under number 1, the answer to item 2 under number 2, etc., for all items, using the appropriate keys to represent the responses.

4. Type the answers from the second paper on row two. Do this for each paper in the group, using a different row for each answer sheet.

5. Count the number of times "a" appears in column 1, and record this as the frequency for response 1 of item 1. In the same column count and record the number of times "s" occurs and record as response 2, the number of times "d" occurs and record as response 3, the number of times "f" occurs and record as response 4, the number of times "g" occurs and record as response 5.

6. Repeat this counting procedure for each column and record the results on the appropriate item analysis card.

7. Repeat steps 1 through 6 for the lower group.

8. Use Fig. E.1 to obtain the indices of discrimination and difficulty for each item.

Stability of Item Analysis Data

The stability of item analysis data from test administration to test administration depends on the comparability of the examinees from year to year, the comparability of the methods and content of instruction from year to year, and the size of the group used to calculate the indices of difficulty and discrimination. Usually one can expect relatively stable indices when the number of examinees approaches 100. Nevertheless, item analysis data obtained from classes of about 30 are still valuable for use in the revision and selection of items, even though they are relatively unstable. A rough gauge is better than none at all.

Evaluating and Refining Items

Item analysis data is used in the selection and revision of items, and principles have been developed to aid in the interpretation of indices of difficulty and indices of discrimination. A few item examples are now presented to show how item analysis data can be used in evaluating and revising items. As indicated by its item analysis data, the item illustrated in Fig. 13.3 is a relatively difficult, poorly discriminating item. A closer examination of this item reveals that a foil, alternate "c," was chosen more often by the upper group than by the lower group. In reading the item, it can be seen that the keyed response is the best choice but that "c" is also

Topic: *Characteristics of gases*

Level: *Understanding*

1. Why is helium used in balloons?

   a. It will not expand at high altitudes.

  *b. It will not explode easily.

   c. It is lighter than air.

   d. It is lighter than hydrogen.

1. 3/3/71–50
$\overline{\text{(date, } N_U)}$

	R_U	R_L	V
a	0	10	$-.20$
b	25	15	$.20$
c	20	10	$.20$
d	5	15	$-.20$
e			

$$D = .40$$
$$V = .20$$

Fig. 13.3. Item analysis data revealing a difficult, poorly discriminating item.

Topic: *Advantages/disadvantages
of various test formats*

Level: *Understanding*

2. As compared with essay examinations, the primary advantage of multiple-choice tests is:

  *a. Better sampling.

   b. Ease of construction.

   c. Measures organizational skill.

   d. Measures creativity.

1. 3/26/60 — 50
$\overline{\text{(date, } N_U)}$

	R_U	R_L	V
a	49	45	$.08$
b	1	3	$-.04$
c	0	2	$-.04$
d	0	0	$.00$
e			

$$D = .94$$
$$V = .08$$

Fig. 13.4 Item analysis data revealing an easy, poorly discriminating item.

correct. If both "b" and "c" were keyed as correct, D would become .70 and V would become .40, resulting in a definite improvement in the item. However, it would be better either to substitute a new alternate for choice "c" or to change the stem. Changing the stem to read "Why is helium, instead of hydrogen, used in balloons?" might be the better approach.

    The item in Fig. 13.4 is too easy ($D = .94$) and, for this reason, fails to discriminate. If one is interested in determining whether or not the class knows

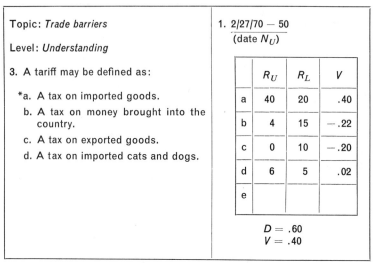

Topic: *Trade barriers*

Level: *Understanding*

1. 2/27/70 — 50
   (date N_U)

3. A tariff may be defined as:

   *a. A tax on imported goods.
   b. A tax on money brought into the country.
   c. A tax on exported goods.
   d. A tax on imported cats and dogs.

	R_U	R_L	V
a	40	20	.40
b	4	15	−.22
c	0	10	−.20
d	6	5	.02
e			

$D = .60$
$V = .40$

Fig. 13.5. Item analysis data of a discriminating item.

the "primary advantage" of this test format, the item might be improved by making the alternatives more homogeneous. The examinees could be required to select, from among *bona fide* advantages, the primary one. For example, one foil could be: "ease of scoring."

The indices of difficulty and validity for the next item (Fig. 13.5) are quite satisfactory. However, since the upper group seemed more favorably inclined toward choice "d" than did the lower group and since alternate "d," although less satisfactory, is a correct response, one might be inclined to revise this foil. A simple revision of foil "d" would be to substitute the word "exported" for "imported."

After looking at the index of difficulty (.30) and the index of discrimination (.12) of the item shown in Fig. 13.6, one can conclude that this is a difficult, poorly discriminating item. Why is this so? Perhaps the question is too trivial or ambiguous; it may be that there is no correct answer; or perhaps the concept being tested here was not properly covered in the course of instruction. However, after carefully reading the stem and alternates, one can see that "d" is the only incorrect response to the question. If "most" were inserted before "appropriate" in the stem, the item would then have only one correct response. Even with this change, alternative "b" might still prove to be a poor foil and, perhaps, should be revised.

Other Selection-Type Item Formats

The traditional true-false item is, in one sense, a multiple-choice item with only two alternatives: agree and disagree. Consequently, one would expect good items to have item difficulties near .75 and item validities somewhat lower than for multiple-choice items, around .20. However, when the true-false format is modified so that the examinee is asked to indicate the extent of agreement by choosing a

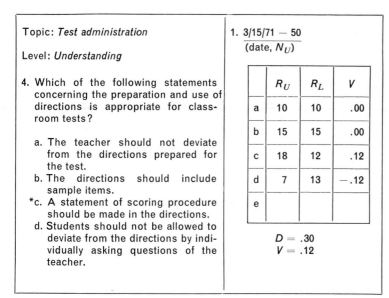

Topic: *Test administration*

Level: *Understanding*

4. Which of the following statements concerning the preparation and use of directions is appropriate for classroom tests?

    a. The teacher should not deviate from the directions prepared for the test.
    b. The directions should include sample items.
   *c. A statement of scoring procedure should be made in the directions.
    d. Students should not be allowed to deviate from the directions by individually asking questions of the teacher.

1. 3/15/71 — 50
$\overline{\text{(date, } N_U)}$

	R_U	R_L	V
a	10	10	.00
b	15	15	.00
c	18	12	.12
d	7	13	−.12
e			

$D = .30$
$V = .12$

Fig. 13.6 Item analysis data of an ambiguous, poorly discriminating item.

position on a five-point scale from "strongly disagree" through "no opinion" to "strongly agree," the item can then be treated, for item analysis purposes, as a five-choice, multiple-choice item with each position on the scale as an alternate. In both cases, the procedures appropriate for calculating item analysis data for multiple-choice items can be used.

When the multiple-choice format is used for a multiple-answer item, each alternate must be independently answered as agreeing or disagreeing with the stem, making a true or false statement. Consequently, for item analysis purposes each alternate should be treated as an independent true-false question. In the example shown in Fig. 13.7, note that alternates 2 and 4 are both false and that their V-values are negative. A multiple-answer item with the below characteristics should be a good item.

The matching question is another variation of the multiple-choice format where, for a series of items, the same alternates are offered. If, as in the traditional approach, an alternate can be correct for only one item, the indices of difficulty and validity are interrelated and the elimination of one item from the series can be expected to influence the item analysis data for each of the other items. However, if an alternate may be correct for more than one item, the indices are more independent. Item analysis data should be obtained for each item in the series separately (i.e. each item with all alternates should have a separate item analysis card) and the procedures appropriate for multiple-choice items should be used to obtain the indices of validity and difficulty. Because the modification of any alternate influences the functioning of all items, the cards of a series should be stapled together. Any revision must be done with the whole series in mind.

Topic: *Advantages/disadvantages of various test formats*	1. 9/29/69 — 10
	(date, N_U)

Level: *Understanding*

5. As compared with multiple-choice tests, the advantages of essay tests are:

   *1. Ease of construction.
   2. Better sampling.
  *3. Measures organizational skills.
   4. Ease of scoring.

	R_U	R_L	V	D
1	10	6	.40	.80
2	6	9	−.30	.75
3	9	7	.20	.80
4	5	10	−.50	.75
5				

Fig. 13.7 Item analysis card for a multiple-answer item.

Completion Tests

The completion item format is somewhat adaptable to item analysis techniques. If the completion item requires only one point per answer, it can be scored 0 or 1; indices of difficulty and validity can be obtained by the direct application of the procedures employed with multiple-choice items. Since chance is not a factor, indices of difficulty should cluster around .50.

Essay Tests

Although it is not a common practice to subject essay tests to item analysis, it is certainly advantageous to examine each question in light of the responses received in order to determine the validity of the question and of the question format. If the poorer students did as well or better on a particular question than the better pupils, the question does not contribute to the differentiation between good and poor pupils. Such a question might have been ambiguous, although it could have required detail not thought important by the better student. If nearly all the students did quite well (or quite poorly) on the question, the degree of difficulty reduces the possibility that the question will discriminate. If the responses required and obtained by the question were such as to be amenable to the multiple-choice format, the question was probably written in the wrong format.

It is possible to obtain item analysis data on essay tests in a manner similar to that presented for selection type tests. The index of difficulty would be the average number of points received on the question divided by the number of possible points. Thus D may be found by use of the formula

$$D = \frac{R_U + R_L}{X_{\max}(N_U + N_L)},$$

where R_U is the number of points received by the upper group, R_L is the number of points received by the lower group, X_{max} is the maximum number of points an individual could receive on the question, N_U is the number of examinees in the upper group, and N_L is the number of examinees in the lower group Similarly, the index of discrimination may be found by use of the formula

$$V = \frac{R_U}{(X_{max})N_U} - \frac{R_L}{(X_{max})N_L}, \quad \text{since } N_U = N_L,$$

$$V = \frac{R_U - R_L}{(X_{max})N_U}.$$

Mastery Tests

A mastery test, sometimes called a criterion reference test, is designed to divide examinees into two groups: those who have mastered the fundamentals of a skill or skills and those who have not mastered the fundamentals and are, consequently, not prepared for more advanced instruction in the use of these skills. In a mastery test, one would expect most examinees to answer the majority of the items correctly. Thus, appropriate items for a mastery test should have indices of difficulty grouped closely around .90. The indices of discrimination will, of necessity, be quite low but should not be negative.

A mastery test can be extremely useful when administered both before and after the learning experience. Analysis of the pre-test results can aid in determining the prior learning brought to the learning situation. It may yield information concerning particular strengths or weaknesses of the group which can aid in developing lesson plans and learning activities. Analysis of the post-test results can be used to assess the effectiveness of the learning experiences. Areas of particular difficulty and success can be determined. By examining the frequencies with which various item responses are chosen, as well as the overall item difficulties and validities, the item data can be used to diagnose difficulties and misconceptions which are troublesome to the learners. This use of item data can enhance learning, regardless of the type of test administered to the learners. Comparisons between the pre-test and post-test can be used to assess the degree of successfulness of the learning situation. Item validity data can be determined by calculating the difference between the proportion of students who successfully completed the item on the post-test and the proportion of students who successfully completed the item on the pre-test. This index of discrimination may be found by using the formula

$$V' = \frac{R_{post}}{N_{post}} - \frac{R_{pre}}{N_{pre}}, \quad \text{since } N_{pre} = N_{post} = N,$$

$$V' = \frac{R_{post} - R_{pre}}{N}.$$

Example: Mastery Test, Early Childhood

The test illustrated in this section was used to evaluate student achievement following the first teaching unit in mathematics at the kindergarten level.[13] The unit was designed to teach kindergarten children to abstractly add and multiply single-digit numbers and the numer 10.

A test at this level must be oral, with the teacher asking the questions and recording the responses. This particular test was administered individually, with about five minutes allotted to each child. The rest of the children enjoyed quiet play activities while the teacher administered the examination.

The test was designed for one basic purpose: to differentiate between those children who had mastered the fundamentals of single-digit addition and multiplication from those children who had not mastered these fundamentals and were, consequently, not prepared for the more advanced instruction which required the use of these elementary skills. Therefore, the test was designed to be a *mastery test*. One would expect this type of test to be fairly easy, with the better students obtaining consistently higher scores than the poorer students. The test is shown in Table 13.2 and the test analysis data are listed in Tables 13.3 and 13.4.

Table 13.2 Mathematics test

Test items administered orally to 16 kindergarten children as an individual performance test

---

1. Give me 6 ways to make 10
   a) 4 "plus" ways*
   b) 2 "of the" ways†

2. Give me 3 ways to make 1
   a) 2 "plus" ways
   b) 1 "of the" ways

3. Give me 4 ways to make 4
   a) 2 "plus" ways
   b) 2 "of the" ways

4. Give me 4 ways to make 7
   a) 2 "plus" ways
   b) 2 "of the" ways

5. Give me 5 ways to make 8
   a) 3 "plus" ways
   b) 2 "of the" ways

All correct combinations were given credit, for example,
$1 + 1 + 1 + 1 + 1 + 1 + 1 + 1 + 1 + 1$
was given credit as one of the "plus" ways to make 10, as was
$5 + 5$.

---

* "plus" refers to addition.
† "of the" refers to multiplication.

---

[13] The test was prepared by Nancy Petering, undergraduate at the University of Missouri–St. Louis, and it was administered to 16 kindergarten children at Meramel Elementary School, Clayton, Missouri.

Table 13.3 Obtained scores on the mathematics test

Score	Frequency		
	Total	"Plus"	"Of the"
22	4	—	—
21	1	—	—
20	2	—	—
19	3	—	—
18	1	—	—
17	1	—	—
16	1	—	—
15	0	—	—
14	0	—	—
13	0	7	—
12	1	2	—
11	0	0	—
10	0	2	—
9	1	1	7
8	0	0	2
7	0	2	3
6	0	0	1
5	0	0	2
4	0	1	0
3	0	0	0
2	0	0	0
1	0	0	0
0	1	1	1
Possible score	22	13	9
Average score	17.4	10.1	7.3

If a student is having no difficulty with these skills, he would be expected to obtain a score of at least 18 (80% × 22) and preferably 20 (90% × 22) of the items correct. This would indicate that at least five students and possibly nine students should have additional help with these skills. Similarly, seven students obtained a score less than 12 (90% × 13) on the "plus" items and seven students obtained a score less than 8 (90% × 9) on the "of the" items. The fact that nine students overall scored less than 90% correct and only seven students scored less than 90% on each of the two subparts indicates that there are at least two students who are having more difficulty with one of the skills than the other. Furthermore, special attention should be given to the student who had zero correct responses.

SUMMARY

Item analysis data are used to eliminate weak test items, to find weaknesses in other test items, and to aid in the selection of items for a test. The data indicate the difficulty of each item for the class and the extent that each item discriminates between the better and the poorer students.

Table 13.4 Item analysis data on the mathematics test

Item	Part	*Number of points correct Upper	Lower	N_U†	D‡	§V'
	Total	47	34	8	.87	+.27
1	"Plus"	32	21	8	.83	+.34
	"Of the"	16	12	8	.87	+.25
	Total	23	9	8	.67	+.58
2	"Plus"	15	5	8	.67	+.62
	"Of the"	7	5	8	.75	+.25
	Total	30	22	8	.81	+.25
3	"Plus"	16	11	8	.84	+.31
	"Of the	16	9	8	.78	+.56
	Total	29	22	8	.78	+.25
4	"Plus"	16	11	8	.84	+.31
	"Of the"	16	7	8	.72	+.56
	Total	39	24	8	.79	+.37
5	"Plus"	24	11	8	.73	+.54
	"Of the"	16	12	8	.87	+.25

The item analysis data indicate that on the whole this test was very good. On three out of five items, the difficulty index was greater than .80, which means that more than 80% of the students got the item correct. Furthermore, the fourth item approaches this value. The validities (V') of the items are high for a mastery test. Further analyses of these indices indicate that additional work on these skills should be undertaken if mastery is desired (assuming that mastery refers to about 90% of the students getting each item correct). The difficulty index of Item 2 indicates that the students have difficulty working with the number "1." Therefore, further instruction on this concept is indicated.

* The students were divided into two groups: the top eight students on the test (upper group) and the bottom eight students on the test (lower group). The part scores being analyzed (i.e., total score, "plus" score, or "of the" score) were used for these divisions.
† N_U = number of upper group = 8.
‡ D = item difficulty = proportion of possible points obtained.
§ V' = proportion of possible points obtained by the upper group minus proportion of points obtained by the lower group.

The *index of difficulty* (D) is the proportion of the examinees who answered the item correctly: the larger the proportion, the easier the item. The maximum number of discriminations an item can make occurs at .50 difficulty. A test designed to obtain maximum differentiation among examinees should be of about 50 percent difficulty, with the mean score falling midway between chance score and 100 percent of the items.

The net D *index of discrimination*, item validity (V), is the difference between the proportion in the better group who responded correctly to the item and the proportion in the poorer group who responded correctly to it. Membership in the groups is dependent upon total test score. The upper 27 percent of the examinees is placed in the better group and the lower 27 percent is placed in the poorer group. Other common methods for determining the index of discrimination are: Flanagan's r, Davis' indices, and tetrachoric r.

The item analysis card is a record of information on an item for up to four administrations. The card contains the item, topic, level, date of administration, number in the upper group, item difficulty, and alternative validities. The item analysis data can aid in evaluating and refining items.

Utilization of selection-type tests introduces the possibility that correct responses might be chosen entirely by guessing. A student's total test score might be expected to include a few points resulting from chance selections when answers are not known. A correction for guessing formula may be applied to obtain estimated "true" scores. However, the correction procedure does not improve the reported scores, and, therefore, it should not be applied to them.

PROBLEMS

1. Define the following terms:
   a) Item difficulty   b) Test difficulty   c) Item discrimination
2. What is the relationship between item difficulty and item discrimination?
3. Why are 27 percent upper- and lower-groups used in item analysis?
4. Explain why items of 50 difficulty will not necessarily produce the best discriminatory test.
5. List five reasons why the correction for guessing formula should *not* be applied to scores.
6. List two advantages of the net D procedure for determining item discrimination as compared to the other three procedures outlined in this chapter.
7. Analyze and revise the following test item:

The Good Neighbor Policy was started by which Presidents?	$N_U\,15$		
	N_U	N_L	V
a. Coolidge and Hoover			
a.	13	11	
b. Johnson and Nixon			
b.	2	1	
c. Washington and Jefferson			
c.	0	1	
d. Wilson and Harding			
d.	0	2	
	D_____		
	V_____		

8. Using the typewriter method, prepare an item analysis for a classroom test.

LIST OF SYMBOLS USED IN CHAPTER 13

Symbols	Verbal equivalents
D	Index of difficulty
L	Subscript used to represent the lower group of examinees
N_L	Number of examinees in lower group
N_{post}	Number of examinees taking post-test
N_{pre}	Number of examinees taking pre-test
N_U	Number of examinees in upper group
R_L	Number of examinees in the lower group who answered an item correctly; number of points obtained on an item by the lower group
R_{post}	Number of examinees taking post-test who answered an item correctly
R_{pre}	Number of examinees taking pre-test who answered an item correctly
R_U	Number of examinees in the upper group who answered an item correctly; number of points obtained on an item by the upper group
U	Subscript used to represent the upper group of examinees
V	Item validity; index of discrimination; Net D
X_{max}	The number of points possible for a test item
NDM	Number of discriminations made by an item
k	Number of item alternates in the correction for chance formula
S	"True" score based on the correction for chance formula
R	Number of examinees who answered an item correctly; Number of points received by examinees; Number of correct responses received by examinees
W	Number of incorrect responses by an examinee

SUGGESTED READING

Ahmann, J. Stanley, and Marvin D. Glock, *Evaluating Pupil Growth: Principles of Tests and Measurement*. Allyn and Bacon, Boston, 1967, Chapter 6.

Cox, R. C., "Item Selection Techniques and Evaluation of Instructional Objectives." *Journal of Educational Measurement*, **2**, 1965, 181–185.

Davis, Frederick B., "Item Selection Techniques," in E. F. Lindquist (Ed.), *Educational Measurement*. American Council on Education, Washington, D.C., 1951, Chapter 9.

Diederich, Paul B., *Short-Cut Statistics for Teacher-Made Tests* (2nd ed.). Educational Testing Service Evaluation and Advisory Service Series, No. 5, Princeton, N.J., 1964, pp. 2–8.

Ebel, Robert L., *Measuring Educational Achievement*. Prentice-Hall, Englewood Cliffs, N.J., 1965, Chapter 11.

Findley, Warren G., "A Rationale for Evaluation of Item Discrimination Statistics." *Educational and Psychological Measurement*, **16**, 1956, 175–180.

Thorndike, Robert L., and Elizabeth Hagen, *Measurement and Evaluation in Psychology and Education*. (3rd. ed.) John Wiley and Sons, New York, 1969, pp. 124–127.

LITERATURE ON EXAMINATIONS

Early Literature

During the early periods of testing, the oral examination was the primary method of measurement. On examination day an instructor of a class of fifteen students might have thirty examination questions prepared. During the examination period, each student might be asked two questions. Then, upon the teacher's judgment of a student's responses, a grade would be assigned. This system had many weaknesses, ranging from the fact that no two students were asked the same questions to the inherent gross subjectivity in evaluating the responses. Horace Mann seemed to recognize some of these problems when he wrote, "Suppose, under the form of oral examination, an hour is assigned to a class of thirty pupils, this gives two minutes apiece. But under the late mode of examination, we have the paradox, that an hour for thirty is sixty minutes apiece." (Mann, 1924,[1] p. 40) Furthermore, he considered this new type of essay examination impartial as compared to the old oral examination since the same questions were submitted to all examinees (Mann, 1924).

During the second half of the nineteenth century, the feeling that the examination system was inadequate permeated the thinking of many scholars. Concern was transferred from the topic, "Which form of test is the best?" to the more general topic, "Is the examination system inherently bad?" For over thirty years, this question served as a topic of debate in many professional journals. The debates centered around the following four areas: (1) the effect of the examination system

---

[1] The references cited are listed at the end of this appendix.

on student health, (2) the effect of the examination system on teaching, (3) the validity and reliability of the examinations used, and (4) the college entrance examinations.

Some educators argued that nervous strain on a student during an examination period would be detrimental to his physical health (Hewitt, 1939; Scoones, 1888). Ignatieff (1898), in a study of weight loss of students during extended examination periods, found the weight loss to be similar to that which could be expected during a prolonged illness.

Some educators (Farrand, 1895–1896; Given, 1894–1895; Herbert *et al.*, 1888, 1889) maintained that the use of examinations was deterimental to good teaching. They felt that the pressures exerted by the system tended to destroy individuality in teaching. Teachers were being forced to adhere closely to prepared texts and outlines in an effort to prepare students for such examinations as those required for college admission. Although recognizing that educational tests were imperfect, others (Kiddle and Schem, 1877) felt that there was no other way to ascertain the efficacy of the teacher's work or the proficiency of the student. Proponents of the examination system pointed out that, in a structure as heterogeneous as the educational system, there is no other way to test the achievement of pupils (Maxwell, 1890). When content examinations of students were flagrantly used to judge their instructor's ability to teach, the vigorous attacks on the examination system were well deserved ("How Examiners are Made," 1898). Others (Sayrs, 1921) pointed out that an examination can be useful if it is used to measure a student's memory and ability to generalize, and if original problems are contained in the examination.

The reliability and validity of the college entrance examinations were questioned. Given (1894–1895) argued that "All the immediate circumstances of the examination are unfair: the unfamiliar room, the crowd of strange companions, the limited time, the inevitable nervous excitement. . . . The whole method is unfair" (p. 75). Conversely, some educators (Eliot, 1895–1896; Lathan, 1886; Seymour, 1896) felt that examinations were necessary even if they left a great amount to be desired. In their defense, Richardson stated that "A written examination subjects all the members of a class to the same trial. It tests their knowledge, and trains them in the important area of expressing their thoughts correctly, precisely, clearly, and briefly, throwing them upon their own resources for ideas, words, and sentence-forms" (Richardson, 1887, p. 417). The most severe criticism of examinations came from the secondary school systems which were responsible for preparing students to take these examinations. These secondary school teachers seemed to feel that the examinations were a personal insult, and that they tended to have an undesirable influence upon the curriculum (Gabsby, 1894–1895).

It is interesting to note that many of these arguments are prevalent in the literature today. The controversy has permeated both professional and non-professional literature.

Recent Literature

THE STATUS OF TESTING

Even though many educators (Cooke, 1959; Grant and Grant, 1957; Sheridan, 1962; Stalnaker, 1951) have extolled the use of essay examinations, this type of examination seems to be losing ground to more objective testing techniques. Thomas (1939), for example, found that 28 percent of the students he inventoried had never taken an essay examination in their high school history, 59 percent of the students had less than one-fourth of their tests in the essay form while in high school, and 13 percent of the students could not recall having ever taken an essay examination in high school.

French (1957) studied the reactions of English teachers to the use of essay items in the *College Entrance Examination Board*. He sent a questionnaire to teachers in both public and private schools. He concluded that the essay was used about as often then as it was ten years previously in public schools, but that there had been a high increase in its use during that decade (1947–1957) in private schools. However, only about half of the teachers seemed to be in favor of continuing to use essay items in the *CEEB*.

Sims (1952) analyzed a sample of essay examination questions used by classroom teachers. He found that the questions fell into three categories: simple-recall, short-answer, and discussion. He reported that across the first twelve grade levels 35 percent of the questions were simple-recall, 35 percent were short-answer, and 30 percent were discussions. Elementary and secondary school examinations were different in that 42 percent, 40 percent and 18 percent, respectively, of these three types were found in the elementary school examinations; and 25 percent, 29 percent, and 46 percent, respectively, of these three types were found in the secondary school examinations.

SUPPLY VERSUS SELECTION TESTS

In most of the early comparisons between supply and selection tests, discussion-type essay examinations and true-false type objective examinations were collated. Crawford and Raynaldo (1925) attempted to distinguish between groups with both essay and true-false tests after dividing students into groups according to the following list of criteria: (1) two levels of achievement in French and in Spanish; (2) three groups according to the study method used in studying new material—

(a) read new material, (b) skimmed new material, (c) did not see new material; and (3) two groups according to whether or not they took lecture notes. The essay examinations did a better job of differentiating between the two achievement groups than did the objective tests. When using a valid test to differentiate between the three groups set up according to the second criterion, group "a" should do better than group "b," and group "b" should do better than group "c". Of the thirteen comparisons made, five favored the true-false tests and eight favored the essay examinations. In the third set of analyses, the true-false tests slightly favored the non-notetakers, while the essay tests favored the notetakers.

Tharp (1927), on the other hand, found that in language skills the objective test seemed to do slightly better than the essay test in determining student achievement. An examination which contained both essay and objective items was given to a group of foreign language students. The objective test correctly placed 64 percent of the students according to their letter grade in the foreign language course, and correctly placed 98 percent within one letter grade; the essay test correctly placed 53 percent and 97 percent, respectively. Similarly, McKee (1934) found that an objective-type examination was superior to an essay type of examination for predicting student success in college English.

One of the methods used to compare objective and essay tests has been to calculate the reliability of the two and then to compare these reliabilities. This has generally been done by comparing the internal consistency correlations or by comparing the reader reliability of the essay test with the internal consistency of the objective test. Regardless of the method of comparison, the objective type of tests obtained significantly greater reliability than the essay tests (Corey, 1930; Gilliland and Misbach, 1933; Huddleston, 1954). Similar comparisons have been made between oral and written examinations, with the former obtaining relatively low results (Barnes and Pressley, 1929; Trimble, 1934).

Peters and Martz (1931) compared students' final grades with their scores on essay, multiple-choice, true-false, and completion tests. They concluded that the various tests were about equally valid for predicting grades. At the elementary level, the true-false test was the least valid and the completion test was the most valid. At the secondary level, the essay test was slightly more valid than the multiple-choice test.

Another point of contention between objective and essay test enthusiasts has been whether or not the two types of tests measure the same mental functions. The objective test enthusiast asserts that since the two types of tests can be used to measure the same objectives, the more reliable objective test should be used (Laird, 1923; Lemper, 1925; Weaver and Traxler, 1931). The essay test proponent, on the other hand, claims that since the two types of tests cannot be used to measure the same objectives, the essay test should be used in order to measure those objectives for which it is most appropriate (Roback, 1921; Weidemann, 1941a).

In a given situation, with tests developed to measure the same factors, which is easier, the subjective test or the objective test? Remmers *et al.* (1923) reported finding that true-false and completion tests were significantly more difficult than the multiple-choice test. Arnold (1927) compared the essay test with the true-false test in both heterogeneous and homogeneous groups. He found that the recall-type test was more difficult than the true-false type test; and that the former was the most reliable when heterogeneous groups were tested, while the latter was most reliable when homogeneous groups were tested.

Still another mode of comparison has been to sample the opinion of students as to which type of examination they prefer. It was found that students prefer subjective to objective examinations and that the more able students seem to believe that objective tests are easier to prepare for but not as personally satisfying as subjective tests (Marcus, 1950; Ozanne, 1926; Albright, 1950). Other educators (Pease and Beardsley, 1950) contended that this difference was not actually true.

SUPPLY-TYPE TESTS

The literature on supply-type examinations has been marked by both the depth of pessimism and the height of optimism. The pros and cons of this conflict can be presented in five categories: (1) marking, (2) weighting of questions, (3) objectives for testing, (4) item sample, and (5) study methods.

Marking

Regardless of the impartiality of the teacher, the grade he assigns to an essay or oral examination will reflect preconceived ideas and prejudices which are so much a part of him that he is not even aware of them. Furthermore, the grades assigned to a set of examination papers will vary according to the whims of the teacher, his attitude, his level of fatigue, and other similar factors (Matimore, 1926; Peters, 1933).

Edgeworth (1888, 1890), one of the first educators to examine the reliability of essay test scores, found that, when he graded papers in haste rather than at leisure, there was a probable error of over $2\frac{1}{2}$ percent in the scores due to the negligence of haste. He asserted that, on a percentage scale, a difference between two candidates of 25 percent may be accidental and liable to reversal. Furthermore, he contended that on an examination such as the *Tripos*, which is used as the graduating honor examination in the British University system, two examiners marking the same paper occasionally differ from one another to the extent of 50 percent or more.

The pioneer study which initiated a landslide of criticism of the essay examination as a measurement technique was reported by Starch and Elliott in 1912. They asked both education students and active teachers to grade two English papers on the percentage basis. No passing grade was stipulated, but all the graders happened to use either 70 percent or 75 percent as the passing mark. The ranges of the scores on the two papers were 35 and 40 points, and, on each, the semi-interquartile range was about five points. It is interesting that the probable error was about

4.5 percentage points, yet one teacher marked as fine as to the tenth of a percent. Furthermore, the investigators found that students tended to grade more leniently than did the active teachers; the median scores for the examinations scored by the students were five to six points higher. In a similar study, Starch and Elliott (1913b) reported an even higher degree of variability in the marks assigned to a geometry paper than to the English papers cited in the previous study. This type of paper was used because of the assumption that mathematics papers can be graded with a high degree of precision. However, the marks were again normally distributed with a probable error of 7.5 percent—somewhat higher than the probable errors of 4.0 percent and 4.5 percent found for the English papers. The investigators noted that one of the possible explanations for the high variability of the marks assigned to the geometry paper might be that the appearance of the paper was of poor quality, thus leading to two different methods of evaluation—one based on content and the other based on quality of composition. In a third study (Starch and Elliott, 1913a), the investigators found that the variability of the marks assigned to a history paper was as great as the variability of the marks assigned to the geometry paper. Ruch (1929) reported that similar results were obtained in a study which used three geography and three history papers. Hence, it would appear that the variability of marks is more a function of the examiner and the method of examination than it is a function of the subject being measured.

In an attempt to reduce the variability of the marks assigned to essay examinations, Starch (1915) experimented with a five-point grading scale. A set of 24 papers written on the topic "Roads" was graded twice by 12 teachers. These papers were first graded on a percentage scale with 70 as the passing mark. Then they were graded on a five-point scale with the proportion of papers falling at each point conforming to the normal curve, and the scores were converted to percentage scores with 70 as the passing mark. The variability of the scores was reduced by half when the latter method of scoring was used. Furthermore, it was noted that the greatest variability seemed to occur in those papers which were generally assigned scores below the median.

The great variability of marks assigned to an essay examination response can be seen in the following ironical experience. Several expert readers were grading examination papers in history when one of the readers constructed what he considered to be a model paper. The model somehow got mixed with the ungraded papers and was scored by several of the readers. The marks ranged from a high of 90 to a low of 40, with the first reader assigning a below-passing mark to the model paper (Wood, 1921).

Hudelson (1925) had 17 English teachers in the same school judge the merits of 17 compositions. The greatest variability was found in the first theme with an average deviation of 9.8 percent (over four years in composition development). The largest range of scores was 45 points and the smallest range of scores was 12 points. Ballard (1923) pointed out that over a period of one year the essays written by a single student may vary in merit as much as six mental years.

Eells (1930) had 61 teachers score elementary school essay examination papers in geography and history on a 21-point (0–20) scale. The papers were regraded by the same teachers after an interval of ten weeks. Although 10 of the teachers gave the same mark twice, 27 of the teachers gave a high mark on one grading and a low mark on the other. One teacher changed his mark from a 5 on the first grading to a 15 on the second grading. Thirteen of the teachers assigned a mark of 10 to a paper on the first grading. These same teachers assigned marks ranging from 5 to 15 to the same paper on the second grading. The correlations between the two gradings for the four papers used in the investigation ranged from .25 to .51.

Ashburn (1938) reported a study of the reader reliability of a 15-minute essay examination administered to 65 students. The average grades given by three professors were D, D, and D+, and failing grades being given to 24, 23, and 21 papers, respectively. While each reader gave about the same number of failing grades, they were not assigned to the same papers. In the assignment of failing grades, they agreed on only eight papers, five of which were blank. Failing grades by at least one of the readers were assigned to 44 of the 65 students taking the test, while 36 of these 44 students were assigned passing grades by at least one of the readers. In three cases, papers were assigned grades of both A and D, and in two cases, papers were assigned grades of both B and E. The inter-grader[2] reliability was found to be .67. The reliabilities of an essay type question in history and in English were also determined. The former had an inter-grader reliability of .70. The latter had both inter-grader and intra-grader[3] (two-week interval between gradings) reliabilities of .80.

Fenlayson (1951) had 197 children write on two equivalent essay questions. These essays were marked by six experienced teachers. The inter-grader reliability was .74, and the intra-grader (two-month interval between gradings) reliability was .81. The average equivalent forms reliability was .691, and the pooled (across readers) equivalent forms reliability was .863. A factor analysis showed only one factor. The investigator concluded that all the graders used the same criterion for marking the papers.

Using a factorial design, Anderson (1960) studied the following variables: (1) testing occasions, (2) tests, (3) markers, and (4) marking occasions. Significant differences were found in all but the last variable (marking occasions). The markers–marking occasions interaction was the only interaction which was significant. Anderson concluded that the greatest variability in marking was among markers and among testing occasions. Markers differed in the grades they assigned and students performed differently at different times. Furthermore, markers did not react to different questions in the same manner and were not the same in their consistency of grading from time to time.

Drake (1940) reported that percentage scores on essay examinations were highly unreliable. After being scored by six readers, one paper received percentage

---

[2] Among different graders of the same set of papers.
[3] Between two readings of the same papers by one grader.

scores ranging from 44 to 98. However, the average rank-order coefficient of correlation between readers was .87, with a range of .81 to .99. Grant and Grant (1957) reported similar findings, with reader reliabilities ranging from a low of .82 for "understanding questions" to a high of .98 for "factual questions." Furthermore, they reported internal consistency reliabilities of .91 and .92.

Bolton (1927) pointed out that most of the studies of the reliability of essay examinations involved heterogeneous groups of teachers; they differed in age, experience, training, job, and other pertinent factors. He attempted to rectify this situation in his study of the reliability of the marks assigned to essay examination papers. His sample of readers consisted of 22 teachers who were teaching the same unit of sixth-grade arithmetic. The teachers submitted questions from which a ten-item arithmetic test was developed. The teachers then administered this test to their classes. Twenty-four of the papers were scored by all 22 teachers. The only grading restriction was that each question was to be graded on the basis of ten points. The investigator found that about half of the teachers' ratings varied by 3 percent or less, and that the average of all variations was only 5.1 percent. When the individual answers on three of the papers (two high and one low) were compared, over 85 percent of the differences were within two points out of a possible ten points. It was noted that the greatest variability of scores was found in the case of poor students.

Frutchey (1933) found close agreement among the marks assigned to essay examinations. After making the objectives on which to rate the test clear to the markers, correlations ranged from .85 to .95, with an average of .90. After noting the extreme variability in scores assigned to history and biology papers, Osburn (1934) had the graders of these essays write keys for what they expected in perfect papers. He found that most of the graders did not use the same objectives for grading the essays.

The "halo effect" has been referred to as one of the sources of error when grading essay examinations. Starch and Elliott (1913b), in their study of the grading of a geometry examination, noted that one of the possible explanations for the high variability of marks assigned to the paper might be that the appearance of the paper was of poor quality. In several studies (Chase, 1968; Klein and Hart, 1968; Marshall and Powers, 1969), writing readability has been identified as a factor significantly affecting the grades assigned to essay responses. Scannell and Marshall (1966) reported a study of the relative influence of selected composition errors on the grades assigned to essay examinations. The following five forms of an essay examination response, differing only in the type of composition errors contained in the paper, were graded by prospective teachers: (1) no composition errors, (2) grammar errors, (3) punctuation errors, (4) spelling errors, and (5) combination of the three types of errors. Significant differences were found between each of the latter two forms (spelling and combination) and the form containing no composition errors. A follow-up study (Marshall, 1967) indicated that if a "B" level, 350-word response to an essay test item contained as many as 12 grammar or 12 spelling errors, it would be assigned a significantly lower letter grade (about "C" level) by classroom teachers. The investigator concluded that teachers are influenced by the quality of composition on an essay examination, and that teachers are not aware of this influence. If a teacher believes that grades should reflect composition skill, the differences indicated in this study might even be enhanced since a deliberate penalty would be added to the unconscious penalty already present. Furthermore, the results of this study indicated that the influence of the different composition errors is not additive.

Several of the supply test enthusiasts have endeavored to develop scoring procedures which would enable graders to score supply-type examinations more reliably. Sims (1931) found average inter-grader and alternate forms reliabilities of .77 and .72 respectively, when papers were graded according to a sorting technique in which the graders were to sort the papers into five categories conforming to a predetermined distribution. Using this same technique when grading discussion, completion and short-answer questions, Sims (1932a) found the average inter-reader reliability to be .94, with the average inter-grader reliability for discussion questions to be .92. Sims (1933a) reported that the variability in marks assigned to essay examination responses was reduced by one-half when scores were converted to grades according to a system which removed the differences between graders arising from differences in standards of grading.

For a study using several short-answer tests to measure specific concepts in writing, rather than extended-answer-type tests, Stalnaker (1934) reported inter-reader reliabilities of .70 to .98. Stalnaker (1938) further asserted that almost any essay test could be graded with reliabilities of .80 and over. He reported that the English examinations at the University of Chicago were graded with an average reliability of .92. Weidemann (1941b) reported a still different procedure. The raters read a few of the papers to get a general idea of the type of answers to expect. Then they established a minimum number of points for scoring and a set of extra points, up to the maximum possible, for extras that a paper might contain. The average inter-grader and intra-grader (five-week interval between gradings) reliabilities were .56 and .80, respectively, when the papers were read by inexperienced graders. However, the intra-grader reliability was .997 after a seven-week interval and .91 after a six-month interval when the papers were read by experienced graders. Ellis (1950) tried a technique in which the students participated in the scoring of the tests. After the examination was given, the students helped prepare the final answers. Then the papers were read aloud to the class, and each student rated every paper except his own. The correlation between the average of the students' ratings and the instructor's rating was .91, and there was no significant relation between the ratings of a student by the other students and the way he rated the other students. Stanley (1962) proposed using analysis of variance techniques to free grades from reader biases. Hudelson (1925) proposed the use of a standard scale for the grading of composition themes. Sims (1933b) found that the variability in scoring essay questions was significantly reduced by using scoring rules and by converting the raw scores into grades. The combination of these methods resulted in an even greater reduction in variability.

Phillips (1965) proposed a method for reducing the time involved in the scoring of essay questions. He divided the class randomly (using a deck of cards containing student numbers) into two sections. On the first test he graded the papers of one of the groups, and on the second test he graded the papers of the other group. Then the deck of cards was reshuffled, the class redivided into two groups, and the whole process repeated. The tests were returned only after the cycle had been completed. Thus, no student knew which test he was going to be graded on. This procedure has the obvious pitfalls of grading students on different questions administered at different times. Nedelsky (1953) described an even different procedure. An essay examination was given as usual. On the next day the students were given a multiple-choice test on their answers. The student would check the responses which corresponded to his essay answers (the items would refer the student to particular essay question numbers). If the essay was of the extended answer type, a matching format could be used where the student would check those concepts discussed in the essay and record the line and page of discussion. The test score could be derived by scoring the objective test or by scoring both the objective and essay tests.

Many (Eurich, 1931; Weidemann, 1940; Zimmerman and Humphreys, 1953) have agreed that reliable scoring of essay type examinations can be accomplished if: (1) a restricted essay type question is used, (2) the questions are designed to measure specific objectives of instruction, and (3) definite scoring procedures are accepted by all readers.

Similar procedures have been recommended for oral-type examinations. Brody and Powell (1947) suggested placing students in more natural situations when administering oral examinations. They proposed setting up discussion groups in which the examinees would be scored on their contributions to the discussion and on the manner in which they handled themselves in the group. Household (1963) reported using tapes with oral English examinations. The tapes of students' responses were sent to examiners who listened to them, scoring them separately, and then comparing the scores for the final grades. This procedure eliminated the bias caused by the examinee's personal appearance as well as the necessity for snap, on-the-spot evaluation. Still another procedure recommended by Dunwiddie (1953) is to set up a student evaluation committee consisting of students previously examined by the teacher. The committee is seated in the back of the class while the test is administered. Each examiner is given a specific point to grade, and after the examination is completed, these grades are combined to obtain students' final grades.

Weighting of Questions

Supply-type examinations have been criticized on the grounds that the questions generally are not equal in difficulty (Rugg, 1923). Comin (1916) had 20 teachers rank 23 arithmetic problems in order of difficulty. The variability of ranks assigned was relatively large. For example, the easiest question was assigned a median rank of five by the teachers, and a second question was ranked first by one teacher and twenty-first by another. The investigator concluded that the questions used on an essay examination should be carefully weighted.

On the other hand, it has been concluded by several educators that the weighting of supply-type examination questions is a waste of time. Using simple weighting procedures, Monroe (1922) reported correlations of .96 and .97 between weighted and unweighted scores, and correlations of .87 and .91 between weighted and unweighted scores when a more complicated system of weighting was used. Charters (1920), using language and grammar scales, found that the correlations between weighted and unweighted scores ran above .90. Similarly, Archer (1963) stated that the correlations between weighted and unweighted scores would run above .95, and therefore the weighting of test items is unnecessary. Stalnaker (1938) discounted the practice of weighting not only because it produced results similar to unweighted scores, but also because the use of simple weights is nothing more than using linear weights in a multiple situation. He also reported that the correlation between commonly weighted and mathematically weighted scores was .97. If the true weights are of interest, there are mathematical formulas for finding them. However, it would appear that the use of weighted scores is nothing more than a useless expenditure of time.

Objectives for Testing

The main contention of supply-type examination advocates has been that these tests can be used to measure certain educational objectives such as a student's ability to organize ideas, his ability to evaluate, and composition skills which cannot be measured as effectively by the more objective types of examinations (Carpenter, 1957; Kinney and Eurich, 1932; Kirby, 1948; Cason, 1931; Weidemann and Wilkinson, 1935). Sims (1932a) contended that the exclusive use of objective tests rests on the assumption that learning consists of a large number of relatively simple and independent habits and that the number of such habits are an indication of the total learning in the field. He argued that the first assumption is supported by empirical evidence that standardized tests seem to have high relations with other indications of achievement; however, the latter assumption is true only if the learning is independent of the test. That is, the test items have to be randomly drawn from the population of habits that could be tested. This independence does not exist in the classroom. Thus, the exclusive use of the objective types of examinations would actually pervert the ends of instruction.

Some educators have contended that the type of examination used by a teacher should be dependent upon the teacher's objectives, and that essay examinations are not suited for testing facts (Keesey, 1951; Sims, 1948; Wrightstone, 1937). The following list contains a summary of the objectives for which the essay examination is particularly adaptable, as reported by various investigators (Alilunas, 1943; Cooke, 1962; Eurich, 1931; Hanchett, 1964; Hannig, 1926; Hewitt, 1939; Keelan, 1964; Shideler, 1960; Sims, 1948; Weidemann and Morris, 1938; Wrightstone, 1937).

1. Attitudes, interests, personality
2. Organization ability
3. Ingenuity or originality
4. Point of view
5. Ability to recall material
6. Interpretation ability
7. Evaluation ability
8. Application ability
9. Analysis ability
10. Synthesis ability

Many of these investigators believed that the essay method of testing was advantageous in that it enabled the student to gain practice in self-expression and in composition. However, Lundahl and Mason (1956) reported that essay examinations are of little value as a method of helping students improve their composition skill.

The oral examination appears to be adaptable to the same basic objectives as were previously reported for the essay test. Furthermore, several educators (Dunwiddie, 1953; Kostich and Nixon, 1953; Narcisco, 1964) have identified the following advantages of the oral test: (1) flexibility of questioning; (2) teacher observation of examinee's personal characteristics; (3) elimination of cheating; (4) detection of evasion and bluffing; (5) correction of defective or misleading questions; (6) enhancing student learning; and (7) supplementing other examinations.

Item Sampling

It has been noted by educators that the size and quality of the sampling of material in a test are more important than the type of test used (Wood, 1927). If this is true, essay and oral examinations are obviously inferior to the more objective measurement techniques because it is impossible for an examination to contain a large number of these types of questions. But if the test is used only to measure such objectives as the ability to interpret facts, reasoning ability, and organizational ability, this criticism can be eliminated because the amount of material sampled is no longer a major consideration (MacNeill, 1943).

Teachers often use optional questions on their essay examinations in an attempt to compensate for the inadequate sample of test items. Yet, this procedure logically introduces some unknown quantity of variance into the test scores. Meyer (1939) contends that the use of optional questions implies that the student knows: (1) the difficulty of each question; (2) the scoring standards; and (3) who is to do the scoring. These latter two qualifications can be satisfied. But he found only a slight positive relation ($r = +.1$) between students' actual achievement and ratings of their achievement in answering an essay examination question. Furthermore, when the students were required to answer the questions not originally elected, over

40 percent would have earned better scores if the best of these questions had been included in the total score in place of the least adequately answered elected question. Thus it seems that students do poorly at judging the relative difficulty of the various questions. Similarly, after analyzing two sections of the *CEEB* examinations, Stalnaker (1936) concluded that examinations must not contain optional or choice questions. Wiseman and Wrigley (1958) studied the responses of 137 students on an essay examination on which the students were given their choice of one of five topics. Using a simple randomized design, they found significant differences between titles, and when holding aptitude constant, the variability between titles was reduced but still significantly large.

Study Methods

Early critics of the examination system believed that the essay examination caused the worst form of cramming and the even greater vice of cheating (Baldwin, 1899; G., 1889). The former is not necessarily a vice since cramming can take the form of an orderly review (Monroe and Sanders, 1923). Cheating, on the other hand, can never be tolerated, although it will probably exist wherever evaluation exists.

If one of the purposes of testing is to improve the teaching process (Glenn, 1921), then the essay examination has a major function in education. This function is the effect of the essay examination on the students in their selection of review procedures and their development of study skills (Link, 1963). Terry (1933) was one of the first educators to analyze the differential influences of the various types of examinations on study procedures. The students in two sections of a college course were asked to make notes on their study methods while studying for an objective test, and later they were asked to make notes on their study methods while studying for an essay test. These notes were analyzed and a list of 67 study methods was developed. This list was evaluated by 236 students from several education classes. Over a third of the judgments indicated discrimination as to the effectiveness of different methods of study for essay and for objective tests. The methods that were checked as being better adapted to objective tests were concerned with small units of subject matter. The methods that were checked as being better adapted to essay tests emphasized large units of subject matter, with many of these methods containing terms such as "main points," "main ideas," and "summaries." Similarly, Douglas and Tallmadge (1934) found that when studying for objective tests students focused their attention upon details and exact wording, while when studying for essay tests they emphasized the organization of ideas, perceiving relations, trends, and personal reactions.

Meyer (1934a and 1934b) investigated the relative efficiency of the different study "sets." He divided his sample into the following four groups: (1) those studying for a true-false test; (2) those studying for a multiple-choice test; (3) those studying for a completion test; and (4) those studying for an essay test. The investigation took place in a controlled laboratory setting. The students were given all four types of tests at the close of the study period, and again after a five-week interval. In the original testing, all four groups did equally well on all four types of tests. However, on the retest, both the "completion group" and the "essay group" did decidedly better on all types of tests than did the other two groups. Thus the investigator concluded that, for lasting results, the recall study set was superior to the recognition study set. In the second portion of the study (Meyer, 1935), the different study methods used by the four groups were analyzed. These methods could be divided into the same two groups indicated by Terry (1933): those studying for detail (true-false, multiple-choice, and completion groups), and those studying for general ideas (essay group). Meyer (1936) replicated this investigation, using an actual classroom situation. The general results were the same, with one major exception. Both recall groups did better than the recognition groups, and the essay group did better than the completion group on the original testing.

SELECTION-TYPE TESTS

The literature on the selection-type examination has been characterized by attempts to determine the distinctive traits and construction principles. This research can be examined in four categories: (1) general characteristics; (2) responses; (3) chance scores; and (4) responding.

General Characteristics

It is generally assumed that a student's test score can be divided into two parts: his *true score* and *error*. Cronbach (1950) has pointed out that the error variance can be divided into three parts: (1) chance variance; (2) response tendencies operating during one testing, but shifting on retesting; and (3) response tendencies operating consistently from one testing to another. Type 1 variance is of lesser importance since its effects can be reduced by lengthening the test. Types 2 and 3, on the other hand, are potentially harmful. Since Type 2 variance is unstable, it cannot correlate with stable variables, and therefore lowers the validity coefficient of the test. Type 3 variance will adversely affect the validity of the test unless it is positively related to the intended purpose of the test. Therefore, the influence of variance Types 2 and 3 should be minimized in order to obtain maximum test validity. This necessitates the identification of the causes of these types of variances and then the formulation of procedures to reduce their influence.

Cronbach (1946) identified five response sets which adversely affect the validity of the selection type of tests: (1) tendency to gamble; (2) definition of judgment categories; (3) inclusiveness; (4) bias; and (5) speed versus accuracy. He collated the results of 32 studies in the determination of these response sets, and concluded that the inclusion of response sets always reduces logical validity. Therefore, response sets should be removed where possible. It was pointed out that response sets are reduced whenever the structuration of the test situation is increased, and that the best procedure is to use an item form which does not invite response sets. The multiple-choice format seems to be the only type of selection test free from these sets. It was shown that the bias afforded by the "Yes"—"No" dichotomy of the true-false test was prone to response sets. If in doubt, students generally tend to respond "Yes" to this type of item. This gives the overly critical person a distinct advantage if the majority of items are false. Furthermore, the reliability of the false items is often about as high as the reliability of the total test. Storey (1966), in a more recent study, reached the same conclusions and found that: (1) students choose the true responses more frequently than the false ones; (2) false items proved more reliable than true items; and (3) the validity of the true-false test was low when compared to another general knowledge test. Furthermore, he concluded that his sample of experienced teachers was unable to construct good true-false items and that the introduction of a simple set concerning the students' ability was sufficient to lower the mean score on the test, destroy the reliability of the test, and destroy the students' ability to estimate their own achievement on the test.

> The heterogeneous bits of evidence pieced together here . . . have established several generalizations.
>
> 1. Any objective test form in which the subject marks fixed response alternatives ("Yes–No," "True–False," "a–b–c," etc.) permits the operation of individual differences in response sets. The influence of response sets in the multiple-choice test is, however, of minor importance.
> 2. Response sets have the greatest variance in tests which are difficult for the subjects tested, or where the subject is uncertain how to respond.
> 3. Items having the same ostensible content actually measure more than one trait, if response sets operate in the test. This is true even for tests which, scored as a whole, are "factorially pure."
> 4. Slight alterations in directions, or training in test-taking, alter markedly the influence of response sets. But if the situation is not restructured by the tester, individual differences in response set remain somewhat stable when similar tests are given at different times.
>
> *   *   *
>
> The following recommendations for practice . . . are reinforced by the present findings:
>
> 1. Response sets should be avoided with the occasional exception of some tests measuring carefulness or other personality traits which are psychologically similar to response sets.
> 2. The forced-choice, paired-comparison, or "do-guess" multiple-choice test should be given preference over other forms of test items.
> 3. When a form of item is used in which response sets are possible
>   a) Directions should be worded so as to reduce ambiguity and to force every student to respond with the same set.
>   b) The test should not be given to a group of students for whom it is quite difficult.
>   c) A response-set score should be obtained, and used to identify subjects whose scores are probably invalid.
> 4. Where response sets are present, attempts should be made to correct for or to capitalize on the response set by an appropriate empirical procedure. (Cronbach, 1950, pp. 16, 23, 29).

The general principles for item construction have been formed largely on a logical basis. It has been assumed that determinants such as inconsistency in item form and clues to the correct response would result in increased error variance and thus would reduce the validity of the test. Dunn and Goldstein (1959) analyzed the relation of four such principles to their effects on test difficulty, validity, and reliability: (1) use of incomplete statement versus complete question as item lead; (2) items with no cues versus items with cues to the correct response; (3) items with equal length alternatives versus items with extra long, correct alternatives; and (4) consistency in item grammar. In the latter three comparisons, the test forms containing the errors were easier than the test form in which the items were written according to the rules. The type of lead did not affect test difficulty. Furthermore, violation of any of the four item-writing principles did not affect the reliability or validity of the tests. A further comparison between test-wiseness and general mental ability failed to produce a significant relationship. This may indicate that test-wiseness is not a function of general mental ability.

Calhoun (1962) investigated the influence of extraneous information on item difficulty and discriminating power. The results indicated that the inclusion of extraneous information in multiple-choice item stems has no systematic effect on either of these indices. It was concluded that, since it is a waste of time, the practice should be avoided.

Brenner (1964) and Mollenkopf (1950) reported on the relationship between item order and difficulty, reliability and discrimination. Mollenkopf found that items on verbal tests seemed to be slightly easier if placed early in the test although no such position effect was found for mathematics tests. Furthermore, he found that item placement had no effect on item discrimination. Brenner found no relation between item difficulty or reliability. Even though there was some inconsistency, the results also indicated that there was no relation between item difficulty order and test discrimination. These results tend to refute the recommendations made by some educators (Garrett, 1965; Ross, 1947) that items should be arranged in order of difficulty from easiest to hardest.

Responses

The multiple-choice item can be easily changed or modified by altering the possible responses. Yet, to a great extent, response format is still a matter of conjecture or armchair reasoning. Research, for the most part, has dealt with only special response types such as the use of "none of the above."

The research on the use of "none of the above" as an option tends to indicate that it affects the difficulty of the item but that it has little effect on the reliability of the test. Wesman and Bennett (1946) found that when testing nursing students on vocabulary and arithmetic the inclusion of "none of these" as an item response had virtually no effect on either test difficulty or reliability. Rimland (1960), on the other hand, when revising the *U.S. Navy Arithmetic Test*, found that the test form with items containing the alternative "right answer not given" was significantly more difficult than the equivalent form which did not use this alternative. Boynton (1962) reported similar results when studying the use "none of these" in spelling tests. Williamson (1965) investigated the effects of the option "none of these" on the difficulty and reliability of the *SRA, SCAT, CAT,* and *ITBS*. The inclusion of this response did not affect reliability in any of the four tests. However, the results for item difficulty were conflicting. On the former two tests, there was no difference between the experimental and control forms, while, on the latter two tests, the experimental forms were significantly more difficult than the control forms.

A few studies have been reported which indicate that students can be conditioned to respond to certain types of alternatives in multiple-choice items. Wevrick (1962) reported that if a set of easy items in which the correct response repeatedly appears in a single location precedes a set of difficult items, students will tend to select in the more difficult items the response which is in that same location. Thus a student's response pattern on a given set of items can influence his response to succeeding items. It would seem to follow that when a test contains items with "all of the above" or "none of the above" as possible responses, easy items containing these alternatives as correct responses should appear early in the test. Chase (1964), in a similar study investigated the effect of the length of the response on response set. He discovered that the length of the response had to be approximately three times as great as the length of other alternatives before it attracted a disproportionate number of examinees. Furthermore, he found that this long response set was eliminated, and in fact, avoided, by introducing a preceding set of easy items in which the correct response was always one of the short alternatives.

Zimmerman and Humphreys (1953) studied the effect of poor foils on test reliability. The experimental form of the examination consisted of a 100-item, five-choice, multiple-choice test in which 112 of the poorest foils had been eliminated. The actual test contained 40 two-choice, 32 three-choice, and 28 four-choice items. They reported a significant gain in reliability on the experimental form of the test and a reduction in working time per item. It was concluded that the efficiency of a test can be significantly improved by deleting poor foils.

Even though the evidence is somewhat contradictory, it indicates that there is little or no relation between the position of the correct response and the difficulty of the item. McNamara and Weitzman (1945) reported that, when difficulty is considered as a function of the position of the correct response, the difficulty distribution is somewhat flat and negatively skewed, with the mode appearing at the next to last response position. Thus four-choice multiple-choice items tend to be most difficult if the correct response is the third alternative and, similarly, five-choice multiple-choice items tend to be most difficult if the correct response is the fourth alternative. Marcus (1963) and Waite (1964), on the other hand, reported that they found no significant relation between the correctness of the response and the difficulty of the item.

Chance Scores

Gulliksen (1950) gives the following formula for determining the expected average score of a test if all examinees were to randomly guess at the correct response:

$$M_c = \frac{K}{A},$$

where M_c is the mean chance score, K is the number of test items, A is the number of possible responses per item. Furthermore, he gives the following formula for determining the standard deviation of chance scores:

$$S_c = \frac{\sqrt{K(A-1)}}{A}.$$

He surmises that the effective range of test scores has an upper bound equal to K and a lower bound equal to $M_c + 2S_c$. For example, on a 50-tem, five-choice test,

$$M_c = 50/5 = 10, \quad S_c = \frac{\sqrt{50\,(4)}}{5} = 2.8,$$

and the effective range would have an upper bound of 50 and a lower bound of 15.6 [that is, $10 + 2(2.8)$].

This effective range is based on the assumption that scores below 15.6 are obtained by randomly guessing at all the items. If this assumption is correct, scores below this lower-bound should be unstable and have zero relation to a criterion variable. Cliff (1958) tested this assumption using the scores falling at or below chance (M_c) on four subtests of the *SCAT*. The dependent variable was a shorter equating examination. The chance scores were significant predictors at the .10 level on all four tests and at the .005 level on two of the tests. Comparisons between regression coefficients determined for the below-chance groups and for the above-chance groups showed no significant differences on three of the four subtests. Comparisons between the standard errors of estimates for the two groups showed no significant difference on any of the four tests. These results indicate that there may be more operating on chance scores than just random guessing. Consequently, they may be meaningful scores in test interpretation.

Responding

One of the interesting questions concerning responding to selection type tests has been whether or not students will benefit by changing their original answers. Investigations on this topic have consistently shown that students gain more than they lose by changing original answers (Lehman, 1928; Lowe and Crawford, 1929; Matthews, 1929; Reile and Briggs, 1952). Reile and Briggs investigated the effects of students changing their original responses according to the following criteria: (1) all students; (2) by sex; and (3) by grade level. They found that students will usually change two items from wrong to right answers for every one item that is changed from right to wrong, that about half of the changes will result in wrong responses (right to wrong or wrong to wrong), and that a student will tend to gain about one correct response for every four changes. Females tend to make slightly fewer wrong-to-right changes and more wrong-to-wrong changes than do males. They also tend to make about one-third more item changes than do the men. Furthermore, it was found that D- and F-students do not gain (or lose) anything by changing responses even though they change more responses than do the better students; C-students tend to gain at a rate of about one more correct item for every four changes; and A- and B-students tend to gain at a rate of slightly less than one more correct item for every two changes.

Preston (1964) investigated the ability of students to answer reading comprehension items before reading the passages. He used the *Cooperative English Test*: Test C2: Reading Comprehension (Higher Level), Form R, because it avoids content which is generally known to college students. The examination was given in the usual manner except that the first thirty items appeared without their respective passages. Over three-fourths of the examinees obtained a score equal to or greater than chance and about one-fifth of them obtained scores over two standard deviations above chance. Both of these results were significant at the .001 level. The results also indicated that there are small but positive relations between the passageless test scores and the actual level of comprehension for the same items ($r = .20$), the level of comprehension on all items ($r = .26$), and the speed of comprehension ($r = .32$).

Dressel and Schmid (1953) investigated the effects on multiple-choice items of modifying the usual one-item, one-response method of construction. The following test forms were constructed:

1. Conventional test, 44 single-answer, four-response, multiple-choice items
2. Free-choice test, same as conventional test except that the students were instructed to mark as many responses as necessary to ensure that they had marked the correct answer
3. Degree-of-certainty test, same as the conventional test except that the student was instructed to indicate how certain he was that he had selected the correct answer
4. Multiple-answer test, contained five-response, multiple-choice items, any number of which might be correct
5. Two-answer test, contained five response, multiple-choice items, two of which were correct and the students were informed of this.

The results indicated that the students worked at different speeds on the different types of tests. The average number of items attempted on the tests in a 30-minute period were:

1. Conventional, 35.2
2. Degree-of-certainty, 34.5
3. Free choice, 32.9
4. Two-answer, 29.3
5. Multiple-answer, 28.2.

The reliabilities of the tests ranged from a high of .78 to a low of .67, with the tests falling in the following order: multiple-answer, two-answer, degree-of-certainty, conventional, and free-choice. Furthermore, the validities of the tests ranged from a high of .66 to a low of .58, with the test falling in the following order: multiple-answer, two-answer, corrected for chance and degree-of-certainty; conventional; two-answer, number right; and free-choice. The results of this study indicate that modification of the conventional multiple-choice item may bring about some changes in performance, but that a great deal of liberty can be taken in making these modifications without impairing the item's efficiency, and in fact, such modifications might just improve its efficiency.

Smith (1958) reported an investigation of two-choice, multiple-choice items. The reliabilities of several 75-item tests were found to be fairly high, ranging from a low of .66 to a high of .79. It was pointed out by the investigator that the students seemed to like this type of item and that they were relatively easy to construct. No comparative data were reported.

REFERENCES

Albright, Preston B. (1950). "Objective and Subjective Examinations." *School and Society*, **72**, 296.

Alilunas, Leo (1943). "What Do Essay Examinations Show?" *Social Education*, **7**, 313–314.

Anderson, C. C. (1960). "New Step Essay Test as a Measure of Composition Ability." *Educational and Psychological Measurement*, **20**, 95–102.

Archer, N. Sidney (1963). "Weighted Question: Is Assigning Values a Useful Procedure?" *Clearing House*, **37**, 360–362.

Arnold, H. L. (1927). "Analysis of Discrepancies Between True-False and Simple Recall Examinations." *Journal of Educational Psychology*, **18**, 414–420.

Ashburn, Robert (1938). "Experiment in the Essay Type Question." *Journal of Experimental Education*, **7**, 1–3.

Baldwin, Joseph (1899). *School Management and School Methods*. D. Appleton and Company, New York.

Ballard, Philip Baswood (1923). *The New Examiner*. Hodder and Stoughton, London.

Barnes, Elinor J., and Steven L. Pressley (1929). "The Reliability and Validity of Oral Examination." *School and Society*, **3**, 719–722.

Bolton, Frederick E. (1927). "Do Teachers' Marks Vary As Much As Supposed?" *Education*, **48**, 24–29.

Boynton, R. M. (1962). "Spatial Vision." *Annual Review of Psychology*, **13**, 171–182.

Brenner, Marshall H. (1964). "Test Difficulty, Reliability, and Discrimination as Functions of Item Difficulty Order." *Journal of Applied Psychology*, **48**, 98–100.

Brody, William, and Neal J. Powell (1947). "A New Approach to Oral Testing." *Educational and Psychological Measurement*, **7**, 289–298.

Calhoun, Roland Leroy (1962). "Item Form and Item Discriminating Power: an Experimental Study." Unpublished doctoral dissertation, University of Michigan.

Carpenter, Finley (1957). "Some Logical Considerations About the Essay–Objective Test Controversy." *Educational Research Bulletin*, **36**, 9–12.

Cason, Hulsey (1931). "The Essay Examination and the New Type Test." *School and Society*, **34**, 413–418.

Charters, W. W. (1920). "Constructing a Language and Grammar Scale." *Journal of Educational Research*, **1**, 249–258.

Chase, Clinton I. (1964). "Relative Length of Option and Response Set in Multiple-Choice Items." *Educational and Psychological Measurement*, **24**, 861–866.

Chase, Clinton I. (1968). "The Impact of Some Obvious Variables on Essay Test Scores." *Journal of Educational Measurement*, **5**, 315–318.

Cliff, Rosemary (1958). "The Predictive Value of Chance-Level Scores." *Educational and Psychological Measurement*, **43**, 607–616.

Comin, Robert (1916). "Teachers' Estimates of the Abilities of Pupils." *School and Society*, **3**, 67–70.

Cooke, George H. (1959). "A Catechism on Essay Tests." *Peabody Journal of Education*, **37**, 158–163.

Cooke, George H. (1962). "What is a Question but a Quest?" *Peabody Journal of Education*, **39**, 274–282.

Corey, Stephen M. (1930). "The Correlation Between New Type and Essay Examination Scores, and the Relationship Between Them and Intelligence as Measured by Army Alpha." *School and Society*, **32**, 849–850.

Crawford, C. C., and D. A. Raynaldo (1925). "Some Experimental Comparisons of True-False Tests and Traditional Examinations." *School Review*, **33**, 698–706.

Cronbach, Lee J. (1946). "Response Sets and Test Validity." *Educational and Psychological Measurement*, **6**, 475–494.

Cronbach, Lee J. (1950). "Further Evidence on Response Sets and Test Design." *Educational and Psychological Measurement*, **10**, 3–31.

Douglas, Harl R., and Margaret Tallmadge (1934). "How University Students Prepare for New Type of Examinations." *School and Society*, **39**, 318–320.

Drake, C. A. (1940). "Examination-Marking Experiment: Essay vs. Objective-Type of Examinations." *School and Society*, **52**, 95–96.

Dressel, Paul L., and John Schmid (1953). "Some Modifications of the Multiple-Choice Item." *Educational and Psychological Measurement*, **13**, 574–595.

Dunn, Theodore F., and Leon G. Goldstein (1959). "Test Difficulty, Validity, and Reliability as Functions of Selected Multiple-Choice Item Construction Principles." *Educational and Psychological Measurement*, **19**, 171–179.

Dunwiddie, William (1953). "How to Give Oral Examinations." *Social Education*, **17**, 123.

Edgeworth, F. Y. (1888). "The Statistics of Examinations." *Journal of the Royal Statistical Society*, **51**, 599–635.

Edgeworth, F. Y. (1890). "The Element of Chance in Competitive Examinations." *Journal of the Royal Statistical Society*, **53**, 460–473, 644–663.

Eells, Walter C. (1930). "Reliability of Repeated Grading of Essay Type Examinations." *Journal of Educational Psychology*, **21**, 48–52.

Eliot, Charles W. (1895–1896). "Requirements for Admission to College and Scientific Schools," Report, Schoolmasters' Association of New York and Vicinity, pp. 78–106.

Ellis, A. (1950). "Experiment in the Rating of Essay-Type Examination Questions by College Students." *Educational and Psychological Measurement*, **10**, 707–711.

Eurich, Alvin C. (1931). "Improving the Essay Examination." *Minnesota Journal of Education*, **12**, 93–96.

Farrand, Wilson (1895–1896). "The Reform of College Entrance Requirements." Report, Schoolmasters' Association of New York and Vicinity, pp. 19–32.

Fenlayson, Douglas (1951). "The Reliability of Marking of Essays." *British Journal of Educational Psychology*, **21**, 126–134.

French, John W. (1957). "What English Teachers Think of Essay Testing." *English Journal*, **46**, 196–201.

Frutchey, Fred P. (1933). "Close Agreement Found in Marking Essay Examinations." *Journal of Higher Education*, **4**, 376–377.

G., A. G. (1889). "Of the Use and Abuse of Examinations in College." *The Nation*, **48**, 266.

Gabsby, Herbert H. (1894–1895). "Admission to College on Certificate." Report, Schoolmasters' Association of New York and Vicinity, pp. 19–29.

Garrett, Henry E. (1965). *Testing for Teachers* (2nd ed.). American Book Company, New York.

Gilliland, A. R., and L. E. Misbach (1933). "Relative Values of Objective and Essay Type Examinations in General Psychology." *Journal of Educational Psychology*, **24**, 349–361.

Given, E. W. (1894–1895). "Admission to College on Certificate." Report, Schoolmasters' Association of New York and Vicinity, pp. 74–78.

Glenn, E. R. (1921). "The Conventional Examination in Chemistry and Physics Versus the New Types of Tests." *School Science and Mathematics*, **21**, 746–756.

Grant, Donald L., and Nathan Grant (1957). "Studies in the Reliability of the Short-Answer Essay Examination." *Journal of Educational Research*, **51**, 109–116.

Gulliksen, Harold (1950). *Theory of Mental Tests*. John Wiley and Sons, New York.

Hanchett, William (1964). "The Essay Examination: a Plea and a Plan." *Journal of Higher Education*, **35**, 27–31.

Hannig, William A. (1926). "The Relative Worth of Short Answer and Free Answer Material in Elementary Teacher Tests." *Public Personnel Studies*, **4**, 277–278.

Herbert, Auberon, *et al.* (1888, 1889). "The Sacrifice of Education to Examinations." *Nineteenth Century*, **24**, 617–652; **25**, 284–323.

Hewitt, J. E. (1939). "Improving the Construction of the Essay and Objective New Type Examinations." *Research Quarterly, American Association for Health, Physical Education, and Recreation*, **10**, 148–154.

Household, Henry L. M. (1963). "Examining Oral English: Brighton Experiment." *Times Educational Supplement*, No. 2521 (September), 295.

"How Examiners Are Made." *The School Journal* (New York), **57**, 293–294.

Huddleston, E. M. (1954). "Measurement of Writing Ability at the College-Entrance Level: Objective vs. Subjective Testing Techniques." *Journal of Experimental Education*, **22**, 165–213.

Hudelson, Earl (1925). "The Effect of Objective Standards upon Composition Teachers' Judgments." *Journal of Educational Research*, **12**, 329–330.

Ignatieff, W. (1898). "Der Einfluss der Examina auf das Körpergewicht." *Zeitschrift für Schulgesundheitspflege*, **11**, 244–247.

Keelan, Jean (1964). "Pandora's Box—The Essay Test." *English Journal*, **53**, 101–103.

Keesey, R. M. (1951). "How Useful Are Essay Tests?" *Educational Digest*, **16**, 46–48.

Kiddle, Henry, and A. J. Schem (1877). *The Cyclopedia of Education*. E. Steiger, New York. "Examinations," p. 288.

Kinney, L. B., and A. C. Eurich (1932). "Summary Investigation Comparing Different Types of Tests." *School and Society*, **36**, 540–544.

Kirby, Bryon C. (1948). "Essay Test is Best." *Journal of Education*, **131**, 98.

Klein, Stephen P., and Frederick M. Hart (1968). "Chance and Systematic Factors Affecting Essay Grades." *Journal of Educational Measurement*, **5**, 197–206.

Kostich, Michael M., and Bernard M. Nixon (1953). "How to Improve Oral Questioning." *Peabody Journal of Education*, **30**, 209–217.

Laird, Donald A. (1923). "A Comparison of the Essay and Objective Type of Examinations." *Journal of Educational Psychology*, **14**, 123–124.

Lathan, Henry (1886). *On the Action of Examinations*. Willard Small, Boston.

Lehman, H. C. (1928). "Does it Pay to Change Initial Decisions in a True-False Test?" *School and Society*, **28**, 456–458.

Lemper, L. H. (1925). "Objective vs. Subjective Tests in Modern Language." *Modern Language Journal*, **10**, 175–177.

Link, F. R. (1963). "Teacher-Made Tests." *National Education Association Journal*, **52**, 23–25.

Lowe, M. L., and C. C. Crawford (1929). "First Impression vs. Second Thought in True-False Tests." *Journal of Educational Psychology*, **20**, 192–195.

Lundahl, W. S., and J. M. Mason (1956). "Essay Testing in Biological Science as a Means for Supplemental Training in Writing Skills." *Science Education*, **40**, 261–267.

McKee, J. H. (1934). "Subjective and (or Versus) Objective." *English Journal* (*College Edition*), **23**, 127–133.

McNamara, W. J., and E. Weitzman (1945). "The Effect of Choice Placement on the Difficulty of Multiple-Choice Questions." *Journal of Educational Psychology*, **36**, 103–113.

MacNeill, Doris E. (1943). "In Apologia of an Essay Examination." *Social Studies*, **34,** 168–172.

Mann, Horace (1924). in Otis W. Caldwell and Stuart A. Courtis (Eds.), *Then and Now in Education*. World Book Company, New York, pp. 37–46.

Marcus, A. (1963). "Effect of Correct Response Location on the Difficulty Level of Multiple-Choice Questions." *Journal of Applied Psychology*, **47,** 48–51.

Marcus, F. L. (1950). "Objective and Subjective Examinations." *School and Society*, **72,** 136–137.

Marshall, Jon C. (1967). "Essay Tests and Composition Errors Re-examined." *American Educational Research Journal*, **4,** 375–386.

Marshall, Jon C., and Jerry M. Powers (1969). "Writing Readability, Composition Errors and Essay Examination Grades." Paper presented at the annual meeting of the National Council of Measurement in Education.

Matimore, Henry P. (1926). "The New vs. the Old: Objective Versus Subjective Examinations." *Catholic School Interests*, **5,** 358–360.

Matthews, C. O. (1929). "Erroneous First Impressions on Objective Tests." *Journal of Educational Psychology*, **20,** 280–286.

Maxwell, W. H. (1890). "Examinations as Tests for Promotion," in *Journal of Proceedings*, National Education Association, pp. 127–141.

Meyer, George (1934a). "Essay Type Examination." *American School Board Journal*, **89,** 17–18.

Meyer, George (1934b). "An Experimental Study of the Old and New Types of Examinations: I. The Effect of the Examination Set on Memory." *Journal of Educational Psychology*, **25,** 641–661.

Meyer, George (1935). "An Experimental Study of the Old and New Types of Examination: II. Methods of Study." *Journal of Educational Psychology*, **26,** 30–40.

Meyer, George (1936). "The Effect on Recall and Recognition of the Examination Set in Classroom Situations." *Journal of Educational Psychology*, **27,** 81–99.

Meyer, George (1939). "The Choice of Questions on Essay Examinations." *Journal of Educational Psychology*, **30,** 161–171.

Mollenkopf, William G. (1950). "An Experimental Study of the Effects on Item-Analysis Data of Changing Item Placement and Test Time Limit." *Psychometrika*, **15,** 291–315.

Monroe, Walter S. (1922). "Description of Performance of Pupils on Exercises of Varying Difficulty." *School and Society*, **15,** 341–343.

Monroe, Walter S., and Lloyd B. Sanders (1923). "The Present Status of Written Examinations and Suggestions for Their Improvement." *University of Illinois Bulletin*, **21,** No. 13.

Narcisco, John C. (1964). "Note on an Experimental Testing Procedure." *Journal of Educational Research*, **58,** 188.

Nedelsky, Leo (1953). "Evaluation of Essays by Objective Tests." *Journal of General Education*, **7,** 209–210.

Osburn, Worth J. (1934). "Testing Thinking." *Journal of Educational Research*, **27,** 401–411.

Ozanne, Charles E. (1926). "A Study of Different Types of Teachers' Tests." *School Review*, **34**, 54–60.

Pease, Katharine, and Seymour W. Beardsley (1950). "Objective and Subjective Examinations." *School and Society*, **72**, 294–296.

Peters, C. C., and H. B. Martz (1931). "A Study of the Validity of Various Types of Examinations." *School and Society*, **33**, 336–338.

Peters, R. F. (1933). "The Essay Examination." *The American School Board Journal*, **87**, 35+.

Phillips, John L., Jr. (1965). "An Application of Intermittent Grading." *Clearing House*, **39**, 305–306.

Preston, Ralph C. (1964). "Ability of Students to Identify Correct Responses Before Reading." *Journal of Educational Research*, **58**, 181–183.

Reile, Patricia J., and Leslie J. Briggs (1952). "Should Students Change Their Initial Answers on Objective Type Tests? More Evidence Regarding an Old Problem." *Journal of Educational Psychology*, **43**, 110–115.

Remmers, H. H., *et al.* (1923). "An Experimental Study of the Relative Difficulties of True-False, Multiple-Choice and Incomplete Sentence Types of Examination Questions." *Journal of Educational Psychology*, **14**, 367–372.

Richardson, John M. (1887). "How Should Examinations Be Conducted? What Is Their Educational Value?" *Education*, **7**, 416–419.

Rimland, Bernard (1960). "The Effects of Varying Time Limits and of Using Right Answer Not Given in Experimental Forms of the U.S. Navy Arithmetic Test." *Educational and Psychological Measurement*, **20**, 533–539.

Roback, A. A. (1921). "Subjective Tests Versus Objective Tests." *Journal of Educational Psychology*, **13**, 439–444.

Ross, C. C. (1947). *Measurement in Today's Schools* (2nd ed.). Prentice-Hall, Englewood Cliffs, N.J.

Ruch, G. M. (1929). *The Objective or New-Type Examination*. Scott, Foresman and Company, Chicago.

Rugg, Earle (1923). "Evaluating the Aims and Outcomes of History." *Historical Outlook*, **14**, 324–326.

Sayrs, W. C. (1921). "What Should Be the Character of an English Test?" *Educational Review*, **61**, 138–147.

Scannell, Dale P., and Jon C. Marshall (1966). "The Effect of Selected Composition Errors on the Grades Assigned to Essay Examinations." *American Educational Research Journal*, **3**, 125–130.

Scoones, Baptiste W. (1888). "Is Examination a Failure?" *Nineteenth Century*, **25**, 236–255.

Seymour, T. D. (1896). "Entrance Requirements for Yale College." *Journal of Proceedings*, National Education Association, pp. 635–641.

Sheridan, John D. (1962). "Midsummer Nightmare." *High Points*, **44**, 24–28.

Shideler, E. W. (1960). "What Do Examinations Teach?" *American Association of University Professors Bulletin*, **46**, 277–280.

Sims, Verner M. (1931). "The Objectivity, Reliability, and Validity of an Essay Examination Graded by Rating." *Journal of Educational Research*, **24**, 216–223.

Sims, Verner M. (1932a). "Objective Tests and Teachers' Measurements." *School and Society*, **36**, 300–302.

Sims, Verner M. (1932b). "Studies in Reducing the Variability of Marks Given on Essay Examinations." *National Education Association Proceedings*, **30**, 359–360.

Sims, Verner M. (1933a). "Improving the Measuring Qualities of an Essay Examination." *Journal of Educational Research*, **27**, 20–31.

Sims, Verner M. (1933b). "Reducing the Variability of Essay Examination Marks Through Eliminating Variations in Standards in Grading." *Journal of Educational Research*, **26**, 637–647.

Sims, Verner M. (1948). "Essay Examination is a Projective Technique." *Education Digest*, **14**, 28–31.

Sims, Verner M. (1952). "Essay Examination Questions Classified on the Basis of Objectivity." *School and Society*, **35**, 101–102.

Smith, Kendon (1958). "An Investigation of the Use of 'Double-Choice' Items in Testing Achievement." *Journal of Educational Research*, **51**, 387–389.

Stalnaker, John M. (1934). "Tests of Acceptable and Reliable Habits of Writing." *English Journal* (*College Education*), **23**, 37–47.

Stalnaker, John M. (1936). "A Study of Optional Questions on Examinations." *School and Society*, **44**, 829–832.

Stalnaker, John M. (1938). "Weighting Questions in the Essay-Type Examination." *Journal of Educational Psychology*, **29**, 481–490.

Stalnaker, J. M. (1951). "The Essay Type of Examination," in E. F. Lindquist (Ed.), *Educational Measurement*. American Council on Education, Washington, D.C., pp. 495–530.

Stanley, Julien C. (1962). "Analysis-of-Variance Principles Applied to the Grading of Essay Tests." *Journal of Experimental Education*, **30**, 279–283.

Starch, Daniel (1915). "Can the Variability of Marks Be Reduced?" *School and Society*, **2**, 242–243.

Starch, Daniel, and Edward C. Elliott (1912). "Reliability of the Grading of High-School Work in English." *School Review*, **20**, 442–457.

Starch, Daniel, and Edward C. Elliott (1913a). "Reliability of Grading Work in History." *School Review*, **21**, 676–681.

Starch, Daniel, and Edward C. Elliott (1913b). "Reliability of Grading Work in Mathematics." *School Review*, **21**, 254–259.

Storey, Arthur G. (1966). "A Review of Evidence or the Case Against the True-False Item." *Journal of Educational Research*, **59**, 282–285.

Terry, Paul W. (1933). "How Students Review for Objective and Essay Tests." *Elementary School Journal*, **33**, 592–603.

Tharp, J. B. (1927). "The New Examination Versus the Old in Foreign Language." *School and Society*, **26**, 691–694.

Thomas, C. M. (1939). "Disappearance of Essay Type Examinations." *Ohio Schools*, **17**, 362–363.

Trimble, Otis C. (1934). "The Oral Examination: its Validity and Reliability." *School and Society*, **39**, 550–552.

Waite, Birt Ellsworth (1964). "The Relationships Between Correct Response Position and Difficulty of Multiple-Choice Questions. Unpublished master's thesis, University of Tennessee.

Weaver, Robert B., and Arthur E. Traxler (1931). "Essay Examinations and Objective Tests in United States History in the Junior High School." *School Review*, **39**, 689–695.

Weidemann, C. C. (1940). "Scoring the Essay Test." *Journal of Higher Education*, **11**, 490–491.

Weidemann, C. C. (1941a). "Further Studies of the Essay Test." *Journal of Higher Education*, **12**, 437–439.

Weidemann, C. C. (1941b). "Review of Essay Test Studies." *Journal of Higher Education*, **12**, 41–44.

Weidemann, Charles C., and Birdean J. Morris (1938). "The Essay-Type Test." *Review of Educational Research*, **8**, 517–522.

Weidemann, Charles C., and R. Wilkinson (1935). "Recent Developments in the Written Essay Examination." *Review of Educational Research*, **5**, 484–490.

Wesman, A. G., and G. K. Bennett (1946). "The Use of 'None of These' as an Option in Test Construction." *Journal of Educational Psychology*, **37**, 541–549.

Wevrick, L. (1962). "Response Set in a Multiple-Choice Test." *Educational and Psychological Measurement*, **22**, 533–538.

Williamson, Malcolm Lynn (1965). "An Experimental Analysis of the Validity Correlates of 'None of These' and Homogeneous Options on Multiple Response Tests." Unpublished master's thesis, University of Southern California.

Wiseman, Stephen, and Jack Wrigley (1958). "Essay-Reliability: the Effect of Choice of Essay-Title." *Educational and Psychological Measurement*, **18**, 128–138.

Wood, Ben D. (1921). "Measurement of College Work." *Educational Administration and Supervision*, **7**, 301–304.

Wood, Eleanor Perry (1927). "Improving the Validity of Collegiate Achievement Tests." *Journal of Educational Psychology*, **18**, 18–25.

Wrightstone, J. W. (1937). "Are Essay Examinations Obsolete?" *Social Education*, **1**, 401–405.

Zimmermann, Wayne S., and Lloyd G. Humphreys (1953). "Item Reliability as a Function of the Omission of Misleads." Abstracts of Papers, 1953 Program, *American Psychologist*, **8**, 460–461.

ILLUSTRATION OF CLASSROOM
MULTIPLE-CHOICE AND ESSAY TESTS

The tests illustrated in this section were prepared to evaluate student achievement following a teaching unit on *A Separate Peace* in a high school literature course.[1] These tests were presented to one of the authors in partial fulfilment of the requirements of an introductory course in the construction of classroom tests.

OBJECTIVES FOR *A SEPARATE PEACE*

Ia. Can recall (or select) the characteristics and motives of selected characters in *A Separate Peace* (knowledge).

Ib. Can interpret the actions and motives of selected characters in *A Separate Peace* (understanding).

Ic. Can analyze and evaluate the behaviors and motives of selected characters in *A Separate Peace* (application).

IIa. Can recognize the characteristics of the novel as a literary form (knowledge).

IIb. Can identify the literary characteristics of *A Separate Peace* (understanding).

IIIa. Can identify selected symbolisms (knowledge).

IIIb. Can interpret selected symbolisms (understanding).

IIIc. Can analyze and evaluate the use of symbolism in *A Separate Peace* (application).

IVa. Can identify the physical settings for specific selections from *A Separate Peace* (knowledge).

IVb. Can interpret the use of physical settings for specified selections from *A Separate Peace* (understanding).

IVc. Can analyze the use of particular physical settings for specified selections from *A Separate Peace* (application).

Va. Can identify the point of view of the literary work (knowledge).

Vb. Can evaluate the point of view of the literary work (application).

VIa. Can identify selected terms used in *A Separate Peace* (knowledge).

VIb. Can define selected terms used in *A Separate Peace* (understanding).

VIc. Can analyze the use of words in the literary work (application).

VIIa. Can interpret causes and effects developed through character description in literature (understanding).

---

1 This material was initially prepared by Mrs. Helen Klingaman, graduate student at Ohio University, and edited by the authors and Mrs. Klingaman.

VIIb Can analyze causes and effects developed through character descriptions in literature (application).

VIIIa. Can identify the author's purpose in a literary work (knowledge).

VIIIb. Can analyze and evaluate the author's purpose in a literary work (application).

IX. Can apply appropriate criteria in the evaluation of a literary work (application).

Table of Specifications for *A Separate Peace**

Weight theoretical-actual		Content area	Level of cognitive skill		
			Knowledge	Understanding	Application
50%	46%	I. Characters in the novel	34–37–41–42–46	28–31–32–33–35–40–44–47	29–30–36–38–39–43–45–48–49–50
5%	6%	II. Literary form	1–3	2	—
10%	12%	III. Symbolisms	9	6	4–5–7–8
5%	8%	IV. Setting of the novel	10	12	11–13
5%	4%	V. Point of view	14	—	15
10%	8%	VI. Terms (vocabulary)	18	16–19	17
5%	6%	VII. Causes and effects	—	21	20–25
5%	4%	VIII. Purpose	22	—	23
5%	6%	IX. Evaluation criteria	—	—	24–26–27

TOTAL:					
	a) Actual number of items		12	14	24
	b) Theoretical number of items		12.5	12.5	25
	c) Theoretical percent of test		25%	25%	50%
	d) Actual percent of test		24%	28%	48%

* The cell numbers correspond to the multiple-choice test item numbers.

A SEPARATE PEACE

Multiple-Choice Examination

Directions:

This examination contains 50 multiple-choice items of four or five responses each. You are to mark your answers on a separate answer sheet which contains spaces for five responses per item. Read each question carefully and select the best response. Record your choice by shading over the appropriate position on the answer sheet. Each item will contain only one correct or best answer. Do not mark more than one response. If some items seem quite difficult to answer, it may be wise to skip them until you have attempted all the items on the test and then to return to the skipped items if time permits. Be sure to mark a response for each item. You will *not* be penalized for incorrect responses.

DO NOT WRITE ON THIS TEST

Be sure to print your name and class period on the answer sheet.

To help clarify any questions regarding the procedures to be followed, a practice exercise is given below. The shading over the letter on the line below indicates the correct response.

1. Which one of the following writers was the author of *The Black Cat?*

   A. Shakespeare

   B. Poe

   C. Whitman

   D. Tennyson

   E. Wilder

1. A ▓ C D E

1. What is the primary difference between a novel and a short story as literary types?

   A. A novel has a climax.
   B. A short story has no plot.
   C. A novel has more characters.
   D. A short story is fiction.
   *E. A novel is longer.

2. Novels can be classified according to type. Which one of the following types would be the best classification for *A Separate Peace?*

   A. propaganda novel.
   B. stream-of-consciousness or psychological novel.
   *C. apprenticeship or initiation novel.
   D. historical novel.
   E. regional or local-color novel.

3. A novel usually has one character who is more important than the others. What is this character called?

   *A. protagonist.
   B. anathema.
   C. antagonist.
   D. antihero.
   E. archetype.

4. In *A Separate Peace* the summer is a symbol of peace and the winter is a symbol of war. This is best shown by:

   A. the gloss of "varnish" that Gene sees over everything at Devon.
   *B. the return in the fall to Devon School's rules after a summer of careless freedom.
   C. the return of Brinker Hadley.
   D. the winter carnival held on the athletic field.
   E. the temporary summer masters who allowed the boys more freedom.

5. The tree by the river, which is described as ". . . tremendous, an irate, steely black steeple," best symbolizes:

   A. the temptation before the fall.
   B. the reality of war.
   *C. the Biblical tree of knowledge.
   D. the "breaking" power of war.
   E. the physical representation of the bond between Finny and Gene.

6. The Devon River is the river in which Finny and Gene swam during the summer. Why is this appropriate?

   *A. It was clean, friendly, and fringed with pine.
   B. It had the tree from which Finny fell.
   C. The other river was too shallow for diving.
   D. It was salty and fringed with seaweed.

7. Finny's whole personality symbolizes:

   A. selfishness.
   *B. no regard to self.
   C. the role of the follower.
   D. desire to be recognized by others.
   E. the human mixtures of good and bad traits.

8. When the pink shirt was worn by Finny, it was an emblem to "celebrate" the first bombing of Central Europe. When Gene later wore the shirt, it had become a symbol of:

   A. adulthood.
   *B. Finny and his character.
   C. childhood and its freedom from care.
   D. Gene's new status as an adult.
   E. Gene's desire to revert to his childhood.

9. What does Brinker's faith symbolize?

   A. the older generation's authority.

   *B. another generation's opinion of the war.

   C. fatherly love and protection.

   D. the "fat old men" that Finny had discussed.

10. In the beginning of the book the adult Gene visits two places at the school. These are:

   A. the tree over the Devon River and the gymnasium.

   B. the playing fields and the marble steps of the First Academy Building.

   C. the tree over the Devon and his dormitory room.

   *D. the marble stairs of the First Academy Building and the tree over the Devon.

11. The setting of a novel must be carefully chosen to fulfill certain qualifications the author has in mind. The setting of *A Separate Peace* best contributes to:

   *A. providing a background for the action and internal struggle.

   B. portraying the local color of the area which the author was showing.

   C. showing the main character in opposition to his environment.

   D. providing the minor characters with a field for interacting with one another.

12. The use of Devon School as the novel's setting best enables the author to:

   A. make full use of teachers as major characters in a boy's development.

   B. make full use of having boys from all over the country interacting.

   C. concentrate on a few boys as his characters.

   *D. disregard parents and home environment.

   E. show how important physical setting really is.

13. The events in the novel take place during the early months of World War II. Why is this important to the story?

   A. It allows minor characters to express their attitudes toward war.

   *B. It allows the main character's conflict within himself to be contrasted to the conflict of the war.

   C. It enables the author to tell how horrible he feels the war is.

   D. It enables the author to emphasize the helplessness of the physically crippled.

   E. It allows the author to show the ease with which individuals can be mentally broken.

14. What method did the author choose to express his point of view?

   A. stream of consciousness.

   B. omniscient.

   C. third-person.

   *D. first-person.

15. The point of view that the author chose to use in *A Separate Peace* is probably the best for this story because:

   A. the reader is primarily concerned with Finny's feelings and thoughts.

   B. the reader needs to know what everyone is feeling.

   *C. the reader is primarily concerned with Gene's feelings and thoughts.

   D. the reader needs someone to tell him what Leper is thinking.

   E. no one was in a better position to tell the story than Brinker.

16. The author uses the flashback technique to tell the story. This technique can be best defined as:

   A. an intentional departure from the normal order.
   B. an overindulgence in emotion by the author.
   *C. a device by which scenes that occurred before the opening scene of the work can be presented.
   D. a device by which the author hopes to gain his audience's attention early in the story.
   E. a device that an author uses at the end of a story to parallel the beginning.

17. Early in the story, when Finny tries to get Gene to climb the tree, Gene says, ". . . I was damned if I'd climb it." These carefully chosen words illustrate which one of the following techniques?

   A. metaphor.
   *B. foreshadowing.
   C. simile.
   D. flashback.

18. The name of the game of blitzball, invented by Finny, came from the word blitzkrieg. Which of the following is the best definition of blitzkrieg?

   A. football in German.
   B. a type of aerial pass thrown for a long distance.
   C. long, loud applause.
   D. a line rush by the ball carrier.
   *E. a sudden, overpowering attack.

19. "Vagaries" could best be used to describe the actions of:

   A. Brinker, before his senior year at school.
   B. Chet, before his senior year at school.
   C. Gene, before the tree incident.
   D. Finny, before the tree incident.
   *E. Leper, before he went into the service.

20. The effect of the beach trip was to cause Gene to fail a trigonometry test and thereby:

   A. to allow his feelings toward Chet to be exposed.
   B. to enable Chet to move ahead of Gene.
   C. to give Finny superiority over Gene.
   *D. to allow his "hatred" of Finny to enter his conscious mind.

21. What caused Finny's denial of a "real war"?

   A. his personality which wouldn't admit hatred existed.
   *B. his physical disability which caused a limp.
   C. his political convictions as a pacifist.
   D. his religious convictions as a conscientious objector.
   E. his ability to detect practical jokes directed against him.

22. The author illustrates most vividly the effects that war might have on an individual by including a war incident in connection with which one of the following persons?

   A. Brinker.
   B. Gene.
   C. Finny.
   *D. Leper.
   E. Chet.

23. The author's primary purpose is to explain:

    A. how peer relationships mature an individual by allowing him to accept himself.

 *B. flawed human nature which attempts to find similarity between personal betrayal and the impulse to war.

    C. what happens to an individual when he realizes he is not capable of sympathy toward his fellow man.

    D. how an individual can refuse to admit reality to others but must admit it to himself.

    E. the effect war might have on young boys as they anticipate their future roles in the conflict.

24. Fiction usually contains the four elements listed below. Rank these elements in order from the most important to the least important for *A Separate Peace*.

    I. Character.
   II. Action.
  III. Setting.
  IV. Theme.

    A. I, IV, III, II
 *B. IV, I, II, III
    C. III, IV, II, I
    D. II, I, III, IV
    E. IV, III, II, I

25. Which one of the following is the best explanation of Gene's act against Finny?

    A. Gene's extreme nervousness in the tree.

    B. Finny's taunts of cowardice directed toward Gene.

    C. Gene's lack of courage.

 *D. Gene's inability to understand Finny.

    E. The secret agreement between Brinker and Gene.

26. The following four statements reflect recognized criteria for novels. Rank them in order from the most important to the least important for *A Separate Peace*.

    I. The novel offers a large and complex view of life.

   II. The novel gives a deeper understanding of the forces which influence human behavior.

  III. The novel gives the reader an opportunity to "live" with the characters over a long period of time.

  IV. The novel gives the reader an opportunity to take part vicariously in many experiences.

    A. IV, I, II, III
    B. III, II, I, IV
 *C. II, IV, III, I
    D. I, II, IV, III
    E. II, I, III, IV

27. The following list contains four possible functions of minor characters. Rank them in descending order on the basis of their importance to *A Separate Peace*.

    I. They may furnish needed background information about the story situation.

   II. They may provide local color by representing people who are typical of the setting.

  III. They may furnish the main characters with a listening audience to whom they can reveal their thoughts and feelings.

  IV. They may serve as foils, allowing the author to compare or contrast different qualities and traits in order to sharpen his portrayal of the main characters.

    A. IV, II, III, I
    B. III, II, I, IV
 *C. IV, III, II, I
    D. II, IV, III, I
    E. III, I, II, IV

28. Just before Gene tells of his earlier life at Devon, he thinks ". . . anybody could see it was time to come in out of the rain." What does he mean by this statement?

    A. He now understands Finny.
    B. He can now forget the accident ever occurred.
    C. He knows that Finny did understand the accident.
    D. Brinker will now stop trying to have him tried in a legal court of law.
    *E. He can now accept himself.

29. When Finny says, "No, you're the same height I am, five-eight and a half. We're on the short side," Gene thinks Finny is showing:

    A. his pride in himself.
    B. his desire to prevent Gene's claim to be five feet, nine inches tall from standing.
    *C. his simple, shocking self-acceptance.
    D. his worst trait, falsity.

30. In returning to dinner after the first jump from the tree, Gene says Finny trapped him again in his strongest trap; that is, Gene became Finny's collaborator. This indicates that Gene really:

    A. wants to become independent.
    *B. wants to live by Finny's "rules."
    C. does not admire Finny because he breaks the rules.
    D. wants to be more like Brinker and less like Finny.
    E. understands Finny's character at that time.

31. Finny had several conversations with Mr. Prud'homme and the Patch-Withers'. What did Gene hope would happen as a result of these conversations?

    *A. That Phineas would not get away with his explanations.
    B. That Finny would get over his envy of Phineas.
    C. That the adults would not be angry at Finny.
    D. That Phineas could continue to get along with the adults and keep them from bothering Finny and himself (Gene).

32. Several times in the beginning of the book, Gene comments that it was his sarcastic summer. Later he realized that sarcasm was:

    A. the only kind of rebuke Finny understood.
    B. a method of letting his teachers know how he really felt.
    C. a method for dealing with people he dislikes.
    *D. a protest of people who are weak.

33. What occurred in their relationship after the incident when Finny helped Gene regain his balance on the tree limb?

    A. Gene was very grateful to Finny and continually expressed his gratitude.
    *B. Gene at first was grateful to Finny but later decided that his gratitude was *not* needed.
    C. A gulf in their relationship occurred because Finny told everyone he had practically saved Gene's life.
    D. Gene was not grateful to Finny as he felt he was perfectly balanced and was in no danger of falling.
    E. Finny lost respect for Gene because he realized that Gene wasn't as good an athlete as he was.

34. Gene was surprised to find that Finny did abide by certain rules (Finny's own) and that the most outstanding one in his life concerned:

   *A. sports.
   B. religion.
   C. school.
   D. home.
   E. study.

35. Several times in the novel Gene indicates amazement at the way Finny could carry people along with his latest idea. Which of the following incidents does *not* show Finny's ability to enlist the others?

   *A. convincing others that the war is really a practical joke.
   B. making up the game of blitzball.
   C. organizing the Super Suicide Society of the Summer Session.
   D. organizing the winter carnival.

36. The "Ledellier Refusal" that occurred in the blitzball game becomes much more than the name of a play when one takes into account Leper's:

   A. inability to "carry the ball" after he has joined the army.
   B. lack of response to the snow-clearing task.
   C. inability to relate to the boys in the school.
   D. refusal to say who moved first in the tree.
   *E. all of the above.

37. Which of the following is *not* a part of Finny's personal decalogue?

   A. Never accuse a friend of a crime if you only have a feeling he did it.
   *B. Never pressure a friend to accept your personal code if he doesn't accept it on his own.
   C. When you really love something then it loves you back, in whatever way it has to love.
   D. Always say some prayers at night because it might turn out there is a God.

38. The incident of the swimming record shows that Finny:

   A. was afraid to try to break the record the second time.
   B. was always best when he had good competition.
   C. wanted publicity for his actions.
   D. was not proud of his feat.
   *E. did live by his code.

39. Why was Gene's response to the swimming incident one of shock?

   A. He was sure he was a faster swimmer than Finny.
   *B. To keep quiet about it made Finny seem too good for a human being to be.
   C. It made Finny the school hero and therefore he envied Finny.
   D. None of the above.

40. While at the beach, Finny tells Gene that Gene is his best pal. Why is Gene unable to reply?

   *A. Gene is envious of Finny to the point that he hates him.
   B. Gene is too embarrassed by the sincere expression of emotion.
   C. Gene has a best friend at home.
   D. Finny dives into the water, not wating for a reply.
   E. Gene had not been reared to express emotion easily.

41. What conclusion did Gene have to come to before he could "accept" Finny?

    A. He can never beat Finny.
    B. The other boys do not like Finny.
    *C. Finny is envious of Gene's superior ability in school.
    D. Finny is really no better in sports than Gene is.
    E. He does not need to beat Finny.

42. Why did Gene decide that he could beat Chet Douglas as valedictorian of the class?

    *A. Chet was so interested in learning that he pursued his own course of studies.
    B. Finny was willing to help Gene study.
    C. Chet lost valuable study time by the meetings of the Super Suicide Society.
    D. Gene was really interested and excited by learning.
    E. Brinker and Leper offered to tutor him in their strongest subjects.

43. Finny stated that, ". . . if you're really good at something, I mean if there's nobody, or hardly anybody who's as good as you are, then you've got to be serious, about that. Don't mess around, for God's sake." What is he really explaining in this statement?

    A. The reason he dislikes Gene.
    B. Why Leper could not adjust to the army.
    C. Why Brinker changed so drastically his senior year.
    *D. What he feels about sports.

44. After confessing to Phineas that he had jounced the limb, Gene says, "It struck me then that I was injuring him again . . . an even deeper injury than what I had done before." What does Gene mean by this statement?

    A. He was making Finny remember the pain and agony of the accident.
    B. He was making Finny decide whether or not to initiate legal action.
    *C. Finny could not understand nor accept the enmity that had allowed Gene to jounce the limb.
    D. He was forcing Finny to forgive him his crime.
    E. He would get his revenge on Finny.

45. Why does Gene, when returning to school in the fall, want to stay away from sports?

    A. Since Finny cannot participate in sports any more, he chooses not to participate.
    B. He feels that sports are not worth the time away from his studies.
    C. If he can't win, he chooses not to play.
    *D. He is afraid that his uncontrollable feelings may come to the surface in the heat of an athletic contest.
    E. Finny asks him not to participate without him.

46. How was Gene able to escape the charges made by Brinker in the Butt Room?

    A. by fighting Brinker until Brinker gave up.
    B. by swearing that he had not knocked Finny off the limb.
    *C. by building up a fanciful story about deliberately injuring Phineas
    D. by leaving the room as soon as possible.
    E. by swearing that he had not been in the tree when Finny fell.

47. On the night of the snow clearing, Gene decided to enlist in the army. Which one of the following was *not* a factor in Gene's decision?

   A. Gene had found something deadly in everything he wanted.
   B. Gene desired to meet the crisis at that time.
   *C. Gene wanted to hurt Phineas by doing something Phineas couldn't.
   D. Gene wanted to break the pattern of his life.
   E. Gene wanted to get away from Devon.

48. What does Gene mean when he tells Finny that he (Finny) would make a "mess, a terrible mess out of the war" even if his leg were not injured?

   A. Finny lacked the discipline necessary for a good soldier.
   *B. Finny lacked the capacity for hatred necessary for war.
   C. Finny lacked the courage necessary for a good solider.
   D. Finny had too much sympathy for the enemy in war time.
   E. Finny would be so unpopular with the other men that he would crack as Leper did.

49. By his actions after Finny's death, Gene is trying to:

   A. revert to his former self and build defenses around himself.
   B. find a way to become more like Brinker.
   C. get into the war as quickly as possible to do his share.
   *D. emulate Finny by telling his true feelings about things.
   E. help Leper recover as fast as possible.

50. Close to the end of the book Gene says, "... I was on active duty all my time at school; I killed my enemy there." What does he mean by this statement?

   *A. He freed himself of hatred.
   B. He had killed Finny, his best friend, and suffered deeply from this act.
   C. He had learned to know himself while attending school.
   D. His enemy was the organized life they had to live at the school.

ANSWER SHEET

1. A B C D O	17. A O C D E	34. O B C D E
2. A B O D E	18. A B C D O	35. O B C D E
3. O B C D E	19. A B C D O	36. A B C D O
4. A O C D E	20. A B C O E	37. A O C D E
5. A B O D E	21. A O C D E	38. A B C D O
6. O B C D E	22. A B C O E	39. A O C D E
7. A O C D E	23. A O C D E	40. O B C D E
8. A O C D E	24. A O C D E	41. A B O D E
9. A O C D E	25. A B C O E	42. O B C D E
10. A B C O E	26. A B O D E	43. A B C O E
11. O B C D E	27. A B O D E	44. A B O D E
12. A B C O E	28. A B C D O	45. A B C O E
13. A O C D E	29. A B O D E	46. A B O D E
14. A B C O E	30. A O C D E	47. A B O D E
15. A B O D E	31. O B C D E	48. A O C D E
16. A B O D E	32. A B C O E	49. A B C O E
	33. A O C D E	50. O B C D E

A SEPARATE PEACE
Essay Examination

DIRECTIONS:

This test contains five essay questions. These questions will require extended answers. Always read the *complete* question before responding. Answer sheets have been provided. Use these sheets for your responses. Be sure you divide your time appropriately so that you are able to consider all the questions. The approximate time limits are given after the questions.

YOUR RESPONSES ARE TO BE DIRECT AND TO THE POINT

Write as clearly as possible. Two separate marks will be assigned to your responses: one mark will be based on how well you answer the questions asked, and the other mark will be based on the accuracy of your composition.

QUESTIONS

 I. There are three pairs of contrasting elements which play prominent roles in *A Separate Peace* and for which one item of a pair symbolizes youth and the other item symbolizes adulthood. List these three pairs of contrasting items. Then explain the differences in symbolism between the items in each pair and compare the similarities in symbolism among the three pairs. Include in your discussion Gene's and Finny's reactions to each of the items. (12 minutes)

 II. At the end of the story Gene states, "I never killed anybody and I never developed an intense level of hatred for the enemy. Because my war ended before I ever put on a uniform, I was on active duty all my time at school; I killed my enemy there." What does Gene mean by this statement? Include in your response (1) what the statement means in terms of Gene's behavior, (2) how it relates, if at all, to Finny, and (3) how it made Gene different from other soldiers during the war. (8 minutes)

III. Explain the similarities between Leper's role in *A Separate Peace* and Gene's role in the story. Include in your response an explanation of the significance of the "Lepellier Refusal." (8 minutes)

IV. Most critics agree that Gene's confession to Finny in the hospital room is the culmination of the novel. Explain what happened in the hospital room between Gene and Finny, what happened to Gene at this time, and why the novel could actually end here. (8 minutes)

 V. After Finny's funeral Gene says, "I did not cry even when I stood watching him being lowered into his family's strait-laced burial ground outside of Boston. I could not escape a feeling that this was my own funeral, and you do not cry in that case." What does Gene mean by this statement? How does the symbolism of Finny's life, death, and burial compare with Gene's life at this point in time? (8 minutes)

ANSWER SHEET

RS _____   Student no. _____

Grade _____   Class period _____

(12 min) I.

ANSWER SHEET
(2)

Student no. _____

(8 min) II.

Class period _____

_____

(8 min) III.

ANSWER SHEET
(3)

Student no. _____

(8 min) IV.   Class period _____

_____

(8 min) V.

POSSIBLE ANSWERS TO ESSAY QUESTIONS

I. The three pairs of contrasting things are (1) the Devon and Naguamsett Rivers, (2) summer and winter, and (3) peace and war. The first item of each pair—the Devon River, summer, and peace—symbolize youth and innocence or at least lack of evil. The other three things—the Naguamsett River, winter, and war—symbolize adulthood or knowledge of evil. Each set of three things is connected. In summer the boys swim in the quiet, lovely Devon River and enjoy the peaceful calm days under the guidance of temporary masters and an acting headmaster. They play pranks and break rules and find that everyone is amused. Then envy, an adult trait, raises its ugly head and the picture changes to the Naguamsett River, winter, and war. The mood is set on Gene's first day back at Devon when he realizes his "baptism" in the Naguamsett begins a new era. Winter is cold and calculating. The reader feels that it is out to get Gene and Finny if it can. The whole winter is one of preparing for war. Leper's enlistment and mental breakdown show the grim aspects of war and its indoctrination in the knowledge of evil. Through all of this winter, Finny refuses to accept the winter and war. He maintains that there is no war, although at the end of the story the reader finds that Finny was really aware of the war and bitterly disappointed that he could not take part. Gene, who wants to believe Finny when he says there is no war, is much more realistic. He accepts, without liking them, both the winter and the war.

II. In saying that "I killed my enemy there," Gene means that he had fought the "evil" thing he had in his heart and won. This was envy or hatred for another person. This does not mean that he killed Finny. Gene means that he fought while at school those characteristics in himself that most men fought while in the war. Gene felt that this thing that most men fought was what caused others to almost "enjoy" war. They could fight their inner demons in an acceptable way. Because he had experienced and conquered his intense level of hatred for the enemy while he was at school, he was not the same as other soldiers when he did go into the service.

III. In a sense Leper's role serves to understate Gene's. Leper is more of everything than Gene. Leper is more quiet, more alone, more afraid, etc. Gene is some of these things, but not to the degree Leper is. He seems to recognize this and "protect" Leper as he does the day of the snow shoveling. In the end, he flees from Leper in the field as Leper tells him the experiences that broke him. Gene really fears that he, too, would break. However, he does not.

The "Lepellier Refusal" begins when Leper refuses the ball in a game, but this really covers his whole personality. He and, in a parallel sense, Gene do "refuse" to face challenges. Leper cannot face the service and cracks. Gene never wants to face things such as diving from the tree or going to help Leper, but usually does face them, thus bringing about his final salvation when he confesses and explains to Finny.

IV. The culmination of the novel takes place in the hospital room when Gene tells Finny he had caused him to fall from the tree purposefully but compulsively. Gene recognizes at this point that he had been a victim of his own envy and hatred. He had wanted to get rid of Finny, the boy who was "good" where he was evil. Up to this point he had not faced his own act truly but had thought only of himself. In the hospital room he thinks of Finny and explains that he had to come to the hospital because he felt he belonged there. Finny recognizes the sincerity at last present in Gene and forgives his act. The story could end there as the reader realizes that Gene now has a chance to become a "good" adult who will recognize fear and hatred but always be able to remain honest with himself and others.

V. Gene could not and did not cry at Finny's funeral because, as he says, he could not escape the feeling that it was his own funeral. By this time Gene has faced and "killed" his enemy—fear. He has become a new individual. Finny was an innocent—he was without evil or a knowledge of evil. Gene no longer was an innocent. He knew evil, had committed evil, but recognized it for what it was. With Finny went Gene's youth and innocence. Gene had "buried" his youth and become an adult who recognizes evil but, hopefully, can rise above it.

ILLUSTRATION OF CLASSROOM
PERFORMANCE TESTS

The tests illustrated in this section were prepared to evaluate student achievement following a teaching unit on pattern alterations for various figure problems in a beginning clothing course at the college level.[1] These tests were presented to one of the authors in partial fulfillment of the requirements of an introductory course in the construction of classroom tests. The first of these tests was considered by Miss McAllister to be a selection-type achievement test. One can easily notice the similarity between this test and the identification-type performance test discussed in Chapter 10. It should be recalled that the distinction between the identification form of the performance test and verbal tests is sometimes unclear. The second test, however, is clearly a performance test of the simulated situations type.

OBJECTIVES OF THE UNIT

After this unit the student should be able to:

1. Alter any pattern to change the length, given the pattern pieces of the garment and a description of the figure problem.
2. Alter any pattern to change the width, given the pattern pieces of the garment and a description of the figure problem.
3. Alter any pattern to change the width of the upper arm or the shoulder height and width, given the pattern pieces of the garment and a description of the figure problem.
4. Alter any pattern to change shape as well as size, given the pattern pieces of the garment and a description of the figure problem.

[1] This material was prepared by Miss Priscilla McAllister, graduate student at Ohio University, and edited by the authors and Miss McAllister.

Table of Specifications

Clothing 110
Winter Quarter 1968–69   Total Number—30 Items or
Alteration Test   5 Problems

Content	Application (100%)	
	Selection test	Performance test
(20%) Alteration for length	6 items	20 points (1 problem)
(25%) Alteration for width	(7.5)* 7 items	25 points (1 problem)
(25%) Alteration for upper arms and shoulders	(7.5)* 8 items	25 points (2 problems)
(30%) Alteration for shape	9 items	30 points (1 problem)
TOTAL	30 items	100 points

* Theoretical number of items.

ALTERATION TEST

Clothing 110
Winter Quarter

DIRECTIONS

This examination contains 30 multiple-choice items of three to five responses each. You are to mark your answers on a separate answer sheet which contains spaces for five responses per item. Read each question carefully and select the best response. Record your choice by shading over the appropriate position on the answer sheet. Each item will contain only one correct or best answer. Do not mark more than one response. If some items seem quite difficult to answer, it may be wise to skip them until you have attempted all the items on the test, and then to return to the skipped items if time permits. Be sure to mark a response for each item. You will *not* be penalized for guessing. DO NOT WRITE ON THIS TEST.

Be sure to print your name and social security number on the answer sheet.

Items 1–6

This is a basic straight skirt with a kick pleat in the center back seam. The skirt is a rectangle between the 7″ hip and the bottom. The skirt must be altered for overall size. The figure is:

OK at the waist; needs 2″ at the 3″ hip; OK at the 7″ hip; and needs 2½″ at the 9″ hip.

Select the answers to the following questions which will best complete the alteration. (Darts B and C are not part of the basic skirt, but are possible answers to Question 5.)

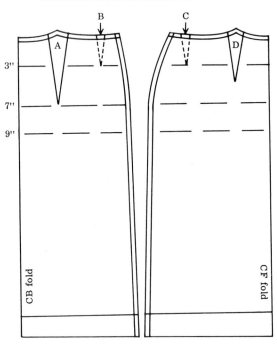

1. How much must be added to the waist and to the 3″ hip at each side edge?
   a) 1″ to the waist; 1″ to the 3″ hip
   b) ½″ to the waist; ½″ to the 3″ hip
   c) ¼″ to the waist; ½″ to the 3″ hip
   d) None to the waist; 1″ to the 3″ hip
   e) None to the waist; ½″ to the 3″ hip

2. How much must be added to the 7″ hip?
   a) Between 1″ and 1¼″
   b) Between ⅝″ and ½″
   c) Between 1½″ and 2″
   d) Nothing

3. How much must be added at the 9″ hip and to the skirt below this level?
   a) 1½″ at the 9″ hip and all the way down
   b) 1½″ at the 9″ hip and return to the original at the bottom
   c) ⅝″ at the 9″ hip and all the way down
   d) ⅝″ at the 9″ hip and return to the original at the bottom
   e) None of above

4. What principle determines the amount to be added below the 9″ hip?
   a) The character of the line
   b) The width at the hem should not be changed.
   c) The lower edge of the skirt must be as wide as the widest hip measure.
   d) Answers (a) and (c)
   e) All of the above

5. What other alteration, if any, is needed?
   a) Darts A and D must be made wider.
   b) Darts B and C should be drafted into the 3″ hip.
   c) Darts B and C should be drafted into the 7″ hip.
   d) The waistband must be increased in length.
   e) No other alteration

6. How should this skirt be altered to increase shape in the hip area?
   a) Slash and spread dart A.
   b) Add two boat-shaped pieces to the side edges.
   c) Alter the same as in Questions 1, 2, and 3.

Choose the figure on the right which illustrates the alteration which should be used to complete the alterations in Questions 7–10.

7. Alter the sleeve to increase the biceps line $\frac{3}{8}''$ for arms that are larger than average.

   a) Figure a
   b) Figure b
   c) Figure c
   d) Figure d
   e) Figure e

8. Alter the sleeve to increase the biceps line $\frac{3}{4}''$ for arms that are larger than average.

   a) Figure a
   b) Figure b
   c) Figure c
   d) Figure d
   e) Figure e

9. An increase of $1\frac{1}{2}''$ is needed at the biceps line for arms which are larger than average. One half inch has been added to the underarm seam edges of the bodice front and back to increase the bust line for overall size. Choose the alteration or alterations which should be used.

   a) Figure b
   b) Figure e
   c) Figures b and d
   d) Figures b and c
   e) Figures d and e

10. An increase of $1\frac{1}{4}''$ is needed at the biceps line for arms which are larger than average.

   a) Figure a
   b) Figure b
   c) Figure c
   d) Figure d
   e) Figure e

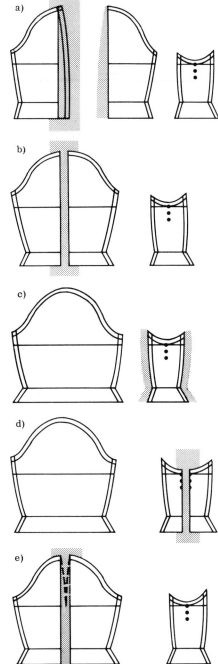

These are the bodice pieces for a typical princess-line dress. Using the basic principles that we have been using for a regulation dress, select the best alterations for each of the situations described in items 11–13.

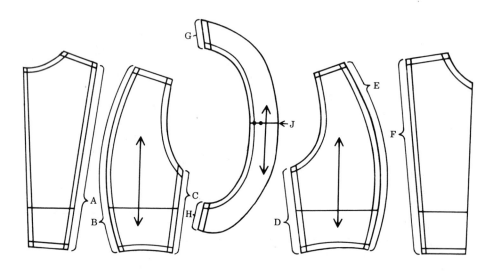

11. The bodice must be altered for a figure that requires an increase in the shape at the bust for a larger than average cup size. An addition of 1″ is needed. How should this alteration be made?

    a) Add a 1″ wide boat-shaped piece to edge E.

    b) Add two ½″ wide boat-shaped pieces, one to edge E and one to F.

    c) Slash through the bust point, spread 1″, and draft in a dart.

    d) Alter the same as for width.

    e) This alteration cannot be attractively accomplished in a princess line garment.

12. In another situation, this bodice must be altered for a figure that has average curves, and needs 1″ added to the bust and to the waist. At what edges and how much must be added at each edge to add 1″ in width?

    a) ½″ at edges C and D

    b) ¼″ at edges C and D

    c) ¼″ at edges A, B, E, and F

    d) ⅛″ at edges A, B, E, and F

    e) $\frac{1}{16}$″ at edges A, B, C, D, E, and F

13. What corresponding alteration is needed for the facing?

    a) Slash and spread 1″ at line J.

    b) Slash and spread ½″ at line J.

    c) Add $\frac{1}{16}$″ to edges G and H.

    d) Add ½″ to edges G and H.

    e) Add ¼″ to edges G and H.

The bodice front has been lengthened ½″ and the bodice back has been shortened ¾″, but the alteration has not been completed. Select the answers to the next five questions (14–18) which will best complete the alteration.

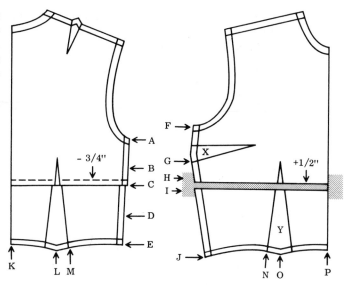

14. The distortions of the cutting lines at the side edges should be corrected by drawing new lines between points
    a) A and E; F and J.
    b) A and E; G and J.
    c) B and D; H and I.
    d) A and C; G and I.

15. What corrections must be made to the bottom of the bodice so that the side seams will be the same length?
    a) Trim ½″ from the front; add ¾″ to back.
    b) Trim 1½″ from front or add 1¼″ to the back.
    c) Trim ⅝″ from the front and add ⅝″ to the back.
    d) Trim ⅝″ from the back and add ⅝″ to the front.

16. The amount in Question 15 is trimmed from the bottom of the bodice at the side edge and restores the patterns to the original measurements at the:
    a) Center front and center back folds.
    b) Center of the darts (L and O).
    c) First seam of the darts (M and N).

17. Which of these figure types would require this alteration?
    a) Person with rounded shoulders
    b) Long-waisted person with a straight back
    c) Short-waisted person with round shoulders
    d) Person whose waistline dips in back

18. Why was the alteration made at a lengthening and shortening line instead of adding or subtracting at the bottom of the bodice?
    a) These are not rectangular-shaped pieces.
    b) This method is never used in any alteration.
    c) The designer had drawn the lengthening and shortening lines and so they must be followed.
    d) This would have been an equally correct alteration.

19. If this bodice needed to be altered to increase the shape in the bust area by ½″, which of the darts should be slashed?
    a) Dart X
    b) Dart Y
    c) Both darts X and Y

This bodice front must be altered for a bust curve which is larger than average. One inch is to be added at the point where it is needed. Select the answers to Questions 20–26 which will best complete the alteration.

20. The bodice must be slashed and spread between what two points?

    a) A and B
    b) A and C
    c) A and D
    d) A and E

21. At what point must the one inch be added?

    a) At A
    b) At B
    c) At C
    d) At D

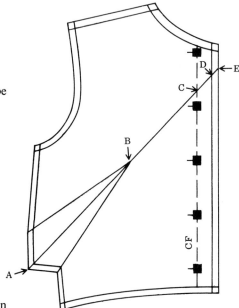

22. What other piece or pieces must be altered to correct for corresponding edges?

    a) The bodice back
    b) The front facing
    c) Both of the above
    d) None of the above

23. Which of the following lines have been distorted by the alteration?

    a) The cutting line of the front edge
    b) The center front line
    c) The buttonhole markings
    d) Answers b and c
    e) All of the above

24. This alteration adds:

    a) Length
    b) Width
    c) Shape
    d) Width and shape
    e) All of the above

25. The shape in this bodice was created by a dart. What other method can be used to create shape?

    a) Gathers
    b) Gussets
    c) Tucks
    d) Seams

26. If it was necessary to shorten this bodice, from what part should the material be removed?

    a) Remove from the bottom so that the dart will not be distorted.

    b) Draw lengthening and shortening lines below the dart but above the seam.

    c) Draw lengthening and shortening lines anywhere between the dart point and the seam allowance so long as it is at right angles to the grain.

The figures below are of a regulation back bodice that has been altered by three different methods. Choose the method which is correct for each of the following examples.

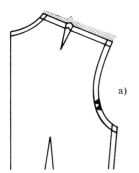
a)

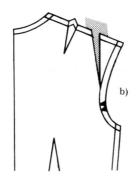
b)

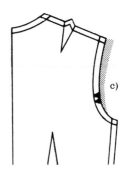
c)

27. Alter for shoulders which are 1″ more square than the average shoulder line.

a) Figure a
b) Figure b
c) Figure c

28. Alter for shoulders that are broader than average.

a) Figure a
b) Figure b
c) Figure c

29. Which of the two alterations performed above requires an addition of height to the cap of the sleeve?

a) Question 27
b) Question 28
c) Questions 27 and 28
d) Neither question

30. Which of these alterations requires that the shoulder line be straightened?

a) Figure a
b) Figure b
c) Figure c
d) Figures a and b
e) Figures a and c

ANSWER KEY[2]

1. c	11. a	21. b
2. b	12. b	22. b
3. c	13. b	23. e
4. d	14. b	24. e
5. b	15. c	25. d
6. a	16. c	26. b
7. b	17. b	27. a
8. e	18. a	28. b
9. c	19. b	29. a
10. a	20. c	30. b

[2] This test is to be machine scored and the answers are to be recorded on a standardized answer sheet.

WINTER QUARTER

Pattern Alteration Test   **Clothing 110**

GENERAL INSTRUCTIONS   **Name** _____

Make the required alterations for the following five problems. Be certain that you understand the problem before you begin your alterations. If it is necessary to cut the pattern pieces out, mount the altered pieces on the blank sheets of paper provided. Mount the pieces for each problem on a separate page. Be certain to label all amounts and to mount all pieces. Write your name in the upper right-hand corner of each page.

Problem 1 (25 points)

This is a basic straight skirt. The skirt is a rectangle between the 7″ hip and the bottom edge. The skirt must be altered in overall size to fit a figure with these irregularities:

the waist measurement is correct;   the 7″ hip measurement is correct;

the 3″ hip must be increased 2″;   the 9″ hip must be increased 2½″.

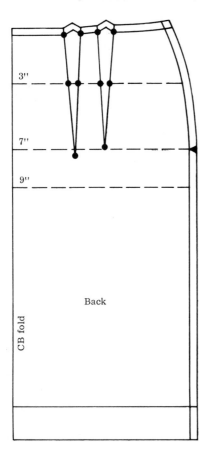

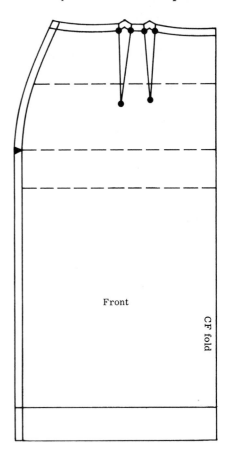

Back   Front

Problem 2 (20 points)

This is the bodice front and back for a regulation dress. Lengthen the bodice front $\frac{1}{2}''$ and shorten the bodice back $\frac{3}{4}''$. Make any other necessary alterations.

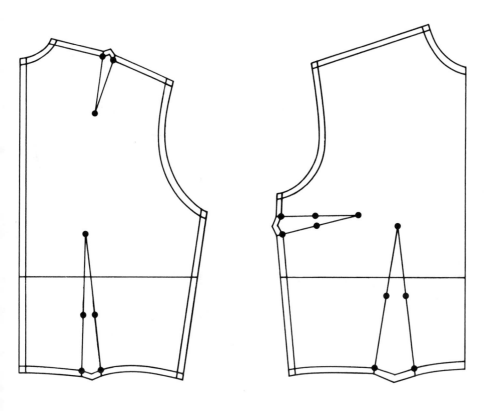

Problem 3 (30 points)

This is the bodice front and facing for a regulation dress that buttons down the front. Alter the pattern for a person who has a larger than average cup size so that the bust curve is increased 1″ at the point where it is needed.

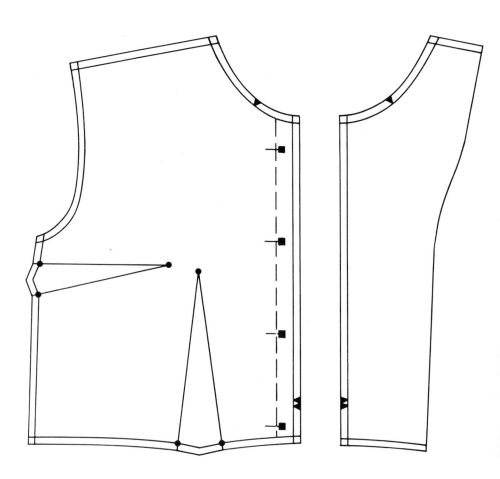

Problem 4 (10 points)

This is a two-piece sleeve pattern. Alter the sleeve to gain $1\frac{1}{2}''$ extra width for large arms.

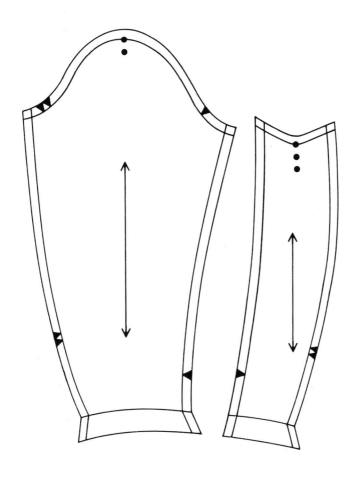

Problem 5 (15 points)

This is the bodice back for a regulation dress. Alter it to fit a figure that has these irregularities:

the shoulders are more square than average and need $\frac{1}{2}''$ in height at the armhole end of the shoulder seam;

the shoulders are broader than average and need an additional $\frac{1}{2}''$ at each side of the figure.

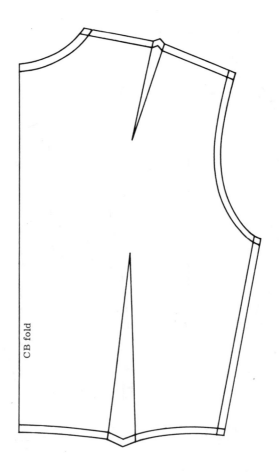

RATING SCALE FOR PATTERN ALTERATION TEST[3]

DIRECTIONS

This rating scale is to be used in scoring the pattern alteration test. In scoring a student's paper, check the appropriateness of the alterations in each problem. For each of the alterations, place a check in the box appropriate to the accuracy of the alteration made. Sum the scores in the boxes checked to obtain a total score.

Problem 1

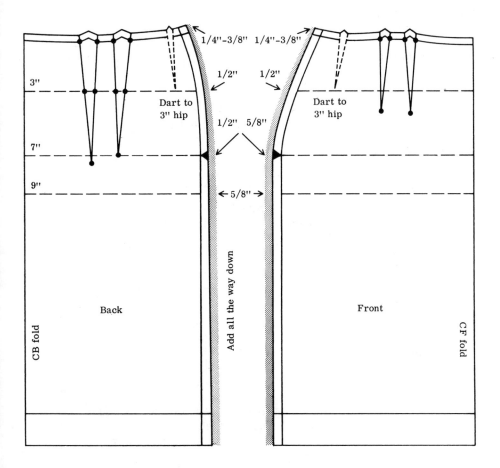

---

[3] By using a rating scale of this type, the student can readily identify the aspect of the task in which she had difficulty. The scale aids the teacher in scoring objectively and permits her to convey the basis for scoring without time-consuming notes.

	No addition	Addition to waist	Added ¼″ to waist
Waist alteration:	0	2	6

Use of darts:

	NO	YES
Right number and location	0	1
Same width as addition to waist	0	1
Darts going to 3″ hip	0	2

	No addition	Addition to hip	Added ½″ to hip
Three-inch hip alteration:	0	1	2

	No addition	Addition to hip	Added ½″ to ⅝″ to hip
Seven-inch hip alteration:	0	2	4

	No addition	Added to hip	Added ⅝″ to hip
Nine-inch hip alteration:	0	1	3

	No addition	Added taper	Added same all the way down	Added ⅝″ all the way down
Below nine-inch hip:	0	1	3	6

[1] Six points are given for the correct addition of ¼ inch to waist; two points are given for any other addition to the waist. This same principle is used on other alteration ratings.

Problem 2

	Correction not made	Correction between wrong points	Perfect correction
Correction of cutting lines:	0	2	5

Back alteration:	NO	YES
Parallel line	0	1
Shortened right amount	0	1
Folded correctly	0	2

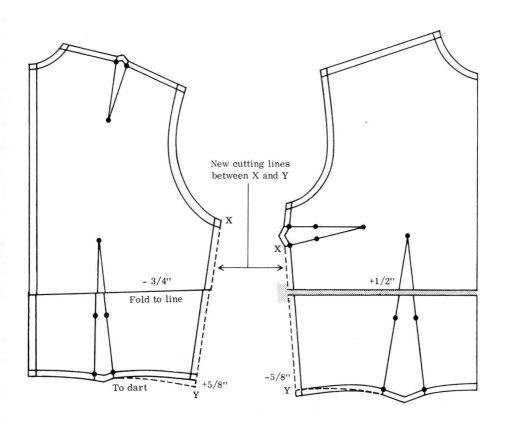

New cutting lines
between X and Y

Front alteration:

	NO	YES
Strip parallel	0	1
Shortened right amount	0	1
Straight of grain line extended	0	1

Bottom correction:

	NO	YES
Line in character	0	1
Proper amount of correction	0	3
Added/subtracted to dart	0	3

Problem 3

	Correction not made	Correction between wrong points	Perfect correction
Cutting line correction:	0	2	4

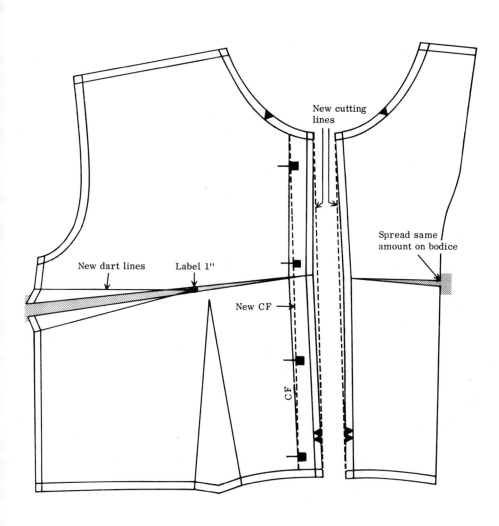

	Correction not made	Attempted the correction	Perfect correction
CF-line correction:	0	2	3

Facing corrected:	NO	YES
Slashed correctly	0	4
Spread same as bodice	0	3
Cutting line corrected	0	2

	NO	YES
Labeled correctly:	0	2

Slashed properly:	NO	YES
Chose correct dart	0	3
Slashed through center of dart	0	2
Slashed only to seam line	0	2

Darts redrawn:	NO	YES
New point between old points	0	2
Lines drawn to original points	0	3

Problem 4

Sleeve slashed properly:	NO	YES
Slashed in right location	0	2
Slashed parallel to grain	0	1
Completely separate pieces	0	3

Lines drawn correctly:	NO	YES
Curves from bicep to cut edge	0	2
Seam allowance	0	1
Right amount added	0	1

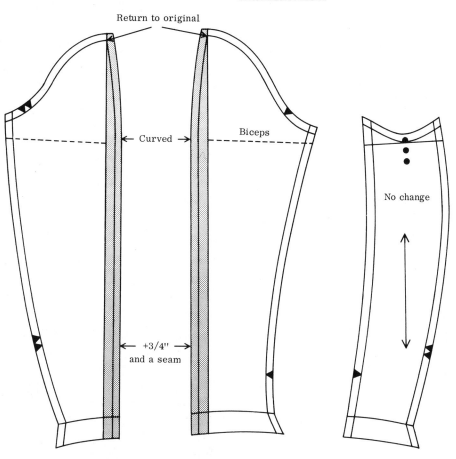

Problem 5

Width added:

	NO	YES
Slashed proper distance from edge	0	2
Slashed to proper point on armhole	0	2
Slashed only to the seam	0	1
Spread proper amount	0	1
Straightened shoulder line	0	2

Height added:

	NO	YES
Added correct amount	0	2
Allowed extra for dart	0	1
Added gradually across	0	4

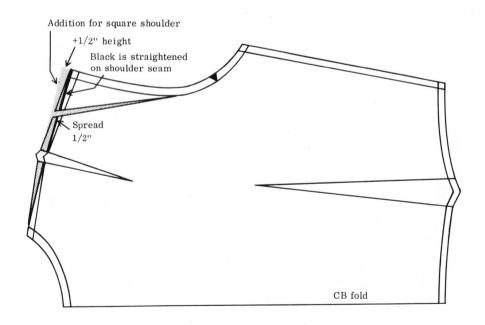

Addition for square shoulder

+1/2" height

Black is straightened
on shoulder seam

Spread
1/2"

CB fold

GRAPH FOR ESTIMATING RELIABILITY

The concept of reliability is explained in Chapter 12. A simplified formula
(KR21) is suggested for use with most objective type examinations:

$$r_{KR21} = \frac{N}{N-1}\left[1 - \frac{(\bar{X}N - \bar{X})}{N \times S^2}\right],$$

where r_{KR21} is the reliability, N is the number of test items, $\bar{X}$ is the mean, and
S is the standard deviation. We can see from this formula that for a test of a given
length, reliability is dependent upon the average test score $(\bar{X})$ and the variability
of the scores (S). That is, r_{KR21} is a function of the mean $(\bar{X})$ and the standard
deviation (S), when N is constant. Furthermore, for a test of a given length with
a constant standard deviation, the reliability function is symmetric about
$\bar{X} = \frac{1}{2}N$. This can be noted from the numerator $\bar{X}(N - \bar{X})$. When $N = 100$,
for example, $\frac{1}{2}N = 50$. If $\bar{X} = 75$, $\bar{X}(N - \bar{X}) = 1875$, and if $\bar{X} = 25$, $\bar{X}(N - \bar{X}) =$
1875. This product is the same whether $\bar{X}$ is 25 points above $\frac{1}{2}N$ or 25 points
below it.

These relationships indicate that the reliability function can be graphed if
N, $\bar{X}$, and S are known. Since the ranges of possible values for $\bar{X}$ and S, as well
as the point of symmetry, are dependent upon N, a separate graph for each value
of N is needed unless proportions between $\bar{X}$ and N and S and N can be obtained.
For this purpose, the formula for KR21 reliability can be rewritten as follows:

$$r_{KR21} = \frac{N}{N-1}\left[1 - \frac{\frac{\bar{X}}{N}\left(\frac{N-\bar{X}}{N}\right)}{N\left(\frac{S}{N}\right)^2}\right].$$

The graphs in Fig. D.1 were obtained using these new values: N, $\bar{X}/N$, and
S/N. The left-hand axis corresponds to N, the bottom-horizontal axis to $\bar{X}/N$,
the top-horizontal axis to S/N, and the right-hand axis is the estimated reliability.
It should be noted that the reliability values read from the chart are only approxi-
mations because the reliability function is not linear. Nevertheless, if care is taken
in reading the graphs, the obtained reliability values should be close to the
calculated KR21 reliability. Furthermore, if $N < 40$, the values in the table at
the bottom should be used for determining the reliability.

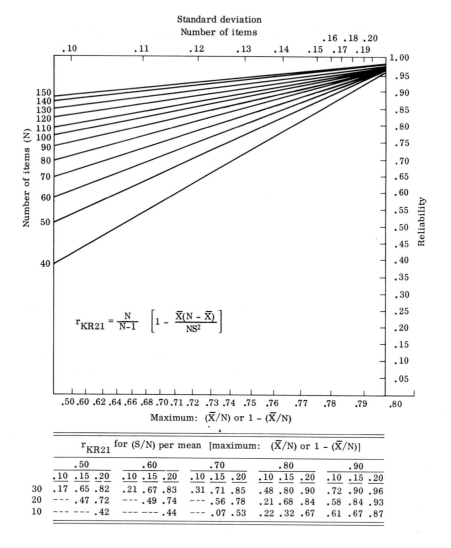

Fig. D.1. Estimated KR21 reliability coefficients.

r_{KR21} for (S/N) per mean [maximum: $(\bar{X}/N)$ or $1 - (\bar{X}/N)$]														
	.50			.60			.70			.80			.90		
	.10	.15	.20	.10	.15	.20	.10	.15	.20	.10	.15	.20	.10	.15	.20
30	.17	.65	.82	.21	.67	.83	.31	.71	.85	.48	.80	.90	.72	.90	.96
20	---	.47	.72	---	.49	.74	---	.56	.78	.21	.68	.84	.58	.84	.93
10	---	---	.42	---	---	.44	---	.07	.53	.22	.32	.67	.61	.67	.87

Reading the Graphs

Use the following steps when determining reliability from Figure D.1.

1. Determine N, $\bar{X}$, and S.
2. Determine the proportion, $\bar{X}/N$ or $1 - (\bar{X}/N)$, whichever is larger.
3. Determine the proportion S/N.
4. With a straightedge, connect these latter two points (X/N and S/N) on the graph.

5. Locate the line corresponding to the number of test items (these lines originate from the left-hand scale).
6. Locate the point where the straightedge intersects this line.
7. From this latter point, read over to the right-hand scale (this value is the estimated KR21 reliability).

Example: N = 50, $\overline{X}$ = 37, S = 5:

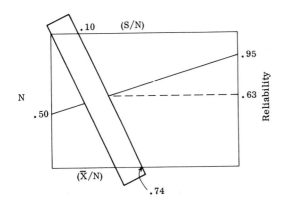

N = 50
(S/N) = .10
($\overline{X}$/N) = .74
rel. = .63

GRAPH FOR ESTIMATING ITEM DIFFICULTY
AND VALIDITY INDICES

The concepts of item difficulty and item validity are explained in Chapter 13. In brief, when analyzing the items on a classroom examination, we divide the scores into three groups—upper 27% of the scores, lower 27% of the scores, and middle 46% of the scores. The two extreme groups are used in the analysis. The two item determinants which are calculated are:

1. *Difficulty*—proportion of examinees who answered the item correctly (or for multiple-scored items, proportion of possible points obtained), and
2. *Validity*—difference between the proportion of the upper group who answered the item correctly and the proportion of the lower group who answered the item correctly (or for multiple-scored items, the difference between the proportion of possible points obtained by the upper group and the proportion of possible points obtained by the lower group).

The formulas for calculating these indices are given in Table E.1.

Table E.1 Formulas for determining item difficulty and item validity

Scoring method	Formula	
	Difficulty	Validity*
Unit-scoring	$D = \dfrac{R_U + R_L}{N_U + N_L}$	$V = \dfrac{R_U - R_L}{N_U}$
Multiple-scoring	$D = \dfrac{R_U + R_L}{X_{max}(N_U + N_L)}$	$V = \dfrac{R_U - R_L}{X_{max}(N_U)}$

where R_U = number of points right, upper-group,
R_L = number of points right, lower-group,
X_{max} = number of points possible on item,
N_U = number of examinees in upper-group,
N_L = number of examinees in lower-group.

* Also referred to as item discrimination.

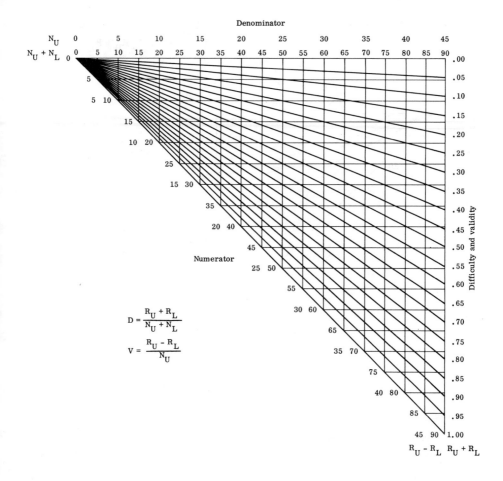

Fig. E.1.

Both item difficulty and item validity can be determined from Fig. E.1, for N_U or $X_{max} \times N_U$ up to and including 45. This graph is therefore adequate for the task of analyzing a multiple-choice test of the one-response per item format for a class of 167 students.

Reading the Graph

The item analysis data can be read from the chart using the following steps. (See also Fig. E.2.)

1. Determine N_U and N_L (actually, $N_U = N_L$).

2. Determine $R_U + R_L$ and $R_U - R_L$.

3. Determine $N_U + N_L$ or $X_{max}(N_U + N_L)$ and $X_{max} \times N_U$.

Example: $N_U = 30$, $N_L = 30$, $R_U = 20$, and $R_L = 10$:

$$N_U = 30 \qquad R_U - R_L = 10$$
$$N_U + N_L = 60 \qquad R_U + R_L = 30$$

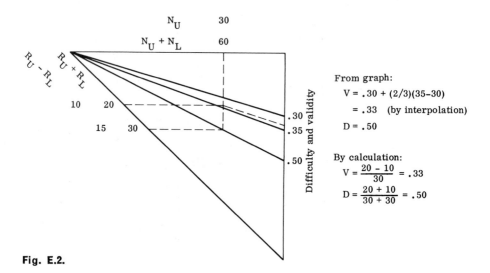

From graph:
$$V = .30 + (2/3)(35-30)$$
$$= .33 \quad \text{(by interpolation)}$$
$$D = .50$$

By calculation:
$$V = \frac{20 - 10}{30} = .33$$
$$D = \frac{20 + 10}{30 + 30} = .50$$

Fig. E.2.

4. *Difficulty*

   a) Locate $N_U + N_L$ on the top-horizontal axis in the second row of numbers.

   b) Locate $R_U + R_L$ on the left-hand diagonal axis in the second column of numbers.

   c) Locate the point where the vertical line through $N_U + N_L$ and the horizontal line through $R_U + R_L$ intersect.

   d) Follow the diagonal line upon which this point falls to the right-hand axis and read the difficulty value from that scale. (If the point falls between two lines, interpolate the value on the difficulty scale.)

5. *Validity—discrimination*

   a) Locate N_U on the top-horizontal axis in the first row of numbers.

   b) Locate $R_U - R_L$ on the left-hand diagonal axis in the first column of numbers.

   c) Locate the point where the vertical line through N_U and the horizontal line through $R_U - R_L$ intersect.

   d) Follow the diagonal line upon which this point falls to the right-hand axis and read the validity value from that scale. (If the point falls between two lines, interpolate the value on the validity scale.)

CONVERSION OF rel TO $\sqrt{1-\text{rel}}$

Table F.1 Conversion of rel to $\sqrt{1-\text{rel}}$

rel	$\sqrt{1-\text{rel}}$	rel	$\sqrt{1-\text{rel}}$	rel	$\sqrt{1-\text{rel}}$
.99	.100	.66	.583	.33	.818
.98	.141	.65	.592	.32	.825
.97	.173	.64	.600	.31	.831
.96	.200	.63	.608	.30	.837
.95	.224	.62	.616	.29	.843
.94	.245	.61	.624	.28	.848
.93	.264	.60	.632	.27	.854
.92	.283	.59	.640	.26	.860
.91	.300	.58	.648	.25	.866
.90	.316	.57	.656	.24	.872
.89	.332	.56	.663	.23	.877
.88	.346	.55	.671	.22	.883
.87	.360	.54	.678	.21	.889
.86	.374	.53	.686	.20	.894
.85	.387	.52	.693	.19	.900
.84	.400	.51	.700	.18	.906
.83	.412	.50	.707	.17	.911
.82	.424	.49	.714	.16	.916
.81	.436	.48	.721	.15	.922
.80	.447	.47	.728	.14	.927
.79	.458	.46	.735	.13	.933
.78	.469	.45	.742	.12	.938
.77	.480	.44	.748	.11	.943
.76	.490	.43	.755	.10	.949
.75	.500	.42	.762	.09	.954
.74	.510	.41	.768	.08	.959
.73	.520	.40	.774	.07	.964
.72	.529	.39	.781	.06	.970
.71	.538	.38	.787	.05	.975
.70	.548	.37	.794	.04	.980
.69	.557	.36	.800	.03	.985
.68	.566	.35	.806	.02	.990
.67	.574	.34	.812	.01	.995

INDEXES

Name Index

Adams, Georgia Sachs, 47, 63, 75, 134, 166, 192, 221
Adkins, Dorothy C., 166
Ahmann, J. Stanley, 27, 47, 63, 75, 122, 134, 166, 248
Albright, Preston B., 254, 269
Alilunas, Leo, 260, 269
Anastasi, Ann, 221
Anderson, C. C., 256, 269
Archer, N. Sidney, 260, 269
Arnold, H. L., 254, 269
Arny, Clara M., 166
Ashburn, Robert, 256, 269

Baldwin, Joseph, 262, 269
Ballard, Phillip Baswood, 265, 269
Barnes, Elinor J., 253, 269
Bean, Kenneth L., 166
Beardsley, Seymour W., 254, 274
Bennett, G. K., 265, 276
Blommers, Paul, 197
Bloom, O. S., 21, 27
Bolton, Fredrick E., 257, 269
Boynton, R. M., 266, 269
Brenner, Marshall, 265, 269
Briggs, Leslie, J., 267, 274
Brody, William, 91, 259, 269

Calhoun, Roland Leroy, 265, 270
Carpenter, Finley, 260, 270
Cason, Hulsey, 260, 270
Charters, W. W., 260, 270
Chase, Clinton I., 197, 257, 266, 270
Clark, Robert B., 197

Cliff, Rosemary, 267, 270
Coladarci, Arthur P., 197
Comin, Robert, 259, 270
Cooke, George H., 252, 260, 270
Cooper, A., 166
Corey, Stephen M., 253, 270
Cowen, E. L., 166
Cox, R. C., 248
Crawford, C. C., 252, 267, 270, 272
Cronbach, Lee, J., 263, 264, 270
Cureton, Edward E., 221, 228

Davis, Fredrick B., 229, 248
Dickinson, Emily, 22, 27
Diederich, Paul B., 249
Dizney, H., 112
Douglas, Harl R., 262, 270
Drake, C. A., 256, 270
Dressel, Paul L., 27, 112, 166, 268, 270
Dunn, Theodore F., 265, 270
Dunviddie, William, 259, 261, 270

Ebel, Robert L., 27, 63, 75, 112, 122, 134, 197, 221, 249
Edgeworth, F. Y., 254, 270, 271
Eells, Walter C., 256, 271
Eliot, Charles W., 251, 271
Elliott, Edward C., 254, 255, 257, 275
Ellis, A., 258, 271
Eurich, Alvin C., 259, 260, 271, 273

Farrand, Wilson, 251, 271
Fenlayson, Douglas, 256, 271
Findley, Warren G., 230, 249

Subject Index

Academic growth, 3
Answer sheets; *see* Test scoring

Balance, 9

Central tendency
  mean, 169–170, 172, 178
  median, 171–172, 175
Chance, 65, 113, 225, 267
Checklist, 81, 87–91, 147–157, 162–165
Clinical experience, evaluation of, 162–165
Clothing test, 295–316
Combining measures, 172–173
Completion item
  association, 68–69
  construction, 66–69
  definition, 64
  incomplete sentence, 67–68
  item analysis, 242
  question, 37, 67
  see also Completion test
Completion test
  reliability, 210
  scoring, 69–71
  scoring economy, 65
  strengths, 65–66
  uses, 66
  weaknesses, 64–65
  see also Completion item
Confidence interval, 206–207
Correction for guessing; *see* Test scoring
Correlation, 183–188

D; see difficulty

Descriptive scale; *see* Performance item
Differences among students, 3
Difficulty
  computation of, 223, 232–233, 246, 320–322
  desired difficulty, 223–224
  equation, 223, 232, 242, 320
  evaluating items, 238–240, 244–245
  factors influencing, 225–226
  graph for estimating, 320–322
  item intercorrelation, 224
  refining items, 238–240
Discrimination
  computation of, 228–229, 231, 233, 243, 246, 320–322
  criterion groups, 226–227
  Davis indices, 229
  desired discrimination, 230, 233–234
  equation, 231, 243, 320
  evaluating items, 238–240, 244–245
  factors influencing, 232–234
  Flanagan's r, 228–229
  graph for estimating, 320–322
  net D. 230–231
  refining items, 238–240
  tetracloric coefficient of correlation, 229
Drafting test, 153–156

Educational objectives
  classification, 19–26
  instructional, 13–19, 277–278, 295
  ultimate, 12–14
Error score, 205–206, 263
Errors of measurement, 8, 200, 205–207